The  do

THE ESSENTIAL WRITINGS OF SRI AUROBINDO

Edited by
Peter Heehs

YMCA Library Building, Jai Singh Road, New Delhi 110001

Oxford University Press is a department of the University of Oxford. It furthers the University's objective of excellence in research, scholarship, and education by publishing worldwide in

Oxford New York
Athens Auckland Bangkok Bogota Buenos Aires Calcutta
Cape Town Chennai Dar es Salaam Delhi Florence Hong Kong Istanbul
Karachi Kuala Lumpur Madrid Melbourne Mexico City Mumbai
Nairobi Paris Sao Paolo Singapore Taipei Tokyo Toronto Warsaw

with associated companies in

Berlin Ibadan

Oxford University Paperbacks 1999

ISBN 0 19 564976 1

Printed at Wadhwa International, New Delhi 110 020
and published by Manzar Khan, Oxford University Press
YMCA Library Building, Jai Singh Road, New Delhi 110 001

Contents

Preface

THIS COMPILATION is an attempt to present a representative selection of the writings of Sri Aurobindo in a single volume. I have tried to give adequate coverage to all major aspects of his work: politics, Indian culture, social theory, philosophy, yoga, and poetry. The six parts devoted to these subjects are introduced by brief notes. The general introduction gives biographical information and an overview of the whole. I have included only complete pieces (essays, letters, poems) or main divisions (chapters, cantos) of long works. The selections have been reproduced as originally published; punctuation, capitalization, etc. have not been modernized. As much as possible, I have avoided writings that draw heavily on the technical vocabulary of yoga. Words from languages other than English that are not defined where they occur are listed in the glossary. Footnotes to the texts explain historical and literary allusions that may be lost on some modern readers.

I am grateful to the Oxford University Press for proposing this volume and to its editorial staff, in particular Anuradha Roy, for helping me bring it to completion. Several of my colleagues at the Sri Aurobindo Ashram Archives and Research Library have given generously of their time in various ways. I would like to thank in particular Medha Gunay, Chaitanya Swain, and Matthijs Cornelissen. The Sri Aurobindo Ashram Trust has kindly granted permission to reproduce the extracts. The selection, introduction and notes are my own responsibility and should not be taken as representing the views of the Ashram.

Introduction

WHEN INDIA achieved independence on 15 August 1947, Sri Aurobindo was asked to write a message for broadcast by All India Radio. He took the opportunity, on a day that coincidentally was his seventy-fifth birthday, to recall the 'five world-movements' he had 'hoped to see fulfilled in his lifetime'. These five 'dreams' sum up his many-sided achievement and provide a gateway to his writings.

The first dream was of 'a revolutionary movement that would achieve a free and independent India'. Around the turn of the century Sri Aurobindo helped organize a secret society that developed into the country's first revolutionary group with a clear political aim. Between 1906 and 1910 he was a leader of the advanced nationalist or Extremist party. His writings and speeches of those years decisively altered the direction of the freedom movement. Part 1 of this compilation includes three examples of his political journalism, two speeches, and two letters that explain his reasons for retiring from politics.

Before, during and after his political career, Sri Aurobindo wrote extensively on Indian civilization and on the key works of the Indian tradition. At a time when most of Asia was dominated by Europe, he dreamed of a 'resurgence and liberation of the peoples of Asia' and a return of their 'great role in the progress of human civilization'. Part 2 features an essay giving an overview of the Indian spiritual tradition, several examples of Sri Aurobindo's interpretations of ancient Indian texts, and three essays dealing with India's role in the cultural confrontations of the present and the future.

For all his championing of Indian civilization, Sri Aurobindo remained internationalist in his outlook. His third dream was of 'a world union forming the outer basis of a fairer, brighter and nobler life for all mankind'. In *The Human Cycle* he showed how humanity's social evolution points towards such a development, and in *The Ideal of Human Unity* described how a union fostering cultural diversity might be effected. Extracts from these works are given in Part 3.

Sri Aurobindo believed that the key to human unity was the spiritual conception of life, present in all civilizations but best preserved and developed in India. It was to help fulfil his dream of a 'spiritual gift of India to the world' that he reinterpreted the Indian tradition in the light of modern knowledge. His own philosophy, articulated in his chief prose work, *The Life Divine*, takes as its basis the omnipresent Reality or *brahman* of the Upanishads, but includes also the European idea of progress through evolution. Extracts from this and other philosophical writings are reproduced in Part 4.

Although the creator of a metaphysical system of remarkable consistency and completeness, Sri Aurobindo insisted that speculative philosophy could never arrive at truth; its role was to prepare the way for intuitive experience. A more direct approach to such experience was the spiritual discipline of yoga. In *The Synthesis of Yoga* and *Letters on Yoga* he traced out a flexible practice that would help in the fulfilment of his last dream, the taking of 'a step in evolution which would raise man to a higher and larger consciousness and begin the solution of the problems that have perplexed and vexed him since he first began to think and to dream of individual perfection and a perfect society'. Sri Aurobindo's 'integral yoga' is rooted in the Indian tradition, but he regarded it as a system of 'practical psychology' appropriate for men and women of all cultures and in all activities of life. Part 5 consists of book-extracts and letters on the integral yoga.

Sri Aurobindo felt that poetry could suggest inner truths that discursive prose could not formulate. His first published writing was a poem; the last book he worked on was an epic based on the Indian legend of Savitri. Part 6 contains a selection of short poems and a complete canto of *Savitri*, as well as an extract from *The Future Poetry* in which he explains his idea of the essence of poetry as revelatory word or *mantra*.

In selecting writings from these six areas of interest, I have attempted to suggest the diversity of Sri Aurobindo's thought. By choosing pieces whose composition straddles six decades — the earliest was written in 1893, the latest in the mid-1940s — I have tried to give an idea of the development of his ideas over an eventful lifetime.

A Brief Life-Sketch

Today, fifty years after India achieved independence, it is difficult to remember that when Sri Aurobindo was born it was a non-self-governing part of the British Empire. A century and a quarter of economic exploitation had reinforced its poverty. British domination of the spheres of technology and education had pushed it to the brink of cultural extinction.

Aurobindo Ghose was born in Calcutta, then the capital of British India, in 1872. His father, a thoroughly Anglicised physician, sent him and his brothers to convent school in Darjeeling and then, in 1879, to England. Aurobindo spoke English from his earliest years; he did not start learning Bengali until he was eighteen. Admitted in 1882 to St Paul's School, London, he excelled in the classical curriculum, which consisted chiefly of Latin and Greek literature. In 1889 he was selected as a probationer to the Indian Civil Service and obtained a scholarship to King's College, Cambridge. There he won prizes for Greek and Latin verse, but neglected to learn horse-riding and as a result was rejected from the civil service.

Finding a job in the administration of the Maharaja of Baroda, Aurobindo returned to India in February 1893. Four months later he contributed the first of several political articles to *Indu Prakash*, an English-Marathi newspaper of Bombay. At the time the annual meetings of the Indian National Congress were the country's only organized expression of nationalist politics. The coterie of lawyers who dominated these meetings each year drew up a timid list of grievances for the government, which each year ignored it. In August 1893 the leaders of public opinion in Bombay were surprised to read in *Indu Prakash*:

> I say, of the Congress, then, this, — that its aims are mistaken, that the spirit in which it proceeds towards their accomplishment is not a spirit of sincerity and whole-heartedness, and that the methods it has chosen are not the right methods, and the leaders in whom it trusts, not the right sort of men to be leaders (page 7).

This was not the right way for a young Indian to ingratiate himself with his elders. Aurobindo was obliged by the editor of the paper to tone down the articles, and soon abandoned them.

During the next twelve years, while he worked in various

state departments, Aurobindo perfected his Bengali and Sanskrit, and wrote literary studies and translations, as well as some poetry. Around 1900 he began to organize a secret revolutionary group and to make contact with nationalist politicians. In 1906, in the wake of the popular agitation against the Partition of Bengal, he left his job in Baroda and went to Calcutta as principal of the newly established Bengal National College. Soon he was enrolled by nationalist leader Bipinchandra Pal as a writer for *Bande Mataram*, an English-language newspaper that became the mouthpiece of a new party of advanced nationalists, dubbed 'Extremists' by their moderate rivals. In the columns of *Bande Mataram*, Bipinchandra and Aurobindo articulated the ideal of complete political independence from Britain. By the end of the year, Aurobindo became editor-in-chief of this influential journal. In it, along with articles on events of the day, he published several statements of policy that helped establish the Extremist programme. The most important of these, 'The Doctrine of Passive Resistance' (pages 12–17), appeared around the same time that Mohandas K. Gandhi began writing on this subject in South Africa. Aurobindo differed from Gandhi in considering passive resistance a means and not an article of faith, and in believing that violent resistance was also a legitimate method for achieving freedom from an imperialist power.

The revolutionary society that Aurobindo had started turned to terrorism under the direction of his brother Barindrakumar. In May 1908, after an unsuccessful assassination attempt, Barindrakumar, Aurobindo and other members of the society were arrested. After a year-long trial, Aurobindo was acquitted for lack of evidence. His brother was condemned to the gallows, but after a successful appeal was instead transported to the Andaman Islands.

Aurobindo had begun the practice of the spiritual discipline of yoga in 1905. During the year he spent in jail he had a series of mystical experiences that transformed his outlook on life. (He described some of these experiences in 'Uttarpara Speech', pages 32–41.) From this moment Aurobindo regarded India's struggle for independence as a part of a global work of spiritual regeneration. As he wrote in *Karmayogin*, a journal he started after his release in 1909, 'It is a spiritual revolution we foresee and the material is only its shadow and reflex' (page 43).

Along with political journalism, Aurobindo wrote and published in *Karmayogin* numerous articles on philosophy and yoga, educational theory, art theory and criticism, and literary criticism, as well as translations and poetry. In April 1910, warned that he was about to be arrested for sedition, he took refuge in the French enclave of Chandernagore, and later went secretly to Pondicherry, the capital of French India. He at first planned to return to the political field when conditions were more favourable, but soon discovered that his yogic practice demanded a full-time commitment. Convinced that the attainment of freedom was now inevitable, he turned his attention to the inner change of consciousness that he believed had to precede any lasting change in the structure and workings of society.

Between 1910 and 1914 Aurobindo worked alone, devoting most of his time to meditation, the study of Sanskrit texts, and the development of new interpretations of the Rig-veda and Upanishads. He believed that these scriptures contained psychological observations of great practical value, and resolved to rescue them from rationalistic European Orientalists and traditional Indian commentators. His interpretation of the Upanishads became the basis of his own philosophy, which began to take shape at this time.

In August 1914 Aurobindo, together with the French writer Paul Richard and his wife Mirra Richard, brought out the first issue of a journal called *Arya*. Over the next seven years Aurobindo published most of his major prose works in monthly instalments in *Arya*. He presented his philosophy in *The Life Divine*, his method of yoga in *The Synthesis of Yoga*, his interpretations of Indian scriptures in *The Secret of the Veda, Essays on the Gita* and other works, his social and political thought in *The Human Cycle* and *The Ideal of Human Unity*, and his theory of poetics in *The Future Poetry*. He also wrote essays on philosophical and other topics, and a series of articles defending Indian culture from foreign detractors. All told, between 1914 and 1921 he published the equivalent of a dozen books, all of which were later brought out separately. Most of the extracts in Parts 2 to 5 are from works first published in *Arya*.

Even after his retirement from politics, Aurobindo remained an influential figure among those who took part in the freedom movement. Writing of the period around the First World War,

Subhas Chandra Bose recalled that Aurobindo was then 'easily the most popular leader in Bengal, despite his voluntary exile'.[1] In 1920 some of Aurobindo's former Extremist colleagues tried to draw him back into the movement. The replies he wrote giving his reasons for staying out of politics (pages 47–53) are important also for outlining the spiritual work he had undertaken. 'I am no longer first and foremost a politician,' he said,

> but have definitely commenced another kind of work with a spiritual basis, a work of spiritual, social, cultural and economic reconstruction of an almost revolutionary kind, and am even making or at least supervising a sort of practical or laboratory experiment in that sense.

This 'laboratory experiment' consisted of a small body of spiritual seekers who had gathered around Aurobindo. He hoped this would become the prototype of a spiritual or 'gnostic' community, such as he had written about in *The Human Cycle* and *The Life Divine*. During the twenties this group began to take organized shape under the guidance of Mirra Richard, who had returned to India in 1920 after a stay in France and Japan. At the end of 1926 Aurobindo stopped meeting with anyone except Mirra and one or two others. More and more exclusively devoted to his yogic practice, he put the management of the community or ashram in Mirra's hands, and asked its members to regard her as their active spiritual guide or 'Mother'. From around this time he became known as 'Sri Aurobindo', the honorific 'Sri' being regarded by his followers as an integral part of his name.

Sri Aurobindo stayed in touch with members of the ashram by means of correspondence. During the thirties he spent several hours a day answering their questions, commenting on their progress, and helping them solve problems of their inner and outer lives. His letters, later collected and published in five volumes, are written in terse and vigorous English, and provide a more accessible introduction to his yoga and philosophy than his formal writings on these subjects.

From the mid 1930s Sri Aurobindo again found time to work on his poetry. His early work had been traditional in form and romantic in style and substance. During his imprisonment he wrote — or rather composed mentally, for he was not allowed

[1] Subhas Chandra Bose, *An Indian Pilgrim* (Delhi: Oxford University Press, 1997), 61.

pen and paper — some short poems giving expression to his inner life. These pieces, later published in *Karmayogin*, show the direction his muse was to take. (One of them, 'Invitation', is reproduced on page 351.) During the early years in Pondicherry he put most of his poetic energy into large dramatic and narrative projects. One of these, *Ilion*, is an account of the fall of Troy written in 'quantitative hexameters' that capture something of the movement of the Greek epic metre. In 1916, before completing *Ilion*, he turned his attention to an Indian theme: the story of Savitri and Satyavan from the *Mahabharata*. The first versions of *Savitri* were narratives in the nineteenth-century style, like others he had written in Baroda. But gradually, through successive revisions, this poem became a record of Sri Aurobindo's inner experiences, written in verse that sought not simply to describe but also to embody the truths of the spiritual life.

Most of the revision of *Savitri* was done during the thirties and forties. At the same time Sri Aurobindo wrote a number of shorter mystical poems. Many of these are in innovative meters, often adapted from European classical forms. During the thirties he composed a series of seventy-three sonnets that are unlike any other examples of this form in English. The most remarkable are first-person accounts of spiritual experiences, seemingly written while the experience was going on. A selection of these mystical lyrics and sonnets has been included in Part 6.

During and after his recovery from an accident in November 1938, Sri Aurobindo revised his major prose works and published them as books. First to be completed was *The Life Divine* (1939–40), followed by part of *The Synthesis of Yoga* (1948), *The Human Cycle* (1949), and *The Ideal of Human Unity* (1950). Separate cantos of *Savitri* began appearing in print in 1946; the entire epic was published in two volumes in 1950 and 1951. Sri Aurobindo died on 5 December 1950 after a brief illness.

The Works of Sri Aurobindo
With Special Reference to the Selections in This Book

The common thread running through Sri Aurobindo's many works is a recognition of the spiritual reality that is the basis of the world and its activities. Life is an expression of this reality, known in English by such names as the Divine, the Absolute, and God. All the activities of life — from poetry and philosophy to politics and social organization — find their deepest meaning when giving form to the divine reality within them. 'All life,' he wrote in *The Human Cycle*, 'is only a lavish and manifold opportunity given us to discover, realise, express the Divine.'[2]

Early in his career, Sri Aurobindo would have avoided such an apparently religious formulation. At the end of his university career he considered himself an agnostic. For a dozen years after his return to his homeland his chief interests were practical politics and imaginative literature. But even then he believed that the Indian tradition preserved spiritual values needed to complement the pragmatic rationalism of the West. India thus had a mission: to transmit the values of its distinctive civilization to the world. It was to fulfil this mission, not just to claim the inherent right of peoples to self-government, that India had to free itself from British domination.

The programme of the Extremist Party, which Sri Aurobindo did much to formulate, consisted of (1) *swaraj* or self-government, (2) *swadeshi* or the use of indigenous goods, (3) the boycott of British products, and (4) national education. It was a programme, in other words, of political, economic and cultural independence. Moderate politicians spoke also of swaraj, interpreting it at best as limited self-rule within the British Empire. Sri Aurobindo insisted unambiguously on the need for political freedom. This was, he wrote in *The Doctrine of Passive Resistance*, 'the life-breath of a nation; to attempt social reform, educational reform, industrial expansion, the moral improvement of the race without aiming first and foremost at political freedom, is the very height of ignorance and futility' (page 13).

[2] Sri Aurobindo, *Social and Political Thought* (Pondicherry: Sri Aurobindo Ashram, 1971), 138.

To achieve this goal it was necessary to take active steps. The Moderates' policy of petitioning the government for small concessions would never lead to freedom. One had to strike where British interests were involved, in the field of commerce. British industry thrived by exploiting Indian raw materials and flooding the market with low-priced products that had driven out traditional manufactures. To set right the balance Indians had to support indigenous producers and to impose a boycott on British goods. A limited boycott had been declared in Bengal when the government went ahead with its unpopular proposal to partition the province. Sri Aurobindo wanted the boycott to be extended to other provinces and used deliberately as a political weapon. He also supported moves to boycott British-run educational institutions and to replace them with national schools and colleges.

The Extremist programme was considered suicidally radical by the leaders of the Moderate Party. They had been trying for twenty years to get a hearing from the British. Now they seemed on the verge of success. The government announced its intention of reforming — without fundamentally changing — the powerless councils in which Indian opinion expressed itself. The Extremists' demand for aggressive action seemed to put these reforms in jeopardy. The struggle between the two parties at meetings of the Indian National Congress intensified. The Moderates were able to retain control of this body for several years, but by excluding the Extremists they deprived Congress of its main source of strength. It was not until 1920 that Congress became an effective instrument, when Gandhi gave it a programme that in many respects was the same as the one put forward by the Extremists fifteen years earlier.

Sri Aurobindo's insistence on the primary importance of independence was his chief contribution to the national movement. He also did much to change its tenor. The movement could no longer remain the armchair occupation of the urban élite; it had to be taken up by everyone in a spirit of complete dedication. As he said in a speech in January 1908, 'Nationalism is not a mere political programme; Nationalism is a religion that has come from God; Nationalism is a creed which you shall have to live' (page 18). He went on to urge his listeners 'to live your Nationalism', to 'realize the strength within you, try to bring it forward so that everything you do may be not your own doing, but the doing of that Truth within you' (page 30).

During his political career Sri Aurobindo was censured by British officials as well as Moderate politicians for mixing up religion and politics. Present-day historians have made similar criticisms, some of them charging him and his associates with giving a Hindu slant to the movement, alienating the Muslims and helping to create India's communal problem. These criticisms are based in part on a misreading of texts such as the one just quoted. When he said that nationalism was a religion, he did not mean it had a special relation to Hinduism or any other traditional faith. What he said was that nationalism was itself a 'religion', that is, a matter of supreme concern guided by the 'great power' that was overseeing India's destiny (page 26). It is true that in the Uttarpara Speech, delivered by invitation to a religious group, he did identify Nationalism with the *sanatana dharma*, the philosophical core of Hinduism that he believed was universal and the basis of a future world cultural synthesis. This is an ethnocentric view but one that is understandable in the context of a political and cultural struggle against an arrogant foreign imperialism.

Sri Aurobindo's writings on Indian culture, a selection of which appear in Part 2, were written in the same historical context and, as a result, now seem unnecessarily polemical. *A Defence of Indian Culture*, begun as a reply to a negative critique of Indian arts and society by a British writer, contains vigorous rebuttals of positions that are no longer seriously held by anyone. Sri Aurobindo intended to remove the polemical portions of these essays when they were republished as a book, but was unable to find time to do so. What is of lasting value in the *Defence* are his sketches of the development of Indian religion, art, literature and polity. Remarkable also are his attempts to seize the 'central motives' of Indian civilization:

> The whole basis of the Indian mind is its spiritual and inward turn, its propensity to seek the things of the spirit and the inner being first and foremost and to look at all else as secondary, dependent, to be handled and determined in the light of the higher knowledge.[3]

[3] Sṛi Aurobindo, *The Foundations of Indian Culture* (Pondicherry: Sri Aurobindo Ashram, 1972), 366.

When Sri Aurobindo examined the products of the Indian mind, he found everywhere the mark of this spirituality. The hymns of the Rig-veda are not the prayers of primitive nature-worshippers but inspired poetry that reveals the truths of existence to those who know its secret. In the Upanishads the veil of secrecy is removed and the mystic contents made explicit. Deeply influenced by the Upanishads, Sri Aurobindo wrote commentaries on two of them, as well as several briefer treatments, such as the beautiful 'Knowledge of Brahman' (pages 93 – 7). In a close reading of the texts freed from dependence on Shankaracharya and other commentators, he showed that they do not teach the exclusive existence of Brahman and the unreality of the world — as the *advaita* school would have it — but the coexistence of the Divine and its multiple manifestations.

Sri Aurobindo was also influenced by the Bhagavad Gita, and in *Essays on the Gita* he brought out its many-sided approach to spiritual truth. The Gita teaches a path of knowledge incorporating elements of Sankhya, Vedanta and Yoga; a path of works; and a path of devotion based on complete self-offering to the Divine. Its 'central interest' to us is its attempt 'to reconcile and even effect a kind of unity between the inner spiritual truth in its most absolute and integral realisation and the outer actualities of man's life and action' (page 105).

This search for a harmony between spirituality and the varied expressions of life is fundamental to Sri Aurobindo's approach to the Indian tradition. While he affirmed that spirituality was 'the master-key of the Indian mind', he insisted also that 'this was not and could not be her whole mentality'. For 'when we look at the past of India, what strikes us next is her stupendous vitality, her inexhaustible power of life and joy of life, her almost unimaginably prolific creativeness.' There was in addition 'a third power of the ancient Indian spirit . . . a strong intellectuality, at once austere and rich, robust and minute, powerful and delicate, massive in principle and curious in detail'.

Thus an ingrained and dominant spirituality, an inexhaustible vital creativeness and gust of life and, mediating between them, a powerful, penetrating and scrupulous intelligence combined of the rational, ethical and aesthetic mind each at a high intensity of action, created the harmony of the ancient Indian culture (pages 120 – 1).

This harmony had to be rediscovered before India could move forward into the future. Never blind to his country's failings, Sri Aurobindo held that 'behind our imperfect cultural figures' were 'certain fundamental motives or essential idea-forces that cannot be thrown aside'. The spirit had to be kept, not necessarily the forms. Even that which was truly great in India's past could not just be 'preserved as it was or repeated for ever' (page 135). If the Upanishads failed to solve the riddle of life, 'we must seek elsewhere for a solution' for 'it is only the ignorant soul that will make itself the slave of a book' (page 101). He was opposed to the 'vulgar and unthinking cultural Chauvinism which holds that whatever we have is good for us because it is Indian or even that whatever is in India is best, because it is the creation of the Rishis.'[4]

India had to move forward into the future and not just try to recover a vanished past because, like it or not, India was locked in a war of cultures with the West. There was a hidden political motive behind Western criticisms of Indian literature, art, society, and polity. The implicit claim was that India must either 'Europeanise, rationalise, materialise her whole being and deserve liberty by the change or else she must be kept in subjection and administered by her cultural superiors' (page 63). Sri Aurobindo's analysis of the culture wars of colonial India finds an echo in the arguments of present-day postcolonial critics. Most of them would find unacceptable his privileging of India's 'spiritual essence' and his neglect of economic and social issues; but they would agree that cultural conflict has an irreducibly political aspect.

Once India was secure 'against the gigantic modern pressure' that made itself felt in cultural conflict, it could turn its attention to a larger problem affecting 'not only ours but all civilizations still in existence'. Sri Aurobindo admitted that 'from the view of the evolutionary future European and Indian civilizations at their best have been only half achievements' while 'the real and perfect civilization yet waits to be discovered'. One step in that direction would be the establishment of 'a unity with the rest of mankind in which we [Indians] shall maintain our spiritual and our outer independence' (pages 127–40).

[4] Ibid., 21.

Sri Aurobindo spoke of the necessity of a united humanity and of the dangers of its imperfect accomplishment in *The Ideal of Human Unity*, his main work of political theory. Unity was inevitable, first, because of 'the increasing closeness of common interests' of the world's nations together with a 'growing unwillingness to face the consequences of collision and ruinous struggle', secondly as a response to 'the force of a common uniting sentiment' (pages 148–9). But if the advent of a world-union was certain, the form it would take was not. One possibility was a world-state, 'the triumph of the idea of mechanical unity or rather uniformity'. Such a formation would be stable, but would tend to crush the life and diversity of the constituent units. A federal system would be better, but would 'allow only a play of minor variations', while a loose confederation, sufficiently free, would lack stability (pages 152–3).

A world-union would only be worth having if it led to 'a better, richer, more happy and puissant individual and collective life' (page 145). The richest, most creative flowerings of the human spirit, Sri Aurobindo observed, took place in small political units, such as the city-states of ancient Greece or the small kingdoms of ancient India. How was one to preserve the sources of creativity while gaining the political and economic advantages of a larger organization? The solution lay in the acceptance of a 'religion of humanity', not the rationalized creed to which Comte gave the name or a universal religious belief, but the recognition of 'a divine Reality, in which we are all one', of which humanity is the 'highest present vehicle on earth' (page 154).

The Ideal of Human Unity is optimistic without being utopian. Its proposals are based on a detailed study of the evolution of the nation that is of considerable interest as a sketch of world political history. The note placed in this compilation after the chapters from the book shows that Sri Aurobindo was aware of the difficulty of establishing a viable world-union. In a world where supranational groupings such as the European Union play an increasingly visible role, his arguments, even if now somewhat dated, retain their interest and relevance.

Sri Aurobindo's approach to the study of humanity and its works was always evolutionary. In book after book he traced the historical development of an institution or form of expression and projected that curve into the future. This is especially clear in *The Human Cycle*. Accepting the phases of social development proposed by the German theorist Karl Lamprecht — ages of symbolic, typal, conventional, individualistic, and subjective thought and action — he showed that they pointed to the start of another age that he called 'spiritual'. The early ages are 'infrarational', governed first by myths evoking 'a hidden, living and mysterious nature of things' (page 159), but later dominated by empty convention. As evolution proceeds, reason has its turn as the ruling faculty of humanity. In the individualistic age, conventions are cast aside as science dethrones religion as the arbiter of truth. But no rational system can be an adequate guide to life, because the sources of life are infrarational and suprarational. A new stage begins in which men and women discover their inner capacities and ultimately their inmost soul. But this subjective turn is not without its dangers. Individuals or nations may mistake the inner self, which is one in all, for the separate ego.

Sri Aurobindo showed in *The Human Cycle* that the emergence of subjectivism was the crucial movement of the present moment. If the perils of false subjectivism could be avoided, humanity might be able to make the transition from the rational to the suprarational curve of the cycle. This would mean the dawning of a spiritual age, one in which the 'inward view', characteristic of the finest periods of Eastern civilization, would be harmonized with the West's attempt to make 'the best we know and can attain the general rule of all life' (page 171). As a result humanity as a whole would 'become divine in consciousness and act', able to 'live inwardly and outwardly the divine life' (page 168).

The bulk of *The Human Cycle* is devoted to a criticism of contemporary civilization in the light of the scheme outlined above. Many of Sri Aurobindo's observations about the inadequacies of reason and the dangers of 'false subjectivism' were borne out by events that took place between the time of writing, during World War I, and book-publication, after World War II. But his hopes for a 'spiritual emergence' have not been fulfilled to any noticeable extent. Such a fulfilment, he showed in his philosophical works, could come about only by means of a general evolutionary change.

Sri Aurobindo undertook to explain the nature and necessity of the spiritual evolution in *The Life Divine*, his principal philosophical work. He began by showing that the materialist's attempt to deny the truth of anything non-physical was as inadequate as the pure idealist's attempt to deny the truth of the material world (pages 185–95). Matter is meaningless without spirit, spirit purposeless without matter. Consciousness and life could never have emerged from matter if there had not been a prior 'involution' of the powers of spirit in the unconsciousness of matter. The process of evolution, by which these powers re-emerge, is fundamentally an evolution of consciousness and only secondarily one of biological forms. As life has emerged from matter and mind from life, so higher powers must emerge from mind.

Mind is the characteristic power of the human being. But mind, even in the form of reason, is inadequate to the task of governing life. It cannot arrive at truth because it works by discerning differences, and truth by its nature lies in identity. Mind presupposes a power of knowledge free from its limitations. This power Sri Aurobindo called 'supermind', 'because to reach it we have to pass beyond and turn upon mind as the mind itself has passed and turned upon life and inconscient matter'. When this happens the human consciousness 'knows and sees, no longer by the reason groping among external data, but by an ever increasing and always more luminous self-illumining and all illuminating experience' (pages 233–4).

Humanity is not the term of the evolutionary process. 'This imperfect being with his hampered, confused, ill-ordered and mostly ineffective consciousness cannot be the end and highest height of the mysterious upward surge of Nature' (page 229). 'Man is a transitional being', a doorway to things beyond him.[5] 'The next approaching achievement in the earth's evolution' is the 'step from man towards superman'. This step is inevitable 'because it is at once the intention of the inner Spirit and the logic of Nature's process' (page 227).

The cosmic process of evolutionary emergence is reflected in every individual who opens herself or himself to its workings. Besides the 'outward visible process of physical evolution with birth as its machinery' and the human body as its result, there is

[5] Like most men and women writing before the 1970s, Sri Aurobindo often used gender-specific language that many today find objectionable. 'Man' was his ordinary term for the human being.

'an invisible process of soul evolution with rebirth into ascending grades of form and consciousness as its machinery' (page 206). Each of us has a permanent psychic entity or soul with its own history of individual development. Rebirth provides the soul with the opportunity for varied experiences in different lives; but for this to have any evolutionary sense, there must be 'a connected sequence from life to life, a result of action and experience, an evolutionary consequence to the soul, a law of Karma' (page 250).

Sri Aurobindo conceded that one 'cannot really assert as against the sceptic' the reality of rebirth; but he showed that it is a logical necessity if one accepts the evolution of consciousness (page 243). His conception has little in common with the naive notions about reincarnation prevalent in India. (For this see especially the letter reproduced on pages 258–9). Similarly, the popular idea of *karma* as the whips and lollipops of a cosmic school-master has little to do with the theory presented in *The Life Divine* and *The Problem of Rebirth*.

Nowhere in his philosophical writings did Sri Aurobindo 'assert as against the sceptic' the truth of his world-view. He simply showed that there was nothing implausible about the idea of an evolution of consciousness, and made a case for the likelihood of the emergence of powers greater than mind. A materialistic philosopher would object that consciousness has no existence apart from matter. Sri Aurobindo reversed the order of priority:

> Consciousness is the great underlying fact, the universal witness for whom the world is a field, the senses instruments. To that witness the worlds and their objects appeal for their reality and for the one world or the many, for the physical equally with the supraphysical we have no other evidence that they exist (page 198).

Viewed from this angle, experiences of the inner consciousness must be given more importance than the bare evidence of the senses. The highest philosophy, Sri Aurobindo insisted, was a transcription of knowledge gained by means of spiritual experience. As he wrote in the letter here entitled 'Metaphysics and Yoga', 'it is not by "thinking out" the entire reality, but by a change of consciousness that one can pass from the ignorance to the Knowledge — the Knowledge by which we become what we know' (page 264). His own philosophy, summarized in the piece called 'Sri Aurobindo's Teaching and Method of Practice', is meant to provide the intellectual basis for a yogic practice aiming at the discovery of the individual's true Self and a participation in the eventual transformation of human nature.

Yoga is often regarded as a thing removed from normal human concerns, suitable perhaps for those disappointed by life but of little value to ordinary men and women. In *The Synthesis of Yoga* Sri Aurobindo tried to correct this misconception. In evolutionary terms life 'is a vast Yoga of Nature' attempting 'to realise her perfection in an ever increasing expression of her yet unrealised potentialities'. Those who practice yoga can compress this evolutionary process 'into a single life or a few years'. They do so not by drawing on supernatural forces but by making 'an intense and exceptional use of powers' that Nature 'has already manifested or is progressively organising in her less exalted but more general operations'. So viewed yoga 'ceases to appear something mystic and abnormal' (pages 268–9). Rather it is life striving to reach its highest potentials.

Over the centuries many specialized paths of yoga have developed in India. They may be classified according to the human faculty they make use of. The path of knowledge harnesses the mind; the path of devotion, the heart; the path of works, the will. Sri Aurobindo discovered that all three paths draw on a 'central dynamic force' that he identified with the *shakti* or divine power of the Tantras. This shakti can become the means of a synthetic spiritual discipline, an 'integral yoga' less specialized and more powerful than any traditional path. His yoga has as its aim not only the liberation of the soul 'from its present natural ignorance and limitation' but also the 'full perfection and enjoyment of the spiritual power, light and joy in the human existence'.[6]

In the four parts of *The Synthesis of Yoga*, Sri Aurobindo considered the paths of works, knowledge and devotion, and the yoga of self-perfection he practised in Pondicherry. He showed that the experiences of all the paths — for example the cosmic consciousness or the *ananda brahman* ('bliss-reality') — could be considered parts of the integral yoga (pages 299–313). But

[6] Sri Aurobindo, *The Synthesis of Yoga* (Pondicherry: Sri Aurobindo Ashram, 1971), 587.

the method he recommended was not confined to the practices of any of these systems. In 'Standards of Conduct and Spiritual Freedom' he showed that human moral standards 'are only temporary, imperfect and evolutive attempts' to formalize 'our stumbling mental progress', but that the 'divine manifestation cannot be bound by our little rules and fragile sanctities' (page 284). Similarly he wrote that the traditional yogas were useful formalizations of practice, but that the shakti of the integral yoga could not 'act according to a fixed system'. 'Without rejecting anything essential', it would compel all to undergo a divine change, making use of 'all life as the means of this integral yoga' (pages 276–7).

In the *Synthesis* Sri Aurobindo laid down the foundations of his integral yoga. In his letters he provided detailed guidance to those engaged in its practice. Dealing with everything from the soul to the sexual impulse, he demonstrated the truth of his maxim, 'All life is Yoga'. His path, although based on traditional Indian practices, was quite new in some of its aspects. In the letter published here under the heading 'The Novelty of the Integral Yoga' he outlined its distinctive characteristics: (1) its purpose is the transformation of life and not an escape from its difficulties, (2) it is done not for the sake of the individual but with an eye to the universal evolutionary process, (3) its method takes hold of the whole of human nature and not just part of it. 'Our yoga,' he summed up, 'is not a retreading of old walks, but a spiritual adventure' (page 339).

Among the techniques of the traditional yogas that Sri Aurobindo recommended to his disciples was *dhyana*, meditation or contemplation. In the letter reproduced on pages 326–8 he presented different methods of meditation, gave the conditions the beginner should try to secure, and suggested objects or ideas to meditate upon. In other letters he showed how the traditional paths of action and devotion could be made parts of an integral practice. But he stressed that success in his yoga did not depend on particular techniques but on an inner surrender to the workings of the divine shakti. The 'central process of the yoga' was a twofold opening to this power: 'an opening inwards of the inner mind, vital, physical to the inmost part of us, the psychic, and an opening upwards to what is above the mind' (page 329).

Some of Sri Aurobindo's letters give a more immediate

impression of the experiences his yoga is based on than the formal prose of *The Life Divine* or *The Synthesis of Yoga*. An even more direct sense of the spiritual life comes through his poetry. Like the Vedic rishis, like Yeats and Heidegger, Sri Aurobindo believed that the rhythmic language of poetry could convey meanings that went much deeper than the intellectual significance of the words. The rishis embodied their vision in 'Mantras, revealed verses of power, not of an ordinary but of a divine inspiration and source'.[7] In *The Future Poetry* Sri Aurobindo showed that this heightened power of speech was not the prerogative of Sanskrit scriptures, but could be found to some degree in the poetry of any language with a developed literature. English poetry had passed through evolutionary stages of primarily physical (Chaucer), vital (Shakespeare) and mental (Pope) inspiration. In the work of Wordsworth, Blake and other so-called Romantic poets it had sometimes risen to heights of inspiration close to what he called the mantra. He hoped that this tendency would be continued in contemporary poetry, and saw hints of this in the work of Yeats and George Russell (A.E.). But he was disappointed by most poetry published between the two world wars, considering much of the work of Eliot and other Modernists to be a relapse into mere intellectuality.

Sri Aurobindo's own poetry was written in almost complete isolation from the main trends of twentieth-century poetry in English. In so far as he emulated others, he looked to the classical ages of Greek, Latin, and Sanskrit literature, and to the Romantic and post-Romantic poets of England. As a result his work now appears dated, and has attracted little attention outside the circle of his admirers. This is unfortunate, because the poetry he wrote in Pondicherry after 1930 gives voice to an unusual inspiration in verse of great elegance and power. This can best be seen in a short lyric like 'Trance' (page 352), but is sustained to a remarkable degree throughout the twenty-four thousand lines of *Savitri*. In the comparatively short canto reproduced in this compilation, Savitri makes the discovery of her psychic being or soul. This leads to a descent of the Divine Force and an answering ascent of the *kundalini* power hidden in the Inconscient. The process,

[7] Sri Aurobindo, *Hymns to the Mystic Fire* (Pondicherry: Sri Aurobindo Ashram, 1971), 1.

explained in plain prose in 'The Central Process of the Yoga', is in the poem rendered living and almost palpable,

For every symbol was a reality
And brought the presence which had given it life.

In his message of 15 August 1947, Sri Aurobindo expressed the hope that India's independence day might come to be regarded as 'an important date in a new age opening for the whole world, for the political, social, cultural and spiritual future of humanity'.[8] His own writings in the fields of politics, society and spirituality stand among modern India's most significant contributions to world culture.

PETER HEEHS

8 Sri Aurobindo's independence day message is reproduced on pages 369–71.

The Essential Writings of Sri Aurobindo

The Spiritual Revolution

ALL WOULD change if man could once consent to be spiritualised; but his nature mental and vital and physical is rebellious to the higher law. He loves his imperfections.

The Spirit is the truth of our being; mind and life and body in their imperfection are its masks, but in their perfection should be its moulds. To be spiritual only is not enough; that prepares a number of souls for heaven, but leaves the earth very much where it was. Neither is a compromise the way of salvation.

The world knows three kinds of revolution. The material has strong results, the moral and intellectual are infinitely larger in their scope and richer in their fruits, but the spiritual are the great sowings.

If the triple change could coincide in a perfect correspondence, a faultless work would be done; but the mind and body of mankind cannot hold perfectly a strong spiritual inrush: most is spilt, much of the rest is corrupted. Many intellectual and physical upturnings of our soil are needed to work out a little result from a large spiritual sowing.

Each religion has helped mankind. Paganism increased in man the light of beauty, the largeness and height of his life, his aim at a many-sided perfection; Christianity gave him some vision of divine love and charity; Buddhism has shown him a noble way to be wiser, gentler, purer, Judaism and Islam how to be religiously faithful in action and zealously devoted to God; Hinduism has opened to him the largest and profoundest spiritual possibilities. A great thing would be done if all these God-visions could embrace and cast themselves into each other; but intellectual dogma and cult egoism stand in the way.

All religions have saved a number of souls, but none yet has been able to spiritualise mankind. For that there is needed not cult and creed, but a sustained and all-comprehending effort at spiritual self-evolution.

The changes we see in the world today are intellectual, moral, physical in their ideal and intention: the spiritual revolution waits for its hour and throws up meanwhile its waves here and there. Until it comes the sense of the others cannot be understood and till then all interpretation of present happening and forecast of man's future are vain things. For its nature, power, event are that which will determine the next cycle of our humanity.

Part One
Nationalism and Beyond

Our ideal is that of Swaraj or absolute autonomy free from foreign control. We claim the right of every nation to live its own life by its own energies according to its own nature and ideals. We reject the claim of aliens to force upon us a civilisation inferior to our own or to keep us out of our inheritance on the untenable ground of a superior fitness. . . . We demand the realisation of our corporate existence as a distinct race and nation because that is the only way in which the ultimate brotherhood of humanity can be achieved.

An Open Letter to My Countrymen

PART ONE consists of articles and speeches from Sri Aurobindo's political career (1906–10), a political article written a number of years earlier, and two letters of 1920 declining invitations to reenter the political field.

• In *New Lamps for Old* the twenty-one-year-old Aurobindo, just returned from England, criticized the aims, activities and leadership of the Indian National Congress. Representing only the small English-educated middle class, the Congress had no right to call itself 'national'. An effective national movement had to draw its strength from the masses.

• Written when Aurobindo had emerged as one of the leaders of the Extremist Party in Bengal, *The Doctrine of Passive Resistance* sketched the three strategies open to a country trying to gain political freedom, 'the life-breath of a nation'. The first was petitioning, the highly ineffective method of the Congress; the second, self-help, a policy advocated by the Extremists; the third, resistance, passive and active. Active resistance was difficult to organize in a country circumstanced like India (although Aurobindo was making secret revolutionary preparations). Passive resistance was therefore an attractive option, though, as Aurobindo said in another article, his party had 'no intention of stressing the passivity at the expense of the resistance'.

• Aurobindo felt that India had to be free not only for itself, but in order to give its spiritual values to the world. Therefore, as he said in *The Present Situation*, the national movement was not a mere political movement but a 'religion', that is, a high endeavour demanding dedication and self-sacrifice.

• After a series of mystic experiences, some of which he spoke of in his *Uttarpara Speech* for the first and only time in public, Aurobindo came to feel the spiritual side of India's mission on a more personal level. He told the religious group that invited him to Uttarpara that a free Indian nationality was part of the fulfilment of the *sanatana dharma*, the universal core of the Indian religious tradition.

• This universal religion, he wrote in *The Ideal of the Karmayogin*, was not limited to what is called Hinduism. It was a search for the inner truth of existence. The solution of the problems of humanity could only come by union with this truth, not by outer, mechanical expedients.

• It was to seek this inner foundation that Aurobindo withdrew from the national movement in 1910. To those who invited him to resume his leadership in 1920, he replied that he saw his work now as one with 'a spiritual basis, a work of social, cultural and economic reconstruction'. What was needed was a spiritual, not merely a political revolution.

New Lamps for Old

'Thou art weighed in the balance and found wanting.'

'The little that is done seems nothing when we look forward and see how much we have yet to do.'

THUS FAR I have been making a circuit, in my disinclination to collide too abruptly with the prepossessions of my countrymen and now that I am compelled to handle my subject more intimately and with a firmer grasp, nothing but my deliberate conviction that it is quite imperative for someone to speak out, has at all persuaded me to continue. I have at the very outset to make distinct the grounds on which I charge the Congress with inadequacy. In the process I find myself bound to say many things that cannot fail to draw obloquy upon me: I shall be compelled to outrage many susceptibilities; compelled to advance many unacceptable ideas; compelled, — worst of all, — to stroke the wrong way many powerful persons, who are wont to be pampered with unstinted flattery and worship. But at all risks the thing must be done, and since it is on me that the choice has fallen, I can only proceed in the best fashion at my command and with what boldness I may. I say, of the Congress, then, this, — that its aims are mistaken, that the spirit in which it proceeds towards their accomplishment is not a spirit of sincerity and whole-heartedness, and that the methods it has chosen are not the right methods, and the leaders in whom it trusts, not the right sort of men to be leaders; — in brief, that we are at present the blind led, if not by the blind, at any rate by the one-eyed.

The third of a series of nine articles published under this title in the *Indu Prakash*, a weekly newspaper of Bombay, in 1893 and 1894.

To begin with, I should a little while ago have had no hesitation in saying that the National Congress was not really national and had not in any way attempted to become *national.* But that was before I became a student of Mr Pherozshah Mehta's speeches.[1] Now to deal with this vexed subject, one must tread on very burning ground, and I shall make no apology for treading with great care and circumspection. The subject is wrapped in so thick a dust of controversy, and legal wits have been so busy drawing subtle distinctions about it, that a word which was once perfectly straightforward and simple, has become almost as difficult as the Law itself. It is therefore incumbent on me to explain what I wish to imply, when I say that the Congress is not really national. Now I do not at all mean to re-echo the Anglo-Indian catchword about the Hindus and Mahomedans. Like most catchwords it is without much force, and has been still further stripped of meaning by the policy of the Congress. The Mahomedans have been as largely represented on that body as any reasonable community could desire, and their susceptibilities, far from being denied respect, have always been most assiduously soothed and flattered. It is entirely futile then to take up the Anglo-Indian refrain; but this at least I should have imagined, that in an era when democracy and similar big words slide so glibly from our tongues, a body like the Congress, which represents not the mass of the population, but a single and very limited class, could not honestly be called national. It is perfectly true that the House of Commons represents not the English nation, but simply the English aristocracy and middle class and yet is none the less national. But the House of Commons is a body legally constituted and empowered to speak and act for the nation, while the Congress is self-created and it is not justifiable for a self-created body representing only a single and limited class to call itself national. It would be just as absurd if the Liberal Party, because it allows within its limits all sorts and conditions of men, were to hold annual meetings and call itself the English National Congress. When therefore I said that the Congress was not really national, I simply meant that it did not represent the mass of the population.

[1] Pherozshah Mehta (1845–1915), a barrister of Bombay, was for many years one of the most influential figures in the Indian National Congress. As President of 1890 session, held in Calcutta, he delivered the address Sri Aurobindo refers to below.

But Mr Pherozshah Mehta will have nothing to do with this sense of the word. In his very remarkable and instructive Presidential address at Calcutta, he argued that the Congress could justly arrogate this epithet without having any direct support from the proletariate; and he went on to explain his argument with the profound subtlety expected from an experienced advocate. 'It is because the masses are still unable to articulate definite political demands that the functions and duty devolve upon their educated and enlightened compatriots to feel, to understand and to interpret their grievances and requirements, and to suggest and indicate how these can best be redressed and met.'

This formidable sentence is, by the way, typical of Mr Mehta's style and reveals the secret of his oratory, which like all great inventions is exceedingly simple: it is merely to say the same thing twice over in different words. But its more noteworthy feature is the idea implied that because the Congress professes to discharge this duty, it may justly call itself national. Nor is this all; Calcutta comes to the help of Bombay in the person of Mr Manmohan Ghose, who repeats and elucidates Mr Mehta's idea.[2] The Congress, he says, asserting the rights of that body to speak for the masses, represents the thinking portion of the Indian people, whose duty it is to guide the ignorant, and this in his opinion sufficiently justifies the Congress in calling itself national. To differ from a successful barrister and citizen, a man held in high honour by every graduate in India, and above all a future member of the Viceroy's Council, would never have been a very easy task for a timid man like myself. But when he is reinforced by so respectable and weighty a citizen as Mr Manmohan Ghose, I really cannot find the courage to persevere. I shall therefore amend the obnoxious phrase and declare that the National Congress may be as national as you please, but it is not a popular body and has not in any way attempted to become a popular body.

But at this point some one a little less learned than Mr Pherozshah Mehta may interfere and ask how it can be true that the Congress is not a popular body. I can only point his attention to a previous statement of mine that the Congress represents not

2 Manmohan Ghose (1844–1896), a barrister of Calcutta active in Congress politics, who as chairman of the reception committee at the 1890 session delivered the address Sri Aurobindo comments on below.

the mass of the population, but a single and limited class. No doubt the Congress tried very hard in the beginning to believe that it really represented the mass of the population, but if it has not already abandoned, it ought now at least to abandon the pretension as quite untenable. And indeed when Mr Pherozshah Mehta and Mr Manmohan Ghose have admitted this patent fact — not as delegates only, but as officials of the Congress — and have even gone so far as to explain the fact away, it is hardly requisite for me to combat the fallacy. But perhaps the enquirer, not yet satisfied, may go on to ask what is that single and limited class which I imagine the Congress to represent. Here it may be of help to us to refer again to the speeches of the Congress leaders and more especially to the talented men from whom I have already quoted. In his able official address Mr Manmohan Ghose asks himself this very question and answers that the Congress represents the thinking portion of the Indian people. 'The delegates present here today,' he goes on, 'are the chosen representatives of that section of the Indian people who have learnt to think, and whose number is daily increasing with marvellous rapidity.' Perhaps Mr Ghose is a little too facile in his use of the word 'thinking'. So much at the mercy of their instincts and prejudices are the generality of mankind, that we hazard a very high estimate when we call even one man out of ten thousand a thinking man. But evidently by the thinking portion Mr Ghose would like to indicate the class to which he himself belongs; I mean those of us who have got some little idea of the machinery of English politics and are eager to import it into India along with cheap Liverpool cloths, shoddy Brummagem wares, and other useful and necessary things which have killed the fine and genuine textures. If this is a true interpretation he is perfectly correct in what he says. For it is really from this class that the Congress movement draws its origin, its support and its most enthusiastic votaries. And if I were asked to describe their class by a single name, I should not hesitate to call it our new middle class. For here too English goods have driven out native goods: our society has lost its old landmarks and is being demarcated on the English model. But of all the brand new articles we have imported, inconceivably the most important is that large class of people — journalists, barristers, doctors, officials, graduates and traders — who have grown up and are increasing with prurient rapidity under the aegis of the British rule: and this class I call the middle class: for, when we are so proud of our imported English goods, it would be absurd, when we want labels for them, not to import their English names as well. Besides this name which I have chosen is really a more accurate description than phrases like 'thinking men' or 'the educated class' which are merely expressions of our own boundless vanity and self-conceit. However largely we may choose to indulge in vague rhetoric about the all-pervading influence of the Congress, no one can honestly doubt that here is the constituency from which it is really empowered. There is indeed a small contingent of aristocrats and a smaller contingent of the more well-to-do ryots: but these are only two flying-wheels in the great middle class machine. The fetish-worshipper may declare as loudly as he pleases that it represents all sorts and conditions of people, just as the Anglo-Indians used to insist that it represented no one but the Bengali Babu. Facts have been too strong for the Anglo-Indian and they will be too strong in the end for the fetish-worshipper. Partisans on either side can in no way alter the clear and immutable truth — these words were put on paper long before the recent disturbances in Bombay and certainly without any suspicion that the prophecy I then hazarded would be fortified by so apt and striking a comment. Facts are already beginning to speak in a very clear and unambiguous voice. How long will the Congress sit like careless Belshazzar, at the feast of mutual admiration?[3] Already the decree has gone out against it; already even the eyes that are dim can discern, — for has it not been written in blood? — the first pregnant phrase of the handwriting upon the wall. 'God has numbered the kingdom and finished it.' Surely after so rough a lesson, we shall not wait to unseal our eyes and unstop our ears, until the unseen finger moves on and writes the second and sterner sentence: 'Thou art weighed in the balance and found wanting.' Or must we sit idle with folded hands and only bestir ourselves when the short hour of grace is past and the kingdom given to another more worthy than we?

[3] In the Bible (*Daniel*, chapter 5) Belshazzar is king of Babylon, son of Nebuchadnezzar. At a feast at his palace appeared mysterious handwriting on the wall. He called the prophet Daniel to read and interpret it. According to Daniel the first word, *mene*, meant 'God hath numbered thy kingdom, and finished it,' and the second word *tekel*, meant 'Thou art weighed in the balances and art found wanting.'

The Doctrine of Passive Resistance

Introduction

IN A series of articles, published in this paper soon after the Calcutta session of the Congress, we sought to indicate our view both of the ideal which the Congress had adopted, the ideal of Swaraj or Self-Government as it exists in the United Kingdom or the Colonies, and of the possible lines of policy by which that ideal might be attained.[1] There are, we pointed out, only three possible policies: petitioning, an unprecedented way of attempting a nation's liberty, which cannot possibly succeed except under conditions which have not yet existed among human beings; self-development and self-help; and the old orthodox historical method of organised resistance to the existing form of Government. We acknowledge that the policy of self-development which the New Party had forced to the front, was itself a novel departure under the circumstances of modern India. Self-development of an independent nation is one thing; self-development from a state of servitude under an alien and despotic rule without the forcible or peaceful removal of that rule as an indispensable preliminary, is quite another. No national self-development is possible without the support of *rāja-śakti*, organised political strength, commanding, and whenever necessary compelling general allegiance and obedience. A caste may develop, a particular community may develop, by its own

The first of seven articles published under this title in April 1907 in *Bande Mataram*, an English-language daily newspaper of Calcutta, then edited by Sri Aurobindo.

[1] At the Calcutta session of the Indian National Congress (December 1906), it was resolved that 'the system of Government obtaining in the self-governing British Colonies should be extended to India'. The president of the session, Dadabhai Naoroji (1825–1917), later equated such self-government with 'Swaraj', a term used by the New Party in the sense of 'entire self-government'.

efforts supported by a strong social organisation; a nation cannot. Industrially, socially, educationally, there can be no genuine progress carrying the whole nation forward, unless there is a central force representing either the best thought and energy of the country or else the majority of its citizens and able to enforce the views and decisions of the nation on all its constituent members. Because Japan had such a central authority, she was able in thirty years to face Europe as an equal; because we in India neither had such an authority nor tried to develop it, but supported each tottering step by clinging to the step-motherly apron-strings of a foreign Government, our record of more than seventy years has not been equal to one year of Japan. We have fumbled through the nineteenth century, prattling of enlightenment and national regeneration; and the result has been not national progress, but national confusion and weakness. Individuals here and there might emancipate themselves and come to greatness; particular communities might show a partial and one-sided development, for a time only; but the nation instead of progressing, sank into a very slough of weakness, helplessness and despondency. Political freedom is the life-breath of a nation; to attempt social reform, educational reform, industrial expansion, the moral improvement of the race without aiming first and foremost at political freedom, is the very height of ignorance and futility. Such attempts are foredoomed to disappointment and failure; yet when the disappointment and failure come, we choose to attribute them to some radical defect in the national character; as if the nation were at fault and not its wise men who would not or could not understand the first elementary conditions of success. The primary requisite for national progress, national reform, is the free habit of free and healthy national thought and action which is impossible in a state of servitude. The second is the organisation of the national will in a strong central authority.

How impossible it is to carry out efficiently any large national object in the absence of this authority was shown by the fate of the Boycott in Bengal.[2] It is idle to disguise from

[2] In August 1905 thousands of Bengalis resolved to boycott British products unless the government's proposal to partition their province was dropped. For a short time this boycott had limited success in hurting British commercial interests.

ourselves that the Boycott is not as yet effective except spasmodically and in patches. Yet to carry through the Boycott was a solemn national decision which has not been reversed but rather repeatedly confirmed. Never indeed has the national will been so generally and unmistakably declared; but for the want of a central authority to work for the necessary conditions, to support by its ubiquitous presence the weak and irresolute and to coerce the refractory, it has not been properly carried out. For the same reason national education languishes. For the same reason every attempt at large national action has failed. It is idle to talk of self-development unless we first evolve a suitable central authority or Government which all will or must accept. The Japanese perceived this at a very early stage and leaving aside all other matters, devoted their first energies to the creation of such an authority in the person of the Mikado and his Government, holding it cheaply purchased even at the price of temporary internal discord and civil slaughter. We also must develop a central authority, which shall be a popular Government in fact though not in name. But Japan was independent; we have to establish a popular authority which will exist side by side and in rivalry with a despotic foreign bureaucracy — no ordinary rough-riding despotism, but quiet, pervasive and subtle — one that has fastened its grip on every detail of our national life and will not easily be persuaded to let go, even in the least degree, its octopus-like hold. This popular authority will have to dispute every part of our national life and activity, one by one, step by step, with the intruding force to the extreme point of entire emancipation from alien control. This and no less than this is the task before us. A Moderate critic characterised it at the time as an unheroic programme; but to us it seems so heroic that we frankly acknowledge its novelty and audacity and the uncertainty of success. For success depends on the presence of several very rare conditions. It demands in the first place a country for its field of action in which the people are more powerfully swayed by the fear of social ex-communication and the general censure of their fellows than by the written law. It demands a country where the capacity for extreme self-denial is part of the national character or for centuries has taken a prominent place in the national discipline. These conditions exist in India. But it requires also an iron endurance, tenacity, doggedness, far above anything that is needed for the more usual military revolt or sanguinary revolution. These qualities we have not as yet developed at least in Bengal; but they are easily generated by suffering and necessity and hardened into permanence by a prolonged struggle with superior power. There is nothing like a strong pressure from above to harden and concentrate what lies below — always provided that the superior pressure is not such as to crush the substance on which it is acting. The last requisite therefore for the success of the policy of self-development against the pressure of foreign rule is that the bureaucracy will so far respect its former traditions and professions as not to interfere finally with any course of action of the popular authority which does not itself try violently to subvert the connection of the British Empire with India. It is extremely doubtful whether this last condition will be satisfied. It is easy to see how the bureaucracy might put a summary end to National Education or an effective check on industrial expansion or do away arbitrarily with popular Arbitration Courts. It is easy to see how the temptation to resort to Russian methods on a much larger and effective scale than that of mere Fullerism might prove too strong for a privileged class which felt power slipping from its hold.[3] We therefore said in our previous articles that we must carry on the attempt at self-development as long as we were permitted. What would be our next resource if it were no longer permitted, it is too early to discuss.

The attempt at self-development by self-help is absolutely necessary for our national salvation, whether we can carry it peacefully to the end or not. In no other way can we get rid of the fatal dependence, passivity and helplessness in which a century of all-pervasive British control has confirmed us. To recover the habit of independent motion and independent action is the first necessity. It was for this reason that after extreme provocation and full conviction of the hopelessness otherwise of inducing any change of policy in the older politicians, the leaders of the New School decided to form an independent party and place

[3] After the partition of Bengal (October 1905), Joseph Bampfylde Fuller (1854–1935) was appointed the first lieutenant-governor (administrative head) of the new province of Eastern Bengal and Assam. For several months, until his forced retirement in August 1906, Fuller pursued a policy of intimidation and repression, particularly against those active in the boycott movement.

their views as an independent programme before the country.[4] Their action, though much blamed at the time, has been thoroughly justified by results. The National Congress has not indeed broken with the old petitioning traditions, but it has admitted the new policy as an essential part of the national programme. Swadeshi and National Education have been recognised, and, in all probability, Arbitration will be given its proper prominence at the next session; Boycott has been admitted as permissible in principle to all parts of India though the recommendation to extend it in practice as an integral part of the national policy was not pressed. It only remained to develop the central authority which will execute the national policy and evolve with time into a popular Government. It was for this object that the New Party determined not to be satisfied with any further evasion of the constitution question, though they did not press for the adoption of their own particular scheme. It is for this object that a Central National Committee has been formed; that Conferences are being held in various districts and sub-divisions and Committees created; that the Provincial Conferences are expected to appoint a Provincial Committee for all Bengal. The mere creation of these Committees will not provide us with our central authority, nor will they be really effective for the purpose until the new spirit and the new views are paramount in the whole country. But it is the first step which costs and the first step has been taken.

So far, well; but the opposition of the bureaucracy to the national self-development must be taken into account. Opposition, not necessarily final and violent, will undoubtedly be offered; and we have not as yet considered the organisation of any means by which it can be effectually met. Obviously, we shall have to fall back on the third policy of organised resistance, and have only to decide what form the resistance should take, passive or active, defensive or aggressive. It is well known that the New Party long ago formulated and all Bengal has in theory accepted, the doctrine of passive, or, as it might be more comprehensively

[4] The programme of the New Party (generally known as the Extremist Party) consisted chiefly of (1) the acceptance of Swaraj or self-government as the goal of the national movement, (2) the encouragement of the use of Swadeshi or indigenous products, (3) a boycott of British products, and (4) the establishment of national schools and colleges. Among its other proposals was the setting up of arbitration courts to replace British law courts.

termed, defensive resistance. We have therefore not only to organise a central authority, not only to take up all branches of our national life into our hands, but, in order to meet bureaucratic opposition and to compel the alien control to remove its hold on us, if not at once, then tentacle by tentacle, we must organise defensive resistance.

The Present Situation

MY FELLOW countrymen, Mr Ranade has said that there is no President here, but that God Himself is our President. I accept that remark in the most reverent spirit, and before addressing you, I ask Him first to inspire me. I have been asked to speak on the 'Needs of the Present Situation'. What is the present situation? What is the situation of this country today? Just as I was coming in, this paper [*showing a copy of the 'Bande Mataram' newspaper*] was put into my hands, and looking at the first page of it, I saw two items of news, 'The "Yugantar" Trial, Judgment delivered, the Printer convicted and sentenced to two years' rigorous imprisonment.' The other is 'Another Newspaper Prosecution, The "Navasakti" Office sacked and searched, Printer let out on a bail of Rs. 10,000.' This is the situation of the country today. Do you realise what I mean? There is a creed in India today which calls itself Nationalism, a creed which has come to you from Bengal. This is a creed which many of you have accepted, and you accepted it when you called yourselves Nationalists. Have you realised, have you yet realised what that means? Have you realised what it is that you have taken in hand? Or is it that you have merely accepted it in the pride of a superior intellectual conviction? You call yourselves Nationalists. What is Nationalism? Nationalism is not a mere political programme; Nationalism is a religion that has come from God; Nationalism is a creed in which you shall have to live. Let no man dare to call himself a Nationalist if he does so merely with a sort of intellectual pride, thinking that he is more patriotic, thinking that he is something higher than those who do not call themselves by that name. If you

A speech delivered in Bombay on 19 January 1907 at the invitation of the Bombay National Union.

are going to be a Nationalist, if you are going to assent to this religion of Nationalists, you must do it in the religious spirit. You must remember that you are the instrument of God for the salvation of your own country. You must live as the instruments of God. What is this that has happened in Bengal? You call yourselves Nationalists, but when this happens to you, what will you do? This thing is happening daily in Bengal, because, in Bengal, Nationalism has come to the people as a religion, and it has been accepted as a religion. But certain forces which are against that religion are trying to crush its rising strength. It always happens when a new religion is preached, when God is going to be born in the people, that such forces rise with all their weapons in their hands to crush this religion. In Bengal too a new religion, a religion divine and sattwic has been preached, and this religion they are trying with all the weapons at their command to crush. By what strength are we in Bengal able to survive? Nationalism has not been crushed. Nationalism is not going to be crushed. Nationalism survives in the strength of God and it is not possible to crush it, whatever weapons are brought against it. Nationalism is immortal; Nationalism cannot die; because it is no human thing. It is God who is working in Bengal. God cannot be killed, God cannot be sent to jail. When these things happen among you, I say to you solemnly, what will you do? Will you do as they do in Bengal? [*Cries of* 'Yes'.] Don't lightly say 'yes'. It is a solemn thing; and suppose that God puts you this question, how will you answer it? Have you got a real faith? Or is it merely a political aspiration? Is it merely a larger kind of selfishness? Or is it merely that you wish to be free to oppress others, as you are being oppressed? Do you hold your political creed from a higher source? Is it God that is born in you? Have you realised that you are merely the instruments of God, that your bodies are not your own? You are merely instruments of God for the work of the Almighty. Have you realised that? If you have realised that, then you are truly Nationalists; then alone will you be able to restore this great nation. In Bengal it has been realised clearly by some, more clearly by others, but it has been realised and you on this side of the country must also realise it; then there will be a blessing on our work, and this great nation will rise again and become once more what it was in the days of its spiritual greatness. [*Applause*] You are the instruments of God to save the light, to save the spirit of India from lasting obscuration and abasement.

Let me tell you what it is that has happened in Bengal. You all know what Bengal used to be; you all know that 'Bengali' used to be a term of reproach among the nations; when people spoke of Bengal, with what feelings did they speak of it? Was it with feelings of respect? Was it with feelings of admiration? You know very well what people of other countries used to say of the Bengali. You know well what you yourselves used to say of the Bengali. Do you think that now? If anybody had told you that Bengal would come forward as the saviour of India, how many of you would have believed it? You would have said, 'No. The saviour of India cannot be Bengal; it may be Maharashtra; it may be Punjab; but it will not be Bengal; the idea is absurd.' What has happened then? What has caused this change? What has made the Bengali so different from his old self? One thing has happened in Bengal, and it is this, that Bengal is learning to believe. Bengal was once drunk with the wine of European civilisation and with the purely intellectual teaching that it received from the West. It began to see all things, to judge all things through the imperfect instrumentality of the intellect. When it was so, Bengal became atheistic, it became a land of doubters and cynics. But still in Bengal there was an element of strength. Whatever the Bengali believed, if he believed at all—many do not believe—but if he believed at all, there was one thing about the Bengali, that he lived what he believed. If he was a Brahmo, or if he was a social reformer, no matter whether what he believed was true or not, but if he believed, he lived that belief. If he believed that one thing was necessary for the salvation of the country, if he believed that a thing was true and that it should be done, he did not stop to think about it. He would not stop to consider from all intellectual standpoints whether the truth in it was merely an ideal and to balance whether he would do honestly what he believed or whether he could hold the belief intellectually without living it, but without regard to consequences to himself, he went and did what he believed. And if he was not a Brahmo, if he was an orthodox Hindu, still if he really believed what the Hindu shastras taught then he never hesitated to drive even his dearest away, rather than aid by his weakness in corrupting society. He never hesitated to enforce what he believed to the uttermost without thinking of the consequences to himself.

Well, what was the one saving element in the Bengali nature? The Bengali has the faculty of belief. Belief is not a merely intellectual process, belief is not a mere persuasion of the mind, belief is something that is in our heart, and what you believe, you must do, because belief is from God. It is to the heart that God speaks, it is in the heart that God resides. This saved the Bengali. Because of this capacity of belief, we were chosen as the people who were to save India, the people who were to stand foremost, the people who must suffer for their belief, the people who must meet everything in the faith that God was with them and that God is in them. Such a people need not be politically strong, it need not be a people sound in physique, it need not be a people of the highest intellectual standing. It must be a people who can believe. In Bengal there came a flood of religious truth. Certain men were born, men whom the educated world would not have recognised if that belief, if that God within them had not been there to open their eyes, men whose lives were very different from what our education, our Western education, taught us to admire. One of them, the man who had the greatest influence and has done the most to regenerate Bengal, could not read and write a single word.[1] He was a man who had been what they call absolutely useless to the world. But he had this one divine faculty in him, that he had more than faith and had realised God. He was a man who lived what many would call the life of a mad man, a man without intellectual training, a man without any outward sign of culture or civilisation, a man who lived on the alms of others, such a man as the English-educated Indian would ordinarily talk of as one useless to society; even if he does not call him a bane to society, he will call him useless to society. He will say, 'This man is ignorant. What does he know? What can he teach me who have received from the West all that it can teach?' But God knew what he was doing. He sent that man to Bengal and set him in the temple of Dakshineshwar in Calcutta, and from North and South and East and West, the educated men, men who were the pride of the university, who had studied all

[1] The reference is to Ramakrishna Paramhansa (1836–1886), the Bengali mystic and saint.

that Europe can teach, came to fall at the feet of this ascetic. The work of salvation, the work of raising India was begun.

Consider the men who are really leading the movement. One thing I will ask you to observe and that is that there are very few who have not been touched by the touch of the sadhu. If you ask who influenced Babu Bipin Chandra Pal, it was a sadhu.[2] Among other men who lead in Bengal is the man who started this paper which is being prosecuted.[3] He is also one of the leading men. You may not know his name here, but he is well-known throughout Bengal, and he had done much to forward this movement [*cries of* 'Bande Mataram']; he is a man who has lived the life of a sadhu, and taken his inspiration and strength from that only source from which inspiration and strength can come. I spoke to you the other day about national education, and I spoke of a man who had given his life to that work, the man who really organised the National College in Calcutta, and that man also is a disciple of a *sannyāsin*,[4] that man also though he lives in the world lives like a sannyasin, and if you take the young workers in Bengal, men that have come forward to do the work of God, what will you find? What is their strength? What is the strength which enables them to bear all the obstacles that come in their way and to resist all the oppression that threatens them? Let me speak a word to you about that. There is a certain section of thought in India which regards Nationalism as 'madness'. The men who think like that are men of great intellectual ability, men who have studied deeply, who have studied economics, who have studied history, men who are entitled to respect, men from whom you would naturally accept leading and guidance, and they say that Nationalism will ruin the country. What is it that makes them talk like this? Many of them are patriots, many of them are thoroughly sincere and honest, many of them desire the good of the country. What is it that is wanting in them? This is wanting. They are men who

[2] Bipin Chandra Pal (1858–1932), leader of the Extremist Party in Bengal. A member of the Brahmo Samaj, he came under the influence of the *yogi* Bijoy Goswami (1841–1899).

[3] Manoranjan Guha Thakurta (1858–1919), proprietor of *Navasakti*, a Bengali nationalist newspaper. He also was a disciple of Bijoy Goswami.

[4] Satish Chandra Mukherji (1865–1948), the founder of the Dawn Society and a pioneer in the national education movement.

have lived in the pure intellect only and they look at things purely from the intellectual standpoint. What does the intellect think? What must it tell you if you also consult the intellect merely? Here is a work that you have undertaken, a work so gigantic, so stupendous, the means for which are so poor, the resistance to which will be so strong, so organised, so disciplined, so well-equipped with all the weapons that science can supply, with all the strength that human power and authority can give, and what means have you with which to carry out this tremendous work of yours? If you look at it intellectually, and these men look at it from the intellectual standpoint, it is hopeless. Here are these men who are being prosecuted. How are they going to resist? They cannot resist. They have to go straight to jail. Well, these gentlemen argue and they are arguing straight from the intellect, they ask, 'How long will you be able to resist like that? How long will this passive resistance work? All your leaders, all your strong men will be sent to jail, you will be crushed, and not only will you be crushed, the nation will be completely crushed.' If you argue from the intellect, this seems to be true. I cannot tell you of any material weapon with which you will meet those who are commissioned to resist your creed of Nationalism when you try to live it. If you ask what material weapons we have got, I must tell you that material weapons may help you no doubt but if you rely wholly upon material weapons, then what they say is perfectly true, that Nationalism is a madness.

Of course there is another side to it. If you say that Nationalism cannot avail, then again I ask the intellect of these people, what will avail? Intellectually speaking, speaking from the Moderate's standpoint, what will avail? What do they rely upon? They rely upon a foreign force in the country. If you do not rely upon God, if you do not rely upon something mightier than material strength, then you will have to depend solely upon what others can give. There are men who think that what God cannot give for the salvation of India, the British Government will give. What you cannot expect from God, you are going to expect from the British Government. Your expectation is vain. Their interests are not yours, their interests are very different from yours, and they will do what their interests tell them. You cannot expect anything else. What then does this intellectual process lead you to? This intellectual process, if it is used honestly, if it is followed to the very end, leads you to despair. It leads you to death. You have nothing which can help you, because you have no material strength at present which the adversary cannot crush, and the adversary will certainly not be so foolish as to help you, or to allow you to develop the necessary strength unmolested. What then is the conclusion? The only conclusion is that there is nothing to be done. The only conclusion is that this country is doomed. That is the conclusion to which this intellectual process will lead you.

I was speaking at Poona on this subject, and I told them of my experience in Bengal. When I went to Bengal three or four years before the swadeshi movement was born, to see what was the hope of revival, what was the political condition of the people, and whether there was the possibility of a real movement, what I found there was that the prevailing mood was apathy and despair. People had believed that regeneration could only come from outside, that another nation would take us by the hand and lift us up and that we have nothing to do for ourselves. Now that belief has been thoroughly broken. They had come to realise that help cannot come from this source, and then they had nothing to rely upon. Their intellects could not tell them of any other source from which help could come, and the result was that apathy and despair spread everywhere, and most of the workers who were really honest with themselves were saying that there was no help for this nation and that we were doomed. Well, this state of despair was the best thing that could have happened for Bengal, for it meant that the intellect had done its best, that the intellect had done all that was possible for it, and that the work of the unaided intellect in Bengal was finished. The intellect having nothing to offer but despair became quiescent, and when the intellect ceased to work, the heart of Bengal was open and ready to receive the voice of God whenever He should speak. When the message came at last, Bengal was ready to receive it and she received it in a single moment, and in a single moment the whole nation rose, the whole nation lifted itself out of delusions and out of despair, and it was by this sudden rising, by this sudden awakening from dream that Bengal found the way of salvation and declared to all India that eternal life, immortality and not lasting degradation was our fate. [*Applause*] Bengal lived in that faith. She felt a mightier truth than any that earth can give, because she held that faith from God and was able to live in that faith.

Then that happened which always happens when God brings other forces to fight against the strength which He Himself has inspired. Because it is always necessary for the divinely appointed strength to grow by suffering; without suffering, without the lesson of selflessness, without the moral force of self-sacrifice, God within us cannot grow. Sri Krishna cannot grow to manhood unless he is called upon to work for others, unless the Asuric forces of the world are about him and work against him and make him feel his strength. Therefore in Bengal there came a time, after the first outbreak of triumphant hope, when all the material forces that can be brought to bear against Nationalism were gradually brought into play, and the question was asked of Bengal, 'Can you suffer? Can you survive?' The young men of Bengal who had rushed forward in the frenzy of the moment, in the inspiration of the new gospel they had received, rushed forward rejoicing in the new-found strength and expecting to bear down all obstacles that came in their way, were now called upon to suffer. They were called upon to bear the crown, not of victory, but of martyrdom. They had to learn the real nature of their new strength. It was not their own strength, but it was the force which was working through them, and they had to learn to be the instruments of that force.

What is it that we have learned then? What is the need of the situation of which I am to tell you today? It is not a political programme. I have spoken to you about many things. I have written about many things, about swadeshi, boycott, national education, arbitration and other subjects. But there was one truth that I have always tried, and those who have worked with me have also tried to lay down as the foundation stone of all that we preached. It is not by any mere political programme, not by national education alone, not by swadeshi alone, not by boycott alone, that this country can be saved. Swadeshi by itself may merely lead to a little more material prosperity, and when it does, you might lose sight of the real thing you sought to do in the glamour of wealth, in the attraction of wealth and in the desire to keep it safe. In other subject countries also, there was material development; under the Roman Empire there was material development, there was industrial progress, but industrial progress and material development did not bring life to the nation. When the hour of trial came, it was found that these nations which had been developing industrially, which had been developing materially, were not alive. No, they were dead and at a touch from outside they crumbled to pieces. So, do not think that it is any particular programme or any particular method which is the need of the situation. These are merely ways of working; they are merely particular concrete lines upon which the spirit of God is working in a nation, but they are not in themselves the one thing needful. What is the one thing needful? What is it that has helped the older men who have gone to prison? What is it that has been their strength, that has enabled them to stand against all temptations and against all dangers and obstacles? They have had one and all of them consciously or unconsciously one over-mastering idea, one idea which nothing can shake, and this was the idea that there is a great power at work to help India, and that we are doing what it bids us. Often they do not understand what they are doing. They do not always realise who guides or where he will guide them; but they have this conviction within, not in the intellect but in the heart, that the power that is guiding them is invincible, that it is almighty, that it is an immortal and irresistible power and that it will do its work. They have nothing to do. They have simply to obey that power. They have simply to go where it leads them. They have only to speak the words that it tells them to speak, and to do the thing that it tells them to do. If the finger points them to prison, to the prison they go. Whatever it bids them to endure, they gladly endure. They do not know how that enduring will help, and the worldly-wise people may tell them that it is impolitic, that by doing this they will be wasting the strength of the country, they will be throwing the best workers away, they are not saving up the forces of the country. But we know that the forces of the country are other than outside forces. There is only one force, and for that force, I am not necessary, you are not necessary, he is not necessary. Neither myself nor another, nor Bipin Chandra Pal, nor all these workers who have gone to prison. None of them is necessary. Let them be thrown as so much waste substance, the country will not suffer. God is doing everything. We are not doing anything. What He bids us suffer, we suffer because the suffering is necessary to give others strength. When He throws us away, He does so because we are no longer required. If things become worse, we shall have not only to go to jail, but give up our lives and if those who seem to stand in front or to be absolutely indispensable are called upon to throw their bodies away, we shall then know that that also is wanted, that this is a work that God has asked us to do, and that in the place of those who are thrown away, God will bring many more. He Himself is behind us. He Himself is the worker and the work. [*Applause*] He is immortal in the hearts of His people. Faith then is what we have in Bengal. Some of us may not have it consciously; some may not call it by that particular name. As I said, we have developed intellectuality, we have developed it notably and we are still much dominated by it. Many have come to this belief through the longing to live for their countrymen, to suffer for their countrymen, because God is not only here in me. He is within all of you, it is God whom I love, it is God for whom I wish to suffer. [*Applause*] In that way many have come to do what God bade them do and He knows which way to lead a man. When it is His will, He will lead him aright.

Another thing, which is only another name for faith, is selflessness. This movement in Bengal, this movement of Nationalism is not guided by any self-interest, not at the heart of it. Whatever there may be in some minds, it is not, at the heart of it, a political self-interest that we are pursuing. It is a religion which we are trying to live. It is a religion by which we are trying to realise God in the nation, in our fellow-countrymen. We are trying to realise Him in the three hundred millions of our people. We are trying, some of us consciously, some of us unconsciously, we are trying to live not for our own interests, but to work and to die for others. When a young worker in Bengal has to go to jail, when he is asked to suffer, he does not feel any pang in that suffering, he does not fear suffering. He goes forward with joy. He says, 'The hour of my consecration has come, and I have to thank God now that the time for laying myself on His altar has arrived and that I have been chosen to suffer for the good of my countrymen. This is the hour of my greatest joy and the fulfilment of my life.' [*Loud applause*] This is the second aspect of our religion, and is the absolute denial of the idea of one's separate self, and the finding of one's higher eternal Self in the three hundred millions of people in whom God Himself lives.

The third thing, which is again another name for faith and selflessness, is courage. When you believe in God, when you believe that God is guiding you, believe that God is doing all and that you are doing nothing, what is there to fear? How can you fear when it is your creed, when it is your religion, to throw yourself away, to throw your money, your body, your life and all that you have, away for others? What is it that you have to fear? There is nothing to fear. Even when you are called before the tribunals of this world, you can face them with courage. Because your very religion means that you have courage. Because it is not you, it is something within you. What can all these tribunals, what can all the powers of the world do to that which is within you, that Immortal, that Unborn and Undying One, whom the sword cannot pierce, whom the fire cannot burn, whom the water cannot drown? Him the jail cannot confine and the gallows cannot end. What is there that you can fear when you are conscious of Him who is within you? Courage is then a necessity, courage is natural and courage is inevitable. If you rely upon other forces, supposing that you are a Nationalist in the European sense, meaning in a purely materialistic sense, that is to say, if you want to replace the dominion of the foreigner by the dominion of somebody else, it is a purely material change; it is not a religion, it is not that you feel for the three hundred millions of your countrymen, that you want to raise them up, that you want to make them all free and happy. It is not that, but you have got some idea that your nation is different from another nation and that these people are outsiders and that you ought to be ruling in their place. What you want is not freedom for your countrymen, but you want to replace the rule of others by yours. If you go in that spirit, what will happen when a time of trial comes? Will you have courage? Will you face it? You will see that is merely an intellectual conviction that you have, that is merely a reason which your outer mind suggests to you. Well, when it comes to be put to the test, what will your mind say to you? What will your intellect say to you? It will tell you, 'It is all very well to work for the country, but, in the meanwhile, I am going to die, or at least to be given a great deal of trouble, and when the fruit is reaped, I shall not be there to enjoy it. How can I bear all this suffering for a dream?' You have this house of yours, you have this property, you have so many things which will be attacked, and so you say, 'That is not the way for me.' If you have not the divine strength of faith and unselfishness, you will not be able to escape from other attachments, you will not like to bear affliction simply for the sake of a change by which you will not profit. How can courage come from such a source? But when you have a higher idea, when you have realised that you have nothing, that you are nothing and that the three hundred millions of people of this country are God in the nation, something which cannot be measured by so much land, or by so much money, or by so many lives, you will then realise that it is something immortal, that the idea for which you are working is something immortal and that it is an immortal power which is working in you. All other attachments are nothing. Every other consideration disappears from your mind, and, as I said, there is no need to cultivate courage. You are led on by that power. You are protected through life and death by One who survives. In the very hour of death, you feel your immortality. In the hour of your worst sufferings, you feel you are invincible.

Now I have told you that these three things are the need of the present situation, because, as I said, the situation is this: You have undertaken a work, you have committed yourselves to something which seems to be materially impossible. You have undertaken a work which will raise the mightiest enemies whom the earth can bring forward. As in the ancient time, when the avatars came, there were also born the mightiest daityas and asuras to face the avatars, so it always is. You may be sure that if you embrace this religion of Nationalism, you will have to meet such tremendous forces as no mere material power can resist. The hour of trial is not distant, the hour of trial is already upon you. What will be the use of your intellectual conviction? What will be the use of your outward enthusiasm? What will be the use of your shouting 'Bande Mataram'? What will be the use of all the mere outward show when the hour of trial comes? Put yourselves in the place of those people who are suffering in Bengal, and think whether they have the strength, and whether, if it comes to you, you have the strength to meet it. With what strength shall we meet it? How can we work invincibly? How can we meet it and survive? Can you answer that question? I have tried to show you that not by your material strength can you meet it. Have you the other strength in you? Have you realised what Nationalism is?

Have you realised that it is a religion that you are embracing? If you have, then call yourselves Nationalists; and when you have called yourselves Nationalists, then try to live your Nationalism. Try to realise the strength within you, try to bring it forward so that everything you do may be not your own doing, but the doing of that Truth within you. Try so that every hour that you live shall be enlightened by that presence, that every thought of yours shall be inspired from that one fountain of inspiration, that every faculty and quality in you may be placed at the service of that immortal power within you. Then you will not say, as I have heard so many of you say, that people are so slow to take up this idea, that people are so slow to work, that you have no fit leaders, and that all your great men tell you a different thing and none of them is ready to come forward to guide you in the path that is pointed out. You will have no complaints to make against others, because then you will not need any leader. The leader is within yourselves. If you can only find Him and listen to His voice, then you will not find that people will not listen to you, because there will be a voice within the people which will make itself heard. That voice and that strength is within you. If you feel it within yourselves, if you live in its presence, if it has become yourselves, then you will find that one word from you will awake an answering voice in others, that the creed which you preach will spread and will be received by all and that it will not be very long, as in Bengal it has not been very long, it has not taken a century or fifty years, it has only taken three years to change the whole nation, to give it a new spirit and a new heart and to put it in front of all the Indian races. From Bengal has come the creed of Nationalism, and from Bengal has come the example of Nationalism. Bengal which was the least respected and the most looked down on of all the Indian races for its weakness has within these three years changed so much, simply because the men there who were called to receive God within themselves were able to receive Him, were able to bear, to suffer and to live in that power, and by living in that power, they were able to give it out. And so in three years the whole race of Bengal has been changed, and you are obliged to ask in wonder, 'What is going on in Bengal?' You see a movement which no obstacle can stop, you see a great development which no power can resist, you see the birth of the avatar in the nation, and if you have received God within you, if you have received that power within you, you will see that God will change the rest of India in even a much shorter time, because the power has already gone forth, and is declaring itself, and when once declared, it will continue its work with ever greater and greater rapidity. It will continue its work with the matured force of Divinity until the whole world sees and until the whole world understands Him, until Sri Krishna who has now hid himself in Gokul, who is now among the poor and despised of the earth, who is now among the cow-herds of Brindaban, will reveal himself, will declare the Godhead, and the whole nation will rise, the whole people of this great country will rise, filled with divine power, filled with the inspiration of the Almighty, and no power on earth shall resist it, and no danger or difficulty shall stop it in its onward course. [*Loud and continued applause*] Because God is there, and it is His Mission, and He has something for us to do. He has a work for his great and ancient nation. Therefore He has been born again to do it, therefore He is revealing Himself in you, not that you may be like other nations, not that you may rise merely by human strength to trample underfoot the weaker peoples, but because something must come out from you which is to save the whole world. That something is what the ancient rishis knew and revealed, and that is to be known and revealed again today, it has to be revealed to the whole world, and in order that He may reveal Himself, you must first realise Him in yourselves, you must shape your lives, you must shape the life of this great nation so that it may be fit to reveal Him and then your task will be done, and you will realise that what you are doing today is no mere political uprising, no mere political change, but that you have been called upon to do God's work. [*Loud and continued applause*]

Uttarpara Speech

When I was asked to speak to you at the annual meeting of your *sabhā*, it was my intention to say a few words about the subject chosen for today, — the subject of the Hindu religion.[1] I do not know now whether I shall fulfil that intention; for as I sat here, there came into my mind a word that I have to speak to you, a word that I have to speak to the whole of the Indian Nation. It was spoken first to myself in jail and I have come out of jail to speak it to my people.

It was more than a year ago that I came here last.[2] When I came I was not alone; one of the mightiest prophets of Nationalism sat by my side. It was he who then came out of the seclusion to which God had sent him, so that in the silence and solitude of his cell he might hear the word that He had to say. It was he that you came in your hundreds to welcome. Now he is far away, separated from us by thousands of miles. Others whom I was accustomed to find working beside me are absent. The storm that swept over the country has scattered them far and wide. It is I this time who have spent one year in seclusion,[3] and now that I come out I find all changed. One who always sat by my side and was associated in my work is a prisoner in

A speech delivered at Uttarpara (a town lying a little north of Calcutta) on 30 May 1909.

1 Sri Aurobindo was invited to Uttarpara by revolutionary colleagues associated with the town's Dharma Rakshini Sabha (society for the protection of religion).

2 On 5 April 1908 Sri Aurobindo was present at a meeting in Uttarpara held in honour of Bipin Chandra Pal, who had been released from Buxar jail on 9 March. Subsequently Pal went to England.

3 Sri Aurobindo was arrested on 2 May 1908 and charged with conspiring with his brother Barindra Kumar and others to 'wage war against the king'. On 6 May 1909, after a prolonged trial at Alipore, near Calcutta, he was acquitted and released.

Burma; another is in the north rotting in detention.[4] I looked round when I came out, I looked round for those to whom I had been accustomed to look for counsel and inspiration. I did not find them. There was more than that. When I went to jail, the whole country was alive with the cry of 'Bande Mataram', alive with the hope of a nation, the hope of millions of men who had newly risen out of degradation. When I came out of jail I listened for that cry, but there was instead a silence. A hush had fallen on the country and men seemed bewildered; for instead of God's bright heaven full of the vision of the future that had been before us, there seemed to be overhead a leaden sky from which human thunders and lightnings rained. No man seemed to know which way to move, and from all sides came the question, 'What shall we do next? What is there that we can do?' I too did not know which way to move, I too did not know what was next to be done. But one thing I knew, that as it was the Almighty Power of God which had raised that cry, that hope, so it was the same power which had sent down that silence. He who was in the shouting and the movement was also in the pause and the hush. He has sent it upon us, so that the nation might draw back for a moment and look into itself and know His will. I have not been disheartened by that silence, because I had been made familiar with silence in my prison and because I knew it was in the pause and the hush that I had myself learned this lesson through the long year of my detention. When Bipin Chandra Pal came out of jail, he came with a message, and it was an inspired message. I remember the speech he made here. It was a speech not so much political as religious in its bearing and intention. He spoke of his realisation in jail, of God within us all, of the Lord within the nation, and in his subsequent speeches also he spoke of a greater than ordinary force in the movement and a greater than ordinary purpose before it. Now I also meet you again, I also come out of jail, and again it is you of Uttarpara who are the

4 On 11 December 1908 nine political leaders of Bengal and Eastern Bengal and Assam were 'deported', that is, imprisoned without arrest or trial in jails outside their home province. Two of those deported were Shyamsundar Chakravarti, who was imprisoned in Burma, and Subodh Chandra Mullick, who was imprisoned in Bareilly and Almora. All nine deportees remained in prison until February 1910, when they were released as a result of public agitation and pressure from certain British MPs.

first to welcome me, not at a political meeting but at a meeting of a society for the protection of our religion. That message which Bipin Chandra Pal received in Buxar jail, God gave to me in Alipore. That knowledge He gave to me day after day during my twelve months of imprisonment and it is that which He has commanded me to speak to you now that I have come out.

I knew I would come out. The year of detention was meant only for a year of seclusion and of training. How could anyone hold me in jail longer than was necessary for God's purpose? He had given me a word to speak and a work to do, and until that word was spoken I knew that no human power could hush me, until that work was done no human power could stop God's instrument, however weak that instrument might be or however small. Now that I have come out, even in these few minutes, a word has been suggested to me which I had no wish to speak. The thing I had in my mind He has thrown from it and what I speak is under an impulse and a compulsion.

When I was arrested and hurried to the Lal Bazar hajat, I was shaken in faith for a while, for I could not look into the heart of His intention. Therefore I faltered for a moment and cried out in my heart to Him, 'What is this that has happened to me? I believed that I had a mission to work for the people of my country and until that work was done, I should have Thy protection. Why then am I here and on such a charge?' A day passed and a second day and a third, when a voice came to me from within, 'Wait and see.' Then I grew calm and waited. I was taken from Lal Bazar to Alipore and was placed for one month in a solitary cell apart from men. There I waited day and night for the voice of God within me, to know what He had to say to me, to learn what I had to do. In this seclusion the earliest realisation, the first lesson came to me. I remembered then that a month or more before my arrest, a call had come to me to put aside all activity, to go into seclusion and to look into myself, so that I might enter into closer communion with Him. I was weak and could not accept the call. My work was very dear to me and in the pride of my heart I thought that unless I was there it would suffer or even fail and cease; therefore I would not leave it. It seemed to me that He spoke to me again and said, 'The bonds you had not strength to break, I have broken for you, because it is not my will nor was it ever my intention that that should continue. I have another thing for you to do and it is for that I have brought you here, to teach you what you could not learn for yourself and to train you for my work.' Then He placed the Gita in my hands. His strength entered into me and I was able to do the *sadhana* of the Gita. I was not only to understand intellectually but to realise what Srikrishna demanded of Arjuna and what He demands of those who aspire to do His work, to be free from repulsion and desire, to do work for Him without the demand for fruit, to renounce self-will and become a passive and faithful instrument in His hands, to have an equal heart for high and low, friend and opponent, success and failure, yet not do His work negligently. I realised what the Hindu religion meant. We speak often of the Hindu religion, of the Sanatana Dharma, but few of us really know what that religion is. Other religions are preponderatingly religions of faith and profession, but the Sanatana Dharma is life itself; it is a thing that has not so much to be believed as lived. This is the *dharma* that for the salvation of humanity was cherished in the seclusion of this peninsula from of old. It is to give this religion that India is rising. She does not rise as other countries do, for self or when she is strong, to trample on the weak. She is rising to shed the eternal light entrusted to her over the world. India has always existed for humanity and not for herself and it is for humanity and not for herself that she must be great.

Therefore this was the next thing He pointed out to me, — He made me realise the central truth of the Hindu religion. He turned the hearts of my jailers to me and they spoke to the Englishman in charge of the jail, 'He is suffering in his confinement; let him at least walk outside his cell for half an hour in the morning and in the evening.' So it was arranged, and it was while I was walking that His strength again entered into me. I looked at the jail that secluded me from men and it was no longer by its high walls that I was imprisoned; no, it was Vasudeva who surrounded me. I walked under the branches of the tree in front of my cell, but it was not the tree, I knew it was Vasudeva, it was Srikrishna whom I saw standing there and holding over me His shade. I looked at the bars of my cell, the very grating that did duty for a door and again I saw Vasudeva. It was Narayana who was guarding and standing sentry over me. Or I lay on the coarse blankets that were given me for a couch and felt the arms of Srikrishna around me, the arms of my Friend and Lover. This was the first use of the deeper vision He gave me. I looked at the prisoners in the jail, the thieves, the murderers, the swindlers, and as I looked at them I saw Vasudeva, it was Narayana whom I found in these darkened souls and misused bodies. Amongst these thieves and dacoits there were many who put me to shame by their sympathy, their kindness, the humanity triumphant over such adverse circumstances. One I saw among them especially who seemed to me a saint, a peasant of my nation who did not know how to read and write, an alleged dacoit sentenced to ten years' rigorous imprisonment, one of those whom we look down upon in our Pharisaical pride of class as *chhotalok*. Once more He spoke to me and said, 'Behold the people among whom I have sent you to do a little of my work. This is the nature of the nation I am raising up and the reason why I raise them.'

When the case opened in the lower court and we were brought before the Magistrate, I was followed by the same insight. He said to me, 'When you were cast into jail, did not your heart fail and did you not cry out to me, where is Thy protection? Look now at the Magistrate, look now at the Prosecuting Counsel.' I looked and it was not the Magistrate whom I saw, it was Vasudeva, it was Narayana who was sitting there on the bench. I looked at the Prosecuting Counsel and it was not the Counsel for the prosecution that I saw; it was Srikrishna who sat there, it was my Lover and Friend who sat there and smiled. 'Now do you fear?' He said, 'I am in all men and I overrule their actions and their words. My protection is still with you and you shall not fear. This case which is brought against you, leave it in my hand. It is not for you. It was not for the trial that I brought you here but for something else. The case itself is only a means for my work and nothing more.' Afterwards when the trial opened in the Sessions Court, I began to write many instructions for my Counsel as to what was false in the evidence against me and on what points the witnesses might be cross-examined. Then something happened which I had not expected. The arrangements which had been made for my defence were suddenly changed and another Counsel stood there to defend me. He came unexpectedly, — a friend of mine, but I did not know he was coming. You have all heard the name of the man who put away from him all other thoughts and abandoned all his practice, who sat up half the night day after day for months and broke his health to save me, — Srijut Chittaranjan Das.[5] When I saw him, I was satisfied, but I still thought it necessary to write instructions. Then all that was put from me and I had the message from within, 'This is the man who will save you from the snares put around your feet. Put aside those papers. It is not you who will instruct him. I will instruct him.' From that time I did not of myself speak a word to my Counsel about the case or give a single instruction and if ever I was asked a question, I always found that my answer did not help the case. I had left it to him and he took it entirely into his hands, with what result you know. I knew all along what He meant for me, for I heard it again and again, always I listened to the voice within: 'I am guiding, therefore fear not. Turn to your own work for which I have brought you to jail and when you come out, remember never to fear, never to hesitate. Remember that it is I who am doing this, not you nor any other. Therefore whatever clouds may come, whatever dangers and sufferings, whatever difficulties, whatever impossibilities, there is nothing impossible, nothing difficult. I am in the nation and its uprising and I am Vasudeva, I am Narayana, and what I will, shall be, not what others will. What I choose to bring about, no human power can stay.'

Meanwhile He had brought me out of solitude and placed me among those who had been accused along with me. You have spoken much today of my self-sacrifice and devotion to my country. I have heard that kind of speech ever since I came out of jail, but I hear it with embarrassment, with something of pain. For I know my weakness, I am a prey to my own faults and backslidings. I was not blind to them before and when they all rose up against me in seclusion, I felt them utterly. I knew then that I the man was a mass of weakness, a faulty and imperfect instrument, strong only when a higher strength entered into me. Then I found myself among these young men and in many of them I discovered a mighty courage, a power of self-effacement in comparison with which I was simply nothing. I saw one or two who were not only superior to me in force and character,

[5] C. R. Das (1870–1925), was Sri Aurobindo's defence attorney in the Alipore Bomb Trial. Subsequently he became a prominent nationalist leader.

— very many were that, — but in the promise of that intellectual ability on which I prided myself. He said to me, 'This is the young generation, the new and mighty nation that is arising at my command. They are greater than yourself. What have you to fear? If you stood aside or slept, the work would still be done. If you were cast aside tomorrow, here are the young men who will take up your work and do it more mightily than you have ever done. You have only got some strength from me to speak a word to this nation which will help to raise it.' This was the next thing He told me.

Then a thing happened suddenly and in a moment I was hurried away to the seclusion of a solitary cell.[6] What happened to me during that period I am not impelled to say, but only this that day after day, He showed me His wonders and made me realise the utter truth of the Hindu religion. I had had many doubts before. I was brought up in England amongst foreign ideas and an atmosphere entirely foreign. About many things in Hinduism I had once been inclined to believe that it was all imagination, that there was much of dream in it, much that was delusion and *maya*. But now day after day I realised in the mind, I realised in the heart, I realised in the body the truths of the Hindu religion. They became living experiences to me, and things were opened to me which no material science could explain. When I first approached Him, it was not entirely in the spirit of the Bhakta, it was not entirely in the spirit of the Jnani. I came to Him long ago in Baroda some years before the Swadeshi began and I was drawn into the public field.

When I approached God at that time, I hardly had a living faith in Him. The agnostic was in me, the atheist was in me, the sceptic was in me and I was not absolutely sure that there was a God at all. I did not feel His presence. Yet something drew me to the truth of the Vedas, the truth of the Gita, the truth of the Hindu religion. I felt there must be a mighty truth somewhere in this Yoga, a mighty truth in this religion based on the Vedanta. So when I turned to the yoga and resolved to practise it and

[6] On 31 August 1908 Narendranath Goswami, an accused in the Alipore Bomb Case who had turned King's Evidence, was shot dead by Kanailal Dutt and Satyendranath Bose. After this the other prisoners, who had been permitted to stay in one large ward, were placed in cells, some, like Sri Aurobindo, in solitary confinement.

find out if my idea was right, I did it in this spirit and with this prayer to Him, 'If Thou art, then Thou knowest my heart. Thou knowest that I do not ask for mukti, I do not ask for anything which others ask for. I ask only for strength to uplift this nation, I ask only to be allowed to live and work for this people whom I love and to whom I pray that I may devote my life.' I strove long for the realisation of yoga and at last to some extent I had it, but in what I most desired, I was not satisfied. Then in the seclusion of the jail, of the solitary cell I asked for it again. I said, 'Give me Thy *adesh*. I do not know what work to do or how to do it. Give me a message.' In the communion of Yoga two messages came. The first message said, 'I have given you a work and it is to help to uplift this nation. Before long the time will come when you will have to go out of jail; for it is not my will that this time either you should be convicted or that you should pass the time as others have to do, in suffering for their country. I have called you to work, and that is the *adesh* for which you have asked. I give you the *adesh* to go forth and do my work.' The second message came and it said, 'Something has been shown to you in this year of seclusion, something about which you had your doubts and it is the truth of the Hindu religion. It is this religion that I am raising up before the world, it is this that I have perfected and developed through the *rishis*, saints and *avatars*, and now it is going forth to do my work among the nations. I am raising up this nation to send forth my word. This is the Sanatana Dharma, this is the eternal religion which you did not really know before, but which I have now revealed to you. The agnostic and the sceptic in you have been answered, for I have given you proofs within and without you, physical and subjective, which have satisfied you. When you go forth, speak to your nation always this word that it is for the sanatana dharma that they arise, it is for the world and not for themselves that they arise. I am giving them freedom for the service of the world. When therefore it is said that India shall rise, it is the Sanatana Dharma that shall rise. When it is said that India shall be great, it is the Sanatana Dharma that shall be great. When it is said that India shall expand and extend herself, it is the Sanatana Dharma that shall expand and extend itself over the world. It is for the *dharma* and by the *dharma* that India exists. To magnify the religion means to magnify the country. I have shown you that I am everywhere and in all men and in all things, that I am in this movement and I am not only working in those who are striving for the country but I am working also in those who oppose them and stand in their path. I am working in everybody and whatever men may think or do they can do nothing but help in my purpose. They also are doing my work; they are not my enemies but my instruments. In all your actions you are moving forward without knowing which way you move. You mean to do one thing and you do another. You aim at a result and your efforts subserve one that is different or contrary. It is shakti that has gone forth and entered into the people. Since long ago I have been preparing this uprising and now the time has come and it is I who will lead it to its fulfilment.'

This then is what I have to say to you. The name of your society is 'Society for the Protection of Religion'.[7] Well, the protection of the religion, the protection and upraising before the world of the Hindu religion, that is the work before us. But what is the Hindu religion? What is this religion which we call Sanatana, eternal? It is the Hindu religion only because the Hindu nation has kept it, because in this peninsula it grew up in the seclusion of the sea and the Himalayas, because in this sacred and ancient land it was given as a charge to the Aryan race to preserve through the ages. But it is not circumscribed by the confines of a single country, it does not belong peculiarly and for ever to a bounded part of the world. That which we call the Hindu religion is really the eternal religion, because it is the universal religion which embraces all others. If a religion is not universal, it cannot be eternal. A narrow religion, a sectarian religion, an exclusive religion can live only for a limited time and a limited purpose. This is the one religion that can triumph over materialism by including and anticipating the discoveries of science and the speculations of philosophy. It is the one religion which impresses on mankind the closeness of God to us and embraces in its compass all the possible means by which man can approach God. It is the one religion which insists every moment on the truth which all religions acknowledge, that He is in all men and all things and that in Him we move and have our being. It is the one religion which enables us not only to

7 Dharma Rakshini Sabha.

understand and believe this truth but to realise it with every part of our being. It is the one religion which shows the world what the world is, that it is the *lila* of Vasudeva. It is the one religion which shows us how we can best play our part in that *lila*, its subtlest laws and its noblest rules. It is the one religion which does not separate life in any smallest detail from religion, which knows what immortality is and has utterly removed from us the reality of death.

This is the word that has been put into my mouth to speak to you today. What I intended to speak has been put away from me, and beyond what is given to me I have nothing to say. It is only the word that is put into me that I can speak to you. That word is now finished. I spoke once before with this force in me and I said then that this movement is not a political movement and that Nationalism is not politics but a religion, a creed, a faith.[8] I say it again today, but I put it in another way. I say no longer that nationalism is a creed, a religion, a faith; I say that it is the Sanatana Dharma which for us is nationalism. This Hindu nation was born with the Sanatana Dharma, with it it moves and with it it grows. When the Sanatana Dharma declines, then the nation declines, and if the Sanatana Dharma were capable of perishing, with the Sanatana Dharma it would perish. The Sanatana Dharma, that is nationalism. This is the message that I have to speak to you.

[8] See 'The Present Situation', page 18.

The Ideal of the Karmayogin

A NATION is building in India today before the eyes of the world so swiftly, so palpably that all can watch the process and those who have sympathy and intuition distinguish the forces at work, the materials in use, the lines of the divine architecture. This nation is not a new race raw from the workshop of Nature or created by modern circumstances. One of the oldest races and greatest civilisations on this earth, the most indomitable in vitality, the most fecund in greatness, the deepest in life, the most wonderful in potentiality, after taking into itself numerous sources of strength from foreign strains of blood and other types of human civilisation, is now seeking to lift itself for good into an organised national unity. Formerly a congeries of kindred nations with a single life and a single culture, always by the law of this essential oneness tending to unity, always by its excess of fecundity engendering fresh diversities and divisions, it has never yet been able to overcome permanently the almost insuperable obstacles to the organisation of a continent. The time has now come when those obstacles can be overcome. The attempt which our race has been making throughout its long history, it will now make under entirely new circumstances. A keen observer would predict its success because the only important obstacles have been or are in the process of being removed. But we go farther and believe that it is sure to succeed because the freedom, unity and greatness of India have now become necessary to the world. This is the faith in which the *Karmayogin* puts its hand to the work and will persist in it, refusing to be discouraged by difficulties however immense and apparently insuperable. We believe that God is with us and in that faith we shall conquer.

Published on 19 June 1909 in the first issue of *Karmayogin*, a weekly newspaper edited by Sri Aurobindo.

We believe that humanity needs us and it is the love and service of humanity, of our country, of the race, of our religion that will purify our heart and inspire our action in the struggle.

The task we set before ourselves is not mechanical but moral and spiritual. We aim not at the alteration of a form of government but at the building up of a nation. Of that task politics is a part, but only a part. We shall devote ourselves not to politics alone, nor to social questions alone, nor to theology or philosophy or literature or science by themselves, but we include all these in one entity which we believe to be all-important, the *dharma*, the national religion which we also believe to be universal. There is a mighty law of life, a great principle of human evolution, a body of spiritual knowledge and experience of which India has always been destined to be guardian, exemplar and missionary. This is the *sanātana dharma*, the eternal religion. Under the stress of alien impacts she has largely lost hold not of the structure of that *dharma*, but of its living reality. For the religion of India is nothing if it is not lived. It has to be applied not only to life, but to the whole of life; its spirit has to enter into and mould our society, our politics, our literature, our science, our individual character, affections and aspirations. To understand the heart of this *dharma*, to experience it as a truth, to feel the high emotions to which it rises and to express and execute it in life is what we understand by Karmayoga. We believe that it is to make the *yoga* the ideal of human life that India rises today; by the *yoga* she will get the strength to realise her freedom, unity and greatness, by the *yoga* she will keep the strength to preserve it. It is a spiritual revolution we foresee and the material is only its shadow and reflex.

The European sets great store by machinery. He seeks to renovate humanity by schemes of society and systems of government; he hopes to bring about the millennium by an act of Parliament. Machinery is of great importance, but only as a working means for the spirit within, the force behind. The nineteenth century in India aspired to political emancipation, social renovation, religious vision and rebirth, but it failed because it adopted Western motives and methods, ignored the spirit, history and destiny of our race and thought that by taking over European education, European machinery, European organisation and equipment we should reproduce in ourselves European prosperity, energy and progress. We of the twentieth century reject the aims, ideals and methods of the Anglicised nineteenth precisely because we accept its experience. We refuse to make an idol of the present; we look before and after, backward to the mighty history of our race, forward to the grandiose destiny for which that history has prepared it.

We do not believe that our political salvation can be attained by enlargement of Councils, introduction of the elective principle, colonial self-government or any other formula of European politics. We do not deny the use of some of these things as instruments, as weapons in a political struggle, but we deny their sufficiency whether as instruments or ideals and look beyond to an end which they do not serve except in a trifling degree. They might be sufficient if it were our ultimate destiny to be an outlying province of the British Empire or a dependent adjunct of European civilisation. That is a future which we do not think it worth making any sacrifice to accomplish. We believe on the other hand that India is destined to work out her own independent life and civilisation, to stand in the forefront of the world and solve the political, social, economical and moral problems which Europe has failed to solve, yet the pursuit of whose solution and the feverish passage in that pursuit from experiment to experiment, from failure to failure she calls her progress. Our means must be as great as our ends and the strength to discover and use the means so as to attain the end can only be found by seeking the eternal source of strength in ourselves.

We do not believe that by changing the machinery so as to make our society the ape of Europe we shall effect social renovation. Widow-remarriage, substitution of class for caste, adult marriage, intermarriages, interdining and the other nostrums of the social reformer are mechanical changes which, whatever their merits or demerits, cannot by themselves save the soul of the nation alive or stay the course of degradation and decline. It is the spirit alone that saves, and only by becoming great and free in heart can we become socially and politically great and free.

We do not believe that by multiplying new sects limited within the narrower and inferior ideas of religion imported from the West or by creating organisations for the perpetuation of the mere dress and body of Hinduism we can recover our spiritual health, energy and greatness. The world moves through an indispensable interregnum of free thought and materialism to a new synthesis of religious thought and experience, a new religious world-life free from intolerance, yet full of faith and fervour, accepting all forms of religion because it has an unshakable faith in the One. The religion which embraces Science and faith, Theism, Christianity, Mahomedanism and Buddhism and yet is none of these, is that to which the World-Spirit moves. In our own, which is the most sceptical and the most believing of all, the most sceptical because it has questioned and experimented the most, the most believing because it has the deepest experience and the most varied and positive spiritual knowledge, — that wider Hinduism which is not a dogma or combination of dogmas but a law of life, which is not a social framework but the spirit of a past and future social evolution, which rejects nothing but insists on testing and experiencing everything and when tested and experienced turning it to the soul's uses, in this Hinduism we find the basis of the future world-religion. This *sanātana dharma* has many scriptures, Veda, Vedanta, Gita, Upanishad, Darshana, Purana, Tantra, nor could it reject the Bible or the Koran; but its real, most authoritative scripture is in the heart in which the Eternal has His dwelling. It is in our inner spiritual experiences that we shall find the proof and source of the world's Scriptures, the law of knowledge, love and conduct, the basis and inspiration of Karmayoga.

Our aim will therefore be to help in building up India for the sake of humanity — this is the spirit of the Nationalism which we profess and follow. We say to humanity, 'The time has come when you must take the great step and rise out of a material existence into the higher, deeper and wider life towards which humanity moves. The problems which have troubled mankind can only be solved by conquering the kingdom within, not by harnessing the forces of Nature to the service of comfort and luxury, but by mastering the forces of the intellect and the spirit, by vindicating the freedom of man within as well as without and by conquering from within external Nature. For that work the resurgence of Asia is necessary, therefore Asia rises. For that work the freedom and greatness of India is essential, therefore she claims her destined freedom and greatness, and it is to the interest of all humanity, not excluding England, that she should wholly establish her claim.'

We say to the nation, 'It is God's will that we should be

ourselves and not Europe. We have sought to regain life by following the law of another being than our own. We must return and seek the sources of life and strength within ourselves. We must know our past and recover it for the purposes of our future. Our business is to realise ourselves first and to mould everything to the law of India's eternal life and nature. It will therefore be the object of the *Karmayogin* to read the heart of our religion, our society, our philosophy, politics, literature, art, jurisprudence, science, thought, everything that was and is ours, so that we may be able to say to ourselves and our nation, "This is our *dharma*". We shall review European civilisation entirely from the standpoint of Indian thought and knowledge and seek to throw off from us the dominating stamp of the Occident; what we have to take from the West we shall take as Indians. And the *dharma* once discovered we shall strive our utmost not only to profess but to live, in our individual actions, in our social life, in our political endeavours.'

We say to the individual and especially to the young who are now arising to do India's work, the world's work, God's work, 'You cannot cherish these ideals, still less can you fulfil them if you subject your minds to European ideas or look at life from the material standpoint. Materially you are nothing, spiritually you are everything. It is only the Indian who can believe everything, dare everything, sacrifice everything. First therefore become Indians. Recover the patrimony of your forefathers. Recover the Aryan thought, the Aryan discipline, the Aryan character, the Aryan life. Recover the Vedanta, the Gita, the Yoga. Recover them not only in intellect or sentiment but in your lives. Live them and you will be great and strong, mighty, invincible and fearless. Neither life nor death will have any terrors for you. Difficulty and impossibility will vanish from your vocabularies. For it is in the spirit that strength is eternal and you must win back the kingdom of yourselves, the inner Swaraj, before you can win back your outer empire. There the Mother dwells and She waits for worship that She may give strength. Believe in Her, serve Her, lose your wills in Hers, your egoism in the greater ego of the country, your separate selfishness in the service of humanity. Recover the source of all strength in yourselves and all else will be added to you; social soundness, intellectual pre-eminence, political freedom, the mastery of human thought, the hegemony of the world.'

Letter to Joseph Baptista

Pondicherry
Jan. 5, 1920

Dear Baptista,

Your offer is a tempting one, but I regret that I cannot answer it in the affirmative. It is due to you that I should state explicitly my reasons. In the first place I am not prepared at present to return to British India. This is quite apart from any political obstacle. I understand that up to last September the Government of Bengal (and probably the Government of Madras also) were opposed to my return to British India and that practically this opposition meant that if I went back I should be interned or imprisoned under one or other of the beneficent Acts which are apparently still to subsist as helps in ushering in the new era of trust and cooperation.[1] I do not suppose other Governments would be any more delighted by my appearance in their respective provinces. Perhaps the King's Proclamation may make a difference, but that is not certain since, as I read it, it does not mean an amnesty, but an act of gracious concession and benevolence limited by the discretion of the Viceroy.[2] Now I have too much work on my hands to waste my time in the

Joseph Baptista (1864–1930) was a barrister, labour organizer and politician associated with Extremist leader Bal Gangadhar Tilak (1856–1920). Towards the end of 1919 Baptista attempted to organize a new 'Social Democratic' party. In December he wrote to Sri Aurobindo, who had taken no active part in politics since 1910, asking him to become the editor of a newspaper meant to be the organ of this party.

[1] During the First World War the British Government passed emergency measures such as the Defense of India Act that allowed internment of suspected persons without arrest or trial. After the war, in an attempt to contain anti-British terrorism, some of the same provisions were included in the so-called 'Rowlatt Acts'.

[2] On 23 December 1919, a month after the conclusion of the war, King George V gave his Royal Assent to a Government of India act granting amnesty to selected political prisoners.

leisured ease of an involuntary Government guest. But even if I were assured of an entirely free action and movement, I should yet not go just now. I came to Pondicherry in order to have freedom and tranquillity for a fixed object having nothing to do with present politics — in which I have taken no direct part since my coming here, though what I could do for the country in my own way I have constantly done, — and until it is accomplished, it is not possible for me to resume any kind of public activity. But if I were in British India, I should be obliged to plunge at once into action of different kinds. Pondicherry is my place of retreat, my cave of tapasya, not of the ascetic kind, but of a brand of my own invention. I must finish that, I must be internally armed and equipped for my work before I leave it.

Next in the matter of the work itself. I do not at all look down on politics or political action or consider I have got above them. I have always laid a dominant stress and I now lay an entire stress on the spiritual life, but my idea of spirituality has nothing to do with ascetic withdrawal or contempt or disgust of secular things. There is to me nothing secular, all human activity is for me a thing to be included in a complete spiritual life, and the importance of politics at the present time is very great. But my line and intention of political activity would differ considerably from anything now current in the field. I entered into political action and continued it from 1903 to 1910 with one aim and one alone, to get into the mind of the people a settled will for freedom and the necessity of a struggle to achieve it in place of the futile ambling Congress methods till then in vogue. That is now done and the Amritsar Congress is the seal upon it.[3] The will is not as practical and compact nor by any means as organised and sustained in action as it should be, but there is the will and plenty of strong and able leaders to guide it. I consider that in spite of the inadequacy of the Reforms,[4] the will to self-determination, if

[3] At the 1919 session of the Indian National Congress, held at Amritsar in December, it was resolved 'That this Congress further urges that Parliament should take early steps to establish full Responsible Government in India in accordance with the principle of Self-determination.'

[4] In December 1919 the Government of India Act, generally referred to as the Montagu-Chelmsford Reforms, was passed. The Act granted limited self-rule to India in the form of 'dyarchy' or dual government, in which certain subjects were transferred to elected legislative councils.

the country keeps its present temper, as I have no doubt it will, is bound to prevail before long. What preoccupies me now is the question what it is going to do with its self-determination, how will it use its freedom, on what lines is it going to determine its future?

You may ask why not come out and help, myself, so far as I can, in giving a lead? But my mind has a habit of running inconveniently ahead of the times, — some might say, out of time altogether into the world of the ideal. Your party, you say, is going to be a social democratic party. Now I believe in something which might be called social democracy, but not in any of the forms now current, and I am not altogether in love with the European kind, however great an improvement it may be on the past. I hold that India having a spirit of her own and a governing temperament proper to her own civilisation, should in politics as in everything else strike out her own original path and not stumble in the wake of Europe. But this is precisely what she will be obliged to do, if she has to start on the road in her present chaotic and unprepared condition of mind. No doubt people talk of India developing on her own lines, but nobody seems to have very clear or sufficient ideas as to what those lines are to be. In this matter I have formed ideals and certain definite ideas of my own, in which at present very few are likely to follow me, — since they are governed by an uncompromising spiritual idealism of an unconventional kind and would be unintelligible to many and an offence and stumbling-block to a great number. But I have not as yet any clear and full idea of the practical lines; I have no formed programme. In a word, I am feeling my way in my mind and am not ready for either propaganda or action. Even if I were, it would mean for some time ploughing my lonely furrow or at least freedom to take my own way. As the editor of your paper, I should be bound to voice the opinion of others and reserve my own, and while I have full sympathy with the general ideas of the advanced parties so far as concerns the action of the present moment and, if I were in the field, would do all I could to help them, I am almost incapable by nature of limiting myself in that way, at least to the extent that would be requisite.

Excuse the length of this screed. I thought it necessary to explain fully so as to avoid giving you the impression that I declined your request from any affectation or reality of spiritual aloofness or wish to shirk the call of the country or want of sympathy with the work you and others are so admirably doing. I repeat my regret that I am compelled to disappoint you.

Yours sincerely,

AUROBINDO GHOSE

Letter to Balakrishna Shivaram Munje

Pondicherry
Aug. 30, 1920

Dear Dr Munje,

As I have already wired to you, I find myself unable to accept your offer of the Presidentship of the Nagpur Congress. There are reasons even within the political field itself which in any case would have stood in my way. In the first place I have never signed and would never care to sign as a personal declaration of faith the Congress creed, as my own is of a different character. In the next place since my retirement from British India I have developed an outlook and views which have diverged a great deal from those I held at the time and, as they are remote from present actualities and do not follow the present stream of political action, I should find myself very much embarrassed what to say to the Congress. I am entirely in sympathy with all that is being done so far as its object is to secure liberty for India, but I should be unable to identify myself with the programme of any of the parties. The President of the Congress is really a mouthpiece of the Congress and to make from the presidential chair a purely personal pronouncement miles away from what the Congress is thinking and doing would be grotesquely out of place. Not only so, but nowadays the President has a responsibility in connection with the All India Congress Committee and the policy of the Congress during the year and other emergencies that may arise which, apart from my constitutional objection and, probably, incapacity to discharge official duties of any kind

Dr B. K. Munje (usually spelled Moonje, 1872–1948) was an ophthalmologist and politician of Nagpur, whom Sri Aurobindo met on several occasions in 1907 and 1908. As head of the reception committee of the Nagpur session of the Indian National Congress, Moonje wrote to Sri Aurobindo in August 1920 asking him to preside over the session.

or to put on any kind of harness, I should be unable to fulfil, since it is impossible for me to throw over suddenly my fixed programme and settle at once in British India. These reasons would in any case have come in the way of my accepting your offer.

The central reason however is this that I am no longer first and foremost a politician, but have definitely commenced another kind of work with a spiritual basis, a work of spiritual, social, cultural and economic reconstruction of an almost revolutionary kind, and am even making or at least supervising a sort of practical or laboratory experiment in that sense which needs all the attention and energy that I can have to spare. It is impossible for me to combine political work of the current kind and this at the beginning. I should practically have to leave it aside, and this I cannot do, as I have taken it up as my mission for the rest of my life. This is the true reason of my inability to respond to your call.

I may say that in any case I think you would be making a wrong choice in asking me to take Tilak's place at your head.[1] No one now alive in India, or at least no one yet known, is capable of taking that place, but myself least of all. I am an idealist to the marrow, and could only be useful when there is something drastic to be done, a radical or revolutionary line to be taken, (I do not mean revolutionary by violence) a movement with an ideal aim and direct method to be inspired and organized. Tilak's policy of 'responsive cooperation', continued agitation and obstruction whenever needed — and that would be oftener than not in the present circumstances — is, no doubt, the only alternative to some form of non-cooperation or passive resistance. But it would need at its head a man of his combined suppleness, skill and determination to make it effective. I have not the suppleness and skill — at least of the kind needed — and could only bring the determination, supposing I accepted the policy, which I could not do practically, as, for any reasons of my own, nothing could induce me to set my foot in the new Councils. On the other hand a gigantic movement of non-cooperation merely to get some Punjab officials punished or to

[1] On 1 August 1920 B. G. Tilak, long the most prominent leader of the advanced wing of the Indian National Congress, died in Bombay.

set up again the Turkish Empire which is dead and gone, shocks my ideas both of proportion and of common sense.[2] I could only understand it as a means of 'embarrassing the Government' and seizing hold of immediate grievances in order to launch an acute struggle for autonomy after the manner of Egypt and Ireland, — though no doubt without the element of violence. All the same, it could be only on a programme involving an entire change of the creed, function and organisation and policy of the Congress, making it a centre of national reconstruction and not merely of political agitation that I could — if I had not the other reason I have spoken of — re-enter the political field. Unfortunately the political mind and habits created by the past methods of the Congress do not make that practicable at the moment. I think you will see that, holding these ideas, it is not possible for me to intervene and least of all on the chair of the President.

Might I suggest that the success of the Congress can hardly depend on the presence of a single person and one who has long been in obscurity? The friends who call on me are surely wrong in thinking that the Nagpur Congress will be uninspiring without me. The national movement is surely strong enough now to be inspired with its own idea especially at a time of stress like the present. I am sorry to disappoint, but I have given the reasons that compel me and I cannot see how it is avoidable.

Yours sincerely,

AUROBINDO GHOSE

[2] Also on 1 August, Mohandas K. Gandhi launched the Non-Cooperation movement to protest the lenient treatment accorded those responsible for the Jallianwalla Bag massacre in Amritsar (13 April 1919) and to oppose the dismantling of the Turkish Caliphate (Khilafat) by the treaty ending the First World War. This marked the beginning of Gandhi's ascendancy over the national movement.

Part Two

The Indian Tradition and the Future

The traditions of the past are very great in their own place, in the past, but I do not see why we should merely repeat them and not go farther. In the spiritual development of the consciousness upon earth, the great past ought to be followed by a greater future.

Extract from a letter

PART TWO consists of writings on Indian culture in general and commentaries on some of the major texts of the Indian spiritual tradition.

• Beginning practically as a review of a book by John Woodroffe with the same title, *'Is India Civilised?'* develops into a consideration of intercultural conflict, and of the importance of preserving India's spiritual essence in the face of Western cultural aggression.

• In *The Evolution of Indian Spirituality*, Sri Aurobindo sketches the features of the main epochs of Indian spiritual culture: the symbolic stage of the Vedas and Upanishads, the intellectual and ethical stage of the philosophers and epic poets, and the Purano-Tantric stage of devotional religion.

• The Vedas, as Sri Aurobindo shows in *The Secret of the Veda*, conceal a psychological significance—a doctrine of the mystics—behind their invocation of divine powers.

• In the Upanishads the mystic poets speak plainly of the one Eternal or Brahman upholding the world's myriad appearances. In *Readings in the Taittiriya Upanishad*, Sri Aurobindo shows that a complete knowledge of Brahman brings not a denial of the world but a joyous affirmation of life's possibilities.

• If any scripture, even one as remarkable as the *Kena Upanishad* (whose sense is summarized in *A Last Word*), falls short of such an affirmation, it is necessary for the seeker to pass beyond.

• Of all the texts of the Indian tradition, the Bhagavad Gita, finest flower of the epic period, comes closest to meeting the demand of contemporary humanity for a reconciliation of inner spiritual truth and the creative possibilities of life and action. To point the way towards a union of the Spirit and its manifestations is *The Core of the Gita's Meaning*.

• In the later stages of India's spiritual development it fell away from this ideal; but since the late nineteenth century there has been a resurgence on the spiritual as well as the artistic and intellectual planes which some have called *The Renaissance in India*.

• If, in the midst of this resurgence, India could preserve its spiritual essence, it would have, Sri Aurobindo believed, a special role to play in the future development of humanity. But, as he admitted in *Indian Civilisation and the Evolutionary Future*, no single culture contained everything that was needed to meet the challenge of the future. The fulfilment of humankind's highest possibilities could only come about through a concert or union of the world's cultural groupings—a subject dealt with in depth in the selections of Part Three.

‘Is India Civilised?’

A BOOK under this rather startling title was published some years ago by Sir John Woodroffe, the well-known scholar and writer on Tantric philosophy,[1] in answer to an extravagant *jeu d'esprit* by Mr William Archer. That well-known dramatic critic leaving his safe natural sphere for fields in which his chief claim to speak was a sublime and confident ignorance, assailed the whole life and culture of India and even lumped together all her greatest achievements, philosophy, religion, poetry, painting, sculpture, Upanishads, Mahabharata, Ramayana in one wholesale condemnation as a repulsive mass of unspeakable barbarism.[2] It was argued by many at the time that to reply to a critic of this kind was to break a butterfly, or it might be in this instance a bumble-bee upon the wheel. But Sir John Woodroffe insisted that even an attack of this ignorant kind ought not to be neglected; he took it as a particularly useful type in the general kind, first, because it raised the question from the rationalistic and not from the Christian and missionary standpoint and, again, because it betrayed the grosser underlying motives of all such attacks. But his book was important, not so

The first of three articles published under this title in the *Arya*, a monthly review edited by Sri Aurobindo, in 1918 and 1919. The articles were revised slightly during the 1920s or early 1930s. The phrase ‘some years ago’ in the first sentence is part of the revision.

[1] John Woodroffe was a British judge in India best known, under the name of Arthur Avalon, as an expositor and popularizer of the Tantra. His *Is India Civilized? Essays on Indian Culture* was published by Ganesh & Co., Madras, in 1918.

[2] William Archer, British writer (1856–1924), best known for his theatre criticism and translations of Ibsen. His *India and the Future* was published by Hutchinson & Co., London, in 1917. In writing this chapter Sri Aurobindo seems to have followed Woodroffe's account of Archer's book, which he probably had not yet read. While patronizing and generally negative about Indian culture, *India and the Future* was not unreservedly condemnatory.

much as an answer to a particular critic, but because it raised with great point and power the whole question of the survival of Indian civilisation and the inevitability of a war of cultures.

The question whether there has been or is a civilisation in India is not any longer debatable; for everyone whose opinion counts recognises the presence of a distinct and a great civilisation unique in its character. Sir John Woodroffe's purpose was to disclose the conflict of European and Asiatic culture and, in greater prominence, the distinct meaning and value of Indian civilisation, the peril it now runs and the calamity its destruction would be to the world. The author held its preservation to be of an immense importance to mankind and he believed it to be in great danger. In the stupendous rush of change which is coming on the human world as a result of the present tornado of upheaval, ancient India's culture, attacked by European modernism, overpowered in the material field, betrayed by the indifference of her children, may perish for ever along with the soul of the nation that holds it in its keeping. The book was an urgent invitation to us to appreciate better this sacred trust and the near peril which besets it and to stand firm and faithful in the hour of the ordeal. It will be useful to state briefly its gist as an introduction to this all-important issue.

A true happiness in this world is the right terrestrial aim of man, and true happiness lies in the finding and maintenance of a natural harmony of spirit, mind and body. A culture is to be valued to the extent to which it has discovered the right key of this harmony and organised its expressive motives and movements. And a civilisation must be judged by the manner in which all its principles, ideas, forms, ways of living work to bring that harmony out, manage its rhythmic play and secure its continuance or the development of its motives. A civilisation in pursuit of this aim may be predominantly material like modern European culture, predominantly mental and intellectual like the old Graeco-Roman or predominantly spiritual like the still persistent culture of India. India's central conception is that of the Eternal, the Spirit here incased in matter, involved and immanent in it and evolving on the material plane by rebirth of the individual up the scale of being till in mental man it enters the world of ideas and realm of conscious morality, *dharma*. This achievement, this victory over unconscious matter develops its lines, enlarges its scope, elevates its levels until the increasing manifestation of the sattwic or spiritual portion of the vehicle of mind enables the individual mental being in man to identify himself with the pure spiritual consciousness beyond Mind. India's social system is built upon this conception; her philosophy formulates it; her religion is an aspiration to the spiritual consciousness and its fruits; her art and literature have the same upward look; her whole dharma or law of being is founded upon it. Progress she admits, but this spiritual progress, not the externally self-unfolding process of an always more and more prosperous and efficient material civilisation. It is her founding of life upon this exalted conception and her urge towards the spiritual and the eternal that constitute the distinct value of her civilisation. And it is her fidelity, with whatever human shortcomings, to this highest ideal that has made her people a nation apart in the human world.

But there are other cultures led by a different conception and even an opposite motive. And by the law of struggle which is the first law of existence in the material universe, varying cultures are bound to come into conflict. A deep-seated urge in Nature compels them to attempt to extend themselves and to destroy, assimilate and replace all disparates or opposites. Conflict is not indeed the last and ideal stage; for that comes when various cultures develop freely, without hatred, misunderstanding or aggression and even with an underlying sense of unity, their separate special motives. But so long as the principle of struggle prevails, one must face the lesser law; it is fatal to disarm in the midmost of the battle. The culture which gives up its living separateness, the civilisation which neglects an active self-defence will be swallowed up and the nation which lived by it will lose its soul and perish. Each nation is a Shakti or power of the evolving spirit in humanity and lives by the principle which it embodies. India is the Bharata Shakti, the living energy of a great spiritual conception, and fidelity to it is the very principle of her existence. For by its virtue alone she has been one of the immortal nations; this alone has been the secret of her amazing persistence and perpetual force of survival and revival.

The principle of struggle has assumed the large historical aspect of an agelong clash and pressure of conflict between Asia and Europe. This clash, this mutual pressure has had its material side, but has borne also its cultural and spiritual aspect. Both materially and spiritually Europe has thrown herself repeatedly upon Asia, Asia too upon Europe, to conquer, assimilate and dominate. There has been a constant alternation, a flowing backward and forward of these two seas of power. All Asia has always had the spiritual tendency in more or less intensity, with more or less clearness; but in this essential matter India is the quintessence of the Asiatic way of being. Europe too in mediaeval times had a culture in which by the dominance of the Christian idea — but Christianity was of Asiatic origin — the spiritual motive took the lead; then there was an essential similarity as well as a certain difference. Still the differentiation of cultural temperament has on the whole been constant. Since some centuries Europe has become material, predatory, aggressive, and has lost the harmony of the inner and outer man which is the true meaning of civilisation and the efficient condition of a true progress. Material comfort, material progress, material efficiency have become the gods of her worship. The modern European civilisation which has invaded Asia and which all violent attacks on Indian ideals represent, is the effective form of this materialistic culture. India, true to her spiritual motive, has never shared in the physical attacks of Asia upon Europe; her method has always been an infiltration of the world with her ideas, such as we today see again in progress. But she has now been physically occupied by Europe and this physical conquest must necessarily be associated with an attempt at cultural conquest; that invasion too has also made some progress. On the other hand English rule has enabled India still to retain her identity and social type; it has awakened her to herself and has meanwhile, until she became conscious of her strength, guarded her against the flood which would otherwise have submerged and broken her civilisation.[3] It is for her now to recover herself, defend her cultural existence against the alien penetration, preserve her distinct spirit, essential principle and

[3] This contention cannot be accepted in an unqualified sense. English rule has by its general principle of social and religious non-interference prevented any direct and violent touch, any deliberate and purposeful social pressure; but it has undermined and deprived of living strength all the preexisting centres and instruments of Indian social life and by a sort of unperceived rodent process left it only a rotting shell without expansive power or any better defensive force than the force of inertia. [Sri Aurobindo's note]

characteristic forms for her own salvation and the total welfare of the human race.

But many questions may arise, — and principally whether such a spirit of defence and attack is the right spirit, whether union, harmony, interchange are not our proper temperament for the coming human advance. Is not a unified world-culture the large way of the future? Can either an exaggeratedly spiritual or an excessively temporal civilisation be the sound condition of human progress or human perfection? A happy or just reconciliation would seem to be a better key to a harmony of Spirit, Mind and Body. And there is the question too whether the forms of Indian culture must be preserved intact as well as the spirit. To these queries the reply of the author is to be found in his law of graduality of the spiritual advance of humanity, its need of advancing through three successive stages.[4]

The first stage is the period of conflict and competition which has been ever dominant in the past and still overshadows the present of mankind. For even when the crudest forms of material conflict are mitigated, the conflict itself still survives and the cultural struggle comes into greater prominence. The second step brings the stage of concert. The third and last is marked by the spirit of sacrifice in which, because all is known as the one Self, each gives himself for the good of others. The second stage has hardly at all commenced for most; the third belongs to the indeterminate future. Individuals have reached the highest stage; the perfected Sannyasin, the liberated man, the soul that has become one with the Spirit, knows all being as himself and for him all self-defence and attack are needless. For strife does not belong to the law of his seeing; sacrifice and self-giving are the whole principle of his action. But no people has reached that level, and to follow a law or principle involuntarily or ignorantly or contrary to the truth of one's consciousness is a falsehood and a self-destruction. To allow oneself to be killed, like the lamb attacked by the wolf, brings no growth, farthers no development, assures no spiritual merit. Concert or unity may come in good time, but it must be an underlying unity with a free differentiation, not a swallowing up of one by another or an incongruous and inharmonious mixture. Nor can it come before

[4] Woodroffe presents this notion in the fifth chapter of his book.

the world is ready for these greater things. To lay down one's arms in a state of war is to invite destruction and it can serve no compensating spiritual purpose.

Spiritual and temporal have indeed to be perfectly harmonised, for the spirit works through mind and body. But the purely intellectual or heavily material culture of the kind that Europe now favours, bears in its heart the seed of death; for the living aim of culture is the realisation on earth of the kingdom of heaven. India, though its urge is towards the Eternal, since that is always the highest, the entirely real, still contains in her own culture and her own philosophy a supreme reconciliation of the eternal and the temporal and she need not seek it from outside. On the same principle the form of the interdependence of mind, body and spirit in a harmonious culture is important as well as the pure spirit; for the form is the rhythm of the spirit. It follows that to break up the form is to injure the spirit's self-expression or at least to put it into grave peril. Change of forms there may and will be, but the novel formation must be a new self-expression or self-creation developed from within; it must be characteristic of the spirit and not servilely borrowed from the embodiments of an alien nature.

Where then does India actually stand in this critical hour of her necessity and how far can she be said to be still firmly seated on her eternal foundations? Already she has been largely affected by European culture and the peril is far from over; on the contrary it will be greater, more insistent, more imperatively violent in the immediate future. Asia is rearising; but that very fact will intensify and is already intensifying the attempt, natural and legitimate according to the law of competition, of European civilisation to assimilate Asia. For if she is culturally transformed and conquered, then when she again counts in the material order of the world, it will not be with any menace of the invasion of Europe by the Asiatic ideal. It is a cultural quarrel complicated with a political question. Asia must become culturally a province of Europe and form politically one part of a Europeanised if not a European concert; otherwise Europe may become culturally a province of Asia, Asiaticised by the dominant influence of wealthy, enormous, powerful Asiatic peoples in the new world-system. The motive of Mr Archer's attack is frankly a political motive. This is the burden of all his song that the reconstruction of the world must take place in the forms and follow the canons of a rationalistic and materialistic European civilisation. On his reasoning, India if she adheres to her own civilisation, if she cherishes its spiritual motive, if she clings to its spiritual principle of formation, will stand out as a living denial, a hideous 'blot' upon this fair, luminous, rationalistic world. Either she must Europeanise, rationalise, materialise her whole being and deserve liberty by the change or else she must be kept in subjection and administered by her cultural superiors: her people of three hundred million religious savages must be held down firmly, taught and civilised by her noble and enlightened Christian-atheistic European warders and tutors. A grotesque statement in form, but in substance it has in it the root of the matter. As against the attack — not universal, for understanding and appreciation of Indian culture are now more common than before, — India is indeed awaking and defending herself, but not sufficiently and not with the whole-heartedness, the clear sight and the firm resolution which can alone save her from the peril. Today it is close; let her choose, — for the choice is imperatively before her, to live or to perish.

The warning cannot be neglected; recent utterances of European publicists and statesmen, recent books and writings against India and the joyful and enthusiastic welcome they have received from the public of occidental countries, point to the reality of the danger. It arises indeed as a necessity from the present political situation and cultural trend of humanity at this moment of enormous decisive change. It is not necessary to follow the writer in all the viewpoints expressed in his book. I cannot myself accept in full his eulogy of the mediaeval civilisation of Europe. Its interest, the beauty of its artistic motives, its deep and sincere spiritual urgings are marred for me by its large strain of ignorance and obscurantism, its cruel intolerance, its revolting early-Teutonic hardness, brutality, ferocity and coarseness. He seems to me to hit a little too hard at the later European culture. This predominantly economic type of civilisation has been ugly enough in its strain of utilitarian materialism, which we shall err grossly if we imitate; still it has been uplifted by some nobler ideals that have done much for the race. But even these are crude and imperfect in their form and need to be spiritualised in their meaning before they can be wholly admitted by the mind of India. I think too that the author has a little underrated the force of the Indian revival. I do not mean its outward realised strength, for that is very deficient, but the inevitability of its drive, its spiritual and potential force. And he has made a little too much of the servile type of Indian who is capable of mouthing the portentously obsequious imagination that 'European institutions are the standard by which the aspirations of India are set.' That, except for the rapidly dwindling class to which this spokesman belongs, has its truth now only in a single field, the political, — a very important exception, I admit, and one which opens the door to a peril of stupendous proportions. But even there a deep change of spirit is foreshadowed although it has not yet taken definite form and has now to meet a fresh invasion of furious Europeanism inspired by the militant crudeness of proletarian Russia. Again he does not attach a sufficient importance to the increasing infiltration of India's spiritual thought into Europe and America, which is her characteristic retort to the European invasion. It is from this point of view that the whole question takes on a different aspect.

Sir John Woodroffe invites us to a vigorous self-defence. But defence by itself in the modern struggle can only end in defeat, and, if battle there must be, the only sound strategy is a vigorous aggression based on a strong, living and mobile defence; for by that aggressive force alone can the defence itself be effective. Why are a certain class of Indians still hypnotised in all fields by European culture and why are we all still hypnotised by it in the field of politics? Because they constantly saw all the power, creation, activity on the side of Europe, all the immobility or weakness of a static inefficient defence on the side of India. But wherever the Indian spirit has been able to react, to attack with energy and to create with éclat, the European glamour has begun immediately to lose its hypnotic power. No one now feels the weight of the religious assault from Europe which was very powerful at the outset, because the creative activities of the Hindu revival have made Indian religion a living and evolving, a secure, triumphant and self-assertive power.[5] But the seal was put to this work by

[5] The term 'Hindu revival' is applied both to the late-nineteenth-century orthodox reaction against Hindu reform movements, and to new religious formations like the Arya Samaj (founded by Swami Dayanand in 1875) and the Ramakrishna Mission (founded by Swami Vivekananda in 1897).

two events, the Theosophical movement and the appearance of Swami Vivekananda at Chicago.[6] For these two things showed the spiritual ideas for which India stands no longer on their defence but aggressive and invading the materialised mentality of the Occident. All India had been vulgarised and anglicised in its aesthetic notions by English education and influence, until the brilliant and sudden dawn of the Bengal school of art cast its rays so far as to be seen in Tokio, London and Paris. That significant cultural event has already effected an aesthetic revolution in the country, not yet by any means complete, but irresistible and sure of the future. The same phenomenon extends to other fields. Even in the province of politics that was the internal sense of the policy of the so-called extremist party in the Swadeshi movement; for it was a movement which attempted to override the previous apparent impossibility of political creation by the Indian spirit upon other than imitative European lines. If it failed for the time being, not by any falsity in its inspiration, but by the strength of a hostile pressure and the weakness still left by a past decadence, if its incipient creations were broken or left languishing and deprived of their original significance, yet it will remain as a finger-post on the roads. The attempt is bound to be renewed as soon as a wider gate is opened under more favourable conditions. Till that attempt comes and succeeds, a serious danger besets the soul of India; for a political Europeanisation would be followed by a social turn of the same kind and bring a cultural and spiritual death in its train. Aggression must be successful and creative if the defence is to be effective.

This great question must be given its larger world-wide import if we are to see it in its true lines. The principle of struggle, conflict and competition still governs and for some time will still govern international relations; for even if war is abolished in the near future by some as yet improbable good fortune of the race, conflict will take other forms. At the same time a certain growing mutual closeness of the life of humanity is the most prominent phenomenon of the day. The War has brought it into violent

[6] The Theosophical Society was founded in New York in 1875. Swami Vivekananda (1863–1902), the most prominent of Ramakrishna Paramhansa's disciples, attracted considerable attention as a speaker at the World's Parliament of Religions in Chicago in 1893.

relief; but the after-war is bringing out all its implications as well as the mass of its difficulties. This is as yet no real concert, still less the beginning of a true unity, but only a compelling physical oneness forced on us by scientific inventions and modern circumstances. But this physical oneness must necessarily bring its mental, cultural and psychological results. At first it will probably accentuate rather than diminish conflict in many directions, enhance political and economic struggles of many kinds and hasten too a cultural struggle. There it may bring about in the end a swallowing unification and a destruction of all other civilisations by one aggressive European type: whether that type will be bourgeois economical or labour materialistic or a rationalistic intellectualism cannot easily be foreseen, but at present in one form or another this is the actuality that is most in the front. On the other hand it may lead to a free concert with some underlying oneness. But the ideal of the entire separateness of the peoples each developing its sharply separatist culture with an alien exclusion law for other leading ideas and cultural forms, although it has been for some time abroad and was growing in vigour, is not likely to prevail. For that to happen the whole aim of unification preparing in Nature must fall to pieces, an improbable but not quite impossible catastrophe. Europe dominates the world and it is natural to forecast a Westernised world with such petty differences as might be permissible in a European unity given up to the rigorous scientific pursuit of the development and organisation of material life. Across this possibility falls the shadow of India.

Sir John Woodroffe quotes the dictum of Professor Lowes Dickinson that the opposition is not so much between Asia and Europe as between India and the rest of the world.[7] There is a truth behind that dictum; but the cultural opposition of Europe and Asia remains an unabolished factor. Spirituality is not the

[7] Goldsworthy Lowes Dickinson (1862–1932), British scholar, wrote several books on international affairs. His *Essay on the Civilisations of India, China & Japan* (London: Dent, 1914) opens: 'The first thing I have to note is that the East is not a unity, as implied in the familiar antithesis of East and West. Between India, on the one hand, and China or Japan, on the other, there is as great a difference as between India and any western country. The contrast that has struck me is that between India and the rest of the world.'

monopoly of India; however it may hide submerged in intellectualism or hid in other concealing veils, it is a necessary part of human nature. But the difference is between spirituality made the leading motive and the determining power of both the inner and the outer life and spirituality suppressed, allowed only under disguises or brought in as a minor power, its reign denied or put off in favour of the intellect or of a dominant materialistic vitalism. The former way was the type of the ancient wisdom at one time universal in all civilised countries — literally, from China to Peru. But all other nations have fallen away from it and diminished its large pervasiveness or fallen away from it altogether as in Europe. Or they are now, as in Asia, in danger of abandoning it for the invading economic, commercial, industrial, intellectually utilitarian modern type. India alone, with whatever fall or decline of light and vigour, has remained faithful to the heart of the spiritual motive. India alone is still obstinately recalcitrant; for Turkey and China and Japan, say her critics, have outgrown that foolishness, by which it is meant that they have outgrown rationalistic and materialistic. India alone as a nation, whatever individuals or a small class may have done, has till now refused to give up her worshipped Godhead or bow her knee to the strong reigning idols of rationalism, commercialism and economism, the successful iron gods of the West. Affected she has been, but not yet overcome. Her surface mind rather than her deeper intelligence has been obliged to admit many Western ideas, liberty, equality, democracy and others, and to reconcile them with her Vedantic Truth; but she has not been altogether at ease with them in the Western form and she seeks about already in her thought to give to them an Indian which cannot fail to be a spiritualised turn. The first passion to imitate English ideas and culture has passed; but another more dangerous has recently taken its place, the passion to imitate continental European culture at large and in particular the crude and vehement turn of revolutionary Russia. On the other hand one sees a growing revival of this ancient Hindu religion and the immense sweep of a spiritual awakening and its significant movements. And out of this ambiguous situation there can be only one out of two issues. Either India will be rationalised and industrialised out of all recognition and she will be no longer India or else she will be the leader in a new world-phase, aid by her example and cultural infiltration the new tendencies of the West and spiritualise the human race. That is the one radical and poignant question at issue. Will the spiritual motive which India represents prevail on Europe and create there new forms congenial to the West, or will European rationalism and commercialism put an end for ever to the Indian type of culture?

Not, then, whether India is civilised is the query that should be put, but whether the motive which has shaped her civilisation or the old-European intellectual or the new-European materialistic motive is to lead human culture. Is the harmony of the spirit, mind and body to found itself on the gross law of our physical nature, rationalised only or touched at the most by an ineffective spiritual glimmer, or is the dominant power of spirit to take the lead and force the lesser powers of the intellect, mind and body to a more exalted effort after a highest harmony, a victorious ever-developing equipoise? India must defend herself by reshaping her cultural forms to express more powerfully, intimately and perfectly her ancient ideal. Her aggression must lead the waves of the light thus liberated in triumphant self-expanding rounds all over the world which it once possessed or at least enlightened in far-off ages. An appearance of conflict must be admitted for a time, for as long as the attack of an opposite culture continues. But since it will be in effect an assistance to all the best that is emerging from the advanced thought of the Occident, it will culminate in the beginning of concert on a higher plane and a preparation of oneness.

The Evolution of Indian Spirituality

THE TASK of religion and spirituality is to mediate between God and man, between the Eternal and Infinite and this transient, yet persistent finite, between a luminous Truth-consciousness not expressed or not yet expressed here and the Mind's ignorance. But nothing is more difficult than to bring home the greatness and uplifting power of the spiritual consciousness to the natural man forming the vast majority of the race; for his mind and senses are turned outward towards the external calls of life and its objects and never inwards to the Truth which lies behind them. This external vision and attraction are the essence of the universal blinding force which is designated in Indian philosophy the Ignorance. Ancient Indian spirituality recognised that man lives in the Ignorance and has to be led through its imperfect indications to a highest inmost knowledge. Our life moves between two worlds, the depths upon depths of our inward being and the surface field of our outward nature. The majority of men put the whole emphasis of life on the outward and live very strongly in their surface consciousness and very little in the inward existence. Even the choice spirits raised from the grossness of the common vital and physical mould by the stress of thought and culture do not usually get farther than a strong dwelling on the things of the mind. The highest flight they reach — and it is this that the West persistently mistakes for spirituality — is a preference for living in the mind and emotions more than in the gross outward life or else an attempt to subject this rebellious life-stuff to the law of intellectual truth or ethical reason and will or aesthetic beauty or of all three together. But

The eighth instalment of *A Defence of Indian Culture*, published in the *Arya* in September 1919 and subsequently revised. Editorial title. *A Defence of Indian Culture* first appeared as part of a book posthumously in 1953.

spiritual knowledge perceives that there is a greater thing in us; our inmost self, our real being is not the intellect, not the aesthetic, ethical or thinking mind, but the divinity within, the Spirit, and these other things are only the instruments of the Spirit. A mere intellectual, ethical and aesthetic culture does not go back to the inmost truth of the spirit; it is still an Ignorance, an incomplete, outward and superficial knowledge. To have made the discovery of our deepest being and hidden spiritual nature is the first necessity and to have erected the living of an inmost spiritual life into the aim of existence is the characteristic sign of a spiritual culture.

This endeavour takes in certain religions the form of a spiritual exclusiveness which revolts from the outward existence rather than seeks to transform it. The main tendency of the Christian discipline was not only to despise the physical and vital way of living, but to disparage and imprison the intellectual and distrust and discourage the aesthetic thirsts of our nature. It emphasised against them a limited spiritual emotionalism and its intense experiences as the one thing needful; the development of the ethical sense was the sole mental necessity, its translation into act the sole indispensable condition or result of the spiritual life. Indian spirituality reposed on too wide and many-sided a culture to admit as its base this narrow movement; but on its more solitary summits, at least in its later period, it tended to a spiritual exclusiveness loftier in vision, but even more imperative and excessive. A spirituality of this intolerant high-pointed kind, to whatever elevation it may rise, however it may help to purify life or lead to a certain kind of individual salvation, cannot be a complete thing. For its exclusiveness imposes on it a certain impotence to deal effectively with the problems of human existence; it cannot lead it to its integral perfection or combine its highest heights with its broadest broadness. A wider spiritual culture must recognise that the Spirit is not only the highest and inmost thing, but all is manifestation and creation of the Spirit. It must have a wider outlook, a more embracing range of applicability and, even, a more aspiring and ambitious aim of its endeavour. Its aim must be not only to raise to inaccessible heights the few elect, but to draw all men and all life and the whole human being upward, to spiritualise life and in the end to divinise human nature. Not only must it be able to lay hold on his deepest individual being but to inspire too his communal existence. It must turn by a spiritual change all the members of his ignorance into members of the knowledge; it must transmute all the instruments of the human into instruments of a divine living. The total movement of Indian spirituality is towards this aim; in spite of all the difficulties, imperfections and fluctuations of its evolution, it had this character. But like other cultures it was not at all times and in all its parts and movements consciously aware of its own total significance. This large sense sometimes emerged into something like a conscious synthetic clarity, but was more often kept in the depths and on the surface dispersed in a multitude of subordinate and special stand-points. Still, it is only by an intelligence of the total drift that its manifold sides and rich variations of effort and teaching and discipline can receive their full reconciling unity and be understood in the light of its own most intrinsic purpose.

Now the spirit of Indian religion and spiritual culture has been persistently and immovably the same throughout the long time of its vigour, but its form has undergone remarkable changes. Yet if we look into them from the right centre it will be apparent that these changes are the results of a logical and inevitable evolution inherent in the very process of man's growth towards the heights. In its earliest form, its first Vedic system, it took its outward foundation on the mind of the physical man whose natural faith is in things physical, in the sensible and visible objects, presences, representations and the external pursuits and aims of this material world. The means, symbols, rites, figures, by which it sought to mediate between the spirit and the normal human mentality were drawn from these most external physical things. Man's first and primitive idea of the Divine can only come through his vision of external Nature and the sense of a superior Power or Powers concealed behind her phenomena, veiled in the heaven and earth, father and mother of our being, in the sun and moon and stars, its lights and regulators, in dawn and day and night and rain and wind and storm, the oceans and the rivers and the forests, all the circumstances and forces of her scene of action, all that vast and mysterious surrounding life of which we are a part and in which the natural heart and mind of the human creature feel instinctively through whatever bright or dark or confused figures that there is here some divine Multitude or else mighty Infinite, one, manifold and mysterious, which takes these forms and manifests itself in these motions. The Vedic religion took this natural sense and feeling of the physical man; it used the conceptions to which they gave birth, and it sought to lead him through them to the psychic and spiritual truths of his own being and the being of the cosmos. It recognised that he was right when he saw behind the manifestations of Nature great living powers and godheads, even though he knew not their inner truth, and right too in offering to them worship and propitiation and atonement. For that inevitably must be the initial way in which his active physical, vital and mental nature is allowed to approach the Godhead. He approaches it through its visible outward manifestations as something greater than his own natural self, something single or multiple that guides, sustains and directs his life, and he calls to it for help and support in the desires and difficulties and distresses and struggles of his human existence.[1] The Vedic religion accepted also the form in which early man everywhere expressed his sense of the relation between himself and the godheads of Nature; it adopted as its central symbol the act and ritual of a physical sacrifice. However crude the notions attached to it, this idea of the necessity of sacrifice did express obscurely a first law of being. For it was founded on that secret of constant interchange between the individual and the universal powers of the cosmos which covertly supports all the process of life and develops the action of Nature.

But even in its external or exoteric side the Vedic religion did not limit itself to this acceptance and regulation of the first religious notions of the natural physical mind of man. The Vedic Rishis gave a psychic function to the godheads worshipped by the people; they spoke to them of a higher Truth, Right, Law of which the gods were the guardians, of the necessity of a truer

[1] The Gita recognises four kinds or degrees of worshippers and God-seekers. There are first the *arthārthī* and *ārta*, those who seek him for the fulfilment of desire and those who turn for divine help in the sorrow and suffering of existence; there is next the *jijñāsu*, the seeker of knowledge, the questioner who is moved to seek the Divine in his truth and in that to meet him; last and highest, there is the *jñānī* who has already contact with the truth and is able to live in unity with the Spirit. [Sri Aurobindo's note]

knowledge and a larger inner living according to this Truth and Right and of a home of Immortality to which the soul of man could ascend by the power of Truth and of right doing. The people no doubt took these ideas in their most external sense; but they were trained by them to develop their ethical nature, to turn towards some initial development of their psychic being, to conceive the idea of a knowledge and truth other than that of the physical life and to admit even a first conception of some greater spiritual Reality which was the ultimate object of human worship or aspiration. This religious and moral force was the highest reach of the external cult and the most that could be understood or followed by the mass of the people.

The deeper truth of these things was reserved for the initiates, for those who were ready to understand and practise the inner sense, the esoteric meaning hidden in the Vedic scripture. For the Veda is full of words which, as the Rishis themselves express it, are secret words that give their inner meaning only to the seer, *kavaye nivacanā niṇyāni vacāṁsi*. This is a feature of the ancient sacred hymns which grew obscure to later ages; it became a dead tradition and has been entirely ignored by modern scholarship in its laborious attempt to read the hieroglyph of the Vedic symbols. Yet its recognition is essential to a right understanding of almost all the ancient religions; for mostly they started on their upward curve through an esoteric element of which the key was not given to all. In all or most there was a surface cult for the common physical man who was held yet unfit for the psychic and spiritual life and an inner secret of the Mysteries carefully disguised by symbols whose sense was opened only to the initiates. This was the origin of the later distinction between the Shudra, the undeveloped physical-minded man, and the twice-born, those who were capable of entering into the second birth by initiation and to whom alone the Vedic education could be given without danger. This too actuated the later prohibition of any reading or teaching of the Veda by the Shudra. It was this inner meaning, it was the higher psychic and spiritual truths concealed by the outer sense, that gave to these hymns the name by which they are still known, the Veda, the Book of Knowledge. Only by penetrating into the esoteric sense of this worship can we understand the full flowering of the Vedic religion in the Upanishads and in the long later evolution of Indian spiritual seeking and experience. For it is all there in its luminous seed, preshadowed or even prefigured in the verses of the early seers. The persistent notion which through every change ascribed the foundation of all our culture to the Rishis, whatever its fabulous forms and mythical ascriptions, contains a real truth and veils a sound historic tradition. It reflects the fact of a true initiation and an unbroken continuity between this great primitive past and the riper but hardly greater spiritual development of our historic culture.

This inner Vedic religion started with an extension of the psychic significance of the godheads in the Cosmos. Its primary notion was that of a hierarchy of worlds, an ascending stair of planes of being in the universe. It saw a mounting scale of the worlds corresponding to a similar mounting scale of planes or degrees or levels of consciousness in the nature of man. A Truth, Right and Law sustains and governs all these levels of Nature; one in essence, it takes in them different but cognate forms. There is for instance the series of the outer physical light, another higher and inner light which is the vehicle of the mental, vital and psychic consciousness and a highest inmost light of spiritual illumination. Surya, the Sun-God, was the lord of the physical Sun; but he is at the same time to the Vedic seer-poet the giver of the rays of knowledge which illumine the mind and he is too the soul and energy and body of the spiritual illumination. And in all these powers he is a luminous form of the one and infinite Godhead. All the Vedic godheads have this outer and this inner and inmost function, their known and their secret Names. All are in their external character powers of physical Nature; all have in their inner meaning a psychic function and psychological ascriptions; all too are various powers of some one highest Reality, *ekaṁ sat*, the one infinite Existence. This hardly knowable Supreme is called often in the Veda 'That Truth' or 'That One', *tat satyam*, *tad ekam*. This complex character of the Vedic godheads assumes forms which have been wholly misunderstood by those who ascribe to them only their outward physical significance. Each of these gods is in himself a complete and separate cosmic personality of the one Existence and in their combination of powers they form the complete universal power, the cosmic whole, *vaiśvadevyam*. Each again, apart from his special function, is one godhead with the others; each holds in himself the universal divinity, each god is all the other gods. This is the aspect of the Vedic teaching and worship to which a European scholar, mistaking entirely its significance because he read it in the dim and poor light of European religious experience, has given the sounding misnomer, henotheism.[2] Beyond, in the triple Infinite, these godheads put on their highest nature and are names of the one nameless Ineffable.

But the greatest power of the Vedic teaching, that which made it the source of all later Indian philosophies, religions, systems of Yoga, lay in its application to the inner life of man. Man lives in the physical cosmos subject to death and the 'much falsehood' of the mortal existence. To rise beyond this death, to become one of the immortals, he has to turn from the falsehood to the Truth; he has to turn to the Light and to battle with and to conquer the powers of the Darkness. This he does by communion with the divine Powers and their aid; the way to call down this aid was the secret of the Vedic mystics. The symbols of the outer sacrifice are given for this purpose in the manner of the Mysteries all over the world an inner meaning; they represent a calling of the gods into the human being, a connecting sacrifice, an intimate interchange, a mutual aid, a communion. There is a building of the powers of the godheads within man and a formation in him of the universality of the divine nature. For the gods are the guardians and increasers of the Truth, the powers of the Immortal, the sons of the infinite Mother; the way to immortality is the upward way of the gods, the way of the Truth, a journey, an ascent by which there is a growth into the law of the Truth, *ṛtasya panthā*. Man arrives at immortality by breaking beyond the limitations not only of his physical self, but of his mental and his ordinary psychic nature into the highest plane and supreme ether of the Truth: for there is the foundation of immortality and the native seat of the triple Infinite. On these ideas the Vedic sages built up a profound psychological and psychic discipline which led beyond itself to a highest spirituality and contained the nucleus of later Indian Yoga. Already we find in their seed, though not in their full expansion, the

[2] The term 'henotheism' was coined by F. Max Müller (1823–1900), the German editor and translator of the Vedas and historian and philosopher of religion, to denote 'the actual belief in one god combined with a worship of his different forms'

most characteristic ideas of Indian spirituality. There is the one Existence, *ekaṁ sat*, supracosmic beyond the individual and the universe. There is the one God who presents to us the many forms, names, powers, personalities of his Godhead. There is the distinction between the Knowledge and the Ignorance,[3] the greater truth of an immortal life opposed to the much falsehood or mixed truth and falsehood of mortal existence. There is the discipline of an inward growth of man from the physical through the psychic to the spiritual existence. There is the conquest of death, the secret of immortality, the perception of a realisable divinity of the human spirit. In an age to which in the insolence of our external knowledge we are accustomed to look back as the childhood of humanity or at best a period of vigorous barbarism, this was the inspired and intuitive psychic and spiritual teaching by which the ancient human fathers, *pūrve pitaraḥ manuṣyāḥ*, founded a great and profound civilisation in India.

This high beginning was secured in its results by a larger sublime efflorescence. The Upanishads have always been recognised in India as the crown and end of Veda; that is indicated in their general name, Vedanta. And they are in fact a large crowning outcome of the Vedic discipline and experience. The time in which the Vedantic truth was wholly seen and the Upanishads took shape, was, as we can discern from such records as the Chhandogya and Brihadaranyaka, an epoch of immense and strenuous seeking, an intense and ardent seed-time of the Spirit. In the stress of that seeking the truths held by the initiates but kept back from ordinary men broke their barriers, swept through the higher mind of the nation and fertilised the soil of Indian culture for a constant and ever increasing growth of spiritual consciousness and spiritual experience. This turn was not as yet universal; it was chiefly men of the higher classes, Kshatriyas and Brahmins trained in the Vedic system of education, no longer content with an external truth and the works of the outer sacrifice, who began everywhere to seek for the highest word of revealing experience from the sages who possessed the knowledge of the One. But we find too among those who attained to the knowledge and became great teachers men of inferior or

[3] *Cittim acittiṁ cinavad vi vidvān.* 'Let the knower distinguish the Knowledge and the Ignorance.' [Sri Aurobindo's note]

doubtful birth like Janashruti, the wealthy Shudra, or Satyakama Jabali, son of a servant-girl who knew not who was his father. The work that was done in this period became the firm bedrock of Indian spirituality in later ages and from it gush still the life-giving waters of a perennial and never failing inspiration. This period, this activity, this grand achievement created the whole difference between the evolution of Indian civilisation and the quite different curve of other cultures.

For a time had come when the original Vedic symbols must lose their significance and pass into an obscurity that became impenetrable, as did the inner teaching of the Mysteries in other countries. The old poise of culture between two extremes with a bridge of religious cult and symbolism to unite them, the crude or half-trained naturalness of the outer physical man on one side of the line, and on the other an inner and secret psychic and spiritual life for the initiates could no longer suffice as the basis of our spiritual progress. The human race in its cycle of civilisation needed a large-lined advance; it called for a more and more generalised intellectual, ethical and aesthetic evolution to help it to grow into the light. This turn had to come in India as in other lands. But the danger was that the greater spiritual truth already gained might be lost in the lesser confident half-light of the acute but unillumined intellect or stifled within the narrow limits of the self-sufficient logical reason. That was what actually happened in the West, Greece leading the way. The old knowledge was prolonged in a less inspired, less dynamic and more intellectual form by the Pythagoreans, by the Stoics, by Plato and the Neo-Platonists; but still in spite of them and in spite of the only half-illumined spiritual wave which swept over Europe from Asia in an ill-understood Christianity, the whole real trend of Western civilisation has been intellectual, rational, secular and even materialistic, and it keeps this character to the present day. Its general aim has been a strong or a fine culture of the vital and physical man by the power of an intellectualised ethics, aesthesis and reason, not the leading up of our lower members into the supreme light and power of the spirit. The ancient spiritual knowledge and the spiritual tendency it had created were saved in India from this collapse by the immense effort of the age of the Upanishads. The Vedantic seers renewed the Vedic truth by extricating it from its cryptic symbols and casting it into a highest and most direct and powerful language of intuition and inner experience. It was not the language of the intellect, but still it wore a form which the intellect could take hold of, translate into its own more abstract terms and convert into a starting-point for an ever widening and deepening philosophic speculation and the reason's long search after a Truth original, supreme and ultimate. There was in India as in the West a great upbuilding of a high, wide and complex intellectual, aesthetic, ethical and social culture. But left in Europe to its own resources, combated rather than helped by obscure religious emotion and dogma, here it was guided, uplifted and more and more penetrated and suffused by a great saving power of spirituality and a vast stimulating and tolerant light of wisdom from a highest ether of knowledge.

The second or post-Vedic age of Indian civilisation was distinguished by the rise of the great philosophies, by a copious, vivid, many-thoughted, many-sided epic literature, by the beginnings of art and science, by the evolution of a vigorous and complex society, by the formation of large kingdoms and empires, by manifold formative activities of all kinds and great systems of living and thinking. Here as elsewhere, in Greece, Rome, Persia, China, this was the age of a high outburst of the intelligence working upon life and the things of the mind to discover their reason and their right way and bring out a broad and noble fullness of human existence. But in India this effort never lost sight of the spiritual motive, never missed the touch of the religious sense. It was a birth time and youth of the seeking intellect and, as in Greece, philosophy was the main instrument by which it laboured to solve the problems of life and the world. Science too developed, but it came second only as an auxiliary power. It was through profound and subtle philosophies that the intellect of India attempted to analyse by the reason and logical faculty what had formerly been approached with a much more living force through intuition and the soul's experience. But the philosophic mind started from the data these mightier powers had discovered and was faithful to its parent Light; it went back always in one form or another to the profound truths of the Upanishads which kept their place as the highest authority in these matters. There was a constant admission that spiritual experience is a greater thing and its light a truer if more incalculable guide than the clarities of the reasoning intelligence.

The same governing force kept its hold on all the other activities of the Indian mind and Indian life. The epic literature is full almost to excess of a strong and free intellectual and ethical thinking; there is an incessant criticism of life by the intelligence and the ethical reason, an arresting curiosity and desire to fix the norm of truth in all possible fields. But in the background and coming constantly to the front there is too a constant religious sense and an implicit or avowed assent to the spiritual truths which remained the unshakable basis of the culture. These truths suffused with their higher light secular thought and action or stood above to remind them that they were only steps towards a goal. Art in India, contrary to a common idea, dwelt much upon life; but still its highest achievement was always in the field of the interpretation of the religio-philosophical mind and its whole tone was coloured by a suggestion of the spiritual and the infinite. Indian society developed with an unsurpassed organising ability, stable effectiveness, practical insight its communal coordination of the mundane life of interest and desire, *kāma*, *artha*; it governed always its action by a reference at every point to the moral and religious law, the Dharma: but it never lost sight of spiritual liberation as our highest point and the ultimate aim of the effort of Life. In later times when there was a still stronger secular tendency of intellectual culture, there came in an immense development of the mundane intelligence, an opulent political and social evolution, an emphatic stressing of aesthetic, sensuous and hedonistic experience. But this effort too always strove to keep itself within the ancient frame and not to lose the special stamp of the Indian cultural idea. The enlarged secular turn was compensated by a deepening of the intensities of psycho-religious experience. New religious or mystic forms and disciplines attempted to seize not only the soul and the intellect, but the emotions, the senses, the vital and the aesthetic nature of man and turn them into stuff of the spiritual life. And every excess of emphasis on the splendour and richness and power and pleasures of life had its recoil and was balanced by a corresponding potent stress on spiritual asceticism as the higher way. The two trends, on one side an extreme of the richness of life experience, on the other an extreme and pure rigorous intensity of the spiritual life, accompanied each other; their interaction, whatever loss there might be of the earlier deep harmony and large synthesis, yet by their double pull preserved something still of the balance of Indian culture.

Indian religion followed this line of evolution and kept its inner continuity with its Vedic and Vedantic origins; but it changed entirely its mental contents and colour and its outward basis. It did not effectuate this change through any protestant revolt or revolution or with any idea of an iconoclastic reformation. A continuous development of its organic life took place, a natural transformation brought out latent motives or else gave to already established motive-ideas a more predominant place or effective form. At one time indeed it seemed as if a discontinuity and a sharp new beginning were needed and would take place. Buddhism seemed to reject all spiritual continuity with the Vedic religion. But this was after all less in reality than in appearance. The Buddhist ideal of Nirvana was no more than a sharply negative and exclusive statement of the highest Vedantic spiritual experience. The ethical system of the eightfold path taken as the way to release was an austere sublimation of the Vedic notion of the Right, Truth and Law followed as the way to immortality, *ṛtasya panthā*. The strongest note of Mahayana Buddhism, its stress on universal compassion and fellow-feeling, was an ethical application of the spiritual unity which is the essential idea of Vedanta.[4] The most characteristic tenets of the new discipline, Nirvana and Karma, could have been supported from the utterances of the Brahmanas and Upanishads. Buddhism could easily have claimed for itself a Vedic origin and the claim would have been no less valid than the Vedic ascription of the Sankhya philosophy and discipline with which it had some points of intimate alliance. But what hurt Buddhism and determined in the end its rejection, was not its denial of a Vedic origin or authority, but the exclusive trenchancy of its intellectual, ethical and spiritual positions. A result of an intense stress of the union of logical reason with the spiritualised mind — for it was by an intense spiritual search supported on a clear and hard rational thinking that it was born as a separate religion, — its trenchant affirmations and

[4] Buddha himself does not seem to have preached his tenets as a novel revolutionary creed, but as the old Aryan way, the true form of the eternal religion. [Sri Aurobindo's note]

still more exclusive negations could not be made sufficiently compatible with the native flexibility, many-sided susceptibility and rich synthetic turn of the Indian religious consciousness; it was a high creed but not plastic enough to hold the heart of the people. Indian religion absorbed all that it could of Buddhism, but rejected its exclusive positions and preserved the full line of its own continuity, casting back to the ancient Vedanta.

This lasting line of change moved forward not by any destruction of principle, but by a gradual fading out of the prominent Vedic forms and the substitution of others. There was a transformation of symbol and ritual and ceremony or a substitution of new kindred figures, an emergence of things that are only hints in the original system, a development of novel idea-forms from the seed of the original thinking. And especially there was a farther widening and fathoming of psychic and spiritual experience. The Vedic gods rapidly lost their deep original significance. At first they kept their hold by their outer cosmic sense but were overshadowed by the great Trinity, Brahma-Vishnu-Shiva, and afterwards faded altogether. A new pantheon appeared which in its outward symbolic aspects expressed a deeper truth and larger range of religious experience, an intenser feeling, a vaster idea. The Vedic sacrifice persisted only in broken and lessening fragments. The house of Fire was replaced by the temple; the karmic ritual of sacrifice was transformed into the devotional temple ritual; the vague and shifting mental images of the Vedic gods figured in the mantras yielded to more precise conceptual forms of the two great deities, Vishnu and Shiva, and of their Shaktis and their offshoots. These new concepts stabilised in physical images which were made the basis both for internal adoration and for the external worship which replaced sacrifice. The psychic and spiritual mystic endeavour which was the inner sense of the Vedic hymns, disappeared into the less intensely luminous but more wide and rich and complex psycho-spiritual inner life of Puranic and Tantric religion and Yoga.

The Purano-Tantric stage of the religion was once decried by European critics and Indian reformers as a base and ignorant degradation of an earlier and purer religion. It was rather an effort, successful in a great measure, to open the general mind of the people to a higher and deeper range of inner truth and experience and feeling. Much of the adverse criticism once heard proceeded from a total ignorance of the sense and intention of this worship. Much of this criticism has been uselessly concentrated on side-paths and aberrations which could hardly be avoided in this immensely audacious experimental widening of the basis of the culture. For there was a catholic attempt to draw towards the spiritual truth minds of all qualities and people of all classes. Much was lost of the profound psychic knowledge of the Vedic seers, but much also of new knowledge was developed, untrodden ways were opened and a hundred gates discovered into the Infinite. If we try to see the essential sense and aim of this development and the intrinsic value of its forms and means and symbols, we shall find that this evolution followed upon the early Vedic form very much for the same reason as Catholic Christianity replaced the mysteries and sacrifices of the early Pagan religions. For in both cases the outward basis of the early religion spoke to the outward physical mind of the people and took that as the starting-point of its appeal. But the new evolution tried to awaken a more inner mind even in the common man, to lay hold on his inner vital and emotional nature, to support all by an awakening of the soul and to lead him through these things towards a highest spiritual truth. It attempted in fact to bring the mass into the temple of the spirit rather than leave them in the outer precincts. The outward physical sense was satisfied through its aesthetic turn by a picturesque temple worship, by numerous ceremonies, by the use of physical images; but these were given a psycho-emotional sense and direction that was open to the heart and imagination of the ordinary man and not reserved for the deeper sight of the elect or the strenuous tapasya of the initiates. The secret initiation remained but was now a condition for the passage from the surface psycho-emotional and religious to a profounder psychic-spiritual truth and experience.

Nothing essential was touched in its core by this new orientation; but the instruments, atmosphere, field of religious experience underwent a considerable change. The Vedic godheads were to the mass of their worshippers divine powers who presided over the workings of the outward life of the physical cosmos; the Puranic Trinity had even for the multitude a predominant psycho-religious and spiritual significance. Its more external significances, for instance the functions of cosmic creation, preservation and destruction, were only a dependent fringe of these profundities that alone touched the heart of its mystery. The central spiritual truth remained in both systems the same, the truth of the One in many aspects. The Trinity is a triple form of the one supreme Godhead and Brahman; the Shaktis are energies of the one Energy of the highest divine Being. But this greatest religious truth was no longer reserved for the initiated few; it was now more and more brought powerfully, widely and intensely home to the general mind and feeling of the people. Even the so-called henotheism of the Vedic idea was prolonged and heightened in the larger and simpler worship of Vishnu or Shiva as the one universal and highest Godhead of whom all others are living forms and powers. The idea of the Divinity in man was popularised to an extraordinary extent, not only the occasional manifestation of the Divine in humanity which founded the worship of the Avataras, but the Presence discoverable in the heart of every creature. The systems of Yoga developed themselves on the same common basis. All led or hoped to lead through many kinds of psycho-physical, inner vital, inner mental and psycho-spiritual methods to the common aim of all Indian spirituality, a greater consciousness and a more or less complete union with the One and Divine or else an immergence of the individual soul in the Absolute. The Purano-Tantric system was a wide, assured and many-sided endeavour, unparalleled in its power, insight, amplitude, to provide the race with a basis of generalised psycho-religious experience from which man could rise through knowledge, works or love or through any other fundamental power of his nature to some established supreme experience and highest absolute status.

This great effort and achievement which covered all the time between the Vedic age and the decline of Buddhism, was still not the last possibility of religious evolution open to Indian culture. The Vedic training of the physically-minded man made the development possible. But in its turn this raising of the basis of religion to the inner mind and life and psychic nature, this training and bringing out of the psychic man ought to make possible a still larger development and support a greater spiritual movement as the leading power of life. The first stage makes possible the preparation of the natural external man for spirituality; the second takes up his outward life into a deeper mental and psychical living and brings him more directly into contact with the spirit and divinity within him; the third should render him capable of taking up his whole mental, psychical, physical living into a first beginning at least of a generalised spiritual life. This endeavour has manifested itself in the evolution of Indian spirituality and is the significance of the latest philosophies, the great spiritual movements of the saints and bhaktas and an increasing resort to the various paths of Yoga. But unhappily it synchronised with a decline of Indian culture and an increasing collapse of its general power and knowledge, and in these surroundings it could not bear its natural fruit; but at the same time it has done much to prepare such a possibility in the future. If Indian culture is to survive and keep its spiritual basis and innate character, it is in this direction, and not in a mere revival or prolongation of the Puranic system, that its evolution must turn, rising so towards the fulfilment of that which the Vedic seers saw as the aim of man and his life thousands of years ago and the Vedantic sages cast into the clear and immortal forms of their luminous revelation.

Even the psychic-emotional part of man's nature is not the inmost door to religious feeling, nor is his inner mind the highest witness to spiritual experience. There is behind the first the inmost soul of man, in that deepest secret heart, *hṛdaye guhāyām*, in which the ancient seers saw the very tabernacle of the indwelling Godhead and there is above the second a luminous highest mind directly open to a truth of the Spirit to which man's normal nature has as yet only an occasional and momentary access. Religious evolution, spiritual experience can find their true native road only when they open to these hidden powers and make them their support for a lasting change, a divinisation of human life and nature. An effort of this kind was the very force behind the most luminous and vivid of the later movements of India's vast religious cycle. It is the secret of the most powerful forms of Vaishnavism and Tantra and Yoga. The labour of ascent from our half-animal human nature into the fresh purity of the spiritual consciousness needed to be followed and supplemented by a descent of the light and force of the spirit into man's members and the attempt to transform human into divine nature.

But it could not find its complete way or its fruit because it synchronised with a decline of the life force in India and a lowering of power and knowledge in her general civilisation and culture. Nevertheless here lies the destined force of her survival and renewal, this is the dynamic meaning of her future. A widest and highest spiritualising of life on earth is the last vision of all that vast and unexampled seeking and experiment in a thousand ways of the soul's outermost and innermost experience which is the unique character of her past; this in the end is the mission for which she was born and the meaning of her existence.

The Secret of the Veda

The Problem and Its Solution

IS THERE at all or is there still a secret of the Veda? According to current conceptions the heart of that ancient mystery has been plucked out and revealed to the gaze of all, or rather no real secret ever existed.[1] The hymns of the Veda are the sacrificial compositions of a primitive and still barbarous race written around a system of ceremonial and propitiatory rites, addressed to personified Powers of Nature and replete with a confused mass of half-formed myth and crude astronomical allegories yet in the making. Only in the later hymns do we perceive the first appearance of deeper psychological and moral ideas — borrowed, some think, from the hostile Dravidians, the 'robbers' and 'Veda-haters' freely cursed in the hymns themselves, — and, however acquired, the first seed of the later Vedantic speculations. This modern theory is in accord with the received idea of a rapid human evolution from the quite recent savage; it is supported by an imposing apparatus of critical research and upheld by a number of Sciences, unhappily still young and still largely conjectural in their methods and shifting in their results, — Comparative Philology, Comparative Mythology and the Science of Comparative Religion.

It is my object in these chapters to suggest a new view of the ancient problem. I do not propose to use a negative and destructive method directed against the received solutions, but

The first chapter of *The Secret of the Veda*, published in the first issue of *Arya*, 15 August 1914. *The Secret of the Veda* first appeared as part of a book posthumously in 1956.

[1] In this paragraph and elsewhere in this chapter Sri Aurobindo refers to the state of Vedic studies in Europe at the end of the nineteenth and beginning of the twentieth century, particularly as exemplified by the works of F. Max Müller.

simply to present, positively and constructively, a larger and, in some sort, a complementary hypothesis built upon broader foundations, — a hypothesis which, in addition, may shed light on one or two important problems in the history of ancient thought and cult left very insufficiently solved by the ordinary theories.

We have in the Rig Veda, — the true and only Veda in the estimation of European scholars, — a body of sacrificial hymns couched in a very ancient language which presents a number of almost insoluble difficulties. It is full of ancient forms and words which do not appear in later speech and have often to be fixed in some doubtful sense by intelligent conjecture; a mass even of the words that it has in common with classical Sanskrit seem to bear or at least to admit another significance than in the later literary tongue; and a multitude of its vocables, especially the most common, those which are most vital to the sense, are capable of a surprising number of unconnected significances which may give, according to our preference in selection, quite different complexions to whole passages, whole hymns and even to the whole thought of the Veda. In the course of several thousands of years there have been at least three considerable attempts, entirely differing from each other in their methods and results, to fix the sense of these ancient litanies. One of these is prehistoric in time and exists only by fragments in the Brahmanas and Upanishads; but we possess in its entirety the traditional interpretation of the Indian scholar Sayana[2] and we have in our own day the interpretation constructed after an immense labour of comparison and conjecture by modern European scholarship. Both of them present one characteristic in common, the extraordinary incoherence and poverty of sense which their results stamp upon the ancient hymns. The separate lines can be given, whether naturally or by force of conjecture, a good sense or a sense that hangs together; the diction that results, if garish in style, if loaded with otiose and decorative epithets, if developing extraordinarily little of meaning in an amazing mass of gaudy figure and verbiage, can be made to run into intelligible sentences; but when we come to read the hymns as a whole we

2 Sayana (fourteenth century), South Indian author of the most respected classical Sanskrit commentary on the Rig Veda.

seem to be in the presence of men who, unlike the early writers of other races, were incapable of coherent and natural expression or of connected thought. Except in the briefer and simpler hymns, the language tends to be either obscure or artificial; the thoughts are either unconnected or have to be forced and beaten by the interpreter into a whole. The scholar in dealing with his text is obliged to substitute for interpretation a process almost of fabrication. We feel that he is not so much revealing the sense as hammering and forging rebellious material into some sort of shape and consistency.

Yet these obscure and barbarous compositions have had the most splendid good fortune in all literary history. They have been the reputed source not only of some of the world's richest and profoundest religions, but of some of its subtlest metaphysical philosophies. In the fixed tradition of thousands of years they have been revered as the origin and standard of all that can be held as authoritative and true in Brahmana and Upanishad, in Tantra and Purana, in the doctrines of great philosophical schools and in the teachings of famous saints and sages. The name borne by them was Veda, the knowledge, — the received name for the highest spiritual truth of which the human mind is capable. But if we accept the current interpretations, whether Sayana's or the modern theory, the whole of this sublime and sacred reputation is a colossal fiction. The hymns are, on the contrary, nothing more than the naive superstitious fancies of untaught and materialistic barbarians concerned only with the most external gains and enjoyments and ignorant of all but the most elementary moral notions or religious aspirations. Nor do occasional passages, quite out of harmony with their general spirit, destroy this total impression. The true foundation or starting-point of the later religions and philosophies is the Upanishads, which have then to be conceived as a revolt of philosophical and speculative minds against the ritualistic materialism of the Vedas.

But this conception, supported by misleading European parallels, really explains nothing. Such profound and ultimate thoughts, such systems of subtle and elaborate psychology as are found in the substance of the Upanishads, do not spring out of a previous void. The human mind in its progress marches from knowledge to knowledge, or it renews and enlarges previous knowledge that has been obscured and overlaid, or it seizes on old imperfect clues and is led by them to new discoveries. The thought of the Upanishads supposes great origins anterior to itself, and these in the ordinary theories are lacking. The hypothesis, invented to fill the gap, that these ideas were borrowed by barbarous Aryan invaders from the civilised Dravidians, is a conjecture supported only by other conjectures. It is indeed coming to be doubted whether the whole story of an Aryan invasion through the Punjab is not a myth of the philologists.

Now, in ancient Europe the schools of intellectual philosophy were preceded by the secret doctrines of the mystics; Orphic and Eleusinian mysteries prepared the rich soil of mentality out of which sprang Pythagoras and Plato.[3] A similar starting-point is at least probable for the later march of thought in India. Much indeed of the forms and symbols of thought which we find in the Upanishads, much of the substance of the Brahmanas supposes a period in India in which thought took the form or the veil of secret teachings such as those of the Greek mysteries.

Another hiatus left by the received theories is the gulf that divides the material worship of external Nature-Powers in the Veda from the developed religion of the Greeks and from the psychological and spiritual ideas we find attached to the functions of the Gods in the Upanishads and Puranas. We may accept for the present the theory that the earliest fully intelligent form of human religion is necessarily,—since man on earth begins from the external and proceeds to the internal,—a worship of outward Nature-Powers invested with the consciousness and the personality that he finds in his own being.

Agni in the Veda is avowedly Fire; Surya is the Sun, Parjanya the Raincloud, Usha the Dawn; and if the material origin or function of some other Gods is less trenchantly clear, it is easy to render the obscure precise by philological inferences or ingenious speculation. But when we come to the worship of the Greeks not much later in date than the Veda, according to modern ideas of chronology, we find a significant change. The material attributes of the Gods are effaced or have become subordinate to psychological conceptions. The impetuous God of Fire has been

[3] The Orphic and Eleusinian Mysteries were the principal secret religious rites of ancient Greece. The philosophies of Pythagoras (sixth century BCE) and of Plato (c. 427–347 BCE) contain many mystic elements.

converted into a lame God of Labour; Apollo, the Sun, presides over poetical and prophetic inspiration; Athene, who may plausibly be identified as in origin a Dawn-Goddess, has lost all memory of her material functions and is the wise, strong and pure Goddess of Knowledge; and there are other deities also, Gods of War, Love, Beauty, whose material functions have disappeared if they ever existed. It is not enough to say that this change was inevitable with the progress of human civilisation: the process also of the change demands inquiry and elucidation. We see the same revolution effected in the Puranas partly by the substitution of other divine names and figures, but also in part by the same obscure process that we observe in the evolution of Greek mythology. The river Saraswati has become the Muse and Goddess of Learning; Vishnu and Rudra of the Vedas are now the supreme Godhead, members of a divine Triad and expressive separately of the conservative and destructive process in the cosmos. In the Isha Upanishad we find an appeal to Surya as a God of revelatory knowledge by whose action we can arrive at the highest truth. This, too, is his function in the sacred Vedic formula of the Gayatri which was for thousands of years repeated by every Brahmin in his daily meditation; and we may note that this formula is a verse from the Rig Veda, from a hymn of the Rishi Vishwamitra.[4] In the same Upanishad, Agni is invoked for purely moral functions as the purifier from sin, the leader of the soul by the good path to the divine Bliss, and he seems to be identified with the power of the will and responsible for human actions. In other Upanishads the Gods are clearly the symbols of sense-functions in man. Soma, the plant which yielded the mystic wine for the Vedic sacrifice, has become not only the God of the moon, but manifests himself as mind in the human being. These evolutions suppose some period, posterior to the early material worship or superior Pantheistic Animism attributed to the Vedas and prior to the developed Puranic mythology, in which the gods became invested with deeper psychological functions, a period which may well have been the Age of the Mysteries. As things stand, a gap is left or else has been created by our exclusive preoccupation with the naturalistic element in the religion of the Vedic Rishis.

[4] The Gayatri is a verse (10) from a hymn of the Rig Veda (3.62) ascribed to the Rishi Vishwamitra.

I suggest that the gulf is of our own creation and does not really exist in the ancient sacred writings. The hypothesis I propose is that the Rig Veda is itself the one considerable document that remains to us from the early period of human thought of which the historic Eleusinian and Orphic mysteries were the failing remnants, when the spiritual and psychological knowledge of the race was concealed, for reasons now difficult to determine, in a veil of concrete and material figures and symbols which protected the sense from the profane and revealed it to the initiated. One of the leading principles of the mystics was the sacredness and secrecy of self-knowledge and the true knowledge of the Gods. This wisdom was, they thought, unfit, perhaps even dangerous to the ordinary human mind or in any case liable to perversion and misuse and loss of virtue if revealed to vulgar and unpurified spirits. Hence they favoured the existence of an outer worship, effective but imperfect, for the profane, an inner discipline for the initiate, and clothed their language in words and images which had, equally, a spiritual sense for the elect, a concrete sense for the mass of ordinary worshippers. The Vedic hymns were conceived and constructed on this principle. Their formulas and ceremonies are, overtly, the details of an outward ritual devised for the Pantheistic Nature-Worship which was then the common religion, covertly the sacred words, the effective symbols of a spiritual experience and knowledge and a psychological discipline of self-culture which were then the highest achievement of the human race. The ritual system recognised by Sayana may, in its externalities, stand; the naturalistic sense discovered by European scholarship may, in its general conceptions, be accepted; but behind them there is always the true and still hidden secret of the Veda,—the secret words, *niṇyā vacāṁsi*, which were spoken for the purified in soul and the awakened in knowledge. To disengage this less obvious but more important sense by fixing the import of Vedic terms, the sense of Vedic symbols and the psychological functions of the Gods is thus a difficult but necessary task, for which these chapters and the translations that accompany them are only a preparation.[5]

[5] *The Secret of the Veda* consists of twenty-three chapters, of which this is the first. They were first published in the monthly review *Arya* between 1914 and 1916. In the same review Sri Aurobindo published many translations of Vedic hymns, often with commentaries.

The hypothesis, if it proves to be valid, will have three advantages. It will elucidate simply and effectively the parts of the Upanishads that remain yet unintelligible or ill-understood as well as much of the origins of the Puranas. It will explain and justify rationally the whole ancient tradition of India; for it will be found that, in sober truth, the Vedanta, Purana, Tantra, the philosophical schools and the great Indian religions do go back in their source to Vedic origins. We can see there in their original seed or in their early or even primitive forms the fundamental conceptions of later Indian thought. Thus a natural starting-point will be provided for a sounder study of Comparative Religion in the Indian field. Instead of wandering amid insecure speculations or having to account for impossible conversions and unexplained transitions we shall have a clue to a natural and progressive development satisfying to the reason. Incidentally, some light may be thrown on the obscurities of early cult and myth in other ancient nations. Finally, the incoherencies of the Vedic texts will at once be explained and disappear. They exist in appearance only, because the real thread of the sense is to be found in an inner meaning. That thread found, the hymns appear as logical and organic wholes and the expression, though alien in type to our modern ways of thinking and speaking, becomes, in its own style, just and precise and sins rather by economy of phrase than by excess, by over-pregnancy rather than by poverty of sense. The Veda ceases to be merely an interesting remnant of barbarism and takes rank among the most important of the world's early Scriptures.

Readings in the Taittiriya Upanishad

The Knowledge of Brahman

The knower of Brahman reacheth that which is supreme. This is that verse which was spoken; 'Truth, Knowledge, Infinity the Brahman, He who knoweth that hidden in the secrecy in the supreme ether, Enjoyeth all desires along with the wise-thinking Brahman.'

This is the burden of the opening sentences of the Taittiriya Upanishad's second section; they begin its elucidation of the highest truth. Or in the Sanskrit,

ब्रह्मविद आप्नोति परम —
तद् एषाभ्युक्ता — सत्यं ज्ञानम् अनन्तं ब्रह्म —
यो वेद निहितं गुहायां — परमे व्योमन —
सोऽश्नुते सर्वान् कामान् — सह ब्रह्मणा विपश्चितेति ।

But what is Brahman?

Whatever reality is in existence, by which all the rest subsists, that is Brahman. An Eternal behind all instabilities, a Truth of things which is implied, if it is hidden in all appearances, a Constant which supports all mutations, but is not increased, diminished, abrogated, — there is such an unknown X which makes existence a problem, our own self a mystery, the universe a riddle. If we were only what we seem to be to our normal self-awareness, there would be no mystery; if the world were only what it can be made out to be by the perceptions of the senses and their strict analysis in the reason, there would be no riddle; and if to take our life as it is now and the world as it has so far developed to our experience were the whole possibility of our knowing and doing, there would be no problem. Or at best there would be but a shallow mystery, an easily solved riddle, the problem only of a child's puzzle. But there is more, and that more is the hidden head of the Infinite and the secret heart of the Eternal. It is the highest and this highest is the all; there is none beyond and there is none other than it. To know it is to know the highest and by knowing the highest to know all. For as it is the beginning and source of all things, so everything else is its consequence; as it is the support and constituent of all things, so the secret of everything else is explained by its secret; as it is the sum and end of all things, so everything else amounts to it and by throwing itself into it achieves the sense of its own existence.

This is the Brahman.

*
* *

If this unknown be solely an indecipherable, only indefinable X, always unknown and unknowable, the hidden never revealed, the secret never opened to us, then our mystery would for ever remain a mystery, our riddle insoluble, our problem intangible. Its existence, even while it determines all we are, know and do, could yet make no practical difference to us; for our relation to it would then be a blind and helpless dependence, a relation binding us to ignorance and maintainable only by that ignorance. Or again, if it be in some way knowable, but the sole result of knowledge were an extinction or cessation of our being, then within our being it could have no consequences; the very act and fructuation of knowledge would bring the annihilation of all that we now are, not its completion or fulfilment. The mystery, riddle, problem would not be so much solved as abolished, for it would lose all its data. In effect we should have to suppose that there is an eternal and irreconcilable opposition between Brahman and what we now are, between the supreme cause and all its effects or between the supreme source and all its derivations. And it would then seem that all that the Eternal originates, all he supports, all he takes back to himself is a denial or contradiction of his being which, though in itself a negative of that which alone is, has yet in some way become a positive. The two could not coexist in consciousness; if he allowed the world to know him, it would disappear from being.

But the Eternal is knowable, He defines himself so that we may seize him, and man can become, even while he exists as man and in this world and in this body, a knower of the Brahman.

The knowledge of the Brahman is not a thing luminous but otiose, informing to the intellectual view of things but without consequence to the soul of the individual or his living; it is a knowledge that is a power and a divine compulsion to change; by it his existence gains something that now he does not possess in consciousness. What is this gain? It is this that he is conscious now in a lower state only of his being, but by knowledge he gains his highest being.

The highest state of our being is not a denial, contradiction and annihilation of all that we now are; it is a supreme accomplishment of all things that our present existence means and aims at, but in their highest sense and in the eternal values.

*

* *

To live in our present state of self-consciousness is to live and to act in ignorance. We are ignorant of ourselves, because we know as yet only that in us which changes always, from moment to moment, from hour to hour, from period to period, from life to life, and not that in us which is eternal. We are ignorant of the world because we do not know God; we are aware of the law of appearances, but not of the law and truth of being.

Our highest wisdom, our minutest most accurate science, our most effective application of knowledge can be at most a thinning of the veil of ignorance, but not a going beyond it, so long as we do not get at the fundamental knowledge and the consciousness to which that is native. The rest are effective for their own temporal purposes, but prove ineffective in the end, because they do not bring to the highest good; they lead to no permanent solution of the problem of existence.

The ignorance in which we live is not a baseless and wholesale falsehood, but at its lowest the misrepresentation of a Truth, at its highest an imperfect representation and translation into inferior and to that extent misleading values. It is a knowledge of the superficial only and therefore a missing of the secret essential which is the key to all that the superficial is striving for; a knowledge of the finite and apparent, but a missing of all that the apparent symbolises and the finite suggests; a knowledge of inferior forms, but a missing of all that our inferior life and being has above it and to which it must aspire if it is to fulfil its greatest possibilities. The true knowledge is that of the highest, the inmost, the infinite. The knower of the Brahman sees all these lower things in the light of the Highest, the external and superficial as a translation of the internal and essential, the finite from the view of the Infinite. He begins to see and know existence no longer as the thinking animal, but as the Eternal sees and knows it. Therefore he is glad and rich in being, luminous in joy, satisfied of existence.

*

* *

Knowledge does not end with knowing, nor is it pursued and found for the sake of knowing alone. It has its full value only when it leads to some greater gain than itself, some gain of being. Simply to know the eternal and to remain in the pain, struggle and inferiority of our present way of being, would be a poor and lame advantage.

A greater knowledge opens the possibility and, if really possessed, brings the actuality of a greater being. To be is the first verb which contains all the others; knowledge, action, creation, enjoyment are only a fulfilment of being. Since we are incomplete in being, to grow is our aim, and that knowledge, action, creation, enjoyment are the best which most help us to expand, grow, feel our existence.

Mere existence is not fullness of being. Being knows itself as power, consciousness, delight; a greater being means a greater power, consciousness and delight.

If by greater being we incurred only a greater pain and suffering, this good would not be worth having. Those who say that it is, mean simply that we get by it a greater sense of fulfilment which brings of itself a greater joy of the power of existence, and an extension of suffering or a loss of other enjoyment is worth having as a price for this greater sense of wideness, height and power. But this could not be the perfection of being or the highest height of its fulfilment; suffering is the seal of a lower status. The highest consciousness is integrally fulfilled in wideness and power of its existence, but also it is integrally fulfilled in delight.

The knower of Brahman has not only the joy of light, but gains something immense as the result of his knowledge, *brahmavid āpnoti.*

What he gains is that highest, that which is supreme; he gains the highest being, the highest consciousness, the highest wideness and power of being, the highest delight; *brahmavid āpnoti param.*

*
* *

The Supreme is not something aloof and shut up in itself. It is not a mere indefinable, prisoner of its own featureless absoluteness, impotent to define, create, know itself variously, eternally buried in a sleep or a swoon of self-absorption. The Highest is the Infinite and the Infinite contains the All. Whoever attains the highest consciousness, becomes infinite in being and embraces the All.

To make this clear the Upanishad has defined the Brahman as the Truth, Knowledge, Infinity and has defined the result of the knowledge of Him in the secrecy, in the cave of being, in the supreme ether as the enjoyment of all its desires by the soul of the individual in the attainment of its highest self-existence.

Our highest state of being is indeed a becoming one with Brahman in his eternity and infinity, but it is also an association with him in delight of self-fulfilment, *aśnute saha brahmaṇā.* And that principle of the Eternal by which this association is possible, is the principle of his knowledge, his self-discernment and all-discernment, the wisdom by which he knows himself perfectly in all the world and all beings, *brahmaṇā vipaścitā.*

Delight of being is the continent of all the fulfilled values of existence which we now seek after in the forms of desire. To know its conditions and possess it purely and perfectly is the infinite privilege of the eternal Wisdom.

Kena Upanishad: A Last Word

We have now completed our review of this Upanishad; we have considered minutely the bearings of its successive utterances and striven to make as precise as we can to the intelligence the sense of the puissant phrases in which it gives us its leading clues to that which can never be entirely expressed by human speech. We have some idea of what it means by that Brahman, by the Mind of mind, the Life of life, the Sense of sense, the Speech of speech, by the opposition of ourselves and the gods, by the Unknowable who is yet not utterly unknowable to us, by the transcendence of the mortal state and the conquest of immortality.

Fundamentally its teaching reposes on the assertion of three states of existence, the human and mortal, the Brahman-consciousness which is the absolute of our relativities, and the utter Absolute which is unknowable. The first is in a sense a false status of misrepresentation because it is a continual term of apparent opposites and balancings where the truth of things is a secret unity; we have here a bright or positive figure and a dark or negative figure and both are figures, neither the Truth; still in that we now live and through that we have to move to the Beyond. The second is the Lord of all this dual action who is beyond it; He is the truth of Brahman and not in any way a falsehood or misrepresentation, but the truth of it as attained by us in our eternal supramental being; in Him are the absolutes of all that here we experience in partial figures. The Unknowable is beyond our grasp because though it is the same Reality, yet it exceeds even our highest term of eternal being and is beyond

The last chapter of Sri Aurobindo's commentary on the Kena Upanishad, published in the *Arya* in 1916 and subsequently revised. *Kena Upanishad* was published posthumously in 1952.

Existence and Non-existence; it is therefore to the Brahman, the Lord who has a relation to what we are that we must direct our search if we would attain beyond what temporarily seems to what eternally is.

The attainment of the Brahman is our escape from the mortal status into Immortality, by which we understand not the survival of death, but the finding of our true self of eternal being and bliss beyond the dual symbols of birth and death. By immortality we mean the absolute life of the soul as opposed to the transient and mutable life in the body which it assumes by birth and death and rebirth and superior also to its life as the mere mental being who dwells in the world subjected helplessly to this law of death and birth or seems at least by his ignorance to be subjected to this and to other laws of the lower Nature. To know and possess its true nature, free, absolute, master of itself and its embodiments is the soul's means of transcendence, and to know and possess this is to know and possess the Brahman. It is also to rise out of mortal world into immortal world, out of world of bondage into world of largeness, out of finite world into infinite world. It is to ascend out of earthly joy and sorrow into a transcendent Beatitude.

This must be done by the abandonment of our attachment to the figure of things in the mortal world. We must put from us its death and dualities if we would compass the unity and immortality. Therefore it follows that we must cease to make the goods of this world or even its right, light and beauty our object of pursuit; we must go beyond these to a supreme Good, a transcendent Truth, Light and Beauty in which the opposite figures of what we call evil disappear. But still, being in this world, it is only through something in this world itself that we can transcend it; it is through its figures that we must find the absolute. Therefore, we scrutinise them and perceive that there are first these forms of mind, life, speech and sense, all of them figures and imperfect suggestions, and then behind them the cosmic principles through which the One acts. It is to these cosmic principles that we must proceed and turn them from their ordinary aim and movement in the world to find their own supreme aim and absolute movement in their own one Godhead, the Lord, the Brahman; they must be drawn to leave the workings of ordinary mind and find the superconscient Mind, to leave the workings of ordinary speech and sense and find the supramental Sense and original Word, to leave the apparent workings of mundane Life and find the transcendent Life.

Besides the gods, there is our self, the spirit within who supports all this action of the gods. Our spirit too must turn from its absorption in its figure of itself as it sees it involved in the movement of individual life, mind, body and subject to it and must direct its gaze upward to its own supreme Self who is beyond all this movement and master of it all. Therefore the mind must indeed become passive to the divine Mind, the sense to the divine Sense, the life to the divine Life and by receptivity to constant touches and visitings of the highest be transfigured into a reflection of these transcendences; but also the individual self must through the mind's aspiration upwards, through upliftings of itself beyond, through constant memory of the supreme Reality in which during these divine moments it has lived, ascend finally into that Bliss and Power and Light.

But this will not necessarily mean the immersion into an all-oblivious Being eternally absorbed in His own inactive self-existence. For the mind, sense, life going beyond their individual formations find that they are only one centre of the sole Mind, Life, Form of things and therefore they find Brahman in that also and not only in an individual transcendence; they bring down the vision of the superconscient into that also and not only into their own individual workings. The mind of the individual escapes from its limits and becomes the one universal mind, his life the one universal life, his bodily sense the sense of the whole universe and even more as his own indivisible Brahman-body. He perceives the universe in himself and he perceives also his self in all existences and knows it to be the one, the omnipresent, the single-multiple all-inhabiting Lord and Reality. Without this realisation he has not fulfilled the conditions of immortality. Therefore it is said that what the sages seek is to distinguish and see the Brahman in all existences; by that discovery, realisation and possession of Him everywhere and in all they attain to their immortal existence.

Still although the victory of the gods, that is to say, the progressive perfection of the mind, life, body in the positive terms of good, right, joy, knowledge, power is recognised as a victory of the Brahman and the necessity of using life and human works in the world as a means of preparation and self-mastery is admitted, yet a final passing away into the infinite heavenly world or status of the Brahman-consciousness is held out as the goal. And this would seem to imply a rejection of the life of the cosmos. Well then may we ask, we the modern humanity more and more conscious of the inner warning of that which created us, be it Nature or God, that there is a work for the race, a divine purpose in its creation which exceeds the salvation of the individual soul, because the universal is as real or even more real than the individual, we who feel more and more, in the language of the Koran, that the Lord did not create heaven and earth in a jest, that Brahman did not begin dreaming this world-dream in a moment of aberration and delirium, — well may we ask whether this gospel of individual salvation is all the message even of this purer, earlier, more catholic Vedanta. If so, then Vedanta at its best is a gospel for the saint, the ascetic, the monk, the solitary, but it has not a message which the widening consciousness of the world can joyfully accept as the word for which it was waiting. For there is evidently something vital that has escaped it, a profound word of the riddle of existence from which it has turned its eyes or which it was unable or thought it not worth while to solve.

Now certainly there is an emphasis in the Upanishads increasing steadily as time goes on into an over-emphasis, on the salvation of the individual, on his rejection of the lower cosmic life. This note increases in them as they become later in date, it swells afterwards into the rejection of all cosmic life whatever and that becomes finally in later Hinduism almost the one dominant and all-challenging cry. It does not exist in the earlier Vedic revelation where individual salvation is regarded as a means towards a great cosmic victory, the eventual conquest of heaven and earth by the superconscient Truth and Bliss and those who have achieved the victory in the past are the conscious helpers of their yet battling posterity. If this earlier note is missing in the Upanishads, then, — for great as are these Scriptures, luminous, profound, sublime in their unsurpassed truth, beauty and power, yet it is only the ignorant soul that will make itself the slave of a book, — then in using them as an aid to knowledge we must insistently call back that earlier missing note, we must seek elsewhere a solution for the word of the riddle that has been ignored.

The Upanishad alone of extant scriptures gives us without veil or stinting, with plenitude and a noble catholicity the truth of the Brahman; its aid to humanity is therefore indispensable. Only, where anything essential is missing, we must go beyond the Upanishads to seek it, — as for instance when we add to its emphasis on divine knowledge the indispensable ardent emphasis of the later teachings upon divine love and the high emphasis of the Veda upon divine works.

The Vedic gospel of a supreme victory in heaven and on earth for the divine in man, the Christian gospel of a kingdom of God and divine city upon earth, the Puranic idea of progressing Avataras ending in the kingdom of the perfect and the restoration of the Golden Age, not only contain behind their forms a profound truth, but they are necessary to the religious sense in mankind. Without it the teaching of the vanity of human life and of a passionate fleeing and renunciation can only be powerful in passing epochs or else on the few strong souls in each age that are really capable of these things. The rest of humanity will either reject the creed which makes that its foundation or ignore it in practice while professing it in precept or else must sink under the weight of its own impotence and the sense of the illusion of life or of the curse of God upon the world as mediaeval Christendom sank into ignorance and obscurantism or later India into stagnant torpor and the pettiness of a life of aimless egoism. The promise for the individual is well, but the promise for the race is also needed. Our father Heaven must remain bright with the hope of deliverance, but also our mother Earth must not feel herself for ever accursed.

It was necessary at one time to insist even exclusively on the idea of individual salvation so that the sense of a Beyond might be driven into man's mentality, as it was necessary at one time to insist on a heaven of joys for the virtuous and pious so that man might be drawn by that shining bait towards the practice of religion and the suppression of his unbridled animality. But as the lures of earth have to be conquered, so also have the lures of heaven. The lure of a pleasant Paradise of the rewards of virtue has been rejected by man; the Upanishads belittled it ages ago in India and it is now no longer dominant in the mind of the people; the similar lure in popular Christianity and popular Islam has no meaning for the conscience of modern humanity.

The lure of a release from birth and death and withdrawal from the cosmic labour must also be rejected, as it was rejected by Mahayanist Buddhism which held compassion and helpfulness to be greater than Nirvana. As the virtues we practise must be done without demand of earthly or heavenly reward, so the salvation we seek must be purely internal and impersonal; it must be the release from egoism, the union with the Divine, the realisation of our universality as well as our transcendence, and no salvation should be valued which takes us away from the love of God in his manifestation and the help we can give to the world. If need be, it must be taught for a time, 'Better this hell with our other suffering selves than a solitary salvation.'

Fortunately, there is no need to go to such lengths and deny one side of the truth in order to establish another. The Upanishad itself suggests the door of escape from any over-emphasis in its own statement of the truth. For the man who knows and possesses the supreme Brahman as the transcendent Beatitude becomes a centre of that delight to which all his fellows shall come, a well from which they can draw the divine waters. Here is the clue that we need. The connection with the universe is preserved for the one reason which supremely justifies that connection; it must subsist not from the desire of personal earthly joy, as with those who are still bound, but for help to all creatures. Two then are the objects of the high-reaching soul, to attain the Supreme and to be for ever for the good of all the world, — even as Brahman Himself; whether here or elsewhere, does not essentially matter. Still where the struggle is thickest, there should be the hero of the spirit, that is surely the highest choice of the son of Immortality; the earth calls most, because it has most need of him, to the soul that has become one with the universe.

And the nature of the highest good that can be done is also indicated, — though other lower forms of help are not therefore excluded. To assist in the lesser victories of the gods which must prepare the supreme victory of the Brahman may well be and must be in some way or other a part of our task; but the greatest helpfulness of all is this, to be a human centre of the Light, the Glory, the Bliss, the Strength, the Knowledge of the Divine Existence, one through whom it shall communicate itself lavishly to other men and attract by its magnet of delight their souls to that which is the Highest.

The Core of the Gita's Meaning

WHAT THEN is the message of the Gita and what its working value, its spiritual utility to the human mind of the present day after the long ages that have elapsed since it was written and the great subsequent transformations of thought and experience? The human mind moves always forward, alters its viewpoint and enlarges its thought substance, and the effect of these changes is to render past systems of thinking obsolete or, when they are preserved, to extend, to modify and subtly or visibly to alter their value. The vitality of an ancient doctrine consists in the extent to which it naturally lends itself to such a treatment; for that means that whatever may have been the limitations or the obsolescences of the form of its thought, the truth of substance, the truth of living vision and experience on which its system was built is still sound and retains a permanent validity and significance. The Gita is a book that has worn extraordinarily well and it is almost as fresh and still in its real substance quite as new, because always renewable in experience, as when it first appeared in or was written into the frame of the Mahabharata. It is still received in India as one of the great bodies of doctrine that most authoritatively govern religious thinking and its teaching acknowledged as of the highest value if not wholly accepted by almost all shades of religious belief and opinion. Its influence is not merely philosophic or academic but immediate and living, an influence both for thought and action, and its ideas are actually at work as a powerful shaping factor in the revival and renewal of a nation and a culture. It has even been said recently by a great voice that all we need of spiritual

The penultimate chapter of *Essays on the Gita*, published in the *Arya* in 1920. A revised book-edition of *Essays on the Gita* was published in two volumes in 1922 and 1928.

truth for the spiritual life is to be found in the Gita. It would be to encourage the superstition of the book to take too literally that utterance. The truth of the spirit is infinite and cannot be circumscribed in that manner. Still it may be said that most of the main clues are there and that after all the later developments of spiritual experience and discovery we can still return to it for a large inspiration and guidance. Outside India too it is universally acknowledged as one of the world's great scriptures, although in Europe its thought is better understood than its secret of spiritual practice. What is it then that gives this vitality to the thought and the truth of the Gita?

The central interest of the Gita's philosophy and Yoga is its attempt, the idea with which it sets out, continues and closes, to reconcile and even effect a kind of unity between the inner spiritual truth in its most absolute and integral realisation and the outer actualities of man's life and action. A compromise between the two is common enough, but that can never be a final and satisfactory solution. An ethical rendering of spirituality is also common and has its value as a law of conduct; but that is a mental solution which does not amount to a complete practical reconciliation of the whole truth of spirit with the whole truth of life and it raises as many problems as it solves. One of these is indeed the starting-point of the Gita; it sets out with an ethical problem raised by a conflict in which we have on one side the dharma of the man of action, a prince and warrior and leader of men, the protagonist of a great crisis, of a struggle on the physical plane, the plane of actual life, between the powers of right and justice and the powers of wrong and injustice, the demand of the destiny of the race upon him that he shall resist and give battle and establish even though through a terrible physical struggle and a giant slaughter a new era and reign of truth and right and justice, and on the other side the ethical sense which condemns the means and the action as a sin, recoils from the price of individual suffering and social strife, unsettling and disturbance and regards abstention from violence and battle as the only way and the one right moral attitude. A spiritualised ethics insists on Ahinsa, on non-injuring and non-killing as the highest law of spiritual conduct. The battle, if it is to be fought out at all, must be fought on the spiritual plane and by some kind of non-resistance or refusal of participation or only by soul resistance, and if this does not succeed on the external plane, if the force of injustice conquers, the individual will still have preserved his virtue and vindicated by his example the highest ideal. On the other hand a more insistent extreme of the inner spiritual direction, passing beyond this struggle between social duty and an absolutist ethical ideal, is apt to take the ascetic turn and to point away from life and all its aims and standards of action towards another and celestial or supracosmic state in which alone beyond the perplexed vanity and illusion of man's birth and life and death there can be a pure spiritual existence. The Gita rejects none of these things in their place, — for it insists on the performance of the social duty, the following of the dharma for the man who has to take his share in the common action, accepts Ahinsa as part of the highest spiritual-ethical ideal and recognises the ascetic renunciation as a way of spiritual salvation. And yet it goes boldly beyond all these conflicting positions; greatly daring, it justifies all life to the spirit as a significant manifestation of the one Divine Being and asserts the compatibility of a complete human action and a complete spiritual life lived in union with the Infinite, consonant with the highest Self, expressive of the perfect Godhead.

All the problems of human life arise from the complexity of our existence, the obscurity of its essential principle and the secrecy of the inmost power that makes out its determinations and governs its purpose and its processes. If our existence were of one piece, solely material-vital or solely mental or solely spiritual, or even if the others were entirely or mainly involved in one of these or were quite latent in our subconscient or our superconscient parts, there would be nothing to perplex us; the material and vital law would be imperative or the mental would be clear to its own pure and unobstructed principle or the spiritual self-existent and self-sufficient to spirit. The animals are aware of no problems; a mental god in a world of pure mentality would admit none or would solve them all by the purity of a mental rule or the satisfaction of a rational harmony; a pure spirit would be above them and self-content in the infinite. But the existence of man is a triple web, a thing mysteriously physical-vital, mental and spiritual at once, and he knows not what are the true relations of these things, which the real reality of his life and his nature, whither the attraction of his destiny and where the sphere of his perfection.

Matter and life are his actual basis, the thing from which he starts and on which he stands and whose requirement and law he has to satisfy if he would exist at all on earth and in the body. The material and vital law is a rule of survival, of struggle, of desire and possession, of self-assertion and the satisfaction of the body, the life and the ego. All the intellectual reasoning in the world, all the ethical idealism and spiritual absolutism of which the higher faculties of man are capable cannot abolish the reality and claim of our vital and material base or prevent the race from following under the imperative compulsion of Nature its aims and the satisfaction of its necessities or from making its important problems a great and legitimate part of human destiny and human interest and endeavour. And the intelligence of man even, failing to find any sustenance in spiritual or ideal solutions that solve everything else but the pressing problems of our actual human life, often turns away from them to an exclusive acceptance of the vital and material existence and the reasoned or instinctive pursuit of its utmost possible efficiency, well-being and organised satisfaction. A gospel of the will to live or the will to power or of a rationalised vital and material perfection becomes the recognised dharma of the human race and all else is considered either a pretentious falsity or a quite subsidiary thing, a side issue of a minor and dependent consequence.

Matter and life however in spite of their insistence and great importance are not all that man is, nor can he wholly accept mind as nothing but a servant of the life and body admitted to certain pure enjoyments of its own as a sort of reward for its service or regard it as no more than an extension and flower of the vital urge, an ideal luxury contingent upon the satisfaction of the material life. The mind much more intimately than the body and the life is the man, and the mind as it develops insists more and more on making the body and the life an instrument — an indispensable instrument and yet a considerable obstacle, otherwise there would be no problem — for its own characteristic satisfactions and self-realisation. The mind of man is not only a vital and physical, but an intellectual, aesthetic, ethical, psychic, emotional and dynamic intelligence, and in the sphere of each of its tendencies its highest and strongest nature is to strain towards some absolute of them which the frame of life will not allow it to capture wholly and embody and make here entirely real. The mental absolute of our aspiration remains as a partly grasped shining or fiery ideal which the mind can make inwardly very present to itself, inwardly imperative on its effort, and can even effectuate partly, but not compel all the facts of life into its image. There is thus an absolute, a high imperative of intellectual truth and reason sought for by our intellectual being; there is an absolute, an imperative of right and conduct aimed at by the ethical conscience; there is an absolute, an imperative of love, sympathy, compassion, oneness yearned after by our emotional and psychic nature; there is an absolute, an imperative of delight and beauty quivered to by the aesthetic soul; there is an absolute, an imperative of inner self-mastery and control of life laboured after by the dynamic will; all these are there together and impinge upon the absolute, the imperative of possession and pleasure and safe embodied existence insisted on by the vital and physical mind. And the human intelligence, since it is not able to realise entirely any of these things, much less all of them together, erects in each sphere many standards and dharmas, standards of truth and reason, of right and conduct, of delight and beauty, of love, sympathy and oneness, of self-mastery and control, of self-preservation and possession and vital efficiency and pleasure, and tries to impose them on life. The absolute shining ideals stand far above and beyond our capacity and rare individuals approximate to them as best they can: the mass follow or profess to follow some less magnificent norm, some established possible and relative standard. Human life as a whole undergoes the attraction and yet rejects the ideal. Life resists in the strength of some obscure infinite of its own and wears down or breaks down any established mental and moral order. And this must be either because the two are quite different and disparate though meeting and interacting principles or because mind has not the clue to the whole reality of life. The clue must be sought in something greater, an unknown something above the mentality and morality of the human creature.

The mind itself has the vague sense of some surpassing factor of this kind and in the pursuit of its absolutes frequently strikes against it. It glimpses a state, a power, a presence that is near and within and inmost to it and yet immeasurably greater and singularly distant and above it; it has a vision of something more essential, more absolute than its own absolutes, intimate, infinite, one, and it is that which we call God, Self or Spirit. This then the mind attempts to know, enter, touch and seize wholly, to approach it or become it, to arrive at some kind of unity or lose itself in a complete identity with that mystery, *āścaryam*. The difficulty is that this spirit in its purity seems something yet farther than the mental absolutes from the actualities of life, something not translatable by mind into its own terms, much less into those of life and action. Therefore we have the intransigent absolutists of the spirit who reject the mental and condemn the material being and yearn after a pure spiritual existence happily purchased by the dissolution of all that we are in life and mind, a Nirvana. The rest of spiritual effort is for these fanatics of the Absolute a mental preparation or a compromise, a spiritualising of life and mind as much as possible. And because the difficulty most constantly insistent on man's mentality in practice is that presented by the claims of his vital being, by life and conduct and action, the direction taken by this preparatory endeavour consists mainly in a spiritualising of the ethical supported by the psychical mind — or rather it brings in the spiritual power and purity to aid these in enforcing their absolute claim and to impart a greater authority than life allows to the ethical ideal of right and truth of conduct or the psychic ideal of love and sympathy and oneness. These things are helped to some highest expression, given their broadest luminous basis by an assent of the reason and will to the underlying truth of the absolute oneness of the spirit and therefore the essential oneness of all living creatures. This kind of spirituality linked on in some way to the demands of the normal mind of man, persuaded to the acceptance of useful social duty and current law of social conduct, popularised by cult and ceremony and image is the outward substance of the world's greater religions. These religions have their individual victories, call in some ray of a higher light, impose some shadow of a larger spiritual or semi-spiritual rule, but cannot effect a complete victory, end flatly in a compromise and in the act of compromise are defeated by life. Its problems remain and even recur in their fiercest forms — even such as this grim problem of Kurukshetra. The idealising intellect and ethical mind hope always to eliminate them, to discover some happy device born of their own aspiration and made effective by their own imperative insistence, which will annihilate this nether untoward aspect of life; but it endures and is not eliminated. The spiritualised intelligence on the other hand offers indeed by the voice of religion the promise of some victorious millennium hereafter, but meanwhile half convinced of terrestrial impotence, persuaded that the soul is a stranger and intruder upon earth, declares that after all not here in the life of the body or in the collective life of mortal man but in some immortal Beyond lies the heaven or the Nirvana where alone is to be found the true spiritual existence.

It is here that the Gita intervenes with a restatement of the truth of the Spirit, of the Self, of God and of the world and Nature. It extends and remoulds the truth evolved by a later thought from the ancient Upanishads and ventures with assured steps on an endeavour to apply its solving power to the problem of life and action. The solution offered by the Gita does not disentangle all the problem as it offers itself to modern mankind; as stated here to a more ancient mentality, it does not meet the insistent pressure of the present mind of man for a collective advance, does not respond to its cry for a collective life that will at last embody a greater rational and ethical and if possible even a dynamic spiritual ideal. Its call is to the individual who has become capable of a complete spiritual existence; but for the rest of the race it prescribes only a gradual advance, to be wisely effected by following out faithfully with more and more of intelligence and moral purpose and with a final turn to spirituality the law of their nature. Its message touches the other smaller solutions but, even when it accepts them partly, it is to point them beyond themselves to a higher and more integral secret into which as yet only the few individuals have shown themselves fit to enter.

The Gita's message to the mind that follows after the vital and material life is that all life is indeed a manifestation of the universal Power in the individual, a derivation from the Self, a ray from the Divine, but actually it figures the Self and the Divine veiled in a disguising Maya, and to pursue the lower life for its own sake is to persist in a stumbling path and to enthrone our nature's obscure ignorance and not at all to find the true truth and complete law of existence. A gospel of the will to live, the will to power, of the satisfaction of desire, of the glorification of mere force and strength, of the worship of the ego and its vehement acquisitive self-will and tireless self-regarding intellect is the gospel of the Asura and it can lead only to some gigantic ruin and perdition. The vital and material man must accept for his government a religious and social and ideal dharma by which, while satisfying desire and interest under right restrictions, he can train and subdue his lower personality and scrupulously attune it to a higher law both of the personal and the communal life.

The Gita's message to the mind occupied with the pursuit of intellectual, ethical and social standards, the mind that insists on salvation by the observance of established dharmas, the moral law, social duty and function or the solutions of the liberated intelligence, is that this is indeed a very necessary stage, the dharma has indeed to be observed and, rightly observed, can raise the stature of the spirit and prepare and serve the spiritual life, but still it is not the complete and last truth of existence. The soul of man has to go beyond to some more absolute dharma of man's spiritual and immortal nature. And this can only be done if we repress and get rid of the ignorant formulations of the lower mental elements and the falsehood of egoistic personality, impersonalise the action of the intelligence and will, live in the identity of the one self in all, break out of all ego-moulds into the impersonal spirit. The mind moves under the limiting compulsion of the triple lower nature, it erects its standards in obedience to the tamasic, rajasic or at highest the sattwic qualities; but the destiny of the soul is a divine perfection and liberation and that can only be based in the freedom of our highest self, can only be found by passing through its vast impersonality and universality beyond mind into the integral light of the immeasurable Godhead and supreme Infinite who is beyond all dharmas.

The Gita's message to those, absolutist seekers of the Infinite, who carry impersonality to an exclusive extreme, entertain an intolerant passion for the extinction of life and action and would have as the one ultimate aim and ideal an endeavour to cease from all individual being in the pure silence of the ineffable Spirit, is that this is indeed one path of journey and entry into the Infinite, but the most difficult, the ideal of inaction a dangerous thing to hold up by precept or example before the world, this way, though great, yet not the best way for man and this knowledge, though true, yet not the integral knowledge. The Supreme, the all-conscious Self, the Godhead, the Infinite is not solely a spiritual existence remote and ineffable; he is here in the universe at once hidden and expressed through man and the gods and through all beings and in all that is. And it is by finding him not only in some immutable silence but in the world and its beings and in all self and in all Nature, it is by raising to an integral as well as to a highest union with him all the activities of the intelligence, the heart, the will, the life that man can solve at once his inner riddle of self and God and the outer problem of his active human existence. Made Godlike, God-becoming, he can enjoy the infinite breadth of a supreme spiritual consciousness that is reached through works no less than through love and knowledge. Immortal and free, he can continue his human action from that highest level and transmute it into a supreme and all-embracing divine activity,—that indeed is the ultimate crown and significance here of all works and living and sacrifice and the world's endeavour.

This highest message is first for those who have the strength to follow after it, the master men, the great spirits, the God-knowers, God-doers, God-lovers who can live in God and for God and do their work joyfully for him in the world, a divine work uplifted above the restless darkness of the human mind and the false limitations of the ego. At the same time, and here we get the gleam of a larger promise which we may even extend to the hope of a collective turn towards perfection,—for if there is hope for man, why should there not be hope for mankind?—the Gita declares that all can if they will, even to the lowest and sinfullest among men, enter into the path of this Yoga. And if there is a true self-surrender and an absolute unegoistic faith in the indwelling Divinity, success is certain in this path. The decisive turn is needed; there must be an abiding belief in the Spirit, a sincere and insistent will to live in the Divine, to be in self one with him and in Nature—where too we are an eternal portion of his being—one with his greater spiritual Nature, God-possessed in all our members and Godlike.

The Gita in the development of its idea raises many issues, such as the determinism of Nature, the significance of the universal manifestation and the ultimate status of the liberated soul, questions that have been the subject of unending and inconclusive debate. It is not necessary in this series of essays of which the object is a scrutiny and positive affirmation of the substance of the Gita and a disengaging of its contribution to the abiding spiritual thought of humanity and its kernel of living practice, to enter far into these discussions or to consider where we may differ from its standpoint or conclusions, make any reserves in our assent or even, strong in later experience, go beyond its metaphysical teaching or its Yoga. It will be sufficient to close with a formulation of the living message it still brings for man the eternal seeker and discoverer to guide him through the present circuits and the possible steeper ascent of his life up to the luminous heights of his spirit.[1]

[1] The final chapter of *Essays on the Gita*, 'The Message of the Gita', is a running summary of the substance of the Bhagvad Gita as interpreted by Sri Aurobindo.

The Renaissance in India

THERE HAS been recently some talk of a Renaissance in India. A number of illuminating essays with that general title and subject have been given to us by a poet and subtle critic and thinker, Mr James H. Cousins, and others have touched suggestively various sides of the growing movement towards a new life and a new thought that may well seem to justify the description.[1] This Renaissance, this new birth in India, if it is a fact, must become a thing of immense importance both to herself and the world, to herself because of all that is meant for her in the recovery or the change of her time-old spirit and national ideals, to the world because of the possibilities involved in the rearising of a force that is in many respects unlike any other and its genius very different from the mentality and spirit that have hitherto governed the modern idea in mankind, although not so far away perhaps from that which is preparing to govern the future. It is rather the first point of view that I shall put forward at present: for the question what India means to make of her own life must precede the wider question what her new life may mean to the human race. And it is besides likely to become before long an issue of a pressing importance.

There is a first question, whether at all there is really a Renaissance in India. That depends a good deal on what we mean by the word; it depends also on the future, for the thing itself is only in its infancy and it is too early to say to what it may lead. The word carries the mind back to the turning-point of European

The first of four chapters published under this title in the *Arya* in 1918 and reprinted as a booklet in 1920.

[1] James H. Cousins (1873–1956), was an Irish writer and minor figure in the Irish Renaissance. His *Renaissance in India*, a series of essays on contemporary Indian art and culture, was published by Ganesh & Co., Madras, in 1918.

culture to which it was first applied; that was not so much a reawakening as an overturn and reversal, a seizure of Christianised, Teutonised, feudalised Europe by the old Graeco-Latin spirit and form with all the complex and momentous results which came from it. That is certainly not a type of renaissance that is at all possible in India. There is a closer resemblance to the recent Celtic movement in Ireland,[2] the attempt of a reawakened national spirit to find a new impulse of self-expression which shall give the spiritual force for a great reshaping and rebuilding: in Ireland this was discovered by a return to the Celtic spirit and culture after a long period of eclipsing English influences, and in India something of the same kind of movement is appearing and has especially taken a pronounced turn since the political outburst of 1905. But even here the analogy does not give the whole truth.[3]

We have to see moreover that the whole is at present a great formless chaos of conflicting influences with a few luminous points of formation here and there where a new self-consciousness has come to the surface. But it cannot be said that these forms have yet a sufficient hold on the general mind of the people. They represent an advance movement; they are the voices of the vanguard, the torchlights of the pioneers. On the whole what we see is a giant Shakti who awakening into a new world, a new and alien environment, finds herself shackled in all her limbs by a multitude of gross or minute bonds, bonds self-woven by her past, bonds recently imposed from outside, and is struggling to be free from them, to arise and proclaim herself, to cast abroad her spirit and set her seal on the world. We hear on every side a sound of the slow fraying of bonds, here and there a sharp tearing and snapping; but freedom of movement has not yet been attained. The eyes are not yet clear, the bud of the soul

[2] A cultural and literary movement of the late nineteenth and early twentieth centuries, generally known as the Irish Renaissance. It consisted chiefly in an effort to restore Gaelic as the official language of Ireland and in a literary efflorescence whose most notable figures included J. M. Synge, W. B. Yeats, and Sean O'Casey in drama, Yeats and A.E. (George Russell) in poetry, and Liam O'Flaherty and others in fiction.

[3] The Swadeshi movement, begun as a political protest against the Partition of Bengal (1905), stimulated some important Bengali writers, notably Rabindranath Tagore (1861–1941) and artists, notably Abanindranath Tagore (1871–1951).

has only partly opened. The Titaness has not yet arisen.

Mr Cousins puts the question in his book whether the word renaissance at all applies since India has always been awake and stood in no need of reawakening. There is a certain truth behind that and to one coming in with a fresh mind from outside and struck by the living continuity of past and present India, it may be especially apparent; but that is not quite how we can see it who are her children and are still suffering from the bitter effects of the great decline which came to a head in the eighteenth and nineteenth centuries. Undoubtedly there was a period, a brief but very disastrous period of the dwindling of that great fire of life, even a moment of incipient disintegration, marked politically by the anarchy which gave European adventure its chance, inwardly by an increasing torpor of the creative spirit in religion and art, — science and philosophy and intellectual knowledge had long been dead or petrified into a mere scholastic Punditism, — all pointing to a nadir of setting energy, the evening-time from which according to the Indian idea of the cycles a new age has to start. It was that moment and the pressure of a superimposed European culture which followed it that made the reawakening necessary.

We have practically to take three facts into consideration, the great past of Indian culture and life with the moment of inadaptive torpor into which it had lapsed, the first period of the Western contact in which it seemed for a moment likely to perish by slow decomposition, and the ascending movement which first broke into some clarity of expression only a decade or two ago. Mr Cousins has his eye fixed on Indian spirituality which has always maintained itself even in the decline of the national vitality; it was certainly that which saved India always at every critical moment of her destiny, and it has been the starting-point too of her renascence. Any other nation under the same pressure would have long ago perished soul and body. But certainly the outward members were becoming gangrened; the powers of renovation seemed for a moment to be beaten by the powers of stagnation, and stagnation is death. Now that the salvation, the reawakening has come, India will certainly keep her essential spirit, will keep her characteristic soul, but there is likely to be a great change of the body. The shaping for itself of a new body, of new philosophical, artistic, literary, cultural, political, social forms by the same soul rejuvenescent will, I should think, be the type of the Indian renascence, — forms not contradictory of the truths of life which the old expressed, but rather expressive of those truths restated, cured of defect, completed.

What was this ancient spirit and characteristic soul of India? European writers, struck by the general metaphysical bent of the Indian mind, by its strong religious instincts and religious idealism, by its other-worldliness, are inclined to write as if this were all the Indian spirit. An abstract, metaphysical, religious mind overpowered by the sense of the infinite, not apt for life, dreamy, unpractical, turning away from life and action as Maya, this, they said, is India; and for a time Indians in this as in other matters submissively echoed their new Western teachers and masters. They learned to speak with pride of their metaphysics, of their literature, of their religion, but in all else they were content to be learners and imitators. Since then Europe has discovered that there was too an Indian art of remarkable power and beauty; but the rest of what India meant it has hardly at all seen. But meanwhile the Indian mind began to emancipate itself and to look upon its past with a clear and self-discerning eye, and it very soon discovered that it had been misled into an entirely false self-view. All such one-sided appreciations indeed almost invariably turn out to be false. Was it not the general misconception about Germany at one time, because she was great in philosophy and music, but had blundered in life and been unable to make the most of its materials, that this was a nation of unpractical dreamers, idealists, erudites and sentimentalists, patient, docile and industrious certainly, but politically inapt, — 'admirable, ridiculous Germany'? Europe has had a terrible awakening from that error. When the renascence of India is complete, she will have an awakening, not of the same brutal kind, certainly, but startling enough, as to the real nature and capacity of the Indian spirit.

Spirituality is indeed the master-key of the Indian mind; the sense of the infinite is native to it. India saw from the beginning, — and, even in her ages of reason and her age of increasing ignorance, she never lost hold of the insight, — that life cannot be rightly seen in the sole light, cannot be perfectly lived in the sole power of its externalities. She was alive to the greatness of material laws and forces; she had a keen eye for the importance of the physical sciences; she knew how to organise the arts of ordinary life. But she saw that the physical does not get its full sense until it stands in right relation to the supra-physical; she saw that the complexity of the universe could not be explained in the present terms of man or seen by his superficial sight, that there were other powers behind, other powers within man himself of which he is normally unaware, that he is conscious only of a small part of himself, that the invisible always surrounds the visible, the suprasensible the sensible, even as infinity always surrounds the finite. She saw too that man has the power of exceeding himself, of becoming himself more entirely and profoundly than he is, — truths which have only recently begun to be seen in Europe and seem even now too great for its common intelligence. She saw the myriad gods beyond man, God beyond the gods, and beyond God his own ineffable eternity; she saw that there were ranges of life beyond our life, ranges of mind beyond our present mind and above these she saw the splendours of the spirit. Then with that calm audacity of her intuition which knew no fear or littleness and shrank from no act whether of spiritual or intellectual, ethical or vital courage, she declared that there was none of these things which man could not attain if he trained his will and knowledge; he could conquer these ranges of mind, become the spirit, become a god, become one with God, become the ineffable Brahman. And with the logical practicality and sense of science and organised method which distinguished her mentality, she set forth immediately to find out the way. Hence from long ages of this insight and practice there was ingrained in her her spirituality, her powerful psychic tendency, her great yearning to grapple with the infinite and possess it, her ineradicable religious sense, her idealism, her Yoga, the constant turn of her art and her philosophy.

But this was not and could not be her whole mentality, her entire spirit; spirituality itself does not flourish on earth in the void, even as our mountaintops do not rise like those of an enchantment of dream out of the clouds without a base. When we look at the past of India, what strikes us next is her stupendous vitality, her inexhaustible power of life and joy of life, her almost unimaginably prolific creativeness. For three thousand years at least, — it is indeed much longer, — she has been creating abundantly and incessantly, lavishly, with an inexhaustible many-sidedness, republics and kingdoms and empires, philosophies and cosmogonies and sciences and creeds and arts and poems and all kinds of monuments, palaces and temples and public works, communities and societies and religious orders, laws and codes and rituals, physical sciences, psychic sciences, systems of Yoga, systems of politics and administration, arts spiritual, arts worldly, trades, industries, fine crafts, — the list is endless and in each item there is almost a plethora of activity. She creates and creates and is not satisfied and is not tired; she will not have an end of it, seems hardly to need a space for rest, a time for inertia and lying fallow. She expands too outside her borders; her ships cross the ocean and the fine superfluity of her wealth brims over to Judaea and Egypt and Rome; her colonies spread her arts and epics and creeds in the Archipelago; her traces are found in the sands of Mesopotamia; her religions conquer China and Japan and spread westward as far as Palestine and Alexandria, and the figures of the Upanishads and the sayings of the Buddhists are reechoed on the lips of Christ. Everywhere, as on her soil, so in her works there is the teeming of a superabundant energy of life. European critics complain that in her ancient architecture, sculpture and art there is no reticence, no holding back of riches, no blank spaces, that she labours to fill every rift with ore, occupy every inch with plenty. Well, but defect or no, that is the necessity of her superabundance of life, of the teeming of the infinite within her. She lavishes her riches because she must, as the Infinite fills every inch of space with the stirring of life and energy because it is the Infinite.

But this supreme spirituality and this prolific abundance of the energy and joy of life and creation do not make all that the spirit of India has been in its past. It is not a confused splendour of tropical vegetation under heavens of a pure sapphire infinity. It is only to eyes unaccustomed to such wealth that there seems to be a confusion in this crowding of space with rich forms of life, a luxurious disorder of excess or a wanton lack of measure, clear balance and design. For the third power of the ancient Indian spirit was a strong intellectuality, at once austere and rich, robust and minute, powerful and delicate, massive in principle and curious in detail. Its chief impulse was that of order and arrangement, but an order founded upon a seeking for the inner law and truth of things and having in view always the possibility of conscientious practice. India has been preeminently the land of the Dharma and the Shastra. She searched for the inner truth and law of each human or cosmic activity, its dharma; that found, she laboured to cast into elaborate form and detailed law of arrangement its application in fact and rule of life. Her first period was luminous with the discovery of the Spirit; her second completed the discovery of the Dharma; her third elaborated into detail the first simpler formulation of the Shastra; but none was exclusive, the three elements are always present.

In this third period the curious elaboration of all life into a science and an art assumes extraordinary proportions. The mere mass of the intellectual production during the period from Asoka well into the Mahomedan epoch is something truly prodigious, as can be seen at once if one studies the account which recent scholarship gives of it, and we must remember that that scholarship as yet only deals with a fraction of what is still lying extant and what is extant is only a small percentage of what was once written and known. There is no historical parallel for such an intellectual labour and activity before the invention of printing and the facilities of modern science; yet all that mass of research and production and curiosity of detail was accomplished without these facilities and with no better record than the memory and for an aid the perishable palm-leaf. Nor was all this colossal literature confined to philosophy and theology, religion and Yoga, logic and rhetoric and grammar and linguistics, poetry and drama, medicine and astronomy and the sciences; it embraced all life, politics and society, all the arts from painting to dancing, all the sixty-four accomplishments, everything then known that could be useful to life or interesting to the mind, even, for instance, to such practical side minutiae as the breeding and training of horses and elephants, each of which had its Shastra and its art, its apparatus of technical terms, its copious literature. In each subject from the largest and most momentous to the smallest and most trivial there was expended the same all-embracing, opulent, minute and thorough intellectuality. On one side there is an insatiable curiosity, the desire of life to know itself in every detail, on the other a spirit of organisation and scrupulous order, the desire of the mind to tread through life with a harmonised knowledge and in the right rhythm and measure. Thus an ingrained and dominant spirituality, an inexhaustible vital creativeness and gust of life and, mediating between them, a powerful, penetrating and scrupulous intelligence combined of the rational, ethical and aesthetic mind each at a high intensity of action, created the harmony of the ancient Indian culture.

Indeed without this opulent vitality and opulent intellectuality India could never have done so much as she did with her spiritual tendencies. It is a great error to suppose that spirituality flourishes best in an impoverished soil with the life half-killed and the intellect discouraged and intimidated. The spirituality that so flourishes is something morbid, hectic and exposed to perilous reactions. It is when the race has lived most richly and thought most profoundly that spirituality finds its heights and its depths and its constant and many-sided fruition. In modern Europe it is after a long explosion of vital force and a stupendous activity of the intellect that spirituality has begun really to emerge and with some promise of being not, as it once was, the sorrowful physician of the malady of life, but the beginning of a large and profound clarity. The European eye is struck in Indian spiritual thought by the Buddhistic and illusionist denial of life. But it must be remembered that this is only one side of its philosophic tendency which assumed exaggerated proportions only in the period of decline. In itself too that was simply one result, in one direction, of a tendency of the Indian mind which is common to all its activities, the impulse to follow each motive, each specialisation of motive even, spiritual, intellectual, ethical, vital, to its extreme point and to sound its utmost possibility. Part of its innate direction was to seek in each not only for its fullness of detail, but for its infinite, its absolute, its profoundest depth or its highest pinnacle. It knew that without a 'fine excess' we cannot break down the limits which the dull temper of the normal mind opposes to knowledge and thought and experience; and it had in seeking this point a boundless courage and yet a sure tread. Thus it carried each tangent of philosophic thought, each line of spiritual experience to its farthest point, and chose to look from that farthest point at all existence, so as to see what truth or power such a view could give it. It tried to know the whole of divine nature and to see too as high as it could beyond nature and into whatever there might be of supradivine. When it formulated a spiritual atheism, it followed that to its acme of possible vision. When, too, it indulged in materialistic atheism,

— though it did that only with a side glance, as the freak of an insatiable intellectual curiosity, — yet it formulated it straight out, boldly and nakedly, without the least concession to idealism or ethicism.

Everywhere we find this tendency. The ideals of the Indian mind have included the height of self-assertion of the human spirit and its thirst of independence and mastery and possession and the height also of its self-abnegation, dependence and submission and self-giving. In life the ideal of opulent living and the ideal of poverty were carried to the extreme of regal splendour and the extreme of satisfied nudity. Its intuitions were sufficiently clear and courageous not to be blinded by its own most cherished ideas and fixed habits of life. If it was obliged to stereotype caste as the symbol of its social order, it never quite forgot, as the caste-spirit is apt to forget, that the human soul and the human mind are beyond caste. For it had seen in the lowest human being the Godhead, Narayana. It emphasised distinctions only to turn upon them and deny all distinctions. If all its political needs and circumstances compelled it at last to exaggerate the monarchical principle and declare the divinity of the king and to abolish its earlier republican city states and independent federations as too favourable to the centrifugal tendency, if therefore it could not develop democracy, yet it had the democratic idea, applied it in the village, in council and municipality, within the caste, was the first to assert a divinity in the people and could cry to the monarch at the height of his power, 'O king, what art thou but the head servant of the demos?' Its idea of the golden age was a free spiritual anarchism. Its spiritual extremism could not prevent it from fathoming through a long era the life of the senses and its enjoyments, and there too it sought the utmost richness of sensuous detail and the depths and intensities of sensuous experience. Yet it is notable that this pursuit of the most opposite extremes never resulted in disorder; and its most hedonistic period offers nothing that at all resembles the unbridled corruption which a similar tendency has more than once produced in Europe. For the Indian mind is not only spiritual and ethical, but intellectual and artistic, and both the rule of the intellect and the rhythm of beauty are hostile to the spirit of chaos. In every extreme the Indian spirit seeks for a law in that extreme and a rule, measure and structure in its application.

Besides, this sounding of extremes is balanced by a still more ingrained characteristic, the synthetical tendency, so that having pushed each motive to its farthest possibility the Indian mind returns always towards some fusion of the knowledge it has gained and to a resulting harmony and balance in action and institution. Balance and rhythm which the Greeks arrived at by self-limitation, India arrived at by its sense of intellectual, ethical and aesthetic order and the synthetic impulse of its mind and life.

I have dwelt on these facts because they are apt to be ignored by those who look only at certain sides of the Indian mind and spirit which are most prominent in the last epochs. By insisting only upon these we get an inaccurate or incomplete idea of the past of India and of the integral meaning of its civilisation and the spirit that animated it. The present is only a last deposit of the past at a time of ebb; it has no doubt also to be the starting-point of the future, but in this present all that was in India's past is still dormant, it is not destroyed; it is waiting there to assume new forms. The decline was the ebb-movement of a creative spirit which can only be understood by seeing it in the full tide of its greatness; the renascence is the return of the tide and it is the same spirit that is likely to animate it, although the forms it takes may be quite new. To judge therefore the possibilities of the renascence, the powers that it may reveal and the scope that it may take, we must dismiss the idea that the tendency of metaphysical abstraction is the one note of the Indian spirit which dominates or inspires all its cadences. Its real key-note is the tendency of spiritual realisation, not cast at all into any white monotone, but many-faceted, many-coloured, as supple in its adaptability as it is intense in its highest pitches. The note of spirituality is dominant, initial, constant, always recurrent; it is the support of all the rest. The first age of India's greatness was a spiritual age when she sought passionately for the truth of existence through the intuitive mind and through an inner experience and interpretation both of the psychic and the physical existence. The stamp put on her by that beginning she has never lost, but rather always enriched it with fresh spiritual experience and discovery at each step of the national life. Even in her hour of decline it was the one thing she could never lose.

But this spiritual tendency does not shoot upward only to the abstract, the hidden and the intangible; it casts its rays downward and outward to embrace the multiplicities of thought and the richness of life. Therefore the second long epoch of India's greatness was an age of the intellect, the ethical sense, the dynamic will in action enlightened to formulate and govern life in the lustre of spiritual truth. After the age of the Spirit, the age of the Dharma; after the Veda and Upanishads, the heroic centuries of action and social formation, typal construction and thought and philosophy, when the outward forms of Indian life and culture were fixed in their large lines and even their later developments were being determined in the seed. The great classical age of Sanskrit culture was the flowering of this intellectuality into curiosity of detail in the refinements of scholarship, science, art, literature, politics, sociology, mundane life. We see at this time too the sounding not only of aesthetic, but of emotional and sensuous, even of vital and sensual experience. But the old spirituality reigned behind all this mental and all this vital activity, and its later period, the post-classical, saw a lifting up of the whole lower life and an impressing upon it of the values of the spirit. This was the sense of the Puranic and Tantric systems and the religions of Bhakti. Later Vaishnavism, the last fine flower of the Indian spirit, was in its essence the taking up of the aesthetic, emotional and sensuous being into the service of the spiritual. It completed the curve of the cycle.

The evening of decline which followed the completion of the curve was prepared by three movements of retrogression. First there is, comparatively, a sinking of that superabundant vital energy and a fading of the joy of life and the joy of creation. Even in the decline this energy is still something splendid and extraordinary and only for a very brief period sinks nearest to a complete torpor; but still a comparison with its past greatness will show that the decadence was marked and progressive. Secondly, there is a rapid cessation of the old free intellectual activity, a slumber of the scientific and the critical mind as well as the creative intuition; what remains becomes more and more a repetition of ill-understood fragments of past knowledge. There is a petrification of the mind and life in the relics of the forms which a great intellectual past had created. Old authority and rule become rigidly despotic and, as always then happens, lose their real sense and spirit. Finally, spirituality remains but burns no longer with the large and clear flame of knowledge of former times, but in intense jets and in a dispersed action which replaces the old magnificent synthesis and in which certain spiritual truths are emphasised to the neglect of others. This diminution amounts to a certain failure of the great endeavour which is the whole meaning of Indian culture, a falling short in the progress towards the perfect spiritualisation of the mind and the life. The beginnings were superlative, the developments very great, but at a certain point where progress, adaptation, a new flowering should have come in, the old civilisation stopped short, partly drew back, partly lost its way. The essential no doubt remained and still remains in the heart of the race and not only in its habits and memories, but in its action it was covered up in a great smoke of confusion. The causes internal and external we need not now discuss; but the fact is there. It was the cause of the momentary helplessness of the Indian mind in the face of new and unprecedented conditions.

It was at this moment that the European wave swept over India. The first effect of this entry of a new and quite opposite civilisation was the destruction of much that had no longer the power to live, the deliquescence of much else, a tendency to the devitalisation of the rest. A new activity came in, but this was at first crudely and confusedly imitative of the foreign culture. It was a crucial moment and an ordeal of perilous severity; a less vigorous energy of life might well have foundered and perished under the double weight of the deadening of its old innate motives and a servile imitation of alien ideas and habits. History shows us how disastrous this situation can be to nations and civilisations. But fortunately the energy of life was there, sleeping only for a moment, not dead, and, given that energy, the evil carried within itself its own cure. For whatever temporary rotting and destruction this crude impact of European life and culture has caused, it gave three needed impulses. It revived the dormant intellectual and critical impulse; it rehabilitated life and awakened the desire of new creation; it put the reviving Indian spirit face to face with novel conditions and ideals and the urgent necessity of understanding, assimilating and conquering them. The national mind turned a new eye on its past culture, reawoke to its sense and import, but also at the same time saw it in relation to modern knowledge and ideas. Out of this awakening vision and impulse the Indian renaissance is arising, and that must determine its future tendency. The recovery of the old spiritual knowledge and experience in all its splendour, depth and fullness is its first, most essential work; the flowing of this spirituality into new forms of philosophy, literature, art, science and critical knowledge is the second; an original dealing with modern problems in the light of the Indian spirit and the endeavour to formulate a greater synthesis of a spiritualised society is the third and most difficult. Its success on these three lines will be the measure of its help to the future of humanity.

The Spirit is a higher infinite of verities; life is a lower infinite of possibilities which seek to grow and find their own truth and fulfilment in the light of these verities. Our intellect, our will, our ethical and our aesthetic being are the reflectors and the mediators. The method of the West is to exaggerate life and to call down as much — or as little — as may be of the higher powers to stimulate and embellish life.[4] But the method of India is on the contrary to discover the spirit within and the higher hidden intensities of the superior powers and to dominate life in one way or another so as to make it responsive to and expressive of the spirit and in that way increase the power of life. Its tendency with the intellect, will, ethical, aesthetic and emotional being is to sound indeed their normal mental possibilities, but also to upraise them towards the greater light and power of their own highest intuitions. The work of the renaissance in India must be to make this spirit, this higher view of life, this sense of deeper potentiality once more a creative, perhaps a dominant power in the world. But to that truth of itself it is as yet only vaguely awake; the mass of Indian action is still at the moment proceeding under the impress of the European motive and method and, because there is a spirit within us to which they are foreign, the action is poor in will, feeble in form and ineffective in results, for it does not come from the roots of our being. Only in a few directions is there some clear light of self-knowledge. It is when a greater light prevails and becomes general that we shall be able to speak, not only in prospect but in fact, of the renaissance of India.

[4] Mr Cousins' distinction between invocation and evocation. [Sri Aurobindo's note]

Indian Civilisation and the Evolutionary Future

BUT THERE is yet another point of view from which the challenge put in front of us ceases to be an issue crudely and provokingly phrased in a conflict of cultures.[1] Instead it presents itself as a problem with a deep significance; it becomes a thought-provoking suggestion that affects not only ours but all civilisations still in existence.

We can reply on the cultural issue from the view-point of the past and the valuation of different cultures as acquired contributions to the growth of the human race, that Indian civilisation has been the form and expression of a culture as great as any of the historic civilisations of mankind, great in religion, great in philosophy, great in science, great in thought of many kinds, great in literature, art and poetry, great in the organisation of society and politics, great in craft and trade and commerce. There have been dark spots, positive imperfections, heavy shortcomings; what civilisation has been perfect, which has not had its deep stains and cruel abysses? There have been considerable lacunae, many blind alleys, much uncultured or ill-cultured ground: what civilisation has been without its unfilled parts, its negative aspects? But our ancient civilisation can survive the severest comparisons of either ancient or mediaeval times. More high-reaching, subtle, many-sided, curious and profound than the Greek, more noble and humane than the Roman, more large and spiritual than the old Egyptian, more vast and original than any other Asiatic civilisation, more intellectual than the European prior to the eighteenth century, possessing all that these had and more, it

The last of three articles published in the *Arya* under the title 'Is India Civilised?' (see the first selection in this part). Editorial title.

[1] For the 'conflict of cultures' see also 'Is India Civilised?', pages 57–68.

was the most powerful, self-possessed, stimulating and wide in influence of all past human cultures.

And if we look from the view-point of the present and the fruitful workings of the progressive Time-Spirit, we can say that even here in spite of our downfall all is not on the debit side. Many of the forms of our civilisation have become inapt and effete and others stand in need of radical change and renovation. But that can be said equally well of European culture; for all its recently acquired progressiveness and habit of more rapid self-adaptation, large parts of it are already rotten and out of date. In spite of all drawbacks and in spite of downfall the spirit of Indian culture, its central ideas, its best ideals have still their message for humanity and not for India alone. And we in India hold that they are capable of developing out of themselves by contact with new need and idea as good and better solutions of the problems before us than those which are offered to us secondhand from Western sources. But besides the comparisons of the past and the needs of the present there is too a view-point of the ideal future. There are the farther goals towards which humanity is moving, — and the present is only a crude aspiration towards them and the immediate future we now see in hope and strive to bring about in form, only its crude preparatory stage. There is an unrealised standard of the ideas which to the mind of the moment are figments of Utopia, but may become to a more developed humanity the commonplaces of their daily environment, the familiar things of the present which they have to overpass. How stands Indian civilisation with regard to this yet unrealised future of the race? Are its master ideas and dominant powers guiding lights or helping forces towards it or do they end in themselves with no vistas on the evolutionary potentialities of the earth's coming ages?

The very idea of progress is an illusion to some minds; for they imagine that the race moves constantly in a circle. Or even their view is that greatness more often than not is to be found in the past and that the line of our movement is a curve of deterioration, a downward lapse. But that is an illusion created when we look too much upon the highlights of the past and forget its shadows or concentrate too much on the dark spaces of the present and ignore its powers of light and its aspects of happier promise. It is created too by a mistaken deduction from the phenomenon of an uneven progress. For Nature effects her evolution through a rhythm of advance and relapse, day and night, waking and sleep; there is a temporary pushing of certain results at the expense of others not less desirable for perfection and to a superficial eye there may seem to be a relapse even in our advance. Progress admittedly does not march on securely in a straight line like a man sure of his familiar way or an army covering an unimpeded terrain or well-mapped unoccupied spaces. Human progress is very much an adventure through the unknown, an unknown full of surprises and baffling obstacles; it stumbles often, it misses its way at many points, it cedes here in order to gain there, it retraces its steps frequently in order to get more widely forward. The present does not always compare favourably with the past; even when it is more advanced in the mass, it may still be inferior in certain directions important to our inner or our outer welfare. But earth does move forward after all, *eppur si muove*. Even in failure there is a preparation for success: our nights carry in them the secret of a greater dawn. This is a frequent experience in our individual progress, but the human collectivity also moves in much the same manner. The question is whither are we marching or what are the true routes and harbours of our voyage.

Western civilisation is proud of its successful modernism. But there is much that it has lost in the eagerness of its gains and much which men of old strove towards that it has not even attempted to accomplish. There is much too that it has wilfully flung aside in impatience or scorn to its own great loss, to the injury of its life, to the imperfection of its culture. An ancient Greek of the time of Pericles or the philosophers suddenly transported in time to this century would be astonished by the immense gains of the intellect and the expansion of the mind, the modern many-sidedness of the reason and inexhaustible habit of inquiry, the power of endless generalisation and precise detail. He would admire without reserve the miraculous growth of science and its giant discoveries, the abundant power, richness and minuteness of its instrumentation, the wonder-working force of its inventive genius. He would be overcome and stupefied rather than surprised and charmed by the enormous stir and pulsation of modern life. But at the same time he would draw back repelled from its unashamed mass of ugliness and vulgarity, its unchastened external utilitarianism, its vitalistic riot and the morbid exaggeration and unsoundness of many of its growths. He would see in it much ill-disguised evidence of the uneliminated survival of the triumphant barbarian. If he recognised its intellectuality and the scrupulous application of thought and scientific reason to the machinery of life, he would miss in it his own later attempt at the clear and noble application of the ideal reason to the inner life of the mind and the soul. He would find that in this civilisation beauty had become an exotic and the shining ideal mind in some fields a debased and exploited slave and in others a neglected stranger. As for the great spiritual seekers of the past, they would experience in all this huge activity of the intellect and the life the sense of an aching void. A feeling of its illusion and unreality because that which is greatest in man and raises him beyond himself had been neglected, would oppress them at every step. The discovery of the laws of physical Nature would not compensate in their eyes for the comparative decline — for a long time it was the almost absolute cessation — of a greater seeking and finding, the discovery of the freedom of the spirit.

But an unbiassed view will prefer to regard this age of civilisation as an evolutionary stage, an imperfect but important turn of the human advance. It is then possible to see that great gains have been made which are of the utmost value to an ultimate perfection, even if they have been made at a great price. There is not only a greater generalisation of knowledge and more thorough use of intellectual power and activity in multiple fields. There is not only the advance of Science and its application to the conquest of our environment, an immense apparatus of means, vast utilisations, endless minute conveniences, an irresistible machinery, a tireless exploitation of forces. There is too a certain development of powerful if not high-pitched ideals and there is an attempt, however external and therefore imperfect, to bring them to bear upon the working of human society as a whole. Much has been diminished or lost, but it can be recovered, eventually, if not with ease. Once restored to its true movement, the inner life of man will find that it has gained in materials, in power of plasticity, in a new kind of depth and wideness. And we shall have acquired a salutary habit of many-sided thoroughness and a sincere endeavour to shape the outer collective life into an adequate image of our highest ideals. Temporary diminutions will not count before the greater inner expansion that is likely to succeed this age of external turmoil and outward-looking endeavour.

If on the other hand an ancient Indian of the time of the Upanishads, the Buddhist period or the later classical age were to be set down in modern India and note that larger part of its life which belongs to the age of decline, he would experience a much more depressing sensation, the sense of a national, a cultural debacle, a fall from the highest summits to discouragingly low levels. He might well ask himself what this degenerate posterity had done with the mighty civilisation of the past. He would wonder how with so much to inspire, to elevate, to spur them to yet greater accomplishment and self-exceeding, they could have lapsed into this impotent and inert confusion and, instead of developing the high motives of Indian culture to yet deeper and wider issues, allowed them to overload themselves with ugly accretions, to rust, to rot, almost to perish. He would see his race clinging to forms and shells and rags of the past and missing nine-tenths of its nobler values. He would compare the spiritual light and energy of the heroic ages of the Upanishads and the philosophies with the later inertia or small and broken fragmentarily derivative activity of our philosophic thought. After the intellectual curiosity, the scientific development, the creative literary and artistic greatness, the noble fecundity of the classical age he would be amazed by the extent of a later degeneracy, its mental poverty, immobility, static repetition, the comparative feebleness of the creative intuition, the long sterility of art, the cessation of science. He would deplore a prone descent to ignorance, a failing of the old powerful will and tapasya, almost a volitional impotence. In place of the simpler and more spiritually rational order of old times he would find a bewildering chaotic disorganised organisation of things without centre and without any large harmonising idea. He would find not a true social order but a half arrested, half hastening putrescence. In place of the great adaptable civilisation which assimilated with power and was able to return tenfold for what it received, he would meet a helplessness that bore passively or only with a few ineffectual galvanic reactions the forces of the outside world and the stress of adverse circumstance. At one time he would see that there had been even a loss of faith and self-confidence so considerable as to tempt the intellectuals of the nation to scrap the ancient spirit and ideals for an alien and imported culture. He would note indeed the beginning of a change, but might perhaps doubt how deep it had gone or whether it was powerful enough to save, forceful enough to upheave the whole nation from its cherished torpor and weakness, enlightened enough to guide a new and robust creative activity towards the building of new significant forms for the ancient spirit.

Here too a better understanding points to hope rather than to the flat despondency suggested by a too hasty surface glance. This last age of Indian history is an example of the constant local succession of night even to the most long and brilliant day in the evolution of the race. But it was a night filled at first with many and brilliant constellations and even at its thickest and worst it was the darkness of Kalidasa's *viceya-tārakā prabhāta-kalpeva śarvarī*, 'night preparing for dawn, with a few just decipherable stars.' Even in the decline all was not loss; there were needed developments, there were spiritual and other gains of the greatest importance for the future. If the high spiritualised mind and stupendous force of spiritual will, *tapasyā*, that characterised ancient India were less in evidence, there were new gains of spiritual emotion and sensitiveness to spiritual impulse on the lower planes of consciousness, that had been lacking before. Architecture, literature, painting, sculpture lost the grandeur, power, nobility of old, but evoked other powers and motives full of delicacy, vividness and grace. There was a descent from the heights to the lower levels, but a descent that gathered riches on its way and was needed for the fullness of spiritual discovery and experience. And in the worst period of decline and failure the spirit was not dead in India, but only torpid, concealed and shackled; now emerging in answer to a pressure of constant awakening shocks for a strong self-liberation it finds that its sleep was a preparation of new potentialities behind the veil of that slumber. The decline of our past culture may even be regarded as a needed waning and dying of old forms to make way not only for a new, but, if we will that it should be so, a greater and more perfect creation.

For after all it is the will in the being that gives to circumstances their value, and often an unexpected value; the hue of apparent actuality is a misleading indicator. If the will in a race or civilisation is towards death, if it clings to the lassitude of decay and the laissez-faire of the moribund or even in strength insists blindly upon the propensities that lead to destruction or if it cherishes only the powers of dead Time and puts away from it the powers of the future, if it prefers life that was to life that will be, nothing, not even abundant strength and resources and intelligence, not even many calls to live and constantly offered opportunities will save it from an inevitable disintegration or collapse. But if there comes to it a strong faith in itself and a robust will to live, if it is open to the things that shall come, willing to seize on the future and what it offers and strong to compel it where it seems adverse, it can draw from adversity and defeat a force of invincible victory and rise from apparent helplessness and decay in a mighty flame of renovation to the light of a more splendid life. This is what Indian civilisation is now rearising to do as it has always done in the eternal strength of its spirit.

The greatness of the ideals of the past is a promise of greater ideals for the future. A continual expansion of what stood behind past endeavour and capacity is the one abiding justification of a living culture. But it follows that civilisation and barbarism are words of a quite relative significance. For from the view of the evolutionary future European and Indian civilisation at their best have only been half achievements, infant dawns pointing to the mature sunlight that is to come. Neither Europe nor India nor any race, country or continent of mankind has ever been fully civilised from this point of view; none has grasped the whole secret of a true and perfect human living, none has applied with an entire insight or a perfectly vigilant sincerity even the little they were able to achieve. If we define civilisation as a harmony of spirit, mind and body, where has that harmony been entire or altogether real? Where have there not been glaring deficiencies and painful discords? Where has the whole secret of the harmony been altogether grasped in all its parts or the complete music of life evolved into the triumphant ease of a satisfying, durable and steadily mounting concord? Not only are there everywhere positive, ugly, even 'hideous' blots on the life of man, but much that we now accept with equanimity, much in which we take pride, may well be regarded by a future humanity as barbarism or at least as semi-barbarous and immature. The achievements that we regard as ideal, will be condemned as a self-satisfied imperfection blind to its own errors; the ideas that we vaunt as enlightenment will appear as a demi-light or a darkness. Not only will many forms of our life that claim to be ancient or even eternal, as if that could be said of any form of things, fail and disappear; the subjective shapes given to our best principles and ideals will perhaps claim from the future at best an understanding indulgence. There is little that will not have to undergo expansion and mutation, change perhaps beyond recognition or accept to be modified in a new synthesis. In the end the coming ages may look on Europe and Asia of today much as we look on savage tribes or primitive peoples. And this view from the future, if we can get it, is undoubtedly the most illuminating and dynamic standpoint from which we can judge our present; but it does not invalidate our comparative appreciation of past and extant cultures.

For this past and present are creating the greater steps of that future and much of it will survive even in that which supplants it. There is behind our imperfect cultural figures a permanent spirit to which we must cling and which will remain permanent even hereafter; there are certain fundamental motives or essential idea-forces which cannot be thrown aside, because they are part of the vital principle of our being and of the aim of Nature in us, our *svadharma*. But these motives, these idea-forces are, whether for nation or for humanity as a whole, few and simple in their essence and capable of an application always varying and progressive. The rest belongs to the less internal layers of our being and must undergo the changing pressure and satisfy the forward-moving demands of the Time-Spirit. There is this permanent spirit in things and there is this persistent swadharma or law of our nature; but there is too a less binding system of laws of successive formulation,— rhythms of the spirit, forms, turns, habits of the nature, and these endure the mutations of the ages, *yugadharma*. The race must obey this double principle of persistence and mutation or bear the penalty of a decay and deterioration that may attaint even its living centre.

Certainly we must repel with vigour every disintegrating or injurious attack; but it is much more important to form our own true and independent view of our own past achievement, present position and future possibilities,— what we were, what we are and what we may be. In our past we must distinguish all that was great, essential, elevating, vitalising, illuminating, victorious, effective. And in that again we must distinguish what was close to the permanent, essential spirit and the persistent law of our cultural being and separate from it what was temporary and transiently formulative. For all that was great in the past cannot be preserved as it was or repeated for ever; there are new needs, there are other vistas before us. But we have to distinguish too what was deficient, ill-grasped, imperfectly formulated or only suited to the limiting needs of the age or unfavourable circumstances. For it is quite idle to pretend that all in the past, even at its greatest, was entirely admirable and in its kind the highest consummate achievement of the human mind and spirit. Afterwards we have to make a comparison of this past with our present and to understand the causes of our decline and seek the remedy of our shortcomings and ailments. Our sense of the greatness of our past must not be made a fatally hypnotising lure to inertia; it should be rather an inspiration to renewed and greater achievement. But in our criticism of the present we must not be one-sided or condemn with a foolish impartiality all that we are or have done. Neither flattering or glossing over our downfall nor fouling our nest to win the applause of the stranger, we have to note our actual weakness and its roots, but to fix too our eyes with a still firmer attention on our elements of strength, our abiding potentialities, our dynamic impulses of self-renewal.

A second comparison has to be made between the West and India. In the past of Europe and the past of India we can observe with an unbiassed mind the successes of the West, the gifts it brought to humanity, but also its large gaps, striking deficiencies, terrible and even 'hideous' vices and failures. On the other balance we have to cast ancient and mediaeval India's achievements and failures. Here we shall find that there is little for which we need lower our heads before Europe and much in which we rise well and sometimes immeasurably above her. But we have to scrutinise next the present of the West in its strong success, vitality, conquering insolence. What has been great in it we shall allow, but take deep note too of its defects, stumblings and dangers. And with this dangerous greatness we must compare the present of India, her downfall and its causes, her velleities of revival, her elements that still make for superiority now and in the future. Let us see and take account of all that we must inevitably receive from the West and consider how we can assimilate it to our own spirit and ideals. But let us see too what founts of native power there are in ourselves from which we can draw deeper, more vital and fresher streams of the power of life than from anything the West can offer. For that will help us more than occidental forms and motives, because it will be more natural to us, more stimulating to our idiosyncrasy of nature, more packed with creative suggestions, more easily taken up and completely followed in power of practice.

But far more helpful than any of these necessary comparisons will be the forward look from our past and present towards our own and not any foreign ideal of the future. For it is our evolutionary push towards the future that will give to our past and present their true value and significance. India's nature, her mission, the work that she has to do, her part in the earth's destiny, the peculiar power for which she stands is written there in her past history and is the secret purpose behind her present sufferings and ordeals. A reshaping of the forms of our spirit will have to take place; but it is the spirit itself behind past forms that we have to disengage and preserve and to give to it new and powerful thought-significances, culture-values, a new instrumentation, greater figures. And so long as we recognise these essential things and are faithful to their spirit, it will not hurt us to make even the most drastic mental or physical adaptations and the most extreme cultural and social changes. But these changes themselves must be cast in the spirit and mould of India and not in any other, not in the spirit of America or Europe, not in the mould of Japan or Russia. We must recognise the great gulf between what we are and what we may and ought to strive to be. But this we must do not in any spirit of discouragement or denial of ourselves and the truth of our spirits, but in order to measure the advance we have to make. For we have to find its true lines and to find in ourselves the aspiration and inspiration, the fire and the force to conceive them and to execute.

An original truth-seeking thought is needed if we are to take this stand and make this movement, a strong and courageous intuition, an unfailing spiritual and intellectual rectitude. The courage to defend our culture against ignorant occidental criticism and to maintain it against the gigantic modern pressure comes first, but with it there must be the courage to admit not from any European standpoint but from our own outlook the errors of our culture. Apart from all phenomena of decline or deterioration, we should recognise without any sophistical denial those things in our creeds of life and social institutions which are in themselves mistaken and some of them indefensible, things weakening to our national life, degrading to our civilisation, dishonouring to our culture. A flagrant example can be found in the treatment of our outcastes. There are those who would excuse it as an unavoidable error in the circumstances of the past; there are others who contend that it was the best possible solution then available. There are still others who would justify it and, with whatever modifications, prolong it as necessary to our social synthesis. The contention is highly disputable. The excuse was there, but it is no justification for continuance. A solution which condemns by segregation one sixth of the nation to permanent ignominy, continued filth, uncleanliness of the inner and outer life and a brutal animal existence instead of lifting them out of it is no solution but rather an acceptance of weakness and a constant wound to the social body and to its collective spiritual, intellectual, moral and material welfare. A social synthesis which can only live by making a permanent rule of the degradation of our fellowmen and countrymen stands condemned and foredoomed to decay and disturbance. The evil effects may be kept under for a long time and work only by the subtler unobserved action of the law of Karma; but once the light of Truth is let in on these dark spots, to perpetuate them is to maintain a seed of disruption and ruin our chances of eventual survival.

Again, we have to look on our cultural ideas and our social forms and see where they have lost their ancient spirit or real significance. Many of them are now a fiction and no longer in accordance with the ideas they assume or with the facts of life. Others even if good in themselves or else beneficent in their own time are no longer sufficient for our growth. All these must either be transformed or discarded and truer ideas and better formulations must be found in their place. The new turn we must give them will not always be a return upon their old significance. The new dynamic truths we have to discover need not be parked within the limited truth of a past ideal. On our past and present ideals we have to turn the searchlight of the spirit and see whether they have not to be surpassed or enlarged or brought into consonance with new wider ideals. All we do or create must be consistent with the abiding spirit of India, but framed to fit into a greater harmonised rhythm and plastic to the call of a more luminous future. If faith in ourselves and fidelity to the spirit of our culture are the first requisites of a continued and vigorous life, a recognition of greater possibilities is a condition not less indispensable. There cannot be a healthy and victorious survival if we make of the past a fetish instead of an inspiring impulse.

The spirit and ideals of our civilisation need no defence, for in their best parts and in their essence they were of eternal value. India's internal and individual seeking of them was earnest, powerful, effective. But the application in the collective life of society was subjected to serious reserves. Never sufficiently bold and thoroughgoing, it became more and more limited and halting when the life-force declined in her peoples. This defect, this gulf between ideal and collective practice, has pursued all human living and was not peculiar to India; but the dissonance became especially marked with the lapse of time and it put at last on our society a growing stamp of weakness and failure. There was a large effort in the beginning at some kind of synthesis between the inner ideal and the outer life; but a static regulation of society was its latter end. An underlying principle of spiritual idealism, an elusive unity and fixed helpful forms of mutuality remained always there, but also an increasing element of strict bondage and minute division and fissiparous complexity in the social mass. The great Vedantic ideals of freedom, unity and the godhead in man were left to the inner spiritual effort of individuals. The power of expansion and assimilation diminished and when powerful and aggressive forces broke in from outside, Islam, Europe, the later Hindu society was content with an imprisoned and static self-preservation, a mere permission to live The form of living became more and more narrow and it endured a continually restricted assertion of its ancient spirit. Duration, survival was achieved, but not in the end a really secure and vital duration, not a great, robust and victorious survival.

And now survival itself has become impossible without expansion. If we are to live at all, we must resume India's great interrupted endeavour; we must take up boldly and execute thoroughly in the individual and in the society, in the spiritual and in the mundane life, in philosophy and religion, in art and literature, in thought, in political and economic and social formulation the full and unlimited sense of her highest spirit and knowledge. And if we do that, we shall find that the best of what comes to us draped in occidental forms, is already implied in our own ancient wisdom and has there a greater spirit behind it, a profounder truth and self-knowledge and the capacity of a will to nobler and more ideal formations. Only we need to work out thoroughly in life what we have always known in the spirit. There and nowhere else lies the secret of the needed harmony between the essential meaning of our past culture and the environmental requirements of our future.

That view opens out a prospect beyond the battle of cultures which is the immediate dangerous aspect of the meeting of East and West. The Spirit in man has one aim before it in all mankind; but different continents or peoples approach it from different sides, with different formulations and in a differing spirit. Not recognising the underlying unity of the ultimate divine motive, they give battle to each other and claim that theirs alone is the way for mankind. The one real and perfect civilisation is the one in which they happen to be born, all the rest must perish or go under. But the real and perfect civilisation yet waits to be discovered; for the life of mankind is still nine tenths of barbarism to one tenth of culture. The European mind gives the first place to the principle of growth by struggle; it is by struggle that it arrives at some kind of concert. But this concert is itself hardly more than an organisation for growth by competition, aggression and farther battle. It is a peace that is constantly breaking, even within itself, into a fresh strife of principles, ideas, interests, races, classes. It is an organisation precarious at its base and in its centre because it is founded on half-truths that deteriorate into whole falsehoods; but it is still or has been till now vigorous in constant achievement and able to grow powerfully and to devour and assimilate. Indian culture proceeded on the principle of a concert that strove to find its base in a unity and reached out again towards some greater oneness. Its aim was a lasting organisation that would minimise or even eliminate the principle of struggle. But it ended by achieving peace and stable arrangement through exclusion, fragmentation and immobility of status; it drew a magic circle of safety and shut itself up in it for good. In the end it lost its force of aggression, weakened its power of assimilation and decayed within its barriers. A static and limited concert, not always enlarging itself, not plastic becomes in our human state of imperfection a prison or a sleeping-chamber. Concert cannot be anything but imperfect and provisional in its form and can only preserve its vitality and fulfil its ultimate aim if it constantly adapts, expands, progresses. Its lesser unities must widen towards a broader and more comprehensive and above all a more real and spiritual oneness. In the larger statement of our culture and civilisation that we have now to achieve, a greater outward expression of spiritual and psychological oneness, but with a diversity which the mechanical method of Europe does not tolerate, will surely be one leading motive. A concert, a unity with the rest of mankind, in which we shall maintain our spiritual and our outer independence will be another line of our endeavour. But what now appears as a struggle may well be the first necessary step, before we can formulate that unity of mankind which the West sees only in idea, but cannot achieve because it does not possess its spirit. Therefore Europe labours to establish unity by accommodation of conflicting interests and the force of mechanical institutions; but so attempted, it will either not be founded at all or will be founded on sand. Meanwhile she wishes to blot out every other culture, as if hers were the only truth or all the truth of life and there were no such thing as truth of the spirit. India, the ancient possessor of the truth of the spirit, must resist that arrogant claim and aggression and affirm her own deeper truths in spite of heavy odds and against all comers. For in its preservation lies the only hope that mankind instead of marching to a new cataclysm and primitive beginning with a constant repetition of the old blind cycles will at last emerge into the light and accomplish the drive forward which will bring the terrestrial evolution to its next step of ascent in the progressive manifestation of the Spirit.

Part Three
The Individual, Society and Humanity

The greatest future triumph of the thinker will come when he can persuade the individual integer and the collective whole to rest their life-relation and its union and stability upon a free and harmonious consent and self-adaptation, and shape and govern the external by the internal truth rather than to constrain the inner spirit by the tyranny of the external form and structure.

The Synthesis of Yoga

PART THREE includes extracts from *The Ideal of Human Unity* and *The Human Cycle*, Sri Aurobindo's principal works of social and political theory. There is much in these books that might be classified as sociology or history, though in the first selection Sri Aurobindo distinguishes his approach from the normal approach of those disciplines.

• *The Ideal of Human Unity*, written during the course of the First World War, opens with a consideration of *The Turn towards Unity: Its Necessity and Dangers*. The advanced thought of humanity has come to accept the necessity of a supranational union, but a fruitful union cannot be achieved by means of social and political machinery, which would crush the life of the constituent units.

• Towards the end of *The Ideal of Human Unity*, Sri Aurobindo introduces the idea of a 'religion of humanity' as the key to a lasting union of humanity. Discussing this in his *Summary and Conclusion*, he notes that some form of a united humanity is now inevitable — a prediction partially borne out by the establishment of the League of Nations and the United Nations. But he cautions that if this union should take the form of a world-state, the results might be disastrous to human creativity and freedom — as German and Russian attempts to establish such a state have shown. There must be a spiritual oneness creating a psychological oneness before there can be a true outward union.

• *A Note* deals with the international political situation before or during the Second World War, when a colossal attempt to establish a world-state was underway. The conflict and confusion showed that no simple solution was possible, and underlined the need of establishing a 'multiple unity', in which different cultural groupings could learn to respect one another.

• In *The Human Cycle*, originally called *The Psychology of Social Development*, Sri Aurobindo accepts the terminology of the theory of social evolution put forward by the German historian Lamprecht, but goes on to develop his own idea of *The Cycle of Society*. The symbolic, typal, conventional and individualistic stages may be pointing not only to a subjective stage, but to an age of spirituality.

• This possibility, prepared throughout *The Human Cycle*, is developed in its final chapter, *The Advent and Progress of the Spiritual Age*. A spiritualized society would not mean one subjected to a religious order, but one in which each individual lived inwardly and outwardly the divine life.

The Turn towards Unity

Its Necessity and Dangers

THE SURFACES of life are easy to understand; their laws, characteristic movements, practical utilities are ready to our hand and we can seize on them and turn them to account with a sufficient facility and rapidity. But they do not carry us very far. They suffice for an active superficial life from day to day, but they do not solve the great problems of existence. On the other hand, the knowledge of life's profundities, its potent secrets, its great, hidden, all-determining laws is exceedingly difficult to us. We have found no plummet that can fathom these depths; they seem to us a vague, indeterminate movement, a profound obscurity from which the mind recoils willingly to play with the fret and foam and facile radiances of the surface. Yet it is these depths and their unseen forces that we ought to know if we would understand existence; on the surface we get only Nature's secondary rules and practical bye-laws which help us to tide over the difficulties of the moment and to organise empirically without understanding them her continual transitions.

Nothing is more obscure to humanity or less seized by its understanding, whether in the power that moves it or the sense of the aim towards which it moves, than its own communal and collective life. Sociology does not help us, for it only gives us the general story of the past and the external conditions under which communities have survived. History teaches us nothing; it is a confused torrent of events and personalities or a kaleidoscope of changing institutions. We do not seize the real sense of all this change and this continual streaming forward of human

The first chapter of *The Ideal of Human Unity*, published in the *Arya* in 1915. *The Ideal of Human Unity* appeared as a book in 1919 and was revised slightly before the publication of the second edition in 1950.

life in the channels of Time. What we do seize are current or recurrent phenomena, facile generalisations, partial ideas. We talk of democracy, aristocracy and autocracy, collectivism and individualism, imperialism and nationalism, the State and the commune, capitalism and labour; we advance hasty generalisations and make absolute systems which are positively announced today only to be abandoned perforce tomorrow; we espouse causes and ardent enthusiasms whose triumph turns to an early disillusionment and then forsake them for others, perhaps for those that we have taken so much trouble to destroy. For a whole century mankind thirsts and battles after liberty and earns it with a bitter expense of toil, tears and blood; the century that enjoys without having fought for it turns away as from a puerile illusion and is ready to renounce the depreciated gain as the price of some new good. And all this happens because our whole thought and action with regard to our collective life is shallow and empirical; it does not seek for, it does not base itself on a firm, profound and complete knowledge. The moral is not the vanity of human life, of its ardours and enthusiasms and of the ideals it pursues, but the necessity of a wiser, larger, more patient search after its true law and aim.

Today the ideal of human unity is more or less vaguely making its way to the front of our consciousness. The emergence of an ideal in human thought is always the sign of an intention in Nature, but not always of an intention to accomplish; sometimes it indicates only an attempt which is predestined to temporary failure. For Nature is slow and patient in her methods. She takes up ideas and half carries them out, then drops them by the wayside to resume them in some future era with a better combination. She tempts humanity, her thinking instrument, and tests how far it is ready for the harmony she has imagined; she allows and incites man to attempt and fail, so that he may learn and succeed better another time. Still the ideal, having once made its way to the front of thought, must certainly be attempted, and this ideal of human unity is likely to figure largely among the determining forces of the future; for the intellectual and material circumstances of the age have prepared and almost impose it, especially the scientific discoveries which have made our earth so small that its vastest kingdoms seem now no more than the provinces of a single country.

But this very commodity of the material circumstances may bring about the failure of the ideal; for when material circumstances favour a great change, but the heart and mind of the race are not really ready — especially the heart — failure may be predicted, unless indeed men are wise in time and accept the inner change along with the external readjustment. But at present the human intellect has been so much mechanised by physical Science that it is likely to attempt the revolution it is beginning to envisage principally or solely through mechanical means, through social and political adjustments. Now it is not by social and political devices, or at any rate not by these chiefly or only, that the unity of the human race can be enduringly or fruitfully accomplished.

It must be remembered that a greater social or political unity is not necessarily a boon in itself; it is only worth pursuing in so far as it provides a means and a framework for a better, richer, more happy and puissant individual and collective life. But hitherto the experience of mankind has not favoured the view that huge aggregations, closely united and strictly organised, are favourable to a rich and puissant human life. It would seem rather that collective life is more at ease with itself, more genial, varied, fruitful when it can concentrate itself in small spaces and simpler organisms.

If we consider the past of humanity so far as it is known to us, we find that the interesting periods of human life, the scenes in which it has been most richly lived and has left behind it the most precious fruits, were precisely those ages and countries in which humanity was able to organise itself in little independent centres acting intimately upon each other but not fused into a single unity. Modern Europe owes two-thirds of its civilisation to three such supreme moments of human history, the religious life of the congeries of tribes which called itself Israel and, subsequently, of the little nation of the Jews, the many-sided life of the small Greek city states, the similar, though more restricted artistic and intellectual life of mediaeval Italy. Nor was any age in Asia so rich in energy, so well worth living in, so productive of the best and most enduring fruits as that heroic period of India when she was divided into small kingdoms, many of them no larger than a modern district. Her most wonderful activities, her most vigorous and enduring work, that which, if we had to make a choice, we should keep at the sacrifice of all else, belonged to that period; the second best came afterwards in larger, but still comparatively small nations and kingdoms like those of the Pallavas, Chalukyas, Pandyas, Cholas and Cheras. In comparison she received little from the greater empires that rose and fell within her borders, the Moghul, the Gupta or the Maurya — little indeed except political and administrative organisation, some fine art and literature and a certain amount of lasting work in other kinds, not always of the best quality. Their impulse was rather towards elaborate organisation than original, stimulating and creative.

Nevertheless, in this regime of the small city state or of regional cultures there was always a defect which compelled a tendency towards large organisations. The defect was a characteristic of impermanence, often of disorder, especially of defencelessness against the onslaught of larger organisations, even of an insufficient capacity for widespread material well-being. Therefore this earlier form of collective life tended to disappear and give place to the organisation of nations, kingdoms and empires.

And here we notice, first, that it is the groupments of smaller nations which have had the most intense life and not the huge States and colossal empires. Collective life diffusing itself in too vast spaces seems to lose intensity and productiveness. Europe has lived in England, France, the Netherlands, Spain, Italy, the small States of Germany — all her later civilisation and progress evolved itself there, not in the huge mass of the Holy Roman or the Russian Empire. We see a similar phenomenon in the social and political field when we compare the intense life and activity of Europe in its many nations acting richly upon each other, rapidly progressing by quick creative steps and sometimes by bounds, with the great masses of Asia, her long periods of immobility in which wars and revolutions seem to be small, temporary and usually unproductive episodes, her centuries of religious, philosophic and artistic reveries, her tendency towards an increasing isolation and a final stagnancy of the outward life.

Secondly, we note that in this organisation of nations and kingdoms those which have had the most vigorous life have gained it by a sort of artificial concentration of the vitality into some head, centre or capital, London, Paris, Rome. By this device

Nature, while acquiring the benefits of a larger organisation and more perfect unity, preserves to some extent that equally precious power of fruitful concentration in a small space and into a closely packed activity which she had possessed in her more primitive system of the city state or petty kingdom. But this advantage was purchased by the condemnation of the rest of the organisation, the district, the provincial town, the village to a dull, petty and somnolent life in strange contrast with the vital intensity of the *urbs* or metropolis.

The Roman Empire is the historic example of an organisation of unity which transcended the limits of the nation, and its advantages and disadvantages are there perfectly typified. The advantages are admirable organisation, peace, widespread security, order and material well-being; the disadvantage is that the individual, the city, the region sacrifice their independent life and become mechanical parts of a machine; life loses its colour, richness, variety, freedom and victorious impulse towards creation. The organisation is great and admirable, but the individual dwindles and is overpowered and overshadowed; and eventually by the smallness and feebleness of the individual the huge organism inevitably and slowly loses even its great conservative vitality and dies of an increasing stagnation. Even while outwardly whole and untouched, the structure has become rotten and begins to crack and dissolve at the first shock from outside. Such organisations, such periods are immensely useful for conservation, even as the Roman Empire served to consolidate the gains of the rich centuries that preceded it. But they arrest life and growth.

We see, then, what is likely to happen if there were a social, administrative and political unification of mankind, such as some have begun to dream of nowadays. A tremendous organisation would be needed under which both individual and regional life would be crushed, dwarfed, deprived of their necessary freedom like a plant without rain and wind and sunlight, and this would mean for humanity, after perhaps one first outburst of satisfied and joyous activity, a long period of mere conservation, increasing stagnancy and ultimately decay.

Yet the unity of mankind is evidently a part of Nature's eventual scheme and must come about. Only it must be under other conditions and with safeguards which will keep the race intact in the roots of its vitality, richly diverse in its oneness.

The Ideal of Human Unity

Summary and Conclusion

IN OTHER words, — and this is the conclusion at which we arrive, — while it is possible to construct a precarious and quite mechanical unity by political and administrative means, the unity of the human race, even if achieved, can only be secured and can only be made real if the religion of humanity, which is at present the highest active ideal of mankind, spiritualises itself and becomes the general inner law of human life.

The outward unity may well achieve itself, — possibly, though by no means certainly, in a measurable time, — because that is the inevitable final trend of the working of Nature in human society which makes for larger and yet larger aggregations and cannot fail to arrive at a total aggregation of mankind in a closer international system.

This working of Nature depends for its means of fulfilment upon two forces which combine to make the larger aggregation inevitable. First, there is the increasing closeness of common interest or at least the interlacing and interrelation of interests in a larger and yet larger circle which makes old divisions an obstacle and a cause of weakness, obstruction and friction, and the clash and collision that comes out of this friction a ruinous calamity to all, even to the victor who has to pay a too heavy price for his gains; and even these expected gains, as war becomes more complex and disastrous, are becoming more and more difficult to achieve and the success problematical. An increasing perception of this community or interrelation of interests and a growing unwillingness to face the consequences of collision and ruinous struggle must push men to welcome any means for mitigating the

The last chapter of *The Ideal of Human Unity*, published in the *Arya* in 1918 and later revised.

divisions which lead to such disasters. If the trend to the mitigation of divisions is once given a definite form, that commences an impetus which drives towards closer and closer union. If she cannot arrive by these means, if the incoherence is too great for the trend of unification to triumph, Nature will use other means, such as war and conquest or the temporary domination of the powerful State or empire or the menace of such a domination which will compel those threatened to adopt a closer system of union. It is these means and this force of outward necessity which she used to create nation-units and national empires, and, however modified in the circumstances and workings, it is at bottom the same force and the same means which she is using to drive mankind towards international unification.

But, secondly, there is the force of a common uniting sentiment. This may work in two ways; it may come before as an originating or contributory cause or it may come afterwards as a cementing result. In the first case, the sentiment of a larger unity springs up among units which were previously divided and leads them to seek after a form of union which may then be brought about principally by the force of the sentiment and its idea or by that secondarily as an aid to other and more outward events and causes. We may note that in earlier times this sentiment was insufficiently effective, as among the petty clans or regional nations; unity had ordinarily to be effected by outward circumstances and generally by the grossest of them, by war and conquest, by the domination of the most powerful among many warring or contiguous peoples. But in later times the force of the sentiment of unity, supported as it has been by a clearer political idea, has become more effective. The larger national aggregates have grown up by a simple act of federation or union, though this has sometimes had to be preceded by a common struggle for liberty or a union in war against a common enemy; so have grown into one the United States, Italy, Germany, and more peacefully the Australian and South African federations. But in other cases, especially in the earlier national aggregations, the sentiment of unity has grown up largely or entirely as the result of the formal, outward or mechanical union. But whether to form or to preserve the growth of the sentiment, the psychological factor is indispensable; without it there can be no secure and lasting union. Its absence, the failure to create such a sentiment or to make it sufficiently living, natural, forcible has been the cause of the precariousness of such aggregates as Austro-Hungary and of the ephemeral character of the empires of the past, even as it is likely to bring about, unless circumstances change, the collapse or disintegration of the great present-day empires.

The trend of forces towards some kind of international world-organisation eventuating in a possible far-off unification, which is now just beginning to declare itself as an idea or aspiration though the causes which made it inevitable have been for some time at work, is enforced by the pressure of need and environment, by outward circumstances. At the same time, there is a sentiment helped and stimulated by these outward circumstances, a cosmopolitan, international sentiment, still rather nebulous and vaguely ideal, which may accelerate the growth of the formal union. In itself this sentiment would be an insufficient cement for the preservation of any mechanical union which might be created; for it could not easily be so close and forcible a sentiment as national feeling. It would have to subsist on the conveniences of union as its only substantial provender. But the experience of the past shows that this mere necessity of convenience is in the end not strong enough to resist the pressure of unfavourable circumstances and the reassertion of old or the effective growth of new centrifugal forces. There is, however, at work a more powerful force, a sort of intellectual religion of humanity, clear in the minds of the few, vaguely felt in its effects and its disguises by the many, which has largely helped to bring about much of the trend of the modern mind and the drift of its developing institutions. This is a psychological force which tends to break beyond the formula of the nation and aspires to replace the religion of country and even, in its more extreme forms, to destroy altogether the national sentiment and to abolish its divisions so as to create the single nation of mankind.

We may say, then, that this trend must eventually realise itself, however great may be the difficulties; and they are really enormous, much greater than those which attended the national formation. If the present unsatisfactory condition of international relations should lead to a series of cataclysms, either large and world-embracing like the present war or, though each more limited in scope, yet in their sum world-pervading and necessarily, by the growing interrelation of interests, affecting even those who do not fall directly under their touch, then mankind will finally be forced in self-defence to a new, closer and more stringently unified order of things. Its choice will be between that and a lingering suicide. If the human reason cannot find out the way, Nature herself is sure to shape these upheavals in such a way as to bring about her end. Therefore, — whether soon or in the long run, whether brought about by its own growing sentiment of unity, stimulated by common interests and convenience, or by the evolutionary pressure of circumstances, — we may take it that an eventual unification or at least some formal organisation of human life on earth is, the incalculable being always allowed for, practically inevitable.

I have tried to show from the analogy of the past evolution of the nation that this international unification must culminate or at least is likely to culminate in one of two forms. There is likely to be either a centralised World-State or a looser world-union which may be either a close federation or a simple confederacy of the peoples for the common ends of mankind. The last form is the most desirable, because it gives sufficient scope for the principle of variation which is necessary for the free play of life and the healthy progress of the race. The process by which the World-State may come starts with the creation of a central body which will at first have very limited functions, but, once created, must absorb by degrees all the different utilities of a centralised international control, as the State, first in the form of a monarchy and then of a parliament, has been absorbing by degrees the whole control of the life of the nation, so that we are now within measurable distance of a centralised socialistic State which will leave no part of the life of its individuals unregulated. A similar process in the World-State will end in the taking up and the regulation of the whole life of the peoples into its hands; it may even end by abolishing national individuality and turning the divisions that it has created into mere departmental groupings, provinces and districts of the one common State. Such an eventuality may seem now a fantastic dream or an unrealisable idea; but it is one which, under certain conditions that are by no means beyond the scope of ultimate possibility, may well become feasible and even, after a certain point is reached, inevitable. A federal system and still more a confederacy would mean, on the other hand, the preservation of the national basis and a greater or less freedom of national life, but the subordination of the separate national to the larger common interests and of full separate freedom to the greater international necessities.

It may be questioned whether past analogies are a safe guide in a problem so new and whether something else might not be evolved more intimately and independently arising from it and suitable to its complexities. But mankind even in dealing with its new problems works upon past experience and therefore upon past motives and analogies. Even when it seizes on new ideas, it goes to the past for the form it gives to them. Behind the apparent changes of the most radical revolutions we see this unavoidable principle of continuity surviving in the heart of the new order. Moreover, these alternatives seem the only way in which the two forces in presence can work out their conflict, either by the disappearance of the one, the separative national instinct, or by an accommodation between them. On the other hand, it is quite possible that human thought and action may take so new a turn as to bring in a number of unforeseen possibilities and lead to a quite different ending. And one might upon these lines set one's imagination to work and produce perhaps a utopia of a better kind. Such constructive efforts of the human imagination have their value and often a very great value; but any such speculations would evidently have been out of place in the study I have attempted.

Assuredly, neither of the two alternatives and none of the three forms considered are free from serious objections. A centralised World-State would signify the triumph of the idea of mechanical unity or rather of uniformity. It would inevitably mean the undue depression of an indispensable element in the vigour of human life and progress, the free life of the individual, the free variation of the peoples. It must end, if it becomes permanent and fulfils all its tendencies, either in a death in life, a stagnation, or by the insurgence of some new saving but revolutionary force or principle which would shatter the whole fabric into pieces. The mechanical tendency is one to which the logical reason of man, itself a precise machine, is easily addicted and its operations are obviously the easiest to manage and the most ready to hand; its full evolution may seem to the reason desirable, necessary, inevitable, but its end is predestined. A centralised socialistic State may be a necessity of the future, once it is founded, but a reaction from it will be equally an eventual necessity of the future. The greater its pressure, the more certainly will it be met by the spread of the spiritual, the intellectual, the vital and practical principle of Anarchism in revolt against that mechanical pressure. So, too, a centralised mechanical World-State must rouse in the end a similar force against it and might well terminate in a crumbling up and disintegration, even in the necessity for a repetition of the cycle of humanity ending in a better attempt to solve the problem. It could be kept in being only if humanity agreed to allow all the rest of its life to be regularised for it for the sake of peace and stability and took refuge for its individual freedom in the spiritual life, as happened once under the Roman Empire. But even that would be only a temporary solution. A federal system also would tend inevitably to establish one general type for human life, institutions and activities; it could allow only a play of minor variations. But the need of variation in living Nature could not always rest satisfied with that scanty sustenance. On the other hand, a looser confederacy might well be open to the objection that it would give too ready a handle for centrifugal forces, were such to arise in new strength. A loose confederation could not be permanent; it must turn in one direction or the other, end either in a close and rigid centralisation or at last by a break-up of the loose unity into its original elements.

The saving power needed is a new psychological factor which will at once make a united life necessary to humanity and force it to respect the principle of freedom. The religion of humanity seems to be the one growing force which tends in that direction; for it makes for the sense of human oneness, it has the idea of the race, and yet at the same time it respects the human individual and the natural human grouping. But its present intellectual form seems hardly sufficient. The idea, powerful in itself and in its effects, is yet not powerful enough to mould the whole life of the race in its image. For it has to concede too much to the egoistic side of human nature, once all and still nine-tenths of our being, with which its larger idea is in conflict. On the other side, because it leans principally on the reason, it turns too readily to the mechanical solution. For the rational idea ends always as a captive of its machinery, becomes a slave of its own too binding process. A new idea with another turn of the logical machine revolts against it and breaks up its machinery, but only to substitute in the end another mechanical system, another credo, formula and practice.

A spiritual religion of humanity is the hope of the future. By this is not meant what is ordinarily called a universal religion, a system, a thing of creed and intellectual belief and dogma and outward rite. Mankind has tried unity by that means; it has failed and deserved to fail, because there can be no universal religious system, one in mental creed and vital form. The inner spirit is indeed one, but more than any other the spiritual life insists on freedom and variation in its self-expression and means of development. A religion of humanity means the growing realisation that there is a secret Spirit, a divine Reality, in which we are all one, that humanity is its highest present vehicle on earth, that the human race and the human being are the means by which it will progressively reveal itself here. It implies a growing attempt to live out this knowledge and bring about a kingdom of this divine Spirit upon earth. By its growth within us oneness with our fellow-men will become the leading principle of all our life, not merely a principle of cooperation but a deeper brotherhood, a real and an inner sense of unity and equality and a common life. There must be the realisation by the individual that only in the life of his fellow-men is his own life complete. There must be the realisation by the race that only on the free and full life of the individual can its own perfection and permanent happiness be founded. There must be too a discipline and a way of salvation in accordance with this religion, that is to say, a means by which it can be developed by each man within himself, so that it may be developed in the life of the race. To go into all that this implies would be too large a subject to be entered upon here; it is enough to point out that in this direction lies the eventual road. No doubt, if this is only an idea like the rest, it will go the way of all ideas. But if it is at all a truth of our being, then it must be the truth to which all is moving and in it must be found the means of a fundamental, an inner, a complete, a real human unity which would be the one secure base of a unification of human life. A spiritual oneness which would create a psychological oneness not dependent upon any intellectual or outward uniformity and compel a oneness of life not bound up with its mechanical means of unification, but ready always to enrich its secure unity by a free inner variation and a freely varied outer self-expression, this would be the basis for a higher type of human existence.

Could such a realisation develop rapidly in mankind, we might then solve the problem of unification in a deeper and truer way from the inner truth to the outer forms. Until then, the attempt to bring it about by mechanical means must proceed. But the higher hope of humanity lies in the growing number of men who will realise this truth and seek to develop it in themselves, so that when the mind of man is ready to escape from its mechanical bent, — perhaps when it finds that its mechanical solutions are all temporary and disappointing, — the truth of the Spirit may step in and lead humanity to the path of its highest possible happiness and perfection.

A Note

We seem at the present moment to be very far away from such a rational solution and indeed at the opposite pole of human possibility; we have swung back to an extreme of international disorder and to an entire application of the vital and animal principle of the struggle for survival, not of the humanly fittest, but of the strongest.

But the very intensity of this struggle and disorder may be the path Nature has chosen towards the true escape from it; for it is becoming more and more evident that a long continuance of the present international state of humanity will lead not to any survival, but to the destruction of civilisation and the relapse of the race towards barbarism, decadence, an evolutionary failure. The antipathy or hostility or distrust of nations, races, cultures, religions towards each other is due to the past habit of egoistic self-assertion, desire for domination, for encroachment upon the lebensraum one of another and the consequent sense of unfriendly pressure, the fear of subjugation or domination and the oppression of the individuality of one by the other. A state of things must be brought about in which mutual toleration is the law, an order in which many elements, racial, national, cultural, spiritual can exist side by side and form a multiple unity; in such an order all these antipathies, hostilities, distrusts would die from lack of nourishment. That would be a true state of perfectly developed human civilisation, a true basis for the higher progress of the race. In this new order India with her spiritual culture turned towards the highest aims of humanity would find her rightful place and would become one of the leaders of the human evolution by the greatness of her ideals and the capacity of her peoples for the spiritualisation of life.

Sri Aurobindo wrote these observations during the 1930s or 1940s in reference to a proposal for a solution of international problems on the basis of the principles in *The Ideal of Human Unity*, which had been submitted to him by a disciple.

The Cycle of Society

MODERN SCIENCE, obsessed with the greatness of its physical discoveries and the idea of the sole existence of Matter, has long attempted to base upon physical data even its study of Soul and Mind and of those workings of Nature in man and animal in which a knowledge of psychology is as important as any of the physical sciences. Its very psychology founded itself upon physiology and the scrutiny of the brain and nervous system. It is not surprising therefore that in history and sociology attention should have been concentrated on the external data, laws, institutions, rites, customs, economic factors and developments, while the deeper psychological elements so important in the activities of a mental, emotional, ideative being like man have been very much neglected. This kind of science would explain history and social development as much as possible by economic necessity or motive, — by economy understood in its widest sense.[1] There are even historians who deny or put aside as of a very subsidiary importance the working of the idea and the influence of the thinker in the development of human institutions. The French Revolution, it is thought, would have happened just as it did and when it did, by economic necessity, even if Rousseau and Voltaire had never written and the eighteenth-century philosophic movement in the world of thought had never worked out its bold and radical speculations.

Recently, however, the all-sufficiency of Matter to explain Mind and Soul has begun to be doubted and a movement of emancipation from the obsession of physical science has set in,

The first chapter of *The Human Cycle* (originally called *The Psychology of Social Development*), published in the *Arya* in 1916 and revised slightly before *The Human Cycle* was brought out as a book in 1949.

[1] The reference here is primarily to the theories of Karl Marx (1818–83).

although as yet it has not gone beyond a few awkward and rudimentary stumblings. Still there is the beginning of a perception that behind the economic motives and causes of social and historical development there are profound psychological, even perhaps soul factors; and in pre-war Germany, the metropolis of rationalism and materialism but the home also, for a century and a half, of new thought and original tendencies good and bad, beneficent and disastrous, a first psychological theory of history was conceived and presented by an original intelligence.[2] The earliest attempts in a new field are seldom entirely successful, and the German historian, originator of this theory, seized on a luminous idea, but was not able to carry it very far or probe very deep. He was still haunted by a sense of the greater importance of the economic factor, and like most European science his theory related, classified and organised phenomena much more successfully than it explained them. Nevertheless, its basic idea formulated a suggestive and illuminating truth, and it is worthwhile following up some of the suggestions it opens out in the light especially of Eastern thought and experience.

The theorist, Lamprecht, basing himself on European and particularly on German history, supposed that human society progresses through certain distinct psychological stages which he terms respectively symbolic, typal and conventional, individualist and subjective. This development forms, then, a sort of psychological cycle through which a nation or a civilisation is bound to proceed. Obviously, such classifications are likely to err by rigidity and to substitute a mental straight line for the coils and zigzags of Nature. The psychology of man and his societies is too complex, too synthetical of many-sided and intermixed tendencies to satisfy any such rigorous and formal analysis. Nor does this theory of a psychological cycle tell us what is the inner meaning of its successive phases or the necessity of their succession or the term and end towards which they are driving. But still to understand natural laws whether of Mind or Matter it

[2] Karl Lamprecht (1856–1915), German historian, was one of the first to develop a theory of history that took human psychology into account. He presented his ideas in *Moderne Geschichtswissenschaft* (1904, translated into English as *What is History*, 1905). Sri Aurobindo read about Lamprecht's idea of the psychological stages of society in an article by Guglielmo Salvadori published in the May/June 1916 issue of *The Hindustan Review*.

is necessary to analyse their working into its discoverable elements, main constituents, dominant forces, though these may not actually be found anywhere in isolation. I will leave aside the Western thinker's own dealings with his idea. The suggestive names he has offered us, if we examine their intrinsic sense and value, may yet throw some light on the thickly veiled secret of our historic evolution, and this is the line on which it would be most useful to investigate.

Undoubtedly, wherever we can seize human society in what to us seems its primitive beginnings or early stages,—no matter whether the race is comparatively cultured or savage or economically advanced or backward,—we do find a strongly symbolic mentality that governs or at least pervades its thought, customs and institutions. Symbolic, but of what? We find that this social stage is always religious and actively imaginative in its religion; for symbolism and a widespread imaginative or intuitive religious feeling have a natural kinship and especially in earlier or primitive formations they have gone always together. When man begins to be predominantly intellectual, sceptical, ratiocinative he is already preparing for an individualist society and the age of symbols and the age of conventions have passed or are losing their virtue. The symbol then is of something which man feels to be present behind himself and his life and his activities,—the Divine, the Gods, the vast and deep unnameable, a hidden, living and mysterious nature of things. All his religious and social institutions, all the moments and phases of his life are to him symbols in which he seeks to express what he knows or guesses of the mystic influences that are behind his life and shape and govern or at the least intervene in its movements.

If we look at the beginnings of Indian society, the far-off Vedic age which we no longer understand, for we have lost that mentality, we see that everything is symbolic. The religious institution of sacrifice governs the whole society and all its hours and moments, and the ritual of the sacrifice is at every turn and in every detail, as even a cursory study of the Brahmanas and Upanishads ought to show us, mystically symbolic. The theory that there was nothing in the sacrifice except a propitiation of Nature-gods for the gaining of worldly prosperity and of Paradise, is a misunderstanding by a later humanity which had already become profoundly affected by an intellectual and practical bent of mind, practical even in its religion and even in its own mysticism and symbolism, and therefore could no longer enter into the ancient spirit. Not only the actual religious worship but also the social institutions of the time were penetrated through and through with the symbolic spirit. Take the hymn of the Rig Veda which is supposed to be a marriage hymn for the union of a human couple and was certainly used as such in the later Vedic ages. Yet the whole sense of the hymn turns about the successive marriages of Suryā, daughter of the Sun, with different gods and the human marriage is quite a subordinate matter overshadowed and governed entirely by the divine and mystic figure and is spoken of in the terms of that figure. Mark, however, that the divine marriage here is not, as it would be in later ancient poetry, a decorative image or poetical ornamentation used to set off and embellish the human union; on the contrary, the human is an inferior figure and image of the divine. The distinction marks off the entire contrast between that more ancient mentality and our modern regard upon things. This symbolism influenced for a long time Indian ideas of marriage and is even now conventionally remembered though no longer understood or effective.

We may note also in passing that the Indian ideal of the relation between man and woman has always been governed by the symbolism of the relation between the Purusha and Prakriti (in the Veda Nri and Gna), the male and female divine Principles in the universe. Even, there is to some degree a practical correlation between the position of the female sex and this idea. In the earlier Vedic times when the female principle stood on a sort of equality with the male in the symbolic cult, though with a certain predominance for the latter, woman was as much the mate as the adjunct of man; in later times when the Prakriti has become subject in idea to the Purusha, the woman also depends entirely on the man, exists only for him and has hardly even a separate spiritual existence. In the Tantrik Shakta religion which puts the female principle highest, there is an attempt which could not get itself translated into social practice,—even as this Tantrik cult could never entirely shake off the subjugation of the Vedantic idea,—to elevate woman and make her an object of profound respect and even of worship.

Or let us take, for this example will serve us best, the Vedic institution of the fourfold order, *caturvarṇa*, miscalled the system of the four castes, — for caste is a conventional, *varṇa* a symbolic and typal institution. We are told that the institution of the four orders of society was the result of an economic evolution complicated by political causes. Very possibly;[3] but the important point is that it was not so regarded and could not be so regarded by the men of that age. For while we are satisfied when we have found the practical and material causes of a social phenomenon and do not care to look farther, they cared little or only subordinately for its material factors and looked always first and foremost for its symbolic, religious or psychological significance. This appears in the Purushasukta of the Veda, where the four orders are described as having sprung from the body of the creative Deity, from his head, arms, thighs and feet. To us this is merely a poetical image and its sense is that the Brahmins were the men of knowledge, the Kshatriyas the men of power, the Vaishyas the producers and support of society, the Shudras its servants. As if that were all, as if the men of those days would have so profound a reverence for mere poetical figures like this of the body of Brahma or that other of the marriages of Suryā, would have built upon them elaborate systems of ritual and sacred ceremony, enduring institutions, great demarcations of social type and ethical discipline. We read always our own mentality into that of these ancient forefathers and it is therefore that we can find in them nothing but imaginative barbarians. To us poetry is a revel of intellect and fancy, imagination a plaything and caterer for our amusement, our entertainer, the nautch-girl of the mind. But to the men of old the poet was a seer, a revealer of hidden truths, imagination no dancing courtesan but a priestess in God's house commissioned not to spin fictions but to image difficult and hidden truths; even the metaphor or simile in the Vedic style is used with a serious purpose and expected to convey a reality, not to suggest a pleasing artifice of thought. The image was to these seers a revelative symbol of the unrevealed and it was used because it could hint luminously to the mind what the precise intellectual word, apt only for logical or practical thought or to express the physical and the superficial, could not

[3] It is at least doubtful. The Brahmin class at first seem to have exercised all sorts of economic functions and not to have confined themselves to those of the priesthood. [Sri Aurobindo's note]

at all hope to manifest. To them this symbol of the Creator's body was more than an image, it expressed a divine reality. Human society was for them an attempt to express in life the cosmic Purusha who has expressed himself otherwise in the material and the supraphysical universe. Man and the cosmos are both of them symbols and expressions of the same hidden Reality.

From this symbolic attitude came the tendency to make everything in society a sacrament, religious and sacrosanct, but as yet with a large and vigorous freedom in all its forms,—a freedom which we do not find in the rigidity of 'savage' communities because these have already passed out of the symbolic into the conventional stage though on a curve of degeneration instead of a curve of growth. The spiritual idea governs all; the symbolic religious forms which support it are fixed in principle; the social forms are lax, free and capable of infinite development. One thing, however, begins to progress towards a firm fixity and this is the psychological type. Thus we have first the symbolic idea of the four orders, expressing—to employ an abstractly figurative language which the Vedic thinkers would not have used nor perhaps understood, but which helps best our modern understanding—the Divine as knowledge in man, the Divine as power, the Divine as production, enjoyment and mutuality, the Divine as service, obedience and work. These divisions answer to four cosmic principles, the Wisdom that conceives the order and principle of things, the Power that sanctions, upholds and enforces it, the Harmony that creates the arrangement of its parts, the Work that carries out what the rest direct. Next, out of this idea there developed a firm but not yet rigid social order based primarily upon temperament and psychic type[4] with a corresponding ethical discipline and secondarily upon the social and economic function.[5] But the function was determined by its suitability to the type and its helpfulness to the discipline; it was not the primary or sole factor. The first, the symbolic stage of this evolution is predominantly religious and spiritual; the other elements, psychological, ethical, economic, physical are there but subordinated to the spiritual and religious idea. The

4 *guṇa* [Sri Aurobindo's note]
5 *karma* [Sri Aurobindo's note]

second stage, which we may call the typal, is predominantly psychological and ethical; all else, even the spiritual and religious, is subordinate to the psychological idea and to the ethical ideal which expresses it. Religion becomes then a mystic sanction for the ethical motive and discipline, Dharma; that becomes its chief social utility, and for the rest it takes a more and more otherworldly turn. The idea of the direct expression of the divine Being or cosmic Principle in man ceases to dominate or to be the leader and in the forefront; it recedes, stands in the background and finally disappears from the practice and in the end even from the theory of life.

This typal stage creates the great social ideals which remain impressed upon the human mind even when the stage itself is passed. The principal active contribution it leaves behind when it is dead is the idea of social honour; the honour of the Brahmin which resides in purity, in piety, in a high reverence for the things of the mind and spirit and a disinterested possession and exclusive pursuit of learning and knowledge; the honour of the Kshatriya which lives in courage, chivalry, strength, a certain proud self-restraint and self-mastery, nobility of character and the obligations of that nobility; the honour of the Vaishya which maintains itself by rectitude of dealing, mercantile fidelity, sound production, order, liberality and philanthropy; the honour of the Shudra which gives itself in obedience, subordination, faithful service, a disinterested attachment. But these more and more cease to have a living root in the clear psychological idea or to spring naturally out of the inner life of the man; they become a convention, though the most noble of conventions. In the end they remain more as a tradition in the thought and on the lips than a reality of the life.

For the typal passes naturally into the conventional stage. The conventional stage of human society is born when the external supports, the outward expressions of the spirit or the ideal become more important than the ideal, the body or even the clothes more important than the person. Thus in the evolution of caste, the outward supports of the ethical fourfold order, — birth, economic function, religious ritual and sacrament, family custom, — each began to exaggerate enormously its proportions and its importance in the scheme. At first, birth does not seem to have been of the first importance in the social order, for faculty and capacity prevailed; but afterwards, as the type fixed itself, its maintenance by education and tradition became necessary and education and tradition naturally fixed themselves in a hereditary groove. Thus the son of a Brahmin came always to be looked upon conventionally as a Brahmin; birth and profession were together the double bond of the hereditary convention at the time when it was most firm and faithful to its own character. This rigidity once established, the maintenance of the ethical type passed from the first place to a secondary or even a quite tertiary importance. Once the very basis of the system, it came now to be a not indispensable crown or pendent tassel, insisted upon indeed by the thinker and the ideal code-maker but not by the actual rule of society or its practice. Once ceasing to be indispensable, it came inevitably to be dispensed with except as an ornamental fiction. Finally, even the economic basis began to disintegrate; birth, family custom and remnants, deformations, new accretions of meaningless or fanciful religious sign and ritual, the very scarecrow and caricature of the old profound symbolism, became the riveting links of the system of caste in the iron age of the old society. In the full economic period of caste the priest and the Pundit masquerade under the name of the Brahmin, the aristocrat and feudal baron under the name of the Kshatriya, the trader and money-getter under the name of the Vaishya, the half-fed labourer and economic serf under the name of the Shudra. When the economic basis also breaks down, then the unclean and diseased decrepitude of the old system has begun; it has become a name, a shell, a sham and must either be dissolved in the crucible of an individualist period of society or else fatally affect with weakness and falsehood the system of life that clings to it. That in visible fact is the last and present state of the caste system in India.

The tendency of the conventional age of society is to fix, to arrange firmly, to formalise, to erect a system of rigid grades and hierarchies, to stereotype religion, to bind education and training to a traditional and unchangeable form, to subject thought to infallible authorities, to cast a stamp of finality on what seems to it the finished life of man. The conventional period of society has its golden age when the spirit and thought that inspired its forms are confined but yet living, not yet altogether walled in, not yet stifled to death and petrified by the growing hardness of the structure in which they are cased. That golden age is often very beautiful and attractive to the distant view of posterity by its precise order, symmetry, fine social architecture, the admirable subordination of its parts to a general and noble plan. Thus at one time the modern litterateur, artist or thinker looked back often with admiration and with something like longing to the mediaeval age of Europe; he forgot in its distant appearance of poetry, nobility, spirituality the much folly, ignorance, iniquity, cruelty and oppression of those harsh ages, the suffering and revolt that simmered below these fine surfaces, the misery and squalor that was hidden behind that splendid façade. So too the Hindu orthodox idealist looks back to a perfectly regulated society devoutly obedient to the wise yoke of the Shastra, and that is his golden age, — a nobler one than the European in which the apparent gold was mostly hard burnished copper with a thin gold-leaf covering it, but still of an alloyed metal, not the true Satya Yuga. In these conventional periods of society there is much indeed that is really fine and sound and helpful to human progress, but still they are its copper age and not the true golden; they are the age when the Truth we strive to arrive at is not realised, not accomplished,[6] but the exiguity of it eked out or its full appearance imitated by an artistic form, and what we have of the reality has begun to fossilise and is doomed to be lost in a hard mass of rule and order and convention.

For always the form prevails and the spirit recedes and diminishes. It attempts indeed to return, to revive the form, to modify it, anyhow to survive and even to make the form survive; but the time-tendency is too strong. This is visible in the history of religion; the efforts of the saints and religious reformers become progressively more scattered, brief and superficial in their actual effects, however strong and vital the impulse. We see this recession in the growing darkness and weakness of India in her last millennium; the constant effort of the most powerful spiritual personalities kept the soul of the people alive but failed to resuscitate the ancient free force and truth and vigour or permanently revivify a conventionalised and stagnating society; in a generation or two the iron grip of that conventionalism has

[6] The Indian names of the golden age are Satya, the Age of the Truth, and Krita, the Age when the law of the Truth is accomplished. [Sri Aurobindo's note]

always fallen on the new movement and annexed the names of its founders. We see it in Europe in the repeated moral tragedy of ecclesiasticism and Catholic monasticism. Then there arrives a period when the gulf between the convention and the truth becomes intolerable and the men of intellectual power arise, the great 'swallowers of formulas', who, rejecting robustly or fiercely or with the calm light of reason symbol and type and convention, strike at the walls of the prison-house and seek by the individual reason, moral sense or emotional desire the Truth that society has lost or buried in its whited sepulchres. It is then that the individualistic age of religion and thought and society is created; the Age of Protestantism has begun, the Age of Reason, the Age of Revolt, Progress, Freedom. A partial and external freedom, still betrayed by the conventional age that preceded it into the idea that the Truth can be found in outsides, dreaming vainly that perfection can be determined by machinery, but still a necessary passage to the subjective period of humanity through which man has to circle back towards the recovery of his deeper self and a new upward line or a new revolving cycle of civilisation.

The Advent and Progress of the Spiritual Age

If a subjective age, the last sector of a social cycle, is to find its outlet and fruition in a spiritualised society and the emergence of mankind on a higher evolutionary level, it is not enough that certain ideas favourable to that turn of human life should take hold of the general mind of the race, permeate the ordinary motives of its thought, art, ethics, political ideals, social effort, or even get well into its inner way of thinking and feeling. It is not enough even that the idea of the kingdom of God on earth, a reign of spirituality, freedom and unity, a real and inner equality and harmony — and not merely an outward and mechanical equalisation and association — should become definitely an ideal of life; it is not enough that this ideal should be actively held as possible, desirable, to be sought and striven after, it is not enough even that it should come forward as a governing preoccupation of the human mind. That would evidently be a very great step forward, — considering what the ideals of mankind now are, an enormous step. It would be the necessary beginning, the indispensable mental environment for a living renovation of human society in a higher type. But by itself it might only bring about a half-hearted or else a strong but only partially and temporarily successful attempt to bring something of the manifest spirit into human life and its institutions. That is all that mankind has ever attempted on this line in the past. It has never attempted to work out thoroughly even that little, except in the limits of a religious order or a peculiar community, and even there with such serious defects and under such drastic limitations as to make the experiment nugatory and without any bearing on human life. If we do not get beyond the mere holding of the ideal and its general influence in human life, this little is

The last chapter of *The Human Cycle*, published in the *Arya* in July 1918.

all that mankind will attempt in the future. More is needed; a general spiritual awakening and aspiration in mankind is indeed the large necessary motive-power, but the effective power must be something greater. There must be a dynamic re-creating of individual manhood in the spiritual type.

For the way that humanity deals with an ideal is to be satisfied with it as an aspiration which is for the most part left only as an aspiration, accepted only as a partial influence. The ideal is not allowed to mould the whole life, but only more or less to colour it; it is often used even as a cover and a plea for things that are diametrically opposed to its real spirit. Institutions are created which are supposed, but too lightly supposed to embody that spirit and the fact that the ideal is held, the fact that men live under its institutions is treated as sufficient. The holding of an ideal becomes almost an excuse for not living according to the ideal; the existence of its institutions is sufficient to abrogate the need of insisting on the spirit that made the institutions. But spirituality is in its very nature a thing subjective and not mechanical; it is nothing if it is not lived inwardly and if the outward life does not flow out of this inward living. Symbols, types, conventions, ideas are not sufficient. A spiritual symbol is only a meaningless ticket, unless the thing symbolised is realised in the spirit. A spiritual convention may lose or expel its spirit and become a falsehood. A spiritual type may be a temporary mould into which spiritual living may flow, but it is also a limitation and may become a prison in which it fossilises and perishes. A spiritual idea is a power, but only when it is both inwardly and outwardly creative. Here we have to enlarge and to deepen the pragmatic principle that truth is what we create, and in this sense first, that it is what we create within us, in other words, what we become. Undoubtedly, spiritual truth exists eternally beyond independent of us in the heavens of the spirit; but it is of no avail for humanity here, it does not become truth of earth, truth of life until it is lived. The divine perfection is always there above us; but for man to become divine in consciousness and act and to live inwardly and outwardly the divine life is what is meant by spirituality; all lesser meanings given to the word are inadequate fumblings or impostures.

This, as the subjective religions recognise, can only be brought about by an individual change in each human life.

The collective soul is there only as a great half-subconscient source of the individual existence; if it is to take on a definite psychological form or a new kind of collective life, that can only come by the shaping growth of its individuals. As will be the spirit and life of the individuals constituting it, so will be the realised spirit of the collectivity and the true power of its life. A society that lives not by its men but by its institutions, is not a collective soul, but a machine; its life becomes a mechanical product and ceases to be a living growth. Therefore the coming of a spiritual age must be preceded by the appearance of an increasing number of individuals who are no longer satisfied with the normal intellectual, vital and physical existence of man, but perceive that a greater evolution is the real goal of humanity and attempt to effect it in themselves, to lead others to it and to make it the recognised goal of the race. In proportion as they succeed and to the degree to which they carry this evolution, the yet unrealised potentiality which they represent will become an actual possibility of the future.

A great access of spirituality in the past has ordinarily had for its result the coming of a new religion of a special type and its endeavour to impose itself upon mankind as a new universal order. This, however, was always not only a premature but a wrong crystallisation which prevented rather than helped any deep and serious achievement. The aim of a spiritual age of mankind must indeed be one with the essential aim of subjective religions, a new birth, a new consciousness, an upward evolution of the human being, a descent of the spirit into our members, a spiritual reorganisation of our life; but if it limits itself by the old familiar apparatus and the imperfect means of a religious movement, it is likely to register another failure. A religious movement brings usually a wave of spiritual excitement and aspiration that communicates itself to a large number of individuals and there is as a result a temporary uplifting and an effective formation, partly spiritual, partly ethical, partly dogmatic in its nature. But the wave, after a generation or two or at most a few generations, begins to subside; the formation remains. If there has been a very powerful movement with a great spiritual personality as its source, it may leave behind a central influence and an inner discipline which may well be the starting-point of fresh waves; but these will be constantly less powerful and enduring in proportion as the movement gets farther and farther away from its source. For meanwhile in order to bind together the faithful and at the same time to mark them off from the unregenerated outer world, there will have grown up a religious order, a Church, a hierarchy, a fixed and unprogressive type of ethical living, a set of crystallised dogmas, ostentatious ceremonials, sanctified superstitions, an elaborate machinery for the salvation of mankind. As a result spirituality is increasingly subordinated to intellectual belief, to outward forms of conduct and to external ritual, the higher to the lower motives, the one thing essential to aids and instruments and accidents. The first spontaneous and potent attempt to convert the whole life into spiritual living yields up its place to a set system of belief and ethics touched by spiritual emotion; but finally even that saving element is dominated by the outward machinery, the sheltering structure becomes a tomb. The Church takes the place of the spirit and a formal subscription to its creed, rituals and order is the thing universally demanded; spiritual living is only practised by the few within the limits prescribed by their fixed creed and order. The majority neglect even that narrow effort and are contented to replace by a careful or negligent piety the call to a deeper life. In the end it is found that the spirit in the religion has become a thin stream choked by sands; at the most brief occasional floodings of its dry bed of conventions still prevent it from becoming a memory in the dead chapters of Time.

The ambition of a particular religious belief and form to universalise and impose itself is contrary to the variety of human nature and to at least one essential character of the Spirit. For the nature of the Spirit is a spacious inner freedom and a large unity into which each man must be allowed to grow according to his own nature. Again — and this is yet another source of inevitable failure — the usual tendency of these credal religions is to turn towards an afterworld and to make the regeneration of the earthly life a secondary motive; this tendency grows in proportion as the original hope of a present universal regeneration of mankind becomes more and more feeble. Therefore while many new spiritual waves with their strong special motives and disciplines must necessarily be the forerunners of a spiritual age, yet their claims must be subordinated in the general mind of the race and of its spiritual leaders to the recognition that all motives and disciplines are valid and yet none entirely valid since they are means and not the one thing to be done. The one thing essential must take precedence, the conversion of the whole life of the human being to the lead of the Spirit. The ascent of man into heaven is not the key, but rather his ascent here into the spirit and the descent also of the Spirit into his normal humanity and the transformation of this earthly nature. For that and not some post mortem salvation is the real new birth for which humanity waits as the crowning movement of its long obscure and painful course.

Therefore the individuals who will most help the future of humanity in the new age will be those who will recognise a spiritual evolution as the destiny and therefore the great need of the human being. Even as the animal man has been largely converted into a mentalised and at the top a highly mentalised humanity, so too now or in the future an evolution or conversion — it does not greatly matter which figure we use or what theory we adopt to support it — of the present type of humanity into a spiritualised humanity is the need of the race and surely the intention of Nature; that evolution or conversion will be their ideal and endeavour. They will be comparatively indifferent to particular belief and form and leave men to resort to the beliefs and forms to which they are naturally drawn. They will only hold as essential the faith in this spiritual conversion, the attempt to live it out and whatever knowledge — the form of opinion into which it is thrown does not so much matter — can be converted into this living. They will especially not make the mistake of thinking that this change can be effected by machinery and outward institutions; they will know and never forget that it has to be lived out by each man inwardly or it can never be made a reality for the kind. They will adopt in its heart of meaning the inward view of the East which bids man seek the secret of his destiny and salvation within; but also they will accept, though with a different turn given to it, the importance which the West rightly attaches to life and to the making the best we know and can attain the general rule of all life. They will not make society a shadowy background to a few luminous spiritual figures or a rigidly fenced and earth-bound root for the growth of a comparatively rare and sterile flower of ascetic spirituality. They will not accept the theory that the many must necessarily remain for ever on the lower ranges of life and only a few climb into the free air and the light, but will start from the standpoint of the great spirits who have striven to regenerate the life of the earth and held that faith in spite of all previous failure. Failures must be originally numerous in everything great and difficult, but the time comes when the experience of past failures can be profitably used and the gate that so long resisted opens. In this as in all great human aspirations and endeavours, an *a priori* declaration of impossibility is a sign of ignorance and weakness, and the motto of the aspirant's endeavour must be the *solvitur ambulando* of the discoverer. For by the doing the difficulty will be solved. A true beginning has to be made; the rest is a work for Time in its sudden achievements or its long patient labour.

The thing to be done is as large as human life, and therefore the individuals who lead the way will take all human life for their province. These pioneers will consider nothing as alien to them, nothing as outside their scope. For every part of human life has to be taken up by the spiritual,—not only the intellectual, the aesthetic, the ethical, but the dynamic, the vital, the physical; therefore for none of these things or the activities that spring from them will they have contempt or aversion, however they may insist on a change of the spirit and a transmutation of the form. In each power of our nature they will seek for its own proper means of conversion; knowing that the Divine is concealed in all, they will hold that all can be made the spirit's means of self-finding and all can be converted into its instruments of divine living. And they will see that the great necessity is the conversion of the normal into the spiritual mind and the opening of that mind again into its own higher reaches and more and more integral movement. For before the decisive change can be made, the stumbling intellectual reason has to be converted into the precise and luminous intuitive, until that again can rise into higher ranges to overmind and supermind or gnosis. The uncertain and stumbling mental will has to rise towards the sure intuitive and into a higher divine and gnostic will, the psychic sweetness, fire and light of the soul behind the heart, *hṛdaye guhāyām*, has to alchemise our crude emotions and the hard egoisms and clamant desires of our vital nature. All our other members have to pass through a similar conversion under the compelling force and light from above. The leaders of the spiritual march will start from and use the knowledge and the means that past effort has developed in this direction, but they will not take them as they are without any deep necessary change or limit themselves by what is now known or cleave only to fixed and stereotyped systems or given groupings of results, but will follow the method of the Spirit in Nature. A constant rediscovery and new formulation and larger synthesis in the mind, a mighty remoulding in its deeper parts because of a greater enlarging Truth not discovered or not well fixed before, is that Spirit's way with our past achievement when he moves to the greatnesses of the future.

This endeavour will be a supreme and difficult labour even for the individual, but much more for the race. It may well be that, once started, it may not advance rapidly even to its first decisive stage; it may be that it will take long centuries of effort to come into some kind of permanent birth. But that is not altogether inevitable, for the principle of such changes in Nature seems to be a long obscure preparation followed by a swift gathering up and precipitation of the elements into the new birth, a rapid conversion, a transformation that in its luminous moment figures like a miracle. Even when the first decisive change is reached, it is certain that all humanity will not be able to rise to that level. There cannot fail to be a division into those who are able to live on the spiritual level and those who are only able to live in the light that descends from it into the mental level. And below these too there might still be a great mass influenced from above but not yet ready for the light. But even that would be a transformation and a beginning far beyond anything yet attained. This hierarchy would not mean as in our present vital living an egoistic domination of the undeveloped by the more developed, but a guidance of the younger by the elder brothers of the race and a constant working to lift them up to a greater spiritual level and wider horizons. And for the leaders too this ascent to the first spiritual levels would not be the end of the divine march, a culmination that left nothing more to be achieved on earth. For there would be still yet higher levels within the supramental realm, as the old Vedic poets knew when they spoke of the spiritual life as a constant ascent,

brahmāṇas tvā śatakrato
ud vaṁśam iva yemire;
yat sānoḥ sānum āruhat,
bhūri aspaṣṭa kartvam,—

'The priests of the word climb thee like a ladder, O hundred-powered. As one ascends from peak to peak, there is made clear the much that has still to be done.'

But once the foundation has been secured, the rest develops by a progressive self-unfolding and the soul is sure of its way. As again it is phrased by the ancient Vedic singers,—

abhyavasthāḥ pra jāyante,
pra vavrer vavriś ciketa;
upasthe mātur vi caṣṭe,—

'State is born upon state; covering after covering becomes conscious of knowledge; in the lap of the Mother the soul sees.'

This at least is the highest hope, the possible destiny that opens out before the human view, and it is a possibility which the progress of the human mind seems on the way to redevelop. If the light that is being born increases, if the number of individuals who seek to realise the possibility in themselves and in the world grows large and they get nearer the right way, then the Spirit who is here in man, now a concealed divinity, a developing light and power, will descend more fully as the Avatar of a yet unseen and unguessed Godhead from above into the soul of mankind and into the great individualities in whom the light and power are the strongest. There will then be fulfilled the change that will prepare the transition of human life from its present limits into those larger and purer horizons; the earthly evolution will have taken its grand impetus upward and accomplished the revealing step in a divine progression of which the birth of thinking and aspiring man from the animal nature was only an obscure preparation and a far-off promise.

Part Four
The Evolution of Consciousness

Our evolution in the Ignorance with its chequered joy and pain of self-discovery and world-discovery, its half-fulfilments, its constant finding and missing, is only our first state. It must lead inevitably towards an evolution in the Knowledge, a self-finding and self-unfolding of the Spirit, a self-revelation of the Divinity in things in that true power of itself in Nature which is to us still a Supernature.

The Life Divine

PART FOUR consists of chapters from two of Sri Aurobindo's philosophical works, *The Life Divine* and *The Problem of Rebirth*, three posthumously published essays, two letters and a note dealing with philosophical topics.

• *The Teaching of Sri Aurobindo* introduces the main themes of his philosophical thought: the one Reality or Brahman behind the manifested world; the cosmic Ignorance and the Inconscience, in which the powers of the Reality are involved; and the spiritual evolution, culminating in the emergence of the supermind and the transformation of earth-nature.

• *The Human Aspiration* for God, Light, Freedom and Immortality cannot be suppressed either by Spirit-denying materialism or world-denying asceticism.

• Of these *Two Negations*, the first, *The Materialist Denial* fails to see that the material world is real 'precisely because it exists in consciousness', while the second, *The Refusal of the Ascetic*, affirms the essence of the Absolute but not its manifestation.

• The Absolute manifests its multifarious possibilities by means of evolution. In *Man and the Evolution*, Sri Aurobindo shows that this is a dual process: an outward physical development and 'an invisible process of soul evolution'. (In this chapter Sri Aurobindo presents at some length positions not his own before refuting them. Readers unfamiliar with this rhetorical strategy should be on their guard against taking the positions so presented as Sri Aurobindo's.)

• The imperfect human being cannot be the end of the evolutionary process. In *Man and the Supermind, The Involved and Evolving Godhead* and *The Evolution of Consciousness*, Sri Aurobindo shows that the evolution of a higher power of consciousness, the supermind, is inevitable.

• *Rebirth* is an essential part of the process of soul evolution, and together with the law of *karma* provides a simple and symmetrical explanation of things.

• *Rebirth and Karma* go together: successive embodiment is meaningless without a dynamic law of action; that law can have no origin or justification without the possibility of rebirth.

• Something of the personality persists in the soul's new birth, but as Sri Aurobindo explains in *Rebirth and Personality*, what survives is not the surface ego-personality but the inner psychic entity.

• The truth of things can to some extent be given form in a mental system, but mind cannot by its unaided power arrive at spiritual truth. Metaphysical philosophy can at best prepare the way for inner experience, which opens the way to spiritual knowledge.

The Teaching of Sri Aurobindo

THE TEACHING of Sri Aurobindo starts from that of the ancient sages of India that behind the appearances of the universe there is the Reality of a Being and Consciousness, a Self of all things, one and eternal. All beings are united in that One Self and Spirit but divided by a certain separativity of consciousness, an ignorance of their true Self and Reality in the mind, life and body. It is possible by a certain psychological discipline to remove this veil of separative consciousness and become aware of the true Self, the Divinity within us and all.

Sri Aurobindo's teaching states that this One Being and Consciousness is involved here in Matter. Evolution is the method by which it liberates itself; consciousness appears in what seems to be inconscient, and once having appeared is self-impelled to grow higher and higher and at the same time to enlarge and develop towards a greater and greater perfection. Life is the first step of this release of consciousness; mind is the second; but the evolution does not finish with mind, it awaits a release into something greater, a consciousness which is spiritual and supramental. The next step of the evolution must be towards the development of Supermind and Spirit as the dominant power in the conscious being. For only then will the involved Divinity in things release itself entirely and it become possible for life to manifest perfection.

But while the former steps in evolution were taken by Nature without a conscious will in the plant and animal life, in man Nature becomes able to evolve by a conscious will in the instrument. It is not, however, by the mental will in man that

This note was written by Sri Aurobindo for inclusion in an information brochure entitled 'The Teaching and the Asram of Sri Aurobindo' (1934). The brochure was published anonymously: this explains his use of the third person to refer to himself.

this can be wholly done, for the mind goes only to a certain point and after that can only move in a circle. A conversion has to be made, a turning of the consciousness by which mind has to change into the higher principle. This method is to be found through the ancient psychological discipline and practice of Yoga. In the past, it has been attempted by a drawing away from the world and a disappearance into the height of the Self or Spirit. Sri Aurobindo teaches that a descent of the higher principle is possible which will not merely release the spiritual Self out of the world, but release it in the world, replace the mind's ignorance or its very limited knowledge by a supramental Truth-Consciousness which will be a sufficient instrument of the inner Self and make it possible for the human being to find himself dynamically as well as inwardly and grow out of his still animal humanity into a diviner race. The psychological discipline of Yoga can be used to that end by opening all the parts of the being to a conversion or transformation through the descent and working of the higher still concealed supramental principle.

This, however, cannot be done at once or in a short time or by any rapid or miraculous transformation. Many steps have to be taken by the seeker before the supramental descent is possible. Man lives mostly in his surface mind, life and body, but there is an inner being within him with greater possibilities to which he has to awake — for it is only a very restricted influence from it that he receives now and that pushes him to a constant pursuit of a greater beauty, harmony, power and knowledge. The first process of Yoga is therefore to open the ranges of this inner being and to live from there outward, governing his outward life by an inner light and force. In doing so he discovers in himself his true soul which is not this outer mixture of mental, vital and physical elements but something of the Reality behind them, a spark from the one Divine Fire. He has to learn to live in his soul and purify and orientate by its drive towards the Truth the rest of the nature. There can follow afterwards an opening upward and descent of a higher principle of the Being. But even then it is not at once the full supramental Light and Force. For there are several ranges of consciousness between the ordinary human mind and the supramental Truth-Consciousness. These intervening ranges have to be opened up and their power brought down into the mind, life and body. Only afterwards can the full power of the

Truth-Consciousness work in the nature. The process of this self-discipline or Sadhana is therefore long and difficult, but even a little of it is so much gained because it makes the ultimate release and perfection more possible.

There are many things belonging to older systems that are necessary on the way — an opening of the mind to a greater wideness and to the sense of the Self and the Infinite, an emergence into what has been called the cosmic consciousness, mastery over the desires and passions; an outward asceticism is not essential, but the conquest of desire and attachment and a control over the body and its needs, greeds and instincts are indispensable. There is a combination of the principles of the old systems, the way of knowledge through the mind's discernment between Reality and the appearance, the heart's way of devotion, love and surrender and the way of works turning the will away from motives of self-interest to the Truth and the service of a greater Reality than the ego. For the whole being has to be trained so that it can respond and be transformed when it is possible for that greater Light and Force to work in the nature.

In this discipline, the inspiration of the Master, and in the difficult stages his control and his presence are indispensable — for it would be impossible otherwise to go through it without much stumbling and error which would prevent all chance of success. The Master is one who has risen to a higher consciousness and being and he is often regarded as its manifestation or representative. He not only helps by his teaching and still more by his influence and example but by a power to communicate his own experience to others.

This is Sri Aurobindo's teaching and method of practice. It is not his object to develop any one religion or to amalgamate the older religions or to found any new religion — for any of these things would lead away from his central purpose. The one aim of his Yoga is an inner self-development by which each one who follows it can in time discover the One Self in all and evolve a higher consciousness than the mental, a spiritual and supramental consciousness which will transform and divinise human nature.

The Human Aspiration

She follows to the goal of those that are passing on beyond, she is the first in the eternal succession of the dawns that are coming, — Usha widens bringing out that which lives, awakening someone who was dead. . . . What is her scope when she harmonises with the dawns that shone out before and those that now must shine? She desires the ancient mornings and fulfils their light; projecting forwards her illumination she enters into communion with the rest that are to come. *Kutsa Angirasa — Rig Veda.*[1]

Threefold are those supreme births of this divine force that is in the world, they are true, they are desirable; he moves there wide-overt within the Infinite and shines pure, luminous and fulfilling. . . . That which is immortal in mortals and possessed of the truth, is a god and established inwardly as an energy working out in our divine powers. . . . Become high-uplifted, O Strength, pierce all veils, manifest in us the things of the Godhead.

Vamadeva — Rig Veda.[2]

THE EARLIEST preoccupation of man in his awakened thoughts and, as it seems, his inevitable and ultimate preoccupation, — for it survives the longest periods of scepticism and returns after every banishment, — is also the highest which his thought can envisage. It manifests itself in the divination of Godhead, the impulse towards perfection, the search after pure Truth and unmixed Bliss, the sense of a secret immortality. The ancient dawns of human knowledge have left us their witness to this constant aspiration; today we

The first chapter of *The Life Divine*, published in the first issue of the *Arya*, 15 August 1914. No changes were made to this chapter when *The Life Divine* was revised for publication as a book in 1939–40. Each chapter of *The Life Divine* begins with one or more translations from Vedic or Vedantic texts. Other translations and citations occur throughout the chapter. The references were provided by the author.

1 I. 113. 8, 10.
2 IV. 1. 7; IV. 2. 1; IV. 4. 5.

see a humanity satiated but not satisfied by victorious analysis of the externalities of Nature preparing to return to its primeval longings. The earliest formula of Wisdom promises to be its last, — God, Light, Freedom, Immortality.

These persistent ideals of the race are at once the contradiction of its normal experience and the affirmation of higher and deeper experiences which are abnormal to humanity and only to be attained, in their organised entirety, by a revolutionary individual effort or an evolutionary general progression. To know, possess and be the divine being in an animal and egoistic consciousness, to convert our twilit or obscure physical mentality into the plenary supramental illumination, to build peace and a self-existent bliss where there is only a stress of transitory satisfactions besieged by physical pain and emotional suffering, to establish an infinite freedom in a world which presents itself as a group of mechanical necessities, to discover and realise the immortal life in a body subjected to death and constant mutation, — this is offered to us as the manifestation of God in Matter and the goal of Nature in her terrestrial evolution. To the ordinary material intellect which takes its present organisation of consciousness for the limit of its possibilities, the direct contradiction of the unrealised ideals with the realised fact is a final argument against their validity. But if we take a more deliberate view of the world's workings, that direct opposition appears rather as part of Nature's profoundest method and the seal of her completest sanction.

For all problems of existence are essentially problems of harmony. They arise from the perception of an unsolved discord and the instinct of an undiscovered agreement or unity. To rest content with an unsolved discord is possible for the practical and more animal part of man, but impossible for his fully awakened mind, and usually even his practical parts only escape from the general necessity either by shutting out the problem or by accepting a rough, utilitarian and unillumined compromise. For essentially, all Nature seeks a harmony, life and matter in their own sphere as much as mind in the arrangement of its perceptions. The greater the apparent disorder of the materials offered or the apparent disparateness, even to irreconcilable opposition, of the elements that have to be utilised, the stronger is the spur, and it drives towards a more subtle and puissant order than can normally be the result of a less difficult endeavour. The accordance of active Life with a material of form in which the condition of activity itself seems to be inertia, is one problem of opposites that Nature has solved and seeks always to solve better with greater complexities; for its perfect solution would be the material immortality of a fully organised mind-supporting animal body. The accordance of conscious mind and conscious will with a form and a life in themselves not overtly self-conscious and capable at best of a mechanical or sub-conscious will is another problem of opposites in which she has produced astonishing results and aims always at higher marvels; for there her ultimate miracle would be an animal consciousness no longer seeking but possessed of Truth and Light, with the practical omnipotence which would result from the possession of a direct and perfected knowledge. Not only, then, is the upward impulse of man towards the accordance of yet higher opposites rational in itself, but it is the only logical completion of a rule and an effort that seem to be a fundamental method of Nature and the very sense of her universal strivings.

We speak of the evolution of Life in Matter, the evolution of Mind in Matter; but evolution is a word which merely states the phenomenon without explaining it. For there seems to be no reason why Life should evolve out of material elements or Mind out of living form, unless we accept the Vedantic solution that Life is already involved in Matter and Mind in Life because in essence Matter is a form of veiled Life, Life a form of veiled Consciousness. And then there seems to be little objection to a farther step in the series and the admission that mental consciousness may itself be only a form and a veil of higher states which are beyond Mind. In that case, the unconquerable impulse of man towards God, Light, Bliss, Freedom, Immortality presents itself in its right place in the chain as simply the imperative impulse by which Nature is seeking to evolve beyond Mind, and appears to be as natural, true and just as the impulse towards Life which she has planted in certain forms of Matter or the impulse towards Mind which she has planted in certain forms of Life. As there, so here, the impulse exists more or less obscurely in her different vessels with an ever-ascending series in the power of its will-to-be; as there, so here, it is gradually evolving and bound fully to evolve the necessary organs and faculties. As the impulse towards Mind ranges from the more sensitive reactions of Life in the metal and the plant up to its full organisation in man, so in man himself there is the same ascending series, the preparation, if nothing more, of a higher and divine life. The animal is a living laboratory in which Nature has, it is said, worked out man. Man himself may well be a thinking and living laboratory in whom and with whose conscious co-operation she wills to work out the superman, the god. Or shall we not say, rather, to manifest God? For if evolution is the progressive manifestation by Nature of that which slept or worked in her, involved, it is also the overt realisation of that which she secretly is. We cannot, then, bid her pause at a given stage of her evolution, nor have we the right to condemn with the religionist as perverse and presumptuous or with the rationalist as a disease or hallucination any intention she may evince or effort she may make to go beyond. If it be true that Spirit is involved in Matter and apparent Nature is secret God, then the manifestation of the divine in himself and the realisation of God within and without are the highest and most legitimate aim possible to man upon earth.

Thus the eternal paradox and eternal truth of a divine life in an animal body, an immortal aspiration or reality inhabiting a mortal tenement, a single and universal consciousness representing itself in limited minds and divided egos, a transcendent, indefinable, timeless and spaceless Being who alone renders time and space and cosmos possible, and in all these the higher truth realisable by the lower term, justify themselves to the deliberate reason as well as to the persistent instinct or intuition of mankind. Attempts are sometimes made to have done finally with questionings which have so often been declared insoluble by logical thought and to persuade men to limit their mental activities to the practical and immediate problems of their material existence in the universe; but such evasions are never permanent in their effect. Mankind returns from them with a more vehement impulse of inquiry or a more violent hunger for an immediate solution. By that hunger mysticism profits and new religions arise to replace the old that have been destroyed or stripped of significance by a scepticism which itself could not satisfy because, although its business was inquiry, it was unwilling sufficiently to inquire. The attempt to deny or stifle a truth because it is yet obscure in its outward workings and too often represented by obscurantist superstition or a crude faith, is itself a kind of obscurantism. The will to escape from a cosmic necessity because it is arduous, difficult to justify by immediate tangible results, slow in regulating its operations, must turn out eventually to have been no acceptance of the truth of Nature but a revolt against the secret, mightier will of the great Mother. It is better and more rational to accept what she will not allow us as a race to reject and lift it from the sphere of blind instinct, obscure intuition and random aspiration into the light of reason and an instructed and consciously self-guiding will. And if there is any higher light of illumined intuition or self-revealing truth which is now in man either obstructed and inoperative or works with intermittent glancings as if from behind a veil or with occasional displays as of the northern lights in our material skies, then there also we need not fear to aspire. For it is likely that such is the next higher state of consciousness of which Mind is only a form and veil, and through the splendours of that light may lie the path of our progressive self-enlargement into whatever highest state is humanity's ultimate resting-place.

The Two Negations

The Materialist Denial

He energised conscious-force (in the austerity of thought) and came to the knowledge that Matter is the Brahman. For from Matter all existences are born; born, by Matter they increase and enter into Matter in their passing hence. Then he went to Varuna, his father, and said, 'Lord, teach me of the Brahman.' But he said to him: 'Energise (again) the conscious-energy in thee; for the Energy is Brahman.' *Taittiriya Upanishad.*[1]

THE AFFIRMATION of a divine life upon earth and an immortal sense in mortal existence can have no base unless we recognise not only eternal Spirit as the inhabitant of this bodily mansion, the wearer of this mutable robe, but accept Matter of which it is made, as a fit and noble material out of which He weaves constantly His garbs, builds recurrently the unending series of His mansions.

Nor is this, even, enough to guard us against a recoil from life in the body unless, with the Upanishads, perceiving behind their appearances the identity in essence of these two extreme terms of existence, we are able to say in the very language of those ancient writings, 'Matter also is Brahman', and to give its full value to the vigorous figure by which the physical universe is described as the external body of the Divine Being. Nor, — so far divided apparently are these two extreme terms, — is that identification convincing to the rational intellect if we refuse to recognise a series of ascending terms (Life, Mind, Supermind and the grades that link Mind to Supermind) between Spirit and Matter. Otherwise the two must appear as irreconcilable opponents

The second chapter of *The Life Divine*, published in the *Arya* in 1914.

[1] III. 1, 2.

bound together in an unhappy wedlock and their divorce the one reasonable solution. To identify them, to represent each in the terms of the other, becomes an artificial creation of Thought opposed to the logic of facts and possible only by an irrational mysticism.

If we assert only pure Spirit and a mechanical unintelligent substance or energy, calling one God or Soul and the other Nature, the inevitable end will be that we shall either deny God or else turn from Nature. For both Thought and Life, a choice then becomes imperative. Thought comes to deny the one as an illusion of the imagination or the other as an illusion of the senses; Life comes to fix on the immaterial and flee from itself in a disgust or a self-forgetting ecstasy, or else to deny its own immortality and take its orientation away from God and towards the animal. Purusha and Prakriti, the passively luminous Soul of the Sankhyas and their mechanically active Energy, have nothing in common, not even their opposite modes of inertia; their antinomies can only be resolved by the cessation of the inertly driven Activity into the immutable Repose upon which it has been casting in vain the sterile procession of its images. Shankara's wordless, inactive Self and his Maya of many names and forms are equally disparate and irreconcilable entities; their rigid antagonism can terminate only by the dissolution of the multitudinous illusion into the sole Truth of an eternal Silence.

The materialist has an easier field; it is possible for him by denying Spirit to arrive at a more readily convincing simplicity of statement, a real Monism, the Monism of Matter or else of Force. But in this rigidity of statement it is impossible for him to persist permanently. He too ends by positing an unknowable as inert, as remote from the known universe as the passive Purusha or the silent Atman. It serves no purpose but to put off by a vague concession the inexorable demands of Thought or to stand as an excuse for refusing to extend the limits of inquiry.

Therefore, in these barren contradictions the human mind cannot rest satisfied. It must seek always a complete affirmation; it can find it only by a luminous reconciliation. To reach that reconciliation it must traverse the degrees which our inner consciousness imposes on us and, whether by objective method of analysis applied to Life and Mind as to Matter or by subjective synthesis and illumination, arrive at the repose of the ultimate unity without denying the energy of the expressive multiplicity. Only in such a complete and catholic affirmation can all the multiform and apparently contradictory data of existence be harmonised and the manifold conflicting forces which govern our thought and life discover the central Truth which they are here to symbolise and variously fulfil. Then only can our Thought, having attained a true centre, ceasing to wander in circles, work like the Brahman of the Upanishad, fixed and stable even in its play and its world-wide coursing, and our life, knowing its aim, serve it with a serene and settled joy and light as well as with a rhythmically discursive energy.

But when that rhythm has once been disturbed, it is necessary and helpful that man should test separately, in their extreme assertion, each of the two great opposites. It is the mind's natural way of returning more perfectly to the affirmation it has lost. On the road it may attempt to rest in the intervening degrees, reducing all things into the terms of an original Life-Energy or of sensation or of Ideas; but these exclusive solutions have always an air of unreality. They may satisfy for a time the logical reason which deals only with pure ideas, but they cannot satisfy the mind's sense of actuality. For the mind knows that there is something behind itself which is not the Idea; it knows, on the other hand, that there is something within itself which is more than the vital Breath. Either Spirit or Matter can give it for a time some sense of ultimate reality; not so any of the principles that intervene. It must, therefore, go to the two extremes before it can return fruitfully upon the whole. For by its very nature, served by a sense that can perceive with distinctness only the parts of existence and by a speech that, also, can achieve distinctness only when it carefully divides and limits, the intellect is driven, having before it this multiplicity of elemental principles, to seek unity by reducing all ruthlessly to the terms of one. It attempts practically, in order to assert this one, to get rid of the others. To perceive the real source of their identity without this exclusive process, it must either have overleaped itself or must have completed the circuit only to find that all equally reduce themselves to That which escapes definition or description and is yet not only real but attainable. By whatever road we may travel, That is always the end at which we arrive and we can only escape it by refusing to complete the journey.

It is therefore of good augury that after many experiments and verbal solutions we should now find ourselves standing to-day in the presence of the two that have alone borne for long the most rigorous tests of experience, the two extremes, and that at the end of the experience both should have come to a result which the universal instinct in mankind, that veiled judge, sentinel and representative of the universal Spirit of Truth, refuses to accept as right or as satisfying. In Europe and in India, respectively, the negation of the materialist and the refusal of the ascetic have sought to assert themselves as the sole truth and to dominate the conception of Life. In India, if the result has been a great heaping up of the treasures of the Spirit, — or of some of them, — it has also been a great bankruptcy of Life; in Europe, the fullness of riches and the triumphant mastery of this world's powers and possessions have progressed towards an equal bankruptcy in the things of the Spirit. Nor has the intellect, which sought the solution of all problems in the one term of Matter, found satisfaction in the answer that it has received.

Therefore the time grows ripe and the tendency of the world moves towards a new and comprehensive affirmation in thought and in inner and outer experience and to its corollary, a new and rich self-fulfilment in an integral human existence for the individual and for the race.

From the difference in the relations of Spirit and Matter to the Unknowable which they both represent, there arises also a difference of effectiveness in the material and the spiritual negations. The denial of the materialist although more insistent and immediately successful, more facile in its appeal to the generality of mankind, is yet less enduring, less effective finally than the absorbing and perilous refusal of the ascetic. For it carries within itself its own cure. Its most powerful element is the Agnosticism which, admitting the Unknowable behind all manifestation, extends the limits of the unknowable until it comprehends all that is merely unknown. Its premise is that the physical senses are our sole means of Knowledge and that Reason, therefore, even in its most extended and vigorous flights, cannot escape beyond their domain; it must deal always and solely with the facts which they provide or suggest; and the suggestions themselves must always be kept tied to their origins; we cannot go beyond, we cannot use them as a bridge leading us into a domain where more powerful and less limited faculties come into play and another kind of inquiry has to be instituted.

A premise so arbitrary pronounces on itself its own sentence of insufficiency. It can only be maintained by ignoring or explaining away all that vast field of evidence and experience which contradicts it, denying or disparaging noble and useful faculties, active consciously or obscurely or at worst latent in all human beings, and refusing to investigate supraphysical phenomena except as manifested in relation to matter and its movements and conceived as a subordinate activity of material forces. As soon as we begin to investigate the operations of mind and of supermind, in themselves and without the prejudgment that is determined from the beginning to see in them only a subordinate term of Matter, we come into contact with a mass of phenomena which escape entirely from the rigid hold, the limiting dogmatism of the materialist formula. And the moment we recognise, as our enlarging experience compels us to recognise, that there are in the universe knowable realities beyond the range of the senses and in man powers and faculties which determine rather than are determined by the material organs through which they hold themselves in touch with the world of the senses, — that outer shell of our true and complete existence, — the premise of materialistic Agnosticism disappears. We are ready for a large statement and an ever-developing inquiry.

But, first, it is well that we should recognise the enormous, the indispensable utility of the very brief period of rationalistic Materialism through which humanity has been passing. For that vast field of evidence and experience which now begins to reopen its gates to us, can only be safely entered when the intellect has been severely trained to a clear austerity; seized on by unripe minds, it lends itself to the most perilous distortions and misleading imaginations and actually in the past encrusted a real nucleus of truth with such an accretion of perverting superstitions and irrationalising dogmas that all advance in true knowledge was rendered impossible. It became necessary for a time to make a clean sweep at once of the truth and its disguise in order that the road might be clear for a new departure and a surer advance. The rationalistic tendency of Materialism has done mankind this great service.

For the faculties that transcend the senses, by the very fact of their being immeshed in Matter, missioned to work in a physical body, put in harness to draw one car along with the emotional desires and nervous impulses, are exposed to a mixed functioning in which they are in danger of illuminating confusion rather than clarifying truth. Especially is this mixed functioning dangerous when men with unchastened minds and unpurified sensibilities attempt to rise into the higher domains of spiritual experience. In what regions of unsubstantial cloud and semi-brilliant fog or a murk visited by flashes which blind more than they enlighten, do they not lose themselves by that rash and premature adventure! An adventure necessary indeed in the way in which Nature chooses to effect her advance, — for she amuses herself as she works, — but still, for the Reason, rash and premature.

It is necessary, therefore, that advancing Knowledge should base herself on a clear, pure and disciplined intellect. It is necessary, too, that she should correct her errors sometimes by a return to the restraint of sensible fact, the concrete realities of the physical world. The touch of Earth is always reinvigorating to the son of Earth, even when he seeks a supraphysical Knowledge. It may even be said that the supraphysical can only be really mastered in its fullness — to its heights we can always reach — when we keep our feet firmly on the physical. 'Earth is His footing',[2] says the Upanishad whenever it images the Self that manifests in the universe. And it is certainly the fact that the wider we extend and the surer we make our knowledge of the physical world, the wider and surer becomes our foundation for the higher knowledge, even for the highest, even for the Brahmavidya.

In emerging, therefore, out of the materialistic period of human Knowledge we must be careful that we do not rashly condemn what we are leaving or throw away even one tittle of its gains, before we can summon perceptions and powers that are well grasped and secure, to occupy their place. Rather we shall observe with respect and wonder the work that Atheism has done for the Divine and admire the services that Agnosticism has rendered in preparing the illimitable increase of knowledge. In our world error is continually the handmaid and pathfinder of Truth;

[2] '*Padbhyām pṛthivī.*' — *Mundaka Upanishad.* II. 1. 4.
'*Pṛthivī pājasyam.*' — *Brihadaranyaka Upanishad.* I. 1. 1.

for error is really a half-truth that stumbles because of its limitations; often it is Truth that wears a disguise in order to arrive unobserved near to its goal. Well, if it could always be, as it has been in the great period we are leaving, the faithful handmaid, severe, conscientious, clean-handed, luminous within its limits, a half-truth and not a reckless and presumptuous aberration.

A certain kind of Agnosticism is the final truth of all knowledge. For when we come to the end of whatever path, the universe appears as only a symbol or an appearance of an unknowable Reality which translates itself here into different systems of values, physical values, vital and sensational values, intellectual, ideal and spiritual values. The more That becomes real to us, the more it is seen to be always beyond defining thought and beyond formulating expression. 'Mind attains not there, nor speech.'[3] And yet as it is possible to exaggerate, with the Illusionists, the unreality of the appearance, so it is possible to exaggerate the unknowableness of the Unknowable. When we speak of It as unknowable, we mean, really, that It escapes the grasp of our thought and speech, instruments which proceed always by the sense of difference and express by the way of definition; but if not knowable by thought, It is attainable by a supreme effort of consciousness. There is even a kind of Knowledge which is one with Identity and by which, in a sense, It can be known. Certainly, that Knowledge cannot be reproduced successfully in the terms of thought and speech, but when we have attained to it, the result is a revaluation of That in the symbols of our cosmic consciousness, not only in one but in all the ranges of symbols, which results in a revolution of our internal being and, through the internal, of our external life. Moreover, there is also a kind of Knowledge through which That does reveal itself by all these names and forms of phenomenal existence which to the ordinary intelligence only conceal It. It is this higher but not highest process of Knowledge to which we can attain by passing the limits of the materialistic formula and scrutinising Life, Mind and Supermind in the phenomena that are characteristic of them and not merely in those subordinate movements by which they link themselves to Matter.

[3] *Kena Upanishad*. I. 3.

The Unknown is not the Unknowable;[4] it need not remain the unknown for us, unless we choose ignorance or persist in our first limitations. For to all things that are not unknowable, all things in the universe, there correspond in that universe faculties which can take cognisance of them, and in man, the microcosm, these faculties are always existent and at a certain stage capable of development. We may choose not to develop them; where they are partially developed, we may discourage and impose on them a kind of atrophy. But, fundamentally, all possible knowledge is knowledge within the power of humanity. And since in man there is the inalienable impulse of Nature towards self-realisation, no struggle of the intellect to limit the action of our capacities within a determined area can for ever prevail. When we have proved Matter and realised its secret capacities, the very knowledge which has found its convenience in that temporary limitation must cry to us, like the Vedic Restrainers, 'Forth now and push forward also in other fields.'[5]

If modern Materialism were simply an unintelligent acquiescence in the material life, the advance might be indefinitely delayed. But since its very soul is the search for Knowledge, it will be unable to cry a halt; as it reaches the barriers of sense-knowledge and of the reasoning from sense-knowledge, its very rush will carry it beyond and the rapidity and sureness with which it has embraced the visible universe is only an earnest of the energy and success which we may hope to see repeated in the conquest of what lies beyond, once the stride is taken that crosses the barrier. We see already that advance in its obscure beginnings.

Not only in the one final conception, but in the great line of its general results Knowledge, by whatever path it is followed, tends to become one. Nothing can be more remarkable and suggestive than the extent to which modern Science confirms in the domain of Matter the conceptions and even the very formulae of language which were arrived at, by a very different method, in the Vedanta, — the original Vedanta, not of the schools of metaphysical philosophy, but of the Upanishads. And these, on

[4] Other is That than the Known; also it is above the Unknown. — *Kena Upanishad.* 1. 3.

[5] *Rig Veda.* I. 4. 5.

the other hand, often reveal their full significance, their richer contents only when they are viewed in the new light shed by the discoveries of modern Science, — for instance, that Vedantic expression which describes things in the Cosmos as one seed arranged by the universal Energy in multitudinous forms.[6] Significant, especially, is the drive of Science towards a Monism which is consistent with multiplicity, towards the Vedic idea of the one essence with its many becomings. Even if the dualistic appearance of Matter and Force be insisted on, it does not really stand in the way of this Monism. For it will be evident that essential Matter is a thing non-existent to the senses and only, like the Pradhana of the Sankhyas, a conceptual form of substance; and in fact the point is increasingly reached where only an arbitrary distinction in thought divides form of substance from form of energy.

Matter expresses itself eventually as a formulation of some unknown Force. Life, too, that yet unfathomed mystery, begins to reveal itself as an obscure energy of sensibility imprisoned in its material formulation; and when the dividing ignorance is cured which gives us the sense of a gulf between Life and Matter, it is difficult to suppose that Mind, Life and Matter will be found to be anything else than one Energy triply formulated, the triple world of the Vedic seers. Nor will the conception then be able to endure of a brute material Force as the mother of Mind. The Energy that creates the world can be nothing else than a Will, and Will is only consciousness applying itself to a work and a result.

What is that work and result, if not a self-involution of Consciousness in form and a self-evolution out of form so as to actualise some mighty possibility in the universe which it has created? And what is its will in Man if not a will to unending Life, to unbounded Knowledge, to unfettered Power? Science itself begins to dream of the physical conquest of death, expresses an insatiable thirst for knowledge, is working out something like a terrestrial omnipotence for humanity. Space and Time are contracting to the vanishing-point in its works, and it strives in a hundred ways to make man the master of circumstance and so lighten the fetters of causality. The idea of limit, of the

[6] *Swetaswatara Upanishad.* VI. 12.

impossible begins to grow a little shadowy and it appears instead that whatever man constantly wills, he must in the end be able to do; for the consciousness in the race eventually finds the means. It is not in the individual that this omnipotence expresses itself, but the collective Will of mankind that works out with the individual as a means. And yet when we look more deeply, it is not any conscious Will of the collectivity, but a superconscious Might that uses the individual as a centre and means, the collectivity as a condition and field. What is this but the God in man, the infinite Identity, the multitudinous Unity, the Omniscient, the Omnipotent, who having made man in His own image, with the ego as a centre of working, with the race, the collective Narayana,[7] the *viśvamānava*[8] as the mould and circumscription, seeks to express in them some image of the unity, omniscience, omnipotence which are the self-conception of the Divine? 'That which is immortal in mortals is a God and established inwardly as an energy working out in our divine powers.'[9] It is this vast cosmic impulse which the modern world, without quite knowing its own aim, yet serves in all its activities and labours subconsciously to fulfil.

But there is always a limit and an encumbrance, — the limit of the material field in the Knowledge, the encumbrance of the material machinery in the Power. But here also the latest trend is highly significant of a freer future. As the outposts of scientific Knowledge come more and more to be set on the borders that divide the material from the immaterial, so also the highest achievements of practical Science are those which tend to simplify and reduce to the vanishing-point the machinery by which the greatest effects are produced. Wireless telegraphy is Nature's exterior sign and pretext for a new orientation. The sensible physical means for the intermediate transmission of the physical force is removed; it is only preserved at the points of impulsion and reception. Eventually even these must disappear; for when the laws and forces of the supraphysical are studied with the right starting-point, the means will infallibly be found for Mind

7 A name of Vishnu, who, as the God in man, lives constantly associated in a dual unity with Nara, the human being. [Sri Aurobindo's note]

8 The universal man. [Sri Aurobindo's note]

9 *Rig Veda*. IV. 2. 1.

directly to seize on the physical energy and speed it accurately upon its errand. There, once we bring ourselves to recognise it, lie the gates that open upon the enormous vistas of the future.

Yet even if we had full knowledge and control of the worlds immediately above Matter, there would still be a limitation and still a beyond. The last knot of our bondage is at that point where the external draws into oneness with the internal, the machinery of ego itself becomes subtilised to the vanishing-point and the law of our action is at last unity embracing and possessing multiplicity and no longer, as now, multiplicity struggling towards some figure of unity. There is the central throne of cosmic Knowledge looking out on her widest dominion; there the empire of oneself with the empire of one's world;[10] there the life[11] in the eternally consummate Being and the realisation of His divine nature[12] in our human existence.

[10] *Svārājya* and *Sāmrājya*, the double aim proposed to itself by the positive Yoga of the ancients. [Sri Aurobindo's note]

[11] *Sālokya-mukti*, liberation by conscious existence in one world of being with the Divine. [Sri Aurobindo's note]

[12] *Sādharmya-mukti*, liberation by assumption of the Divine Nature. [Sri Aurobindo's note]

The Two Negations

The Refusal of the Ascetic

All this is the Brahman; this Self is the Brahman and the Self is fourfold. Beyond relation, featureless, unthinkable, in which all is still.

Mandukya Upanishad.[1]

AND STILL there is a beyond.

For on the other side of the cosmic consciousness there is, attainable to us, a consciousness yet more transcendent, — transcendent not only of the ego, but of the Cosmos itself, — against which the universe seems to stand out like a petty picture against an immeasurable background. That supports the universal activity, — or perhaps only tolerates it; It embraces Life with Its vastness, — or else rejects it from Its infinitude.

If the materialist is justified from his point of view in insisting on Matter as reality, the relative world as the sole thing of which we can in some sort be sure and the Beyond as wholly unknowable, if not indeed non-existent, a dream of the mind, an abstraction of Thought divorcing itself from reality, so also is the Sannyasin, enamoured of that Beyond, justified from his point of view in insisting on pure Spirit as the reality, the one thing free from change, birth, death, and the relative as a creation of the mind and the senses, a dream, an abstraction in the contrary sense of Mentality withdrawing from the pure and eternal Knowledge.

The third chapter of *The Life Divine*, published in the *Arya* in 1914.

1 Verses 2, 7.

What justification, of logic or of experience, can be asserted in support of the one extreme which cannot be met by an equally cogent logic and an equally valid experience at the other end? The world of Matter is affirmed by the experience of the physical senses which, because they are themselves unable to perceive anything immaterial or not organised as gross Matter, would persuade us that the suprasensible is the unreal. This vulgar or rustic error of our corporeal organs does not gain in validity by being promoted into the domain of philosophical reasoning. Obviously, their pretension is unfounded. Even in the world of Matter there are existences of which the physical senses are incapable of taking cognisance. Yet the denial of the suprasensible as necessarily an illusion or a hallucination depends on this constant sensuous association of the real with the materially perceptible, which is itself a hallucination. Assuming throughout what it seeks to establish, it has the vice of the argument in a circle and can have no validity for an impartial reasoning.

Not only are there physical realities which are suprasensible, but, if evidence and experience are at all a test of truth, there are also senses which are supraphysical[2] and can not only take cognisance of the realities of the material world without the aid of the corporeal sense-organs, but can bring us into contact with other realities, supraphysical and belonging to another world — included, that is to say, in an organisation of conscious experiences that are dependent on some other principle than the gross Matter of which our suns and earths seem to be made.

Constantly asserted by human experience and belief since the origins of thought, this truth, now that the necessity of an exclusive preoccupation with the secrets of the material world no longer exists, begins to be justified by new-born forms of scientific research. The increasing evidences, of which only the most obvious and outward are established under the name of telepathy with its cognate phenomena, cannot long be resisted except by minds shut up in the brilliant shell of the past, by intellects limited in spite of their acuteness through the limitation of their field of experience and inquiry, or by those who confuse enlightenment and reason with the faithful

[2] *Sūkṣma indriya*, subtle organs, existing in the subtle body (*sūkṣma deha*), and the means of subtle vision and experience (*sūkṣma dṛṣṭi*). [Sri Aurobindo's note]

repetition of the formulas left to us from a bygone century and the jealous conservation of dead or dying intellectual dogmas.

It is true that the glimpse of supraphysical realities acquired by methodical research has been imperfect and is yet ill-affirmed; for the methods used are still crude and defective. But these rediscovered subtle senses have at least been found to be true witnesses to physical facts beyond the range of the corporeal organs. There is no justification, then, for scouting them as false witnesses when they testify to supraphysical facts beyond the domain of the material organisation of consciousness. Like all evidence, like the evidence of the physical senses themselves, their testimony has to be controlled, scrutinised and arranged by the reason, rightly translated and rightly related, and their field, laws and processes determined. But the truth of great ranges of experience whose objects exist in a more subtle substance and are perceived by more subtle instruments than those of gross physical Matter, claims in the end the same validity as the truth of the material universe. The worlds beyond exist: they have their universal rhythm, their grand lines and formations, their self-existent laws and mighty energies, their just and luminous means of knowledge. And here on our physical existence and in our physical body they exercise their influences; here also they organise their means of manifestation and commission their messengers and their witnesses.

But the worlds are only frames for our experience, the senses only instruments of experience and conveniences. Consciousness is the great underlying fact, the universal witness for whom the world is a field, the senses instruments. To that witness the worlds and their objects appeal for their reality and for the one world or the many, for the physical equally with the supraphysical we have no other evidence that they exist. It has been argued that this is no relation peculiar to the constitution of humanity and its outlook upon an objective world, but the very nature of existence itself; all phenomenal existence consists of an observing consciousness and an active objectivity, and the Action cannot proceed without the Witness because the universe exists only in or for the consciousness that observes and has no independent reality. It has been argued in reply that the material universe enjoys an eternal self-existence; it was here before life and mind made their appearance: it will survive after they have disappeared and no longer trouble with their transient strivings and limited thoughts the eternal and inconscient rhythm of the suns. The difference, so metaphysical in appearance, is yet of the utmost practical import, for it determines the whole outlook of man upon life, the goal that he shall assign for his efforts and the field in which he shall circumscribe his energies. For it raises the question of the reality of cosmic existence and, more important still, the question of the value of human life.

If we push the materialist conclusion far enough, we arrive at an insignificance and unreality in the life of the individual and the race which leaves us, logically, the option between either a feverish effort of the individual to snatch what he may from a transient existence, to 'live his life', as it is said, or a dispassionate and objectless service of the race and the individual, knowing well that the latter is a transient fiction of the nervous mentality and the former only a little more long-lived collective form of the same regular nervous spasm of Matter. We work or enjoy under the impulsion of a material energy which deceives us with the brief delusion of life or with the nobler delusion of an ethical aim and a mental consummation. Materialism like spiritual Monism arrives at a Maya that is and yet is not, — is, for it is present and compelling, is not, for it is phenomenal and transitory in its works. At the other end, if we stress too much the unreality of the objective world, we arrive by a different road at similar but still more trenchant conclusions, — the fictitious character of the individual ego, the unreality and purposelessness of human existence, the return into the Non-Being or the relationless Absolute as the sole rational escape from the meaningless tangle of phenomenal life.

And yet the question cannot be solved by logic arguing on the data of our ordinary physical existence; for in those data there is always a hiatus of experience which renders all argument inconclusive. We have, normally, neither any definitive experience of a cosmic mind or supermind not bound up with the life of the individual body, nor, on the other hand, any firm limit of experience which would justify us in supposing that our subjective self really depends upon the physical frame and can neither survive it nor enlarge itself beyond the individual body. Only by an extension of the field of our consciousness or an unhoped-for increase in our instruments of knowledge can the ancient quarrel be decided.

The extension of our consciousness, to be satisfying, must necessarily be an inner enlargement from the individual into the cosmic existence. For the Witness, if he exists, is not the individual embodied mind born in the world, but that cosmic Consciousness embracing the universe and appearing as an immanent Intelligence in all its works to which either world subsists eternally and really as Its own active existence or else from which it is born and into which it disappears by an act of knowledge or by an act of conscious power. Not organised mind, but that which, calm and eternal, broods equally in the living earth and the living human body and to which mind and senses are dispensable instruments, is the Witness of cosmic existence and its Lord.

The possibility of a cosmic consciousness in humanity is coming slowly to be admitted in modern Psychology, like the possibility of more elastic instruments of knowledge, although still classified, even when its value and power are admitted, as a hallucination. In the psychology of the East it has always been recognised as a reality and the aim of our subjective progress. The essence of the passage over to this goal is the exceeding of the limits imposed on us by the ego-sense and at least a partaking, at most an identification with the self-knowledge which broods secret in all life and in all that seems to us inanimate.

Entering into that Consciousness, we may continue to dwell, like It, upon universal existence. Then we become aware — for all our terms of consciousness and even our sensational experience begin to change, — of Matter as one existence and of bodies as its formations in which the one existence separates itself physically in the single body from itself in all others and again by physical means establishes communication between these multitudinous points of its being. Mind we experience similarly, and Life also, as the same existence one in its multiplicity, separating and reuniting itself in each domain by means appropriate to that movement. And, if we choose, we can proceed farther and, after passing through many linking stages, become aware of a supermind whose universal operation is the key to all lesser activities. Nor do we become merely conscious of this cosmic existence, but likewise conscious in it, receiving it in sensation, but also entering into it in awareness. In it we live as we lived before in the ego-sense, active, more and more in contact, even unified more and more with other minds, other lives, other bodies than the organism we call ourselves, producing effects not only on our own moral and mental being and on the subjective being of others, but even on the physical world and its events by means nearer to the divine than those possible to our egoistic capacity.

Real then to the man who has had contact with it or lives in it, is this cosmic consciousness, with a greater than the physical reality; real in itself, real in its effects and works. And as it is thus real to the world which is its own total expression, so is the world real to it; but not as an independent existence. For in that higher and less hampered experience we perceive that consciousness and being are not different from each other, but all being is a supreme consciousness, all consciousness is self-existence, eternal in itself, real in its works and neither a dream nor an evolution. The world is real precisely because it exists only in consciousness; for it is a Conscious Energy one with Being that creates it. It is the existence of material form in its own right apart from the self-illumined energy which assumes the form, that would be a contradiction of the truth of things, a phantasmagoria, a nightmare, an impossible falsehood.

But this conscious Being which is the truth of the infinite supermind, is more than the universe and lives independently in Its own inexpressible infinity as well as in the cosmic harmonies. World lives by That; That does not live by the world. And as we can enter into the cosmic consciousness and be one with all cosmic existence, so we can enter into the world-transcending consciousness and become superior to all cosmic existence. And then arises the question which first occurred to us, whether this transcendence is necessarily also a rejection. What relation has this universe to the Beyond?

For at the gates of the Transcendent stands that mere and perfect Spirit described in the Upanishads, luminous, pure, sustaining the world but inactive in it, without sinews of energy, without flaw of duality, without scar of division, unique, identical, free from all appearance of relation and of multiplicity, —the pure Self of the Adwaitins[3], the inactive Brahmin, the transcendent Silence. And the mind when it passes those gates

[3] The Vedantic Monists. [Sri Aurobindo's note]

suddenly, without intermediate transitions, receives a sense of the unreality of the world and the sole reality of the Silence which is one of the most powerful and convincing experiences of which the human mind is capable. Here, in the perception of this pure Self or of the Non-Being behind it, we have the starting-point for a second negation, — parallel at the other pole to the materialistic, but more complete, more final, more perilous in its effects on the individuals or collectivities that hear its potent call to the wilderness, — the refusal of the ascetic.

It is this revolt of Spirit against Matter that for two thousand years, since Buddhism disturbed the balance of the old Aryan world, has dominated increasingly the Indian mind. Not that the sense of the cosmic illusion is the whole of Indian thought; there are other philosophical statements, other religious aspirations. Nor has some attempt at an adjustment between the two terms been wanting even from the most extreme philosophies. But all have lived in the shadow of the great Refusal and the final end of life for all is the garb of the ascetic. The general conception of existence has been permeated with the Buddhistic theory of the chain of Karma and with the consequent antinomy of bondage and liberation, bondage by birth, liberation by cessation from birth. Therefore all voices are joined in one great consensus that not in this world of the dualities can there be our kingdom of heaven, but beyond, whether in the joys of the eternal Vrindavan[4] or the high beatitude of Brahmaloka[5], beyond all manifestations in some ineffable Nirvana[6] or where all separate experience is lost in the featureless unity of the indefinable Existence. And through many centuries a great army of shining witnesses, saints and teachers, names sacred to Indian memory and dominant in Indian imagination, have borne always the same witness and swelled always the same lofty and distant appeal, — renunciation the sole path of knowledge, acceptation of physical life the act of the ignorant, cessation from birth the right use of human birth, the call of the Spirit, the recoil from Matter.

[4] *Goloka*, the Vaishnava heaven of eternal Beauty and Bliss. [Sri Aurobindo's note]

[5] The highest state of pure existence, consciousness and beatitude attainable by the soul without complete extinction in the Indefinable. [Sri Aurobindo's note]

[6] Extinction, not necessarily of all being, but of being as we know it; extinction of ego, desire and egoistic action and mentality. [Sri Aurobindo's note]

For an age out of sympathy with the ascetic spirit — and throughout all the rest of the world the hour of the Anchorite may seem to have passed or to be passing — it is easy to attribute this great trend to the failing of vital energy in an ancient race tired out by its burden, its once vast share in the common advance, exhausted by its many-sided contribution to the sum of human effort and human knowledge. But we have seen that it corresponds to a truth of existence, a state of conscious realisation which stands at the very summit of our possibility. In practice also the ascetic spirit is an indispensable element in human perfection and even its separate affirmation cannot be avoided so long as the race has not at the other end liberated its intellect and its vital habits from subjection to an always insistent animalism.

We seek indeed a larger and completer affirmation. We perceive that in the Indian ascetic ideal the great Vedantic formula, 'One without a second', has not been read sufficiently in the light of that other formula equally imperative, 'All this is the Brahman'. The passionate aspiration of man upward to the Divine has not been sufficiently related to the descending movement of the Divine leaning downward to embrace eternally Its manifestation. Its meaning in Matter has not been so well understood as Its truth in the Spirit. The Reality which the Sannyasin seeks has been grasped in its full height, but not, as by the ancient Vedantins, in its full extent and comprehensiveness. But in our completer affirmation we must not minimise the part of the pure spiritual impulse. As we have seen how greatly Materialism has served the ends of the Divine, so we must acknowledge the still greater service rendered by Asceticism to Life. We shall preserve the truths of material Science and its real utilities in the final harmony, even if many or even if all of its existing forms have to be broken or left aside. An even greater scruple of right preservation must guide us in our dealing with the legacy, however actually diminished or depreciated, of the Aryan past.

Man and the Evolution

The one Godhead secret in all beings, all-pervading, the inner Self of all, presiding over all action, witness, conscious knower and absolute... the One in control over the many who are passive to Nature, fashions one seed in many ways. *Swetaswatara Upanishad.*[1]

The Godhead moves in this Field modifying each web of things separately in many ways.... One, he presides over all wombs and natures; himself the womb of all, he is that which brings to ripeness the nature of the being and he gives to all who have to be matured their result of development and appoints all qualities to their workings. *Swetaswatara Upanishad.*[2]

He fashions one form of things in many ways. *Katha Upanishad.*[3]

Who has perceived this truth occult, that the Child gives being to the Mothers by the workings of his nature? An offspring from the lap of many Waters, he comes forth from them a seer possessed of his whole law of nature. Manifested, he grows in the lap of their crookednesses and becomes high, beautiful and glorious. *Rig Veda.*[4]

From the non-being to true being, from the darkness to the Light, from death to Immortality. *Brihadaranyaka Upanishad.*[5]

A SPIRITUAL evolution, an evolution of consciousness in Matter in a constant developing self-formation till the form can reveal the indwelling Spirit, is then the keynote, the central significant motive of the terrestrial existence. This significance is concealed at the outset by the involution of the Spirit, the Divine Reality, in a dense material Inconscience; a veil of Inconscience, a veil of insensibility of Matter hides the

Chapter 23 of Book Two, Part II of *The Life Divine*, written in 1940 for inclusion in the revised first edition of the book.

1 VI. 11, 12.
2 V. 3-5.
3 II. 2. 12.
4 I. 95. 4, 5.
5 I. 3. 28.

universal Consciousness-Force which works within it, so that the Energy, which is the first form the Force of creation assumes in the physical universe, appears to be itself inconscient and yet does the works of a vast occult Intelligence. The obscure mysterious creatrix ends indeed by delivering the secret consciousness out of its thick and tenebrous prison; but she delivers it slowly, little by little, in minute infinitesimal drops, in thin jets, in small vibrant concretions of energy and substance, of life, of mind, as if that were all she could get out through the crass obstacle, the dull reluctant medium of an inconscient stuff of existence. At first she houses herself in forms of Matter which appear to be altogether unconscious, then struggles towards mentality in the guise of living Matter and attains to it imperfectly in the conscious animal. This consciousness is at first rudimentary, mostly a half subconscious or just conscious instinct; it develops slowly till in more organised forms of living Matter it reaches its climax of intelligence and exceeds itself in Man, the thinking animal who develops into the reasoning mental being but carries along with him even at his highest elevation the mould of original animality, the dead weight of subconscience of body, the downward pull of gravitation towards the original Inertia and Nescience, the control of an inconscient material Nature over his conscious evolution, its power for limitation, its law of difficult development, its immense force for retardation and frustration. This control by the original Inconscience over the consciousness emerging from it takes the general shape of a mentality struggling towards knowledge but itself, in what seems to be its fundamental nature, an Ignorance. Thus hampered and burdened, mental man has still to evolve out of himself the fully conscious being, a divine manhood or a spiritual and supramental supermanhood which shall be the next product of the evolution. That transition will mark the passage from the evolution in the Ignorance to a greater evolution in the Knowledge, founded and proceeding in the light of the Superconscient and no longer in the darkness of the Ignorance and Inconscience.

This terrestrial evolutionary working of Nature from Matter to Mind and beyond it has a double process: there is an outward visible process of physical evolution with birth as its machinery, — for each evolved form of body housing its own evolved power of consciousness is maintained and kept in continuity by heredity; there is, at the same time, an invisible process of soul evolution with rebirth into ascending grades of form and consciousness as its machinery. The first by itself would mean only a cosmic evolution; for the individual would be a quickly perishing instrument, and the race, a more abiding collective formulation, would be the real step in the progressive manifestation of the cosmic Inhabitant, the universal Spirit: rebirth is an indispensable condition for any long duration and evolution of the individual being in the earth-existence. Each grade of cosmic manifestation, each type of form that can house the indwelling Spirit, is turned by rebirth into a means for the individual soul, the psychic entity, to manifest more and more of its concealed consciousness; each life becomes a step in a victory over Matter by a greater progression of consciousness in it which shall make eventually Matter itself a means for the full manifestation of the Spirit.

But this account of the process and meaning of the terrestrial creation is at every point exposed to challenge in the mind of man himself, because the evolution is still half-way on its journey, is still in the Ignorance, is still seeking in the mind a half-evolved humanity for its own purpose and significance. It is possible to challenge the theory of evolution on the ground that it is insufficiently founded and that it is superfluous as an explanation of the process of terrestrial existence. It is open to doubt, even if evolution is granted, whether man has the capacity to develop into a higher evolutionary being. It is open also to doubt whether the evolution is likely to go any farther than it has gone already or whether a supramental evolution, the appearance of a consummated Truth-Consciousness, a being of Knowledge, is at all probable in the fundamental Ignorance of the earthly Nature. Another construction neither teleological nor evolutionary can be put on the workings of the Spirit in the manifestation here, and it may be as well before proceeding farther to formulate succinctly the line of thinking which makes such a construction possible.

Admitting that the creation is a manifestation of the Timeless Eternal in a Time Eternity, admitting that there are the seven grades of Consciousness and that the material Inconscience has been laid down as a basis for the reascent of the Spirit, admitting that rebirth is a fact, a part of the terrestrial order, still a spiritual evolution of the individual being is not an inevitable consequence of any of these admissions or even of all of them together. It is possible to take another view of the spiritual significance and the inner process of terrestrial existence. If each thing created is a form of the manifest Divine Existence, each is divine in itself by the spiritual presence within it, whatever its appearance, its figure or character in Nature. In each form of manifestation the Divine takes the delight of existence and there is no need of change or progress within it. Whatever ordered display or hierarchy of actualised possibilities is necessitated by the nature of the Infinite Being, is sufficiently provided for by the numberless variation, the teeming multitude of forms, types of consciousness, natures that we see everywhere around us. There is no teleological purpose in creation and there cannot be, for all is there in the Infinite: the Divine has nothing that he needs to gain or that he has not; if there is creation and manifestation, it is for the delight of creation, of manifestation, not for any purpose. There is then no reason for an evolutionary movement with a culmination to be reached or an aim to be worked out and effectuated or a drive towards ultimate perfection.

In fact we see that the principles of creation are permanent and unchanging: each type of being remains itself and does not try nor has any need to become other than itself; granting that some types of existence disappear and others come into being, it is because the Consciousness-Force in the universe withdraws its life-delight from those that perish and turns to create others for its pleasure. But each type of life, while it lasts, has its own pattern and remains faithful with whatever minor variations to that pattern: it is bound to its own consciousness and cannot get away from it into other-consciousness; limited by its own nature, it cannot transgress these boundaries and pass into other-nature. If the Consciousness-Force of the Infinite has manifested Life after manifesting Matter and Mind after manifesting Life, it does not follow that it will proceed to manifest Supermind as the next terrestrial creation. For Mind and Supermind belong to quite different hemispheres, Mind to the lower status of the Ignorance, Supermind to the higher status of the Divine Knowledge. This world is a world of the Ignorance and intended to be that only; there need be no intention to bring down the powers of the higher hemisphere into the lower half of existence or to manifest their concealed presence there; for, if they are at all existent here, it is in an occult incommunicable immanence and only to maintain the creation, not to perfect it. Man is the summit of this ignorant creation; he has reached the utmost consciousness and knowledge of which it is capable: if he tries to go farther, he will only revolve in larger cycles of his own mentality. For that is the curve of his existence here, a finite circling which carries the Mind in its revolutions and returns always to the point from which it started; Mind cannot go outside its own cycle, — all idea of a straight line of movement or of progress reaching infinitely upward or sidewise into the Infinite is a delusion. If the soul of man is to go beyond humanity, to reach either a supramental or a still higher status, it must pass out of this cosmic existence, either to a plane or world of Bliss and Knowledge or into the unmanifest Eternal and Infinite.

It is true that Science now affirms an evolutionary terrestrial existence: but if the facts with which Science deals are reliable, the generalisations it hazards are short-lived; it holds them for some decades or some centuries, then passes to another generalisation, another theory of things. This happens even in physical Science where the facts are solidly ascertainable and verifiable by experiment: in psychology, — which is relevant here, for the evolution of consciousness comes into the picture, — its instability is still greater; it passes there from one theory to another before the first is well-founded; indeed, several conflicting theories hold the field together. No firm metaphysical building can be erected upon these shifting quicksands. Heredity, upon which Science builds its concept of life-evolution, is certainly a power, a machinery for keeping a type of species in unchanged being: the demonstration that it is also an instrument for persistent and progressive variation is very questionable; its tendency is conservative rather than evolutionary, — it seems to accept with difficulty the new character that the Life-Force attempts to force upon it. All the facts show that a type can vary within its own specification of nature, but there is nothing to show that it can go beyond it. It has not yet been really established that ape-kind developed into man; for it would rather seem that a type resembling the ape, but always characteristic of itself and not of apehood, developed within its own tendencies of nature and became what we know as man, the present human being. It is not even established that inferior races of man developed out of themselves the superior races; those of an inferior organisation and capacity perished, but it has not been shown that they left behind the human races of today as their descendants: but still such a development within the type is imaginable. The progress of Nature from Matter to Life, from Life to Mind, may be conceded: but there is no proof yet that Matter developed into Life or Life-energy into Mind-energy; all that can be conceded is that Life has manifested in Matter, Mind in living Matter. For there is no sufficient proof that any vegetable species developed into an animal existence or that any organisation of inanimate Matter developed into a living organism. Even if it be discovered hereafter that under certain chemical or other conditions Life makes its appearance, all that will be established by this coincidence is that in certain physical circumstances Life manifests, not that certain chemical conditions are constituents of Life, are its elements or are the evolutionary cause of a transformation of inanimate into animate Matter. Here as elsewhere each grade of being exists in itself and by itself, is manifested according to its own character by its own proper energy, and the gradations above or below it are not origins and resultant sequences but only degrees in the continuous scale of earth-nature.

If it be asked, how then did all these various gradations and types of being come into existence, it can be answered that, fundamentally, they were manifested in Matter by the Consciousness-Force in it, by the power of the Real-Idea building its own significant forms and types for the indwelling Spirit's cosmic existence: the practical or physical method might vary considerably in different grades or stages, although a basic similarity of line may be visible; the creative Power might use not one but many processes or set many forces to act together. In Matter the process is a creation of infinitesimals charged with an immense energy, their association by design and number, the manifestation of larger infinitesimals on that primary basis, the grouping and association of these together to found the appearance of sensible objects, earth, water, minerals, metals, the whole material kingdom. In Life also the Consciousness-Force begins with infinitesimal forms of vegetable life and infinitesimal animalcules; it creates an original plasm and multiplies it, creates the living cell as a unit, creates other kinds of minute biological apparatus like the seed or the gene, uses always the same method of grouping and association so as to build by a various operation various living organisms. A constant creation of types is visible, but that is no indubitable proof of evolution. The types are sometimes distant from each other, sometimes closely similar, sometimes identical in basis but different in detail; all are patterns, and such a variation in patterns with an identical rudimentary basis for all is the sign of a conscious Force playing with its own Idea and developing by it all kinds of possibilities of creation. Animal species in coming into birth may begin with a like rudimentary embryonic or fundamental pattern for all, it may follow out up to a stage certain similarities of development on some or all of its lines; there may too be species that are twy-natured, amphibious, intermediate between one type and another: but all this need not mean that the types developed one from another in an evolutionary series. Other forces than hereditary variation have been at work in bringing about the appearance of new characteristics; there are physical forces such as food, light-rays and others that we are only beginning to know, there are surely others which we do not yet know; there are at work invisible life-forces and obscure psychological forces. For these subtler powers have to be admitted even in the physical evolutionary theory to account for natural selection; if the occult or subconscious energy in some types answers to the need of the environment, in others remains unresponsive and unable to survive, this is clearly the sign of a varying life-energy and psychology, of a consciousness and a force other than the physical at work making for variation in Nature. The problem of the method of operation is still too full of obscure and unknown factors for any at present possible structure of theory to be definitive.

Man is a type among many types so constructed, one pattern among the multitude of patterns in the manifestation in Matter. He is the most complex that has been created, the richest in content of consciousness and the curious ingeniousness of his building; he is the head of the earthly creation, but he does not exceed it. Even as others, so he too has his own native law, limits, special kind of existence, *svabhāva, svadharma*; within those limits he can extend and develop, but he cannot go outside them. If there is a perfection to which he has to arrive, it must be a perfection in his own kind, within his own law of being, — the full play of it, but by observation of its mode and measure, not by transcendence. To exceed himself, to grow into the superman, to put on the nature and capacities of a god would be a contradiction of his self-law, impracticable and impossible. Each form and way of being has its own appropriate way of the delight of being; to seek through the mind the mastery and use and enjoyment of the environment of which he is capable is rightly man the mental being's objective: but to look beyond, to run after an ulterior object or aim of existence, to aspire to surpass the mental stature is to bring in a teleological element into existence which is not visible in the cosmic structure. If a supramental being is to appear in the terrestrial creation, it must be a new and independent manifestation; just as Life and Mind have manifested in Matter, so Supermind must manifest there and the secret Conscious-Energy must create the necessary patterns for this new grade of its potencies. But there is no sign of any such intention in the operations of Nature.

But if a superior creation is intended, then, certainly, it is not out of man that the new grade, type or pattern can develop; for in that case there would be some race or kind or make of human beings that has already the material of the superman in it, just as the peculiar animal being that developed into humanity had the essential elements of human nature already potential or present in it: there is no such race, kind or type, at most there are only spiritualised mental beings who are seeking to escape out of the terrestrial creation. If by any occult law of Nature such a human development of the supramental being is intended, it could only be by a few in humanity detaching themselves from the race so as to become a first foundation for this new pattern of being. There is no reason to suppose that the whole race could develop this perfection; it cannot be a possibility generalised in the human creature.

If indeed man has evolved in Nature out of the animal, yet now we see that no other animal type shows any signs of an evolution beyond itself; if then there was this evolutionary stress in the animal kingdom, it must have sunk back into quiescence as soon as the object was fulfilled by man's appearance: so too if there is any such stress for a new step in evolution, for self-exceeding, it is likely to subside into quiescence as soon as its object is fulfilled by the supramental being's appearance. But there is no such stress in reality: the idea of human progress itself is very probably an illusion, for there is no sign that man, once emerged from the animal stage, has radically progressed during his race-history; at most he has advanced in knowledge of the physical world, in Science, in the handling of his surroundings, in his purely external and utilitarian use of the secret laws of Nature. But otherwise he is what he always was in the early beginnings of civilisation: he continues to manifest the same capacities, the same qualities and defects, the same efforts, blunders, achievements, frustrations. If progress there has been, it is in a circle, at most perhaps in a widening circle. Man today is not wiser than the ancient seers and sages and thinkers, not more spiritual than the great seekers of old, the first mighty mystics, not superior in arts and crafts to the ancient artists and craftsmen; the old races that have disappeared showed as potent an intrinsic originality, invention, capacity of dealing with life and, if modern man in this respect has gone a little farther, not by any essential progress but in degree, scope, abundance, it is because he has inherited the achievements of his forerunners. Nothing warrants the idea that he will ever hew his way out of the half-knowledge half-ignorance which is the stamp of his kind, or, even if he develops a higher knowledge, that he can break out of the utmost boundary of the mental circle.

It is tempting and not illogical to regard rebirth as the potential means of a spiritual evolution, the factor that makes it possible, but still it is not certain, granting rebirth to be a fact, that this is its significance. All the ancient theories about reincarnation supposed it to be a constant transmigration of the soul from animal to human, but also from human to animal bodies: the Indian idea added the explanation of Karma, of a return for good or evil done, of a result of past will and effort; but there was no suggestion of a progressive evolution from type to higher type, still less of birth into a kind of being that has never yet existed but has still to evolve in the future. If evolution there is, then man is the last stage, because through him there can be the rejection of terrestrial or embodied life and an escape into some heaven or Nirvana. That was the end envisaged by the ancient theories and, since this is fundamentally and unchangeably a world of Ignorance, — even if all cosmic existence is not in its nature a state of Ignorance, — that escape is likely to be the true end of the cycle.

This is a line of reasoning that has a considerable cogency and importance, and it was necessary to state it, even if too briefly for its importance, in order to meet it. For although some of its propositions are valid, its view of things is not complete and its cogency is not conclusive. And first we may without much difficulty get rid of the objection to the teleological element which the idea of a predetermined evolution from inconscience to superconscience, the development of a rising order of beings with a culminating transition from the life of the Ignorance to a life in the Knowledge, brings into the structure of the terrestrial existence. The objection to a teleological cosmos can be based on two very different grounds, — a scientific reasoning proceeding on the assumption that all is the work of an inconscient Energy which acts automatically by mechanical processes and can have no element of purpose in it, and a metaphysical reasoning which proceeds on the perception that the Infinite and Universal has everything in it already, that it cannot have something unaccomplished to accomplish, something to add to itself, to work out, to realise, and there can therefore be in it no element of progress, no original or emergent purpose.

The scientific or materialist objection cannot maintain its validity if there is a secret Consciousness in or behind the apparently inconscient Energy in Matter. Even in the Inconscient there seems to be at least an urge of inherent necessity producing the evolution of forms and in the forms a developing Consciousness, and it may well be held that this urge is the evolutionary will of a secret Conscious-Being and its push of progressive manifestation the evidence of an innate intention in the evolution. This is a teleological element and it is not irrational to admit it: for the conscious or even the inconscient nisus arises from a truth of conscious-being that has become dynamic and set out to fulfil itself in an automatic process of material Nature; the teleology, the element of purpose in the nisus is the translation of self-operative Truth of Being into terms of self-effective Will-Power of that Being, and, if consciousness is there, such a Will-Power must also be there and the translation is normal and inevitable. Truth of Being inevitably fulfilling itself would be the fundamental fact of the evolution, but Will and its purpose must be there as part of the instrumentation, as an element in the operative principle.

The metaphysical objection is more serious; for it seems self-evident that the Absolute can have no purpose in manifestation except the delight of manifestation itself: an evolutionary movement in Matter as part of the manifestation must fall within this universal statement; it can be there only for the delight of the unfolding, the progressive execution, the objectless seried self-revelation. A universal totality may also be considered as something complete in itself; as a totality, it has nothing to gain or to add to its fullness of being. But here the material world is not an integral totality, it is part of a whole, a grade in a gradation; it may admit in it, therefore, not only the presence of undeveloped immaterial principles or powers belonging to the whole that are involved within its Matter, but also a descent into it of the same powers from the higher gradations of the system to deliver their kindred movements here from the strictness of a material limitation. A manifestation of the greater powers of Existence till the whole being itself is manifest in the material world in the terms of a higher, a spiritual creation, may be considered as the teleology of the evolution. This teleology does not bring in any factor that does not belong to the totality; it proposes only the realisation of the totality in the part. There can be no objection to the admission of a teleological factor in a part movement of the universal totality, if the purpose,—not a purpose in the human sense, but the urge of an intrinsic Truth-necessity conscious in the will of the indwelling Spirit,—is the perfect manifestation there of all the possibilities inherent in the total movement. All exists here, no doubt, for the delight of existence, all is a game or Lila; but a game too carries within itself an object to be accomplished and without the fulfilment of that object would have no completeness of significance. A drama without denouement may be an artistic possibility,—existing only for the pleasure of watching the characters and the pleasure in problems posed without a solution or with a forever suspended dubious balance of solution; the drama of the earth evolution might conceivably be of that character, but an intended or inherently predetermined denouement is also and more convincingly possible. Ananda is the secret principle of all being and the support of all activity of being: but Ananda does not exclude a delight in the working out of a Truth inherent in being, immanent in the Force or Will of being, upheld in the hidden self-awareness of its Consciousness-Force which is the dynamic and executive agent of all its activities and the knower of their significance.

A theory of spiritual evolution is not identical with a scientific theory of form-evolution and physical life-evolution; it must stand on its own inherent justification: it may accept the scientific account of physical evolution as a support or an element, but the support is not indispensable. The scientific theory is concerned only with the outward and visible machinery and process, with the detail of Nature's execution, with the physical development of things in Matter and the law of development of Life and Mind in Matter; its account of the process may have to be considerably changed or may be dropped altogether in the light of new discovery, but that will not affect the self-evident fact of a spiritual evolution, an evolution of Consciousness, a progression of the soul's manifestation in material existence. In its outward aspects this is what the theory of evolution comes to, — there is in the scale of terrestrial existence a development of forms, of bodies, a progressively complex and competent organisation of Matter, of Life in Matter, of Consciousness in living Matter; in this scale, the better organised the form, the more it is capable of housing a better organised, a more complex and capable, a more developed or evolved Life and Consciousness. Once the evolutionary hypothesis is put forward and the facts supporting it are marshalled, this aspect of the terrestrial existence becomes so striking as to appear indisputable. The precise machinery by which this is done or the exact genealogy or chronological succession of types of being is a secondary, though in itself an interesting and important question; the development of one form of life out of a precedent less evolved form, natural selection, the struggle for life, the survival of acquired characteristics may or may not be accepted, but the fact of a successive creation with a developing plan in it is the one conclusion which is of primary consequence. Another self-evident conclusion is that there is a graduated necessary succession in the evolution, first the evolution of Matter, next the evolution of Life in Matter, then the evolution of Mind in living Matter, and in this last stage an animal evolution followed by a human evolution. The first three terms of the succession are too evident to be disputable. It may be debated whether there was a succession of man to animal or a simultaneous initial development, man outstripping the animal in Mind-evolution; a theory has even been put forward that man was not the last, but the first and eldest of the animal species. This priority of man is an ancient conception, but it was not universal; it is born of the sense of the clear supremacy of man among earthly creatures, the dignity of this supremacy seeming to demand a priority of birth: but in evolutionary fact the superior is not prior but posterior in appearance, the less developed precedes the more developed and prepares it.

In fact, the idea of the priority of the lower forms of Life is not altogether absent in ancient thinking. Apart from mythical accounts of creation, we find already in ancient and mediaeval thought in India utterances that favour the priority of the animal over man in the time succession in a sense that agrees with the modern evolutionary conception. An Upanishad declares that the Self or Spirit after deciding on life-creation first formed animal kinds like the cow and horse, but the gods, — who are in the thought of the Upanishads powers of Consciousness and powers of Nature, — found them to be insufficient vehicles, and the Spirit finally created the form of man which the gods saw to be excellently made and sufficient and they entered into it for their cosmic functions. This is a clear parable of the creation of more and more developed forms till one was found that was capable of housing a developed consciousness. In the Puranas it is stated that the tamasic animal creation was the first in time. Tamas is the Indian word for the principle of inertia of consciousness and force: a consciousness dull and sluggish and incompetent in its play is said to be tamasic; a force, a Life-energy that is indolent and limited in its capacity, bound to a narrow range of instinctive impulses, not developing, not seeking farther, not urged to a greater kinetic action or a more luminously conscious action, would be assigned to the same category. The animal, in whom there is this less developed force of consciousness, is prior in creation; the more developed human consciousness, in which there is a greater force of kinetic Mind-energy and light of perception, is a later creation. The Tantra speaks of a soul fallen from its status passing through many lacs of births in plant and animal forms before it can reach the human level and be ready for salvation. Here, again, there is implied the conception of vegetable and animal life-forms as the lower steps of a ladder, humanity as the last or culminating development of the conscious being, the form which the soul has to inhabit in order to be capable of the spiritual motive and a spiritual issue out of mentality, life and physicality. This is indeed the normal conception, and it recommends itself so strongly both to reason and intuition that it hardly needs debate, — the conclusion is almost unescapable.

It is against this background of a developing evolutionary process that we have to look at man, his origin and first appearance, his status in the manifestation. There are here two possibilities; either there was the sudden appearance of a human body and consciousness in the earth-nature, an abrupt creation or independent automatic manifestation of reasoning mentality in the material world intervening upon a previous similar manifestation of subconscious life-forms and of living conscious bodies in Matter, or else there was an evolution of humanity out of animal being, slow perhaps in its preparation and in its stages of development, but with strong leaps of change at the decisive points of the transition. The latter theory offers no difficulty: for it is certain that changes of characteristics in the type, though not of the fundamental type itself, can be brought about in species or genus, — indeed this has already been done by man himself and its possibilities are being strikingly worked out on a small scale by experimental Science, — and it may fairly be assumed that the secretly conscious Energy in Nature could effect large-scale operations of the kind and bring about considerable and decisive developments by means of its own creative conventions. The necessary condition for the change from the normal animal to the human character of existence would be a development of the physical organisation which would capacitate a rapid progression, a reversal or turnover of the consciousness, a reaching to a new height and a looking down from it at the lower stages, a heightening and widening of capacity which would enable the being to take up the old animal faculties with a larger and more plastic, a human intelligence, and at the same time or later to develop greater and subtler powers proper to the new type of being, powers of reason, reflection, complex observation, organised invention, thought and discovery. If there is an emergent Consciousness-Force, there would be no difficulty in the transition, the instrument being provided, except the difficulty of the obstruction and resistance of the material Inconscience. The animal has already some of the corresponding qualities on a limited scale, for action only, in a rudimentary organisation crude and simple, with a very inferior scope and plasticity, a narrower and more casual command of the faculty; but especially the working of these faculties is more mechanical, less deliberate, marked with the character of an automatism of Nature-Energy driving an operation of primitive consciousness and not, as in man, of a conscious Energy observing and to a great extent directing and governing and deliberately changing or modifying its own operations. Other animal habits of consciousness are not fundamentally different from man's; all he had to do was to develop and enlarge them on a higher mental level and wherever possible, to mentalise, refine, subtilise, — in brief, to bring to them the enlightenment of his new understanding and intellectual capacity and a power of reasoned control denied to the animal. This change or reversal once effected, the power of the human mind to work upon itself and things, create, know, speculate, would develop in the course of his evolution, even if, as is conceivable, they were at the beginning small in scope, nearer to the animal, still comparatively simple and crude in their action. Such a reversal has been made in each radical transition of Nature: Life-Force emerging turns upon Matter, imposes a vital content on the operations of material Energy while it develops also its own new movements and operations; Life-Mind emerges in Life-Force and Matter and imposes its content of consciousness on their operations while it develops also its own action and faculties; a new greater emergence and reversal, the emergence of humanity, is in line with Nature's precedents; it would be a new application of the general principle.

This theory is therefore easy to accept: its working is intelligible. But the other hypothesis presents considerable difficulties. On the side of consciousness the new manifestation, the human, could be accounted for by an upsurge of concealed Consciousness from the involution in universal Nature. But in that case it must have had some material form already existent for its vehicle of emergence, the vehicle being adapted by the force of the emergence itself to the needs of a new inner creation; or else a rapid divergence from previous physical types or patterns may have brought a new being into existence. But whichever the hypothesis accepted, this means an evolutionary process, — there is only a difference in the method and machinery of the divergence or transition. Or there may have been, on the contrary, not an upsurgence but a descent of mentality from a Mind-plane above us, perhaps the descent of a soul or mental being into terrestrial Nature. The difficulty would then be the appearance of the human body, too complex and difficult an organ to have been suddenly created or manifested; for such a miraculous speed of process, though quite possible on a supraphysical plane of being, does not seem to figure among the normal possibles or potentials of the material Energy. It could only happen there by an intervention of a supraphysical force or law of Nature or by a creator Mind acting with full power and directly on Matter. An action of a supraphysical Force and a creator may be conceded in every new appearance in Matter; each such appearance is at bottom a miracle operated by a secret Consciousness supported by a veiled Mind-Energy or Life-Energy: but the action is nowhere seen to be direct, overt, self-sufficient; it is always superimposed on an already realised physical basis and acts by an extension of some established process of Nature. It is more conceivable that there was an opening of some existing body to a supraphysical influx so that it was transformed into a new body; but no such event can lightly be assumed to have taken place in the past history of material Nature: in order to happen it would seem to need either the conscious intervention of an invisible mental being to form the body he intended to inhabit or else a previous development of a mental being in Matter itself who would be already able to receive a supraphysical power and impose it on the rigid and narrow formulas of his physical existence. Otherwise we must suppose that there was a pre-existent body already so much evolved as to be fitted for the reception of a vast mental influx or capable of a pliable response to the descent into it of a mental being. But this would suppose a previous evolution of mind in body to the point at which such a receptivity would be possible. It is quite conceivable that such an evolution from below and such a descent from above co-operated in the appearance of humanity in earth-nature. The secret psychical entity already there in the animal might have itself called down the mental being, the Mind-Purusha, into the realm of living Matter in order to take up the vital-mental energy already at work and lift it into a higher mentality. But this would still be a process of evolution, the higher plane only intervening to assist the appearance and enlargement of its own principle in terrestrial Nature.

Next, it may be conceded that each type or pattern of consciousness and being in the body, once established, has to be faithful to the law of being of that type, to its own design and rule of nature. But it may also very well be that part of the law of the human type is its impulse towards self-exceeding, that the means for a conscious transition has been provided for among the spiritual powers of man; the possession of such a capacity may be a part of the plan on which the creative Energy has built him. It may be conceded that what man has up till now principally done is to act within the circle of his nature, on a spiral of nature-movement, sometimes descending, sometimes ascending, — there has been no straight line of progress, no indisputable, fundamental or radical exceeding of his past nature: what he has done is to sharpen, subtilise, make a more and more complex and plastic use of his capacities. It cannot truly be said that there has been no such thing as human progress since man's appearance or even in his recent ascertainable history; for however great the ancients, however supreme some of their achievements and creations, however impressive their powers of spirituality, of intellect or of character, there has been in later developments an increasing subtlety, complexity, manifold development of knowledge and possibility in man's achievements, in his politics, society, life, science, metaphysics, knowledge of all kinds, art, literature; even in his spiritual endeavour, less surprisingly lofty and less massive in power of spirituality than that of the ancients, there has been this increasing subtlety, plasticity, sounding of depths, extension of seeking. There have been falls from a high type of culture, a sharp temporary descent into a certain obscurantism, cessations of the spiritual urge, plunges into a barbaric natural materialism; but these are temporary phenomena, at worst a downward curve of the spiral of progress. This progress has not indeed carried the race beyond itself, into a self-exceeding, a transformation of the mental being. But that was not to be expected; for the action of evolutionary Nature in a type of being and consciousness is first to develop the type to its utmost capacity by just such a subtilisation and increasing complexity till it is ready for her bursting of the shell, the ripened decisive emergence, reversal, turning over of consciousness on itself that constitutes a new stage in the evolution. If it be supposed that her next step is the spiritual and supramental being, the stress of spirituality in the race may be taken as a sign that that is Nature's intention, the sign too of the capacity of man to operate in himself or aid her to operate the transition. If the appearance in animal being of a type similar in some respects to the ape-kind but already from the beginning endowed with the elements of humanity was the method of the human evolution, the appearance in the human being of a spiritual type resembling mental-animal humanity but already with the stamp of the spiritual aspiration on it would be the obvious method of Nature for the evolutionary production of the spiritual and supramental being.

It is pertinently suggested that if such an evolutionary culmination is intended and man is to be its medium, it will only be a few especially evolved human beings who will form the new type and move towards the new life; that once done, the rest of humanity will sink back from a spiritual aspiration no longer necessary for Nature's purpose and remain quiescent in its normal status. It can equally be reasoned that the human gradation must be preserved if there is really an ascent of the soul by reincarnation through the evolutionary degrees towards the spiritual summit; for otherwise the most necessary of all the intermediate steps will be lacking. It must be conceded at once that there is not the least probability or possibility of the whole human race rising in a block to the supramental level; what is suggested is nothing so revolutionary and astonishing, but only the capacity in the human mentality, when it has reached a certain level or a certain point of stress of the evolutionary impetus, to press towards a higher plane of consciousness and its embodiment in the being. The being will necessarily undergo by this embodiment a change from the normal constitution of its nature, a change certainly of its mental and emotional and sensational constitution and also to a great extent of the body-consciousness and the physical conditioning of our life and energies; but the change of consciousness will be the chief factor, the initial movement, the physical modification will be a subordinate factor, a consequence. This transmutation of the consciousness will always remain possible to the human being when the flame of the soul, the psychic kindling, becomes potent in heart and mind and the nature is ready. The spiritual aspiration is innate in man; for he is, unlike the animal, aware of imperfection and limitation and feels that there is something to be attained beyond what he now is: this urge towards self-exceeding is not likely ever to die out totally in the race. The human mental status will be always there, but it will be there not only as a degree in the scale of rebirth, but as an open step towards the spiritual and supramental status.

It must be observed that the appearance of human mind and body on the earth marks a crucial step, a decisive change in the course and process of the evolution; it is not merely a continuation of the old lines. Up till this advent of a developed thinking mind in Matter evolution had been effected, not by the self-aware aspiration, intention, will or seeking of the living being, but subconsciously or subliminally by the automatic operation of Nature. This was so because the evolution began from the Inconscience and the secret Consciousness had not emerged sufficiently from it to operate through the self-aware participating individual will of its living creature. But in man the necessary change has been made, — the being has become awake and aware of himself; there has been made manifest in Mind its will to develop, to grow in knowledge, to deepen the inner and widen the outer existence, to increase the capacities of the nature. Man has seen that there can be a higher status of consciousness than his own; the evolutionary oestrus is there in his parts of mind and life, the aspiration to exceed himself is delivered and articulate within him: he has become conscious of a soul, discovered the Self and Spirit. In him, then, the substitution of a conscious for a subconscious evolution has become conceivable and practicable, and it may well be concluded that the aspiration, the urge, the persistent endeavour in him is a sure sign of Nature's will for a higher way to fulfilment, the emergence of a greater status.

In the previous stages of the evolution Nature's first care and effort had to be directed towards a change in the physical organisation, for only so could there be a change of consciousness; this was a necessity imposed by the insufficiency of the force of consciousness already in formation to effect a change in the body. But in man a reversal is possible, indeed inevitable; for it is through his consciousness, through its transmutation and no longer through a new bodily organism as a first instrumentation that the evolution can and must be effected. In the inner reality of things a change of consciousness was always the major fact, the evolution has always had a spiritual significance and the physical change was only instrumental; but this relation was concealed by the first abnormal balance of the two factors, the body of the external Inconscience outweighing and obscuring in importance the spiritual element, the conscious being. But once the balance has been righted, it is no longer the change of body that must precede the change of consciousness; the consciousness itself by its mutation will necessitate and operate whatever mutation is needed for the body. It has to be noted that the human mind has already shown a capacity to aid Nature in the evolution of new types of plant and animal; it has created new forms of its environment, developed by knowledge and discipline considerable changes in its own mentality. It is not an impossibility that man should aid Nature consciously also in his own spiritual and physical evolution and transformation. The urge to it is already there and partly effective, though still incompletely understood and accepted by the surface mentality; but one day it may understand, go deeper within itself and discover the means, the secret energy, the intended operation of the Consciousness-Force within which is the hidden reality of what we call Nature.

All these are conclusions that can be arrived at even from the observation of the outward phenomena of Nature's progression, her surface evolution of being and of consciousness in the physical birth and the body. But there is the other, the invisible factor; there is rebirth, the progress of the soul by ascent from grade to grade of the evolving existence, and in the grades to higher and higher types of bodily and mental instrumentation. In this progression the psychic entity is still veiled, even in man the conscious mental being, by its instruments, by mind and life and body; it is unable to manifest fully, held back from coming to the front where it can stand out as the master of its nature, obliged to submit to a certain determination by the instruments, to a domination of Purusha by Prakriti. But in man the psychic part of the personality is able to develop with a much greater rapidity than in the inferior creation, and a time can arrive when the soul-entity is close to the point at which it will emerge from behind the veil into the open and become the master of its instrumentation in Nature. But this will mean that the secret indwelling spirit, the Daemon, the Godhead within is on the point of emergence; and, when it emerges, it can hardly be doubted that its demand will be, as indeed it already is in the Mind itself when it undergoes the inner psychic influence, for a diviner, a more spiritual existence. In the nature of the earth-life where the Mind is an instrument of the Ignorance, this can only be effected by a change of consciousness, a transition from a foundation in Ignorance to a foundation in Knowledge, from the mental to a supramental consciousness, a supramental instrumentation of Nature.

There is no conclusive validity in the reasoning that because this is a world of Ignorance, such a transformation can only be achieved by a passage to a heaven beyond or cannot be achieved at all and the demand of the psychic entity is itself ignorant and must be replaced by a merger of the soul in the Absolute. This conclusion could only be solely valid if Ignorance were the whole meaning, substance and power of the world-manifestation or if there were no element in World-Nature itself through which there could be an exceeding of the ignorant mentality that still burdens our present status of being. But the Ignorance is only a portion of this World-Nature; it is not the whole of it, not the original power or creator: it is in its higher origin a self-limiting Knowledge and even in its lower origin, its emergence out of the sheer material Inconscience, it is a suppressed Consciousness labouring to find, to recover itself, to manifest Knowledge, which is its true character, as the foundation of existence. In universal Mind itself there are ranges above our mentality which are instruments of the cosmic truth-cognition, and into these the mental being can surely rise; for already it rises towards them in supernormal conditions or receives from them without yet knowing or possessing them intuitions, spiritual intimations, large influxes of illumination or spiritual capacity. All these ranges are conscious of what is beyond them, and the highest of them is directly open to the Supermind, aware of the Truth-Consciousness which exceeds it. Moreover, in the evolving being itself, those greater powers of consciousness are here, supporting Mind-truth, underlying its action which screens them; this Supermind and those Truth-powers uphold Nature by their secret presence: even, truth of Mind is their result, a diminished operation, a representation in partial figures. It is, therefore, not only natural but seems inevitable that these higher powers of Existence should manifest here in Mind as Mind itself has manifested in Life and Matter.

Man's urge towards spirituality is the inner driving of the spirit within him towards emergence, the insistence of the Consciousness-Force of the being towards the next step of its manifestation. It is true that the spiritual urge has been largely other-worldly or turned at its extreme towards a spiritual negation and self-annihilation of the mental individual; but this is only one side of its tendency maintained and made dominant by the necessity of passing out of the kingdom of the fundamental Inconscience, overcoming the obstacle of the body, casting away the obscure vital, getting rid of the ignorant mentality, the necessity to attain first and foremost, by a rejection of all these impediments to spiritual being, to a spiritual status. The other, the dynamic side of the spiritual urge has not been absent,—the aspiration to a spiritual mastery and mutation of Nature, to a spiritual perfection of the being, a divinisation of the mind, the heart and the very body: there has even been the dream or a psychic prevision of a fulfilment exceeding the individual transformation, a new earth and heaven, a city of God, a divine descent upon earth, a reign of the spiritually perfect, a kingdom of God not only within us but outside, in a collective human life. However obscure may have been some of the forms taken by this aspiration, the indication they contain of the urge of the occult spiritual being within to emergence in earth-nature is unmistakable.

If a spiritual unfolding on earth is the hidden truth of our birth into Matter, if it is fundamentally an evolution of consciousness that has been taking place in Nature, then man as he is cannot be the last term of that evolution: he is too imperfect an expression of the Spirit, Mind itself a too limited form and instrumentation; Mind is only a middle term of consciousness, the mental being can only be a transitional being. If, then, man is incapable of exceeding mentality, he must be surpassed and Supermind and superman must manifest and take the lead of the creation. But if his mind is capable of opening to what exceeds it, then there is no reason why man himself should not arrive at Supermind and supermanhood or at least lend his mentality, life and body to an evolution of that greater term of the Spirit manifesting in Nature.

Man and the Supermind

MAN IS a transitional being, he is not final; for in him and high beyond him ascend the radiant degrees which climb to a divine supermanhood.

The step from man towards superman is the next approaching achievement in the earth's evolution. There lies our destiny and the liberating key to our aspiring, but troubled and limited human existence — inevitable because it is at once the intention of the inner Spirit and the logic of Nature's process.

The appearance of a human possibility in a material and animal world was the first glint of a coming divine Light, — the first far-off intimation of a godhead to be born out of Matter. The appearance of the superman in the human world will be the fulfilment of that distant shining promise.

The difference between man and superman will be the difference between mind and a consciousness as far beyond it as thinking mind is beyond the consciousness of plant and animal; the differentiating essence of man is mind, the differentiating essence of superman will be supermind or a divine gnosis.

Man is a mind imprisoned, obscured and circumscribed in a precarious and imperfect living but imperfectly conscious body. The superman will be a supramental spirit which will envelop and freely use a conscious body, plastic to spiritual forces. His physical frame will be a firm support and an adequate radiant instrument for the spirit's divine play and work in Matter.

Mind, even free and in its own unmixed and unhampered element, is not the highest possibility of consciousness; for mind is not in possession of Truth, but only a minor vessel or an instrument and here an ignorant seeker plucking eagerly at a

This and the two essays that follow were written in this order in a single notebook around 1930. They were not published during Sri Aurobindo's lifetime.

mass of falsehoods and half-truths for the unsatisfying pabulum of its hunger. Beyond mind is a supramental or gnostic power of consciousness that is in eternal possession of Truth; all its motion and feeling and sense and outcome are instinct and luminous with the inmost reality of things and express nothing else.

Supermind or gnosis is in its original nature at once and in the same movement an infinite wisdom and an infinite will. At its source it is the dynamic consciousness of the divine Knower and Creator.

When in the process of unfolding of an always greater force of the one Existence, some delegation of this power shall descend into our limited human nature, then and then only can man exceed himself and know divinely and divinely act and create; he will have become at last a conscious portion of the Eternal. The superman will be born, not a magnified mental being, but a supramental power descended here into a new life of the transformed terrestrial body. A gnostic supermanhood is the next distinct and triumphant victory to be won by the spirit descended into earthly nature.

The disk of a secret sun of Power and Joy and Knowledge is emerging out of the material consciousness in which our mind works as a chained slave or a baffled and impotent demiurge; supermind will be the formed body of that radiant effulgence.

Superman is not man climbed to his own natural zenith, not a superior degree of human greatness, knowledge, power, intelligence, will, character, genius, dynamic force, saintliness, love, purity or perfection. Supermind is something beyond mental man and his limits, a greater consciousness than the highest consciousness proper to human nature.

Man is a being from the mental worlds whose mentality works here involved, obscure and degraded in a physical brain, shut off from its own divinest powers and impotent to change life beyond certain narrow and precarious limits. Even in the highest of his kind it is baulked of its luminous possibilities of supreme force and freedom by this dependence. Most often and in most men it is only a servitor, a purveyor of amusements, a caterer of needs and interests to the life and the body. But the superman will be a gnostic king of Nature; supermind in him even in its evolutionary beginnings will appear as a ray of the eternal omniscience and omnipotence. Sovereign and irresistible it will lay hands on the mental and physical instruments, and, standing above and yet penetrating and possessing our lower already manifested parts, it will transform mind, life and body into its own divine and luminous nature.

Man in himself is hardly better than an ambitious nothing. He is a narrowness that reaches towards ungrasped widenesses, a littleness straining towards grandeurs which are beyond him, a dwarf enamoured of the heights. His mind is a darkened ray in the splendours of the universal Mind. His life is a striving exulting and suffering wave, an eager passion-tossed and sorrow-stricken or a blindly and dully toiling petty moment of the universal Life. His body is a labouring perishable speck in the material universe. An immortal soul is somewhere hidden within him and gives out from time to time some sparks of its presence, and an eternal spirit is above and overshadows with its wings and upholds with its power this soul continuity in his nature. But that greater spirit is obstructed from descent by the hard lid of his constructed personality and this inner radiant soul is wrapped, stifled and oppressed in dense outer coatings. In all but a few it is seldom active, in many hardly perceptible. The soul and spirit in man seem rather to exist above and behind his formed nature than to be a part of its visible reality; subliminal in his inner being or superconscient above in some unreached status, they are in his outer consciousness possibilities rather than things realised and present. The spirit is in course of birth rather than born in Matter.

This imperfect being with his hampered, confused, ill-ordered and mostly ineffective consciousness cannot be the end and highest height of the mysterious upward surge of Nature. There is something more that has yet to be brought down from above and is now seen only by broken glimpses through sudden rifts in the giant wall of our limitations. Or else there is something yet to be evolved from below, sleeping under the veil of man's mental consciousness or half visible by flashes, as life once slept in the stone and metal, mind in the plant and reason in the cave of animal memory underlying its imperfect apparatus of emotion and sense-device and instinct. Something there is in us yet unexpressed that has to be delivered by an enveloping illumination from above. A godhead is imprisoned in our depths, one in its being with a greater godhead ready to descend from superhuman summits. In that descent and awakened joining is the secret of our future.

Man's greatness is not in what he is but in what he makes possible. His glory is that he is the closed place and secret workshop of a living labour in which supermanhood is made ready by a divine Craftsman.

But he is admitted to a yet greater greatness and it is this that, unlike the lower creation, he is allowed to be partly the conscious artisan of his divine change. His free assent, his consecrated will and participation are needed that into his body may descend the glory that will replace him. His aspiration is earth's call to the supramental Creator.

If earth calls and the Supreme answers, the hour can be even now for that immense and glorious transformation.

The Involved and Evolving Godhead

THE INVOLUTION of a superconscient Spirit in inconscient Matter is the secret cause of this visible and apparent world. The keyword of the earth's riddle is the gradual evolution of a hidden illimitable consciousness and power out of the seemingly inert yet furiously driven force of insensible Nature. Earth-life is one self-chosen habitation of a great Divinity and his aeonic will is to change it from a blind prison into his splendid mansion and high heaven-reaching temple.

The nature of the Divinity in the world is an enigma to the mind, but to our enlarging consciousness it will appear as a presence simple and inevitable. Freed we shall enter into the immutable stability of an eternal existence that puts on this revealing multitude of significant mutable forms. Illumined we shall become aware of the indivisible light of an infinite consciousness that breaks out here into multiform grouping and detail of knowledge. Sublimated in might, we shall share the illimitable movement of an omnipotent force that works out its marvels in self-imposed limits. Fixed in griefless bliss we shall possess the calm and ecstasy of an immeasurable Delight that creates for ever the multitudinous waves and rhythms and the ever increasing outward-going and inward-drawing intensities of its own creative and communicative world-possessing and self-possessing bliss. This, since we are inwardly souls of that Spirit, will be the nature of our fourfold experience when the evolving Godhead will work here in its own unveiled movement.

If that full manifestation had been from the beginning, there would be no terrestrial problem, no anguish of growth, no baffled seeking out of mind and will and life and body towards knowledge and force and joy and an immortal persistence. But this Godhead, whether within us or outside in things and forces and creatures, started from an involution in inconscience of

Nature and began by the manifestation of its apparent opposites. Out of a vast cosmic inconscience and inertia and insensibility, an initial disguise that is almost non-existence, the Spirit in Matter has chosen to evolve and slowly shape, as if in a grudging and gradually yielding material, its might and light and infinity and beatitude.

The significance of the terrestrial evolution lies in this slow and progressive liberation of some latent indwelling Spirit. The heart of its mystery is the difficult appearance, the tardy becoming of a divine Something or Someone already involved in physical Nature. The Spirit is there with all its potential forces in a first formal basis of its own supporting, yet resistant substance. Its greater subsequent and deliberately emerging movements, life and mind and intuition and soul and supermind and the light of the Godhead are already there, locked up and obscurely compressed into the initial power and first expressive values of Matter.

Before there could be any evolution, there must needs be this involution of the Divine All that is to emerge. Otherwise there would have been not an ordered and significant evolution, but a successive creation of things unforeseeable, not contained in their antecedents, not their inevitable consequences or right followers in sequence.

This world is not an apparent order fortuitously managed by an inexplicable Chance. Neither is it a marvellous mechanism miraculously contrived by a stumblingly fortunate unconscious Force or mechanical Necessity. It is not even a structure built according to his fancy or will by an external and therefore necessarily a limited Creator. Mentally conceivable, each of these solutions can explain one side or appearance of things; but it is a greater truth that can alone successfully join all the aspects and illumine all the facts of the enigma.

If all were indeed a result of cosmic Chance, there would be no necessity of a new advance; nothing beyond mind need appear in the material world, — as indeed there was then no necessity for even mind to arise at all out of the meaningless blind material whirl. Consciousness itself would be only a fortuitous apparition, a strange hallucinating reflection or ghost of Matter.

Or if all were the work of a mechanical Force, then too mind need not have appeared at all as part of the huge grinding engine; there was no indispensable call for this subtler and yet less competent groping mechanic contrivance. No frail thinking brain should have been there to labour over the quite sufficient cogs and springs and pistons of the first unerring machine. A supermind added on this brilliant and painful complication would be still more a superfluity and a luminous insolence; it could be nothing more than a false pretension of transitory consciousness to govern and possess the greater inconscient Force that is its creator.

Or if an experimenting, external and therefore limited Creator were the inventor of the animal's suffering life and man's fumbling mind and this huge mainly unused and useless universe, there was no reason why he should not have stopped short with the construction of a mental intelligence in his creatures, content with the difficult ingenuity of his labour. Even if he were all-powerful and all-wise, he might well pause there, — for if he went farther, the creature would be in danger of rising too near to the level of his Maker.

But if this is the truth of things that an infinite Spirit, an eternal Divine Presence and Consciousness and Force and Bliss is involved and hidden here and slowly emerges, then is it inevitable that its powers or the ascending degrees of its one power should emerge too one after the other till the whole glory is manifested, a mighty divine Fact embodied and dynamic and visible.

All mental ideas of the nature of things, are inconclusive considerations of our insufficient logical reason when it attempts in its limited light and ignorant self-sufficiency to weigh the logical probabilities of a universal order which after all its speculation and discovery must remain obscure to it still and an enigma. The true witness and discoverer is our growing consciousness; for that consciousness is itself the sign and power of the evolving Divine, and its growth out of the apparent inconscience of the material universe is the fundamental, the one abiding, progressive index event of the long earth-story.

Only when this evolving consciousness can grow into its own full divine power will we directly know ourselves and the world instead of catching at tags and tail ends of an insufficient figure of knowledge. This full power of the consciousness is supermind or gnosis, — supermind because to reach it we have to pass beyond and turn upon mind as the mind itself has passed and turned upon life and inconscient matter and gnosis because it is eternally self-possessed of Truth and in its very stuff and nature it is dynamic substance of knowledge.

The true knowledge of things is denied to our reason, because that is not our spirit's greatest essential power but only an expedient, a transitional instrument meant to deal with the appearance of things and their phenomenal process. True knowledge commences only when our consciousness can pass beyond its present normal limit in man: for then it becomes directly aware of its self and of the Power in the world and begins to have at least an initial knowledge by identity which is the sole true knowledge. Henceforward it knows and sees, no longer by the reason groping among external data, but by an ever increasing and always more luminous self-illumining and all illuminating experience. In the end it will become a conscious part of the Divine revealing itself in the world; its life will be a power for the conscious evolution of that which is still unmanifested in the material universe.

The Evolution of Consciousness

ALL LIFE here is a stage or a circumstance in an unfolding progressive evolution of a Spirit that has involved itself in Matter and is labouring to manifest itself in that reluctant substance. This is the whole secret of earthly existence.

But the key of that secret is not to be found in life itself or in the body; its hieroglyph is not in embryo or organism,—for these are only a physical means or base: the one significant mystery of this universe is the appearance and growth of consciousness in the vast mute unintelligence of Matter. The escape of Consciousness out of an apparent initial Inconscience,—but it was there all the time masked and latent, for the inconscience of Matter is itself only a hooded consciousness—its struggle to find itself, its reaching out to its own inherent completeness, perfection, joy, light, strength, mastery, harmony, freedom, this is the prolonged miracle and yet the natural and all-explaining phenomenon of which we are at once the observers and a part, instrument and vehicle.

A Consciousness, a Being, a Power, a Joy was here from the beginning darkly imprisoned in this apparent denial of itself, this original night, this obscurity and nescience of material Nature. That which is and was for ever, free, perfect, eternal and infinite, That which all is, That which we call God, Brahman, Spirit, has here shut itself up in its own self-created opposite. The Omniscient has plunged itself into Nescience, the All Conscious into Inconscience, the All-Wise into perpetual Ignorance. The Omnipotent has formulated itself in a vast cosmic self-driven Inertia that by disintegration creates; the Infinite is self-expressed here in a boundless fragmentation; the All-Blissful has put on a huge insensibility out of which it struggles by pain and hunger and desire and sorrow. Elsewhere the Divine is; here in physical life, in this obscure material world, it would seem almost as if the

Divine is not but is only becoming, *theos ouk estin alla gignetai*. This gradual becoming of the Divine out of its own phenomenal opposites is the meaning and purpose of the terrestrial evolution.

Evolution in its essence is not the development of a more and more organised body or a more and more efficient life — these are only its machinery and outward circumstance. Evolution is the strife of a Consciousness somnambulised in Matter to wake and be free and find and possess itself and all its possibilities to the very utmost and widest, to the very last and highest. Evolution is the emancipation of a self-revealing Soul secret in Form and Force, the slow becoming of a Godhead, the growth of a Spirit.

In this evolution mental man is not the goal and end, the completing value, the highest last significance; he is too small and imperfect to be the crown of all this travail of Nature. Man is not final, but a middle term only, a transitional being, an instrumental intermediate creature.

This character of evolution and this mediary position of man are not at first apparent; for to the outward eye it would seem as if evolution, the physical evolution at least were finished long ago leaving man behind as its poor best result and no new beings or superior creations were to be expected any longer. But this appears to us only so long as we look at forms and outsides only and not at the inner significances of the whole process. Matter, body, life even are the first terms necessary for the work that had to be done. New living forms may no longer be appearing freely, but this is because it is not, or at least it is not primarily, new living forms that the Force of evolution is now busied with evolving, but new powers of consciousness. When Nature, the Divine Power, had formed a body erect and empowered to think, to devise, to inquire into itself and things and work consciously both on things and self, she had what she wanted for her secret aim; relegating all else to the sphere of secondary movements, she turned toward that long-hidden aim her main highest forces. For all till then was a long strenuously slow preparation; but throughout it the development of consciousness in which the appearance of man was the crucial turning point had been kept wrapped within her as her ultimate business and true purpose.

This slow preparation of Nature covered immense aeons of time and infinities of space in which they appeared to be her only business; the real business strikes on our view at least when we look with the outward eye of reason as if it came only as a fortuitous accident, in or near the end, for a span of time and in a speck and hardly noticeable corner of one of the smallest provinces of a possibly minor universe among these many boundless finites, these countless universes. If it were so, we could still reply that time and space matter not to the Infinite and Eternal; it is not a waste of labour for That — as it would be for our brief death-driven existences — to work for trillions of years in order to flower only for a moment. But that paradox too is only an appearance — for the history of this single earth is not all the story of evolution — other earths there are even now elsewhere, and even here many earth-cycles came before us, and many are those that will come hereafter.

Nature laboured for innumerable millions of years to create a material universe of flaming suns and systems; for a lesser but still interminable series of millions she stooped to make this earth a habitable planet. For all that incalculable time she was or seemed busy only with the evolution of Matter; life and mind were kept secret in an apparent non-existence. But the time came when life could manifest, a vibration in the metal, a growing and seeking, a drawing in and a feeling outward in the plant, an instinctive force and sense, a nexus of joy and pain and hunger and emotion and fear and struggle in the animal, — a first organised consciousness, the beginning of the long-planned miracle. Thenceforward she was busy no more exclusively with matter for its own sake, but most with palpitant plasmic matter useful for the expression of life; the evolution of life was now her one intent purpose. And slowly too mind manifested in life, an intensely feeling, a crude thinking and planning vital mind in the animal, but in man the full organisation and apparatus, the developing if yet imperfect mental being, the Manu, the thinking, devising, aspiring, already self-conscient creature. And from that time onward the growth of mind rather than any radical change of life became her shining preoccupation, her wonderful wager. Body appeared to evolve no more; life itself evolved little or only so much in its cycles as would serve to express Mind heightening and widening itself in the living body; an unseen internal evolution was now Nature's great passion and purpose.

And if Mind were all that consciousness could achieve, if

Mind were the secret Godhead, if there were nothing higher, larger, no more miraculous ranges, man could be left to fulfil mind and complete his own being and there would or need be nothing here beyond him, carrying consciousness to its summits, extending it to its unwalled vastnesses, plunging with it into depths unfathomable; he would by perfecting himself consummate Nature. Evolution would end in a Man-God, crown of the earthly cycles.

But Mind is not all; for beyond mind is a greater consciousness; there is a supermind and spirit. As Nature laboured in the animal, the vital being, till she could manifest out of him man, the Manu, the thinker, so she is labouring in man, the mental being till she can manifest out of him a spiritual and supramental godhead, the truth conscious Seer, the knower by identity, the embodied Transcendental and Universal in the individual nature.

From the clod and metal to the plant, from the plant to the animal, from the animal to man, so much has she completed of her journey; a huge stretch or a stupendous leap still remains before her. As from matter to life, from life to mind, so now she must pass from mind to supermind, from man to superman; this is the gulf that she has to bridge, the supreme miracle that she has to perform before she can rest from her struggle and discontent and stand in the radiance of that supreme consciousness, glorified, transmuted, satisfied with her labour.

The subhuman was once here supreme in her, the human replacing it walks now in the front of Time, but still, aim and goal of the future there waits the supramental, the superman, an unborn glory yet unachieved before her.

Rebirth

THE THEORY of rebirth is almost as ancient as thought itself and its origin is unknown. We may according to our prepossessions accept it as the fruit of ancient psychological experience always renewable and verifiable and therefore true or dismiss it as a philosophical dogma and ingenious speculation; but in either case the doctrine, even as it is in all appearance well-nigh as old as human thought itself, is likely also to endure as long as human beings continue to think.

In former times the doctrine used to pass in Europe under the grotesque name of transmigration which brought with it to the Western mind the humorous image of the soul of Pythagoras migrating, a haphazard bird of passage, from the human form divine into the body of a guinea-pig or an ass.[1] The philosophical appreciation of the theory expressed itself in the admirable but rather unmanageable Greek word, metempsychosis, which means the insouling of a new body by the same psychic individual. The Greek tongue is always happy in its marriage of thought and word and a better expression could not be found; but forced into English speech the word becomes merely long and pedantic without any memory of its subtle Greek sense and has to be abandoned. Reincarnation is the now popular term, but the idea in the word leans to the gross or external view of the fact and begs many questions. I prefer 'rebirth', for it renders the sense of the wide, colourless, but sufficient Sanskrit term, *punarjanma*,

Published in *Arya* in 1915; subsequently revised and included in *The Problem of Rebirth*, a book published posthumously in 1952.

[1] Pythagoras (sixth century BCE), Greek mathematician and philosopher. He believed in the transmigration of souls between successive, not necessarily human, bodies.

'again-birth', and commits us to nothing but the fundamental idea which is the essence and life of the doctrine.

Rebirth is for the modern mind no more than a speculation and a theory; it has never been proved by the methods of modern science or to the satisfaction of the new critical mind formed by a scientific culture. Neither has it been disproved; for modern science knows nothing about a before-life or an after-life for the human soul, knows nothing indeed about a soul at all, nor can know; its province stops with the flesh and brain and nerve, the embryo and its formation and development. Neither has modern criticism any apparatus by which the truth or untruth of rebirth can be established. In fact, modern criticism, with all its pretensions to searching investigation and scrupulous certainty, is no very efficient truth-finder. Outside the sphere of the immediate physical it is almost helpless. It is good at discovering data, but except where the data themselves bear on the surface their own conclusion, it has no means of being rightly sure of the generalisations it announces from them so confidently in one generation and destroys in the next. It has no means of finding out with surety the truth or untruth of a doubtful historical assertion; after a century of dispute it has not even been able to tell us yes or no, whether Jesus Christ ever existed. How then shall it deal with such a matter as this of rebirth which is stuff of psychology and must be settled rather by psychological than physical evidence?

The arguments which are usually put forward by supporters and opponents, are often weak or futile and even at their best insufficient either to prove or to disprove anything in the world. One argument, for instance, often put forward triumphantly in disproof is this that we have no memory of our past lives and therefore there were no past lives! One smiles to see such reasoning seriously used by those who imagine that they are something more than intellectual children. The argument proceeds on psychological grounds and yet it ignores the very nature of our ordinary or physical memory which is all that the normal man can employ. How much do we remember of our actual lives which we are undoubtedly living at the present moment? Our memory is normally good for what is near, becomes vaguer or less comprehensive as its objects recede into the distance, farther off seizes only some salient points and, finally, for the beginning of our lives falls into a mere blankness. Do we remember even the mere fact, the simple state of being an infant on the mother's breast? and yet that state of infancy was, on any but a Buddhist theory, part of the same life and belonged to the same individual, — the very one who cannot remember it just as he cannot remember his past lives. Yet we demand that this physical memory, this memory of the brute brain of man which cannot remember our infancy and has lost so much of our later years, shall recall that which was before infancy, before birth, before itself was formed. And if it cannot, we are to cry, 'Disproved your reincarnation theory!' The sapient insipiency of our ordinary human reasoning could go no farther than in this sort of ratiocination. Obviously, if our past lives are to be remembered whether as fact and state or in their events and images, it can only be by a psychical memory awaking which will overcome the limits of the physical and resuscitate impressions other than those stamped on the physical being by physical cerebration.

I doubt whether, even if we could have evidence of the physical memory of past lives or of such a psychical awakening, the theory would be considered any better proved than before. We now hear of many such instances confidently alleged though without that apparatus of verified evidence responsibly examined which gives weight to the results of psychical research. The sceptic can always challenge them as mere fiction and imagination unless and until they are placed on a firm basis of evidence. Even if the facts alleged are verified, he has the resource of affirming that they are not really memories but were known to the person alleging them by ordinary physical means or were suggested to him by others and have been converted into reincarnate memory either by conscious deception or by a process of self-deception and self-hallucination. And even supposing the evidence were too strong and unexceptionable to be got rid of by these familiar devices, they might yet not be accepted as proof of rebirth; the mind can discover a hundred theoretical explanations for a single group of facts. Modern speculation and research have brought in this doubt to overhang all psychical theory and generalisation.

We know for instance that in the phenomena, say, of automatic writing or of communication from the dead, it is disputed whether the phenomena proceed from outside, from disembodied minds, or from within, from the subliminal consciousness, or whether the communication is actual and immediate from the released personality or is the uprising to the surface of a telepathic impression which came from the mind of the then living man but has remained submerged in our subliminal mentality. The same kind of doubts might be opposed to the evidences of reincarnate memory. It might be maintained that they prove the power of a certain mysterious faculty in us, a consciousness that can have some inexplicable knowledge of past events, but that these events may belong to other personalities than ours and that our attribution of them to our own personality in past lives is an imagination, a hallucination, or else an instance of that self-appropriation of things and experiences perceived but not our own which is one out of the undoubted phenomena of mental error. Much would be proved by an accumulation of such evidences but not, to the sceptic at least, rebirth. Certainly, if they were sufficiently ample, exact, profuse, intimate, they would create an atmosphere which would lead in the end to a general acceptance of the theory by the human race as a moral certitude. But proof is a different matter.

After all, most of the things that we accept as truths are really no more than moral certitudes. We have all the profoundest unshakeable faith that the earth revolves on its own axis, but as has been pointed out by a great French mathematician, the fact has never been proved; it is only a theory which accounts well for certain observable facts, no more. Who knows whether it may not be replaced in this or another century by a better — or a worse? All observed astronomical phenomena were admirably accounted for by theories of spheres and I know not what else, before Galileo came in with his 'And yet it moves,' disturbing the infallibility of Popes and Bibles and the science and logic of the learned.[2] One feels certain that admirable theories could be invented to account for the facts of gravitation if our intellects were not prejudiced and prepossessed by the anterior demonstrations of Newton.[3] This is the ever-perplexing and inherent plague of our reason; for it starts by knowing nothing and has to deal with

[2] Galileo Galilei (1564–1642), Italian mathematician and astronomer. His telescopic observations helped establish the heliocentric theory of Copernicus. Forced by the Inquisition to retract the heretical opinion that the earth moves around the sun, he is said to have remarked afterwards, *eppur si mouve*, 'And yet it moves.'

[3] This was written in pre-Einsteinian days. [Sri Aurobindo's note]

infinite possibilities, and the possible explanations of any given set of facts until we actually know what is behind them, are endless. In the end, we really know only what we observe and even that subject to a haunting question, for instance, that green is green and white is white, although it appears that colour is not colour but something else that creates the appearance of colour. Beyond observable fact we must be content with reasonable logical satisfaction, dominating probability and moral certitude, — at least until we have the sense to observe that there are faculties in us higher than the sense-dependent reason and awaiting development by which we can arrive at greater certainties.

We cannot really assert as against the sceptic any such dominant probability or any such certitude on behalf of the theory of rebirth. The external evidence yet available is in the last degree rudimentary. Pythagoras was one of the greatest of sages, but his assertion that he fought at Troy under the name of the Antenorid and was slain by the younger son of Atreus is an assertion only and his identification of the Trojan shield will convince no one who is not already convinced; the modern evidence is not as yet any more convincing than the proof of Pythagoras. In absence of external proof which to our matter-governed sensational intellects is alone conclusive, we have the argument of the reincarnationists that their theory accounts for all the facts better than any other yet advanced. The claim is just, but it does not create any kind of certitude. The theory of rebirth coupled with that of Karma gives us a simple, symmetrical, beautiful explanation of things; but so too the theory of the spheres gave us once a simple, symmetrical, beautiful explanation of the heavenly movements. Yet we have now got quite another explanation, much more complex, much more Gothic and shaky in its symmetry, an inexplicable order evolved out of chaotic infinities, which we accept[4] as the truth of the matter. And yet, if we will only think, we shall perhaps see that even this is not the whole truth; there is much more behind we have not yet discovered. Therefore the simplicity, symmetry, beauty,

[4] Or used to accept, but now it is suggested that this order is only a schema created by our own mind or determined by the constitution of our brain, a syntax and logic of word and thought which we impose on a world that in fact does not or may not contain any such thing. [Sri Aurobindo's note]

satisfactoriness of the reincarnation theory is no warrant of its certitude.

When we go into details, the uncertainty increases. Rebirth accounts, for example, for the phenomenon of genius, inborn faculty and so many other psychological mysteries. But then Science comes in with its all-sufficient explanation by heredity, — though, like that of rebirth, all-sufficient only to those who already believe in it. Without doubt, the claims of heredity have been absurdly exaggerated. It has succeeded in accounting for much, not all, in our physical make-up, our temperament, our vital peculiarities. Its attempt to account for genius, inborn faculty and other psychological phenomena of a higher kind is a pretentious failure. But this may be because Science knows nothing at all that is fundamental about our psychology, — no more than primitive astronomers knew of the constitution and law of the stars whose movements they yet observed with a sufficient accuracy. I do not think that even when Science knows more and better, it will be able to explain these things by heredity; but the scientist may well argue that he is only at the beginning of his researches, that the generalisation which has explained so much may well explain all, and that at any rate his hypothesis has had a better start in its equipment of provable facts than the theory of reincarnation.

Nevertheless, the argument of the reincarnationist is so far a good argument and respect-worthy, though not conclusive. But there is another more clamorously advanced which seems to me to be on a par with the hostile reasoning from absence of memory, at least in the form in which it is usually advanced to attract unripe minds. This is the ethical argument by which it is sought to justify God's ways with the world or the world's ways with itself. There must, it is thought, be a moral governance for the world; or at least some sanction of reward in the cosmos for virtue, some sanction of punishment for sin. But upon our perplexed and chaotic earth no such sanction appears. We see the good man thrust down into the press of miseries and the wicked flourishing like a green bay-tree and *not* cut down miserably in his end. Now this is intolerable. It is a cruel anomaly, it is a reflection on God's wisdom and justice, almost a proof that God is not; we must remedy that. Or if God is not, we must have some other sanction for righteousness.

How comforting it would be if we could tell a good man and even the amount of his goodness, — for should not the Supreme be a strict and honourable accountant? — by the amount of ghee that he is allowed to put into his stomach and the number of rupees he can jingle into his bank and the various kinds of good luck that accrue to him. Yes, and how comforting too if we could point our finger at the wicked stripped of all concealment and cry at him, 'O thou wicked one! for if thou wert not evil, wouldst thou in a world governed by God or at least by good, be thus ragged, hungry, unfortunate, pursued by griefs, void of honour among men? Yes, thou art proved wicked, because thou art ragged. God's justice is established.' The Supreme Intelligence being fortunately wiser and nobler than man's childishness, this is impossible. But let us take comfort! It appears that if the good man has not enough good luck and ghee and rupees, it is because he is really a scoundrel suffering for his crimes, — but a scoundrel in his past life who has suddenly turned a new leaf in his mother's womb; and if yonder wicked man flourishes and tramples gloriously on the world, it is because of his goodness — in a past life, the saint that was then having since been converted — was it by his experience of the temporal vanity of virtue? — to the cult of sin. All is explained, all is justified. We suffer for our sins in another body; we shall be rewarded in another body for our virtues in this; and so it will go on *ad infinitum*. No wonder, the philosophers found this a bad business and proposed as a remedy to get rid of both sin and virtue and even as our highest good to scramble anyhow out of a world so amazingly governed.

Obviously, this scheme of things is only a variation of the old spiritual-material bribe and menace, the bribe of a Heaven of fat joys for the good and the threat of a hell of eternal fire or bestial tortures for the wicked. The idea of the Law of the world as primarily a dispenser of rewards and punishments is cognate to the idea of the Supreme Being as a judge, 'father' and school-master who is continually rewarding with lollipops his good boys and continually caning his naughty urchins. It is cognate also to the barbarous and unthinking system of sometimes savage and always degrading punishment for social offences on which human society, unable still to find out or organise a more satisfactory way, is still founded. Man insists continually on making God in his own image instead of seeking to make himself more and more in the image of God, and all these ideas are the reflection of the child and the savage and the animal in us which we have still failed to transform or outgrow. We should be inclined to wonder how these fancies of children found their way into such profound philosophical religions as Buddhism and Hinduism, if it were not so patent that men will not deny themselves the luxury of tacking on the rubbish from their past to the deeper thoughts of their sages.

No doubt, since these ideas were so prominent, they must have had their use in training humanity. Perhaps even it is true that the Supreme deals with the child soul according to its childishness and allows it to continue its sensational imaginations of heaven and hell for a time beyond the death of the physical body. Perhaps both these ideas of after-life and of rebirth as fields of punishment and reward were needed because suited to our half-mentalised animality. But after a certain stage the system ceases to be really effective. Men believe in Heaven and Hell but go on sinning merrily, quit at last by a Papal indulgence or the final priestly absolution or a death-bed repentance or a bath in the Ganges or a sanctified death at Benares, — such are the childish devices by which we escape from our childishness! And in the end the mind grows adult and puts the whole nursery nonsense away with contempt. The reward and punishment theory of rebirth, if a little more elevated or at least less crudely sensational, comes to be as ineffective. And it is good that it should be so. For it is intolerable that man with his divine capacity should continue to be virtuous for a reward and shun sin out of terror. Better a strong sinner than a selfish virtuous coward or a petty huckster with God; there is more divinity in him, more capacity of elevation. Truly the Gita has said well, *kṛpaṇāḥ phalahetavaḥ*. And it is inconceivable that the system of this vast and majestic world should have been founded on these petty and paltry motives. There is reason in these theories? then reason of the nursery, puerile. Ethics? then ethics of the mud, muddy.

The true foundation of the theory of rebirth is the evolution of the soul, or rather its efflorescence out of the veil of Matter and its gradual self-finding. Buddhism contained this truth involved in its theory of Karma and emergence out of Karma but failed to bring it to light; Hinduism knew it of old, but afterwards missed the right balance of its expression. Now we are again able to restate the ancient truth in a new language and this is already being done by certain schools of thought, though still the old incrustations tend to tack themselves on to the deeper wisdom. And if this gradual efflorescence be true, then the theory of rebirth is an intellectual necessity, a logically unavoidable corollary. But what is the aim of that evolution? Not conventional or interested virtue and the faultless counting out of the small coin of good in the hope of an apportioned material reward, but the continual growth towards a divine knowledge, strength, love and purity. These things alone are real virtue and this virtue is its own reward. The one true reward of the works of love is to grow ever in capacity and delight of love up to the ecstasy of the spirit's all-seizing embrace and universal passion; the one reward of the works of right Knowledge is to grow perpetually into the infinite Light; the one reward of the works of right Power is to harbour more and more of the Force Divine, and of the works of purity to be freed more and more from egoism into that immaculate wideness where all things are transformed and reconciled into the divine equality. To seek other reward is to bind oneself to a foolishness and a childish ignorance; and to regard even these things as a reward is an unripeness and an imperfection.

And what of suffering and happiness, misfortune and prosperity? These are experiences of the soul in its training, helps, props, means, disciplines, tests, ordeals, — and prosperity often a worse ordeal than suffering. Indeed, adversity, suffering may often be regarded rather as a reward to virtue than as a punishment for sin, since it turns out to be the greatest help and purifier of the soul struggling to unfold itself. To regard it merely as the stern award of a Judge, the anger of an irritated Ruler or even the mechanical recoil of result of evil upon cause of evil is to take the most superficial view possible of God's dealings with the soul and the law of the world's evolution. And what of worldly prosperity, wealth, progeny, the outward enjoyment of art, beauty, power? Good, if they be achieved without loss to the soul and enjoyed only as the outflowing of the divine Joy and Grace upon our material existence. But let us seek them first for others or rather for all, and for ourselves only as a part of the universal condition or as one means of bringing perfection nearer.

The soul needs no proof of its rebirth any more than it needs proof of its immortality. For there comes a time when it is consciously immortal, aware of itself in its eternal and immutable essence. Once that realisation is accomplished, all intellectual questionings for and against the immortality of the soul fall away like a vain clamour of ignorance around the self-evident and ever-present truth. *Tato na vicikitsate.* That is the true dynamic belief immortality when it becomes to us not an intellectual dogma but a fact as evident as the physical fact of our breathing and as little in need of proof or argument. So also there comes a time when the soul becomes aware of itself in its eternal and mutable movement; it is then aware of the ages behind that constituted the present organisation of the movement, sees how this was prepared in an uninterrupted past, remembers something of the bygone soul-states, environments, particular forms of activity which built up its present constituents and knows to what it is moving by development in an uninterrupted future. This is the true dynamic belief in rebirth, and there too the play of the questioning intellect ceases; the soul's vision and the soul's memory are all. Certainly, there remains the question of the mechanism of the development and of the laws of rebirth where the intellect and its inquiries and generalisations can still have some play. And here the more one thinks and experiences, the more the ordinary, simple, cut-and-dried account of reincarnation seems to be of doubtful validity. There is surely here a greater complexity, a law evolved with a more difficult movement and a more intricate harmony out of the possibilities of the Infinite. But this is a question which demands long and ample consideration; for subtle is the law of it. *Aṇur hyeṣa dharmaḥ.*

Rebirth and Karma

THE ANCIENT idea of Karma was inseparably connected with a belief in the soul's continual rebirth in new bodies. And this close association was not a mere accident, but a perfectly intelligible and indeed inevitable union of two related truths which are needed for each other's completeness and can with difficulty exist in separation. These two things are the soul side and the nature side of one and the same cosmic sequence. Rebirth is meaningless without karma, and karma has no fount of inevitable origin and no rational and no moral justification if it is not an instrumentality for the sequences of the soul's continuous experience. If we believe that the soul is repeatedly reborn in the body, we must believe also that there is some link between the lives that preceded and the lives that follow and that the past of the soul has an effect on its future; and that is the spiritual essence of the law of Karma. To deny it would be to establish a reign of the most chaotic incoherence, such as we find only in the leaps and turns of the mind in dream or in the thoughts of madness, and hardly even there. And if this existence were, as the cosmic pessimist imagines, a dream or an illusion or, worse, as Schopenhauer would have it, a delirium and insanity of the soul,[1] we might accept some such law of inconsequent consequence. But, taken even at its worst, this world of life differs from dream, illusion and madness by its plan of fine, complex and subtle sequences, the hanging together and utility even of its discords, the general and particular harmony of its relations, which, if they are not the harmony we would have, not our longed-for ideal harmony, has still at every point the stamp

Published in *Arya* in 1919; subsequently revised and included in *The Problem of Rebirth*.

[1] Arthur Schopenhauer (1788–1860), pessimistic German philosopher.

of a Wisdom and an Idea at work; it is not the act of a Mind in tatters or a machine in dislocation. The continuous existence of the soul in rebirth must signify an evolution if not of the self, for that is said to be immutable, yet of its more outward active soul or self of experience. This evolution is not possible if there is not a connected sequence from life to life, a result of action and experience, an evolutionary consequence to the soul, a law of Karma.

And on the side of Karma, if we give to that its integral and not a truncated meaning, we must admit rebirth for the sufficient field of its action. For Karma is not quite the same thing as a material or substantial law of cause and effect, the antecedent and its mechanical consequence. That would perfectly admit of a Karma which could be carried on in time and the results come with certainty in their proper place, their just degree by a working out of the balance of forces, but need not in any way touch the human originator who might have passed away from the scene by the time the result of his acts got into manifestation. A mechanical Nature could well visit the sins of the fathers not on them, but on their fourth or their four-hundredth generation, as indeed this physical Nature does, and no objection of injustice or any other mental or moral objection could rise, for the only justice or reason of a mechanism is that it shall work according to the law of its structure and the fixed eventuality of its force in action. We cannot demand from it a mind or a moral equity or any kind of supraphysical responsibility. The universal energy grinds out inconsciently its effects and individuals are only fortuitous or subordinate means of its workings; the soul itself, if there is a soul, makes only a part of the mechanism of Nature, exists not for itself, but as an utility for her business. But Karma is more than a mechanical law of antecedent and consequence. Karma is action, there is a thing done and a doer and an active consequence; these three are the three joints, the three locks, the three *sandhis* of the connexus of Karma. And it is a complex mental, moral and physical working; for the law of it is not less true of the mental and moral than of the physical consequence of the act to the doer. The will and the idea are the driving force of the action, and the momentum does not come from some commotion in my chemical atoms or some working of ion and electron or some weird biological effervescence. Therefore the act and consequence must have some relation to the will and the idea and there must be a mental and moral consequence to the soul which has the will and idea. That, if we admit the individual as a real being, signifies a continuity of act and consequence to him and therefore rebirth for a field of this working. It is evident that in one life we do not and cannot labour out and exhaust all the values and powers of that life, but only carry on a past thread, weave out something in the present, prepare infinitely more for the future.

This consequence of rebirth would not follow from the very nature of Karma if there were only an All-Soul of the universe. For then it would be that which is carrying on in myriads of forms its past, working out some present result, spinning yarn of karma for a future weft of consequence. It is the All-Soul which would be the originator, would upbear the force of the act, would receive and exhaust or again take up for farther uses the returning force of the consequence. Nothing essential would depend on its doing all these things through the same individual mask of its being. For the individual would only be a prolonged moment of the All-Soul, and what it originated in this moment of its being which I call myself, might very well produce its result on some other moment of the same being which from the point of view of my ego would be somebody quite different from and unconnected with myself. There would be no injustice, no unreason in such an apparently vicarious reaping of the fruit or suffering of the consequence; for what has a mask, though it be a living and suffering mask, to do with these things? And, in fact, in the nature of life in the material universe a working out of the result of the action of one in the lives of many others, an effect of the individual's action on the group or the whole is everywhere the law. What I sow in this hour, is reaped by my posterity for several generations and we can then call it the karma of the family. What the men of today as community or people resolve upon and execute, comes back with a blessing or a sword upon the future of their race when they themselves have passed away and are no longer there to rejoice or to suffer; and that we can speak of as the karma of the nation. Mankind as a whole too has a karma; what it wrought in its past, will shape its future destiny; individuals seem only to be temporary units of human thought, will, nature who act according to the compulsion of the soul in humanity and disappear; but the karma of the race which they have helped to form continues through the centuries, the millenniums, the cycles.

But we can see, when we look into ourselves, that this relation of the individual to the whole has a different significance; it does not mean that I have no existence except as a more or less protracted moment in the cosmic becoming of the All-Soul: that too is only a superficial appearance and much subtler and greater is the truth of my being. For the original and eternal Reality, the Alpha and Omega, the Godhead is neither separate in the individual nor is he only and solely a Pantheos, a cosmic spirit. He is at once the eternal individual and the eternal All-Soul of this and many universes, and at the same time he is much more than these things. This universe might end, but he would still be; and I too, though the universe might end, could still exist in him; and all these eternal souls would still exist in him. But as his being is for ever, so the succession of his creations too is for ever; if one creation were to come to an end, it would be only that another might begin and the new would carry on with a fresh commencement and initiation the possibility that had not been worked out in the old, for there can be no end to the self-manifestation of the Infinite. *Nāsti anto vistarasya me*. The universe finds itself in me, even as I find myself in the universe, because we are this face and that face of the one eternal Reality, and individual being is as much needed as universal being to work out this manifestation. The individual vision of things is as true as the universal vision, both are ways of the self-seeing of the Eternal. I may now see myself as a creature contained in the universe; but when I come to self-knowledge, I see too the universe to be a thing contained in myself, subtly by implication in my individuality, amply in the great universalised self I then become. These are data of an ancient experience, things known and voiced of old, though they may seem shadowy and transcendental to the positive modern mind which has long pored so minutely on outward things that it has become dazed and blind to any greater light and is only slowly recovering the power to see through its folds; but they are for all that always valid and can be experienced today by any one of us who chooses to turn to the deepest way of the inner experience. Modern thought and science, if we look at the new knowledge given us in its whole, do not contradict them, but only trace for us the outward effect and workings of these realities; for always we find in the end that truth of self is not contradicted, but reproduced and made effectual here by law of Energy and law of Matter.

The necessity of rebirth, if we look at it from the outward side, from the side of energy and process, stands upon a persistent and insistent fact which supervenes always upon the generality of common law and kind and constitutes the most intimate secret of the wonder of existence, the uniqueness of the individual. And this uniqueness is everywhere, but appears as a subordinate factor only in the lower ranges of existence. It becomes more and more important and pronounced as we rise in the scale, enlarges in mind, gets to enormous proportions when we come to the things of the spirit. That would seem to indicate that the cause of this significant uniqueness is something bound up with the very nature of spirit; it is something it held in itself and is bringing out more and more as it emerges out of material Nature into self-conscience. The laws of being are at bottom one for all of us, because all existence is one existence; one spirit, one self, one mind, one life, one energy of process is at work; one will and wisdom has planned or has evolved from itself the whole business of creation. And yet in this oneness there is a persistent variety, which we see first in the form of a communal variation. There is everywhere a group energy, group life, group mind, and if soul is, then we have reason to believe that however elusive it may be to our seizing, there is a group-soul which is the support and foundation — some would call it the result — of this communal variety. That gives us a ground for a group karma. For the group or collective soul renews and prolongs itself and in man at least develops its nature and experience from generation to generation. And who knows whether, when one form of it is disintegrated, community or nation, it may not wait for and assume other forms in which its will of being, its type of nature and mentality, its attempt of experience is carried forward, migrates, one might almost say, into new-born collective bodies, in other ages or cycles? Mankind itself has this separate collective soul and collective existence. And on that community the community of karma is founded; the action and development of the whole produces consequence of karma and experience for the individual and the totality even as the action and development of the individual produces consequences and experience for others, for the group, for the whole. And the individual is there; you cannot reduce him to a nullity or an illusion; he is real, alive, unique. The communal soul-variation mounts up from the rest, exceeds, brings in or brings out something more, something new, adds novel powers in the evolution. The individual mounts and exceeds in the same way from the community. It is in him, on his highest heights that we get the flame-crest of self-manifestation by which the One finds himself in Nature.

And the question is how does that come about at all? I enter into birth, not in a separate being, but in the life of the whole, and therefore I inherit the life of the whole. I am born physically by a generation which is a carrying on of its unbroken history; the body, life, physical mentality of all past being prolongs itself in me and I must therefore undergo the law of heredity; the parent, says the Upanishad, recreates himself by the energy in his seed and is reborn in the child. But as soon as I begin to develop, a new, an independent and overbearing factor comes in, which is not my parents nor my ancestry, nor past mankind, but I, my own self. And this is the really important, crowning, central factor. What matters most in my life, is not my heredity; that only gives me my opportunity or my obstacle, my good or my bad material, and it has not by any means been shown that I draw all from that source. What matters supremely is what I make of my heredity and not what my heredity makes of me. The past of the world, bygone humanity, my ancestors are there in me; but still I myself am the artist of my self, my life, my actions. And there is the present of the world, of humanity, there are my contemporaries as well as my ancestors; the life of my environment too enters into me, offers me a new material, shapes me by its influence, lays its direct or its indirect touch on my being. I am invaded, changed, partly recreated by the environing being and action in which I am and act. But here again the individual comes in subtly and centrally as the decisive power. What is supremely important is what I make of all this surrounding and invading present and not what it makes of me. And in the interaction of individual and general Karma in which others are causes and produce an effect in my existence and I am a cause and produce an effect on them, I live for others, whether I would have it so or no, and others live for me and for all. Still the central power of my psychology takes its colour from this seeing that I live for my self, and for others or for the world only as an extension of my self, as a thing with which I am bound up in some kind of oneness. I seem to be a soul, self or spirit who constantly with the assistance of all create out of my past and present my future being and myself too help in the surrounding creative evolution.

What then is this all-important and independent power in me and what is the beginning and the end of its self-creation? Has it, even though it is something independent of the physical and vital present and past which gives to it so much of its material, itself no past and no future? Is it something which suddenly emerges from the All-Soul at my birth and ceases at my death? Is its insistence on self-creation, on making something of itself for itself, for its own future and not only for its fleeting present and the future of the race, a vain preòccupation, a gross parasitical error? That would contradict all that we see of the law of the world-being; it would not reduce our life to a greater consistency with the frame of things, but would bring in a freak element and an inconsistency with the pervading principle. It is reasonable to suppose that this powerful independent element which supervenes and works upon the physical and vital evolution, was in the past and will be in the future. It is reasonable also to suppose that it did not come in suddenly from some unconnected existence and does not pass out after one brief intervention; its close connection with the life of the world is rather a continuation of a long past connection. And this brings in at once the whole necessity of past birth and karma. I am a persistent being who pursue my evolution within the persistent being of the world. I have evolved my human birth and I help constantly in the human evolution. I have created by my past karma my own conditions and my relations with the life of others and the general karma. That shapes my heredity, my environment, my affinities, my connections, my material, my opportunities and obstacles, a part of my predestined powers and results, not arbitrarily predestined but predetermined by my own stage of nature and past action, and on this groundwork I build new karma and farther strengthen or subtilise my power of natural being, enlarge experience, go on with my soul evolution. This process is woven in with the universal evolution and all its lines are included in the web of being, but it is not merely a jutting point or moment of it or a brief tag shot into the tissue. That is what rebirth means in the history of my manifested self and of universal being.

The old idea of rebirth errs on the contrary by an excessive individualism. Too self-concentrated, it treated one's rebirth and karma as too much one's own single affair, a sharply separate movement in the whole, leaned too much on one's own concern with one's self and even while it admitted universal relations and a unity with the whole, yet taught the human being to see in life principally a condition and means of his own spiritual benefit and separate salvation. That came from the view of the universe as a movement which proceeds out of something beyond, something from which each being enters into life and returns out of it to its source, and the absorbing idea of that return as the one thing that at all matters. Our being in the world, so treated, came in the end to be regarded as an episode and in sum and essence an unhappy and discreditable episode in the changeless eternity of the Spirit. But this was too summary a view of the will and the ways of the Spirit in existence. Certain it is that while we are here, our rebirth or karma, even while it runs on its own lines, is intimately one with the same lines in the universal existence. But my self-knowledge and self-finding too do not abolish my oneness with other life and other beings. An intimate universality is part of the glory of spiritual perfection. This idea of universality, of oneness not only with God or the eternal Self in me, but with all humanity and other beings, is growing to be the most prominent strain in our minds and it has to be taken more largely into account in any future idea or computation of the significance of rebirth and karma. It was admitted in old times; the Buddhist law of compassion was a recognition of its importance; but it has to be given a still more pervading power in the general significance.

The self-effectuation of the Spirit in the world is the truth on which we take our foundation, a great, a long self-weaving in time. Rebirth is the continuity of that self-effectuation in the individual, the persistence of the thread; Karma is the process, a force, a work of energy and consequence in the material world, an inner and an outer will, an action and mental, moral, dynamic consequence in the soul evolution of which the material world is a constant scene. That is the conception; the rest is a question of the general and particular laws, the way in which karma works out and helps the purpose of the spirit in birth and life. And whatever those laws and ways may be, they must be subservient to this spiritual self-effectuation and take from it all their meaning and value. The law is a means, a line of working for the spirit, and does not exist for its own sake or for the service of any abstract idea. Idea and law of working are only direction and road for the soul's progress in the steps of its existence.

Rebirth and Personality

YOU MUST avoid a common popular blunder about reincarnation. The popular idea is that Titus Balbus is reborn again as John Smith, a man with the same personality, character, attainments as he had in his former life with the sole difference that he wears coat and trousers instead of a toga and speaks in cockney English instead of popular Latin. That is not the case. What would be the earthly use of repeating the same personality or character a million times from the beginning of time till its end? The soul comes into birth for experience, for growth, for evolution till it can bring the Divine into Matter. It is the central being that incarnates, not the outer personality — the personality is simply a mould that it creates for its figures of experience in that one life. In another birth it will create for itself a different personality, different capacities, a different life and career. Supposing Virgil is born again, he may take up poetry in one or two other lives, but he will certainly not write an epic but rather perhaps slight but elegant and beautiful lyrics such as he wanted to write, but did not succeed, in Rome. In another birth he is likely to be no poet at all, but a philosopher and a yogin seeking to attain and to express the highest truth — for that too was an unrealised trend of his consciousness in that life. Perhaps before he had been a warrior or ruler doing deeds like Aeneas or Augustus before he sang them. And so on — on this side or that the central being develops a new character, a new personality, grows, develops, passes through all kinds of terrestrial experience.

As the evolving being develops still more and becomes more rich and complex, it accumulates its personalities, as it were.

A letter written in June 1933 and published in the booklet *The Riddle of This World* later in 1933.

Sometimes they stand behind the active elements, throwing in some colour, some trait, some capacity here and there, — or they stand in front and there is a multiple personality, a many-sided character or a many-sided, sometimes what looks like a universal capacity. But if a former personality, a former capacity is brought fully forward, it will not be to repeat what was already done, but to cast the same capacity into new forms and new shapes and fuse it into a new harmony of the being which will not be a reproduction of what was before. Thus you must not expect to be what the warrior and the poet were. Something of the outer characteristics may reappear but very much changed and new-cast in a new combination. It is in a new direction that the energies will be guided to do what was not done before.

Another thing. It is not the personality, the character that is of the first importance in rebirth — it is the psychic being who stands behind the evolution of the nature and evolves with it. The psychic when it departs from the body, shedding even the mental and vital on its way to its resting place, carries with it the heart of its experiences, — not the physical events, not the vital movements, not the mental buildings, not the capacities or characters, but something essential that it gathered from them, what might be called the divine element for the sake of which the rest existed. That is the permanent addition, it is that that helps in the growth towards the Divine. That is why there is usually no memory of the outward events and circumstances of past lives — for this memory there must be a strong development towards unbroken continuance of the mind, the vital, even the subtle physical; for though it all remains in a kind of seed memory, it does not ordinarily emerge. What was the divine element in the magnanimity of the warrior, that which expressed itself in his loyalty, nobility, high courage, what was the divine element behind the harmonious mentality and generous vitality of the poet and expressed itself in them, that remains and in a new harmony of character may find a new expression or, if the life is turned towards the Divine, be taken up as powers for the realisation or for the work that has to be done for the Divine.

Metaphysical Thought and the Supreme Truth

European metaphysical thought — even in those thinkers who try to prove or explain the existence and nature of God or of the Absolute — does not in its method and result go beyond the intellect. But the intellect is incapable of knowing the supreme Truth; it can only range about seeking for Truth, and catching fragmentary representations of it, not the thing itself, and trying to piece them together. Mind cannot arrive at Truth; it can only make some constructed figure that tries to represent it or a combination of figures. At the end of European thought, therefore, there must always be Agnosticism, declared or implicit. Intellect, if it goes sincerely to its own end, has to return and give this report: 'I cannot know; there is, or at least it seems to me that there may be or even must be Something beyond, some ultimate Reality, but about its truth I can only speculate; it is either unknowable or cannot be known by me.' Or, if it has received some light on the way from what is beyond it, it can say too: 'There is perhaps a consciousness beyond Mind, for I seem to catch glimpses of it and even to get intimations from it. If that is in touch with the Beyond or if it is itself the consciousness of the Beyond and you can find some way to reach it, then this Something can be known but not otherwise.'

Any seeking of the supreme Truth through intellect alone must end either in Agnosticism of this kind or else in some intellectual system or mind-constructed formula. There have been hundreds of these systems and formulas and there can be hundreds more, but none can be definitive. Each may have its value for the mind, and different systems with their contrary conclusions can have an equal appeal to intelligences of equal power and competence. All this labour of speculation has its

A letter written in 1930 and included in *The Riddle of This World* in 1933.

utility in training the human mind and helping to keep before it the idea of Something beyond and Ultimate towards which it must turn. But the intellectual Reason can only point vaguely or feel gropingly towards it or try to indicate partial and even conflicting aspects of its manifestation here; it cannot enter into and know it. As long as we remain in the domain of the intellect only, an impartial pondering over all that has been thought and sought after, a constant throwing up of ideas, of all the possible ideas, and the formation of this or that philosophical belief, opinion or conclusion is all that can be done. This kind of disinterested search after Truth would be the only possible attitude for any wide and plastic intelligence. But any conclusion so arrived at would be only speculative; it could have no spiritual value; it would not give the decisive experience or the spiritual certitude for which the soul is seeking. If the intellect is our highest possible instrument and there is no other means of arriving at supraphysical Truth, then a wise and large Agnosticism must be our ultimate attitude. Things in the manifestation may be known to some degree, but the Supreme and all that is beyond the Mind must remain forever unknowable.

It is only if there is a greater consciousness beyond Mind and that consciousness is accessible to us that we can know and enter into the ultimate Reality. Intellectual speculation, logical reasoning as to whether there is or is not such a greater consciousness cannot carry us very far. What we need is a way to get the experience of it, to reach it, enter into it, live in it. If we can get that, intellectual speculation and reasoning must fall necessarily into a very secondary place and even lose their reason for existence. Philosophy, intellectual expression of the Truth may remain, but mainly as a means of expressing this greater discovery and as much of its contents as can at all be expressed in mental terms to those who still live in the mental intelligence.

This, you will see, answers your point about the Western thinkers, Bradley and others, who have arrived through intellectual thinking at the idea of an 'Other beyond Thought' or have even, like Bradley, tried to express their conclusions about it in terms that recall some of the expressions in the *Arya*.[1] The idea

[1] Francis Herbert Bradley (1846–1924), British absolute idealist philosopher. In *Appearance and Reality* (1893) and other works he argues that thought and language are incapable of attaining to or expressing true reality.

in itself is not new; it is as old as the Vedas. It was repeated in other forms in Buddhism, Christian Gnosticism, Sufism. Originally, it was not discovered by intellectual speculation, but by the mystics following an inner spiritual discipline. When, somewhere between the seventh and fifth centuries B.C., men began both in the East and West to intellectualise knowledge, this Truth survived in the East; in the West where the intellect began to be accepted as the sole or highest instrument for the discovery of Truth, it began to fade. But still it has there too tried constantly to return; the Neo-Platonists brought it back, and now, it appears, the Neo-Hegelians and others (e.g., the Russian Ouspensky and one or two German thinkers, I believe) seem to be reaching after it.[2] But still there is a difference.

In the East, especially in India, the metaphysical thinkers have tried, as in the West, to determine the nature of the highest Truth by the intellect. But, in the first place, they have not given mental thinking the supreme rank as an instrument in the discovery of Truth, but only a secondary status. The first rank has always been given to spiritual intuition and illumination and spiritual experience; an intellectual conclusion that contradicts this supreme authority is held invalid. Secondly, each philosophy has armed itself with a practical way of reaching to the supreme state of consciousness, so that even when one begins with Thought, the aim is to arrive at a consciousness beyond mental thinking. Each philosophical founder (as also those who continued his work or school) has been a metaphysical thinker doubled with a yogi. Those who were only philosophic intellectuals were respected for their learning but never took rank as truth-discoverers. And the philosophies that lacked a sufficiently powerful means of spiritual experience died out and became things of the past because they were not dynamic for spiritual discovery and realisation.

In the West it was just the opposite that came to pass. Thought, intellect, the logical reason came to be regarded more

[2] Neo-Platonism, a mystico-philosophical school originated by Plotinus (205–270), was a fusion of the thought of Plato, Pythagoras and other classical Greek philosophers with Eastern mysticism. The term 'Neo-Hegelianism' is applied to the thought of late-nineteenth- and early-twentieth-century followers of the German idealist philosopher G. W. F. Hegel (1770–1831), among them Bradley. Peter Ouspensky (1878–1947) is known especially as the foremost intellectual disciple of the mystic Georgei Gurdjieff (c. 1877–1949), with whom he later broke.

and more as the highest means and even the highest end; in philosophy, Thought is the be-all and the end-all. It is by intellectual thinking and speculation that the truth is to be discovered; even spiritual experience has been summoned to pass the tests of the intellect, if it is to be held valid—just the reverse of the Indian position. Even those who see that the mental Thought must be overpassed and admit a supramental 'Other', do not seem to escape from the feeling that it must be through mental Thought, sublimating and transmuting itself, that this other Truth must be reached and made to take the place of the mental limitation and ignorance. And again Western thought has ceased to be dynamic; it has sought after a theory of things, not after realisation. It was still dynamic amongst the ancient Greeks, but for moral and aesthetic rather than spiritual ends. Later on, it became yet more purely intellectual and academic; it became intellectual speculation only without any practical ways and means for the attainment of the Truth by spiritual experiment, spiritual discovery, a spiritual transformation. If there were not this difference, there would be no reason for seekers like yourself to turn to the East for guidance; for in the purely intellectual field, the Western thinkers are as competent as any Eastern sage. It is the spiritual way, the road that leads beyond the intellectual levels, the passage from the outer being to the inmost Self, which has been lost by the over-intellectuality of the mind of Europe.

In the extracts you have sent me from Bradley and Joachim, it is still the intellect thinking about what is beyond itself and coming to an intellectual, a reasoned speculative conclusion about it. It is not dynamic for the change which it attempts to describe. If these writers were expressing in mental terms some realisation, even mental, some intuitive experience of this 'Other than Thought', then one ready for it might feel it through the veil of the language they use and himself draw near to the same experience. Or if, having reached the intellectual conclusion, they had passed on to the spiritual realisation, finding the way or following one already found, then in pursuing their thought, one might be preparing oneself for the same transition. But there is nothing of the kind in all this strenuous thinking. It remains in the domain of the intellect and in that domain it is no doubt admirable; but it does not become dynamic for spiritual experience.

It is not by 'thinking out' the entire reality, but by a change of consciousness that one can pass from the ignorance to the Knowledge—the Knowledge by which we become what we know. To pass from the external to a direct and intimate inner consciousness; to widen consciousness out of the limits of the ego and the body; to heighten it by an inner will and aspiration and opening to the Light till it passes in its ascent beyond Mind; to bring down a descent of the supramental Divine through self-giving and surrender with a consequent transformation of mind, life and body—this is the *integral* way to the Truth.[3] It is this that we call the Truth here and aim at in our yoga.

[3] I have said that the idea of the supermind was already in existence from ancient times. There was in India and elsewhere the attempt to reach it by rising to it; but what was missed was the way to make it integral for the life and to bring it down for transformation of the whole nature, even of the physical nature. [Sri Aurobindo's note]

Part Five
Yoga and Life

It is a great error to suppose that spirituality flourishes best in an impoverished soil with the life half-killed and the intellect discouraged and intimidated. The spirituality that so flourishes is something morbid, hectic and exposed to perilous reactions. It is when the [human] race has lived most richly and thought most profoundly that spirituality finds its heights and its depths and its constant and many-sided fruition.

The Renaissance in India

PART FIVE consists of six chapters from *The Synthesis of Yoga*—two from the introduction and one from each of the book's four parts—as well as five letters on aspects of Sri Aurobindo's integral yoga.

• The processes of Yoga are special developments of natural human powers; there can thus be no rigid distinction between *Life and Yoga*: 'all life is either consciously or subconsciously a Yoga'.

• The different systems of yoga each make use of part of the total human being. A *Synthesis of the Systems* would result in an integral yoga more powerful and comprehensive than any individual path. Such a synthesis could be brought about by means of a surrender to the *shakti* or force of the divine consciousness.

• In the first part of the *Synthesis*, 'The Yoga of Divine Works', Sri Aurobindo discusses the nature of *karmayoga*, the means of which is action done for the sake of the Divine. In *Standards of Conduct and Spiritual Freedom* he considers what relationship human moral standards have with the 'standardless, spiritual and supramental mode of working for which the Yoga seeks'. Besides being essential for an understanding of his yoga, this chapter is an important contribution to the study of the evolution of human societies.

• Part Two of *The Synthesis* is devoted to 'The Yoga of Integral Knowledge'. In *The Cosmic Consciousness* Sri Aurobindo deals with one of the fundamental mystical experiences that can come to seekers who have undergone the necessary preparation.

• Part Three of *The Synthesis* deals with 'The Yoga of Divine Love', which is based on the traditional yoga of *bhakti* or devotion. By means of this yoga one can become aware of *The Ananda Brahman*, the 'bliss-existence' that is the source of all joy, beauty, love, peace and delight.

• The fourth part of the *Synthesis*, 'The Yoga of Self-Perfection', deals with a particular path of yoga that Sri Aurobindo followed in Pondicherry. In *The Integral Perfection* he clarifies what he means by perfection, distinguishing his integral perfection from the mundane and religious ideals.

• *Karmayoga* and *Bhakti* are letters written by Sri Aurobindo to disciples, dealing with aspects of the yogas of work and devotion. *Meditation* is a letter written in answer to a series of questions on meditation and related subjects.

• In *The Central Process of the Yoga*, Sri Aurobindo explains two important processes of his yoga—'opening' and 'descent'—to one of his disciples. In the letter here called *The Novelty of the Integral Yoga*, he clarifies what he means by 'transformation', one of the most distinctive concepts in his yoga.

Life and Yoga

THERE ARE two necessities of Nature's workings which seem always to intervene in the greater forms of human activity, whether these belong to our ordinary fields of movement or seek those exceptional spheres and fulfilments which appear to us high and divine. Every such form tends towards a harmonised complexity and totality which again breaks apart into various channels of special effort and tendency, only to unite once more in a larger and more puissant synthesis. Secondly, development into forms is an imperative rule of effective manifestation; yet all truth and practice too strictly formulated becomes old and loses much, if not all, of its virtue; it must be constantly renovated by fresh streams of the spirit revivifying the dead or dying vehicle and changing it, if it is to acquire a new life. To be perpetually reborn is the condition of a material immortality. We are in an age, full of the throes of travail, when all forms of thought and activity that have in themselves any strong power of utility or any secret virtue of persistence are being subjected to a supreme test and given their opportunity of rebirth. The world today presents the aspect of a huge cauldron of Medea in which all things are being cast, shredded into pieces, experimented on, combined and recombined either to perish and provide the scattered material of new forms or to emerge rejuvenated and changed for a fresh term of existence.[1] Indian Yoga, in its essence a special action or formulation of certain great powers of Nature, itself specialised, divided and variously formulated,

The first chapter of the Introduction to *The Synthesis of Yoga*, published in the *Arya* in 1914. The closing phrase of the chapter, 'All Life is Yoga', is the book's epigraph. *The Synthesis of Yoga* was first brought out as a book posthumously in 1955.

[1] Medea, an enchantress celebrated in Greek mythology, cut an old ram apart, threw the pieces into her cauldron, uttered some magic words, and a lamb came forth.

is potentially one of these dynamic elements of the future life of humanity. The child of immemorial ages, preserved by its vitality and truth into our modern times, it is now emerging from the secret schools and ascetic retreats in which it had taken refuge and is seeking its place in the future sum of living human powers and utilities. But it has first to rediscover itself, bring to the surface the profoundest reason of its being in that general truth and that unceasing aim of Nature which it represents, and find by virtue of this new self-knowledge and self-appreciation its own recovered and larger synthesis. Reorganising itself, it will enter more easily and powerfully into the reorganised life of the race which its processes claim to lead within into the most secret penetralia and upward to the highest altitudes of its own existence and personality.

In the right view both of life and of Yoga all life is either consciously or subconsciously a Yoga. For we mean by this term a methodised effort towards self-perfection by the expression of the secret potentialities latent in the being and — highest conditions of victory in that effort — a union of the human individual with the universal and transcendent Existence we see partially expressed in man and in the Cosmos. But all life, when we look behind its appearances, is a vast Yoga of Nature who attempts in the conscious and the subconscious to realise her perfection in an ever increasing expression of her yet unrealised potentialities and to unite herself with her own divine reality. In man, her thinker, she for the first time upon this Earth devises self-conscious means and willed arrangements of activity by which this great purpose may be more swiftly and puissantly attained. Yoga, as Swami Vivekananda has said, may be regarded as a means of compressing one's evolution into a single life or a few years or even a few months of bodily existence. A given system of Yoga, then, can be no more than a selection or a compression, into narrower but more energetic forms of intensity, of the general methods which are already being used loosely, largely, in a leisurely movement, with a profuser apparent waste of material and energy but with a more complete combination by the great Mother in her vast upward labour. It is this view of Yoga that can alone form the basis for a sound and rational synthesis of Yogic methods. For then Yoga ceases to appear something mystic and abnormal which has no relation to the ordinary processes of the

World-Energy or the purpose she keeps in view in her two great movements of subjective and objective self-fulfilment; it reveals itself rather as an intense and exceptional use of powers that she has already manifested or is progressively organising in her less exalted but more general operations.

Yogic methods have something of the same relation to the customary psychological workings of man as has the scientific handling of the natural force of electricity or of steam to their normal operations in Nature. And they, too, like the operations of Science are formed upon a knowledge developed and confirmed by regular experiment, practical analysis and constant result. All Rajayoga, for instance, depends on this perception and experience that our inner elements, combinations, functions, forces, can be separated or dissolved, can be new-combined and set to novel and formerly impossible workings or can be transformed and resolved into a new general synthesis by fixed internal processes. Hathayoga similarly depends on this perception and experience that the vital forces and functions to which our life is normally subjected and whose ordinary operations seem set and indispensable, can be mastered and the operations changed or suspended with results that would otherwise be impossible and that seem miraculous to those who have not seized the rationale of their process. And if in some other of its forms this character of Yoga is less apparent, because they are more intuitive and less mechanical, nearer, like the Yoga of Devotion, to a supernal ecstasy or, like the Yoga of Knowledge, to a supernal infinity of consciousness and being, yet they too start from the use of some principal faculty in us by ways and for ends not contemplated in its everyday spontaneous workings. All methods grouped under the common name of Yoga are special psychological processes founded on a fixed truth of Nature and developing, out of normal functions, powers and results which were always latent but which her ordinary movements do not easily or do not often manifest.

But as in physical knowledge the multiplication of scientific processes has its disadvantages, as that tends, for instance, to develop a victorious artificiality which overwhelms our natural human life under a load of machinery and to purchase certain forms of freedom and mastery at the price of an increased servitude, so the preoccupation with Yogic processes and their exceptional results may have its disadvantages and losses. The Yogin tends to draw away from the common existence and lose his hold upon it; he tends to purchase wealth of spirit by an impoverishment of his human activities, the inner freedom by an outer death. If he gains God, he loses life, or if he turns his efforts outward to conquer life, he is in danger of losing God. Therefore we see in India that a sharp incompatibility has been created between life in the world and spiritual growth and perfection, and although the tradition and ideal of a victorious harmony between the inner attraction and the outer demand remains, it is little or else very imperfectly exemplified. In fact, when a man turns his vision and energy inward and enters on the path of Yoga, he is popularly supposed to be lost inevitably to the great stream of our collective existence and the secular effort of humanity. So strongly has the idea prevailed, so much has it been emphasized by prevalent philosophies and religions that to escape from life is now commonly considered as not only the necessary condition, but the general object of Yoga. No synthesis of Yoga can be satisfying which does not, in its aim, reunite God and Nature in a liberated and perfected human life or, in its method, not only permit but favour the harmony of our inner and outer activities and experiences in the divine consummation of both. For man is precisely that term and symbol of a higher Existence descended into the material world in which it is possible for the lower to transfigure itself and put on the nature of the higher and the higher to reveal itself in the forms of the lower. To avoid the life which is given him for the realisation of that possibility, can never be either the indispensable condition or the whole and ultimate object of his supreme endeavour or of his most powerful means of self-fulfilment. It can only be a temporary necessity under certain conditions or a specialised extreme effort imposed on the individual so as to prepare a greater general possibility for the race. The true and full object and utility of Yoga can only be accomplished when the conscious Yoga in man becomes, like the subconscious Yoga in Nature, outwardly conterminous with life itself and we can once more, looking out both on the path and the achievement, say in a more perfect and luminous sense: 'All life is Yoga.'

The Synthesis of the Systems

BY THE very nature of the principal Yogic schools, each covering in its operations a part of the complex human integer and attempting to bring out its highest possibilities, it will appear that a synthesis of all of them largely conceived and applied might well result in an integral Yoga. But they are so disparate in their tendencies, so highly specialised and elaborated in their forms, so long confirmed in the mutual opposition of their ideas and methods that we do not easily find how we can arrive at their right union.

An undiscriminating combination in block would not be a synthesis, but a confusion. Nor would a successive practice of each of them in turn be easy in the short span of our human life and with our limited energies, to say nothing of the waste of labour implied in so cumbrous a process. Sometimes, indeed, Hathayoga and Rajayoga are thus successively practised. And in a recent unique example, in the life of Ramakrishna Paramahansa, we see a colossal spiritual capacity first driving straight to the divine realisation, taking, as it were, the kingdom of heaven by violence, and then seizing upon one Yogic method after another and extracting the substance out of it with an incredible rapidity, always to return to the heart of the whole matter, the realisation and possession of God by the power of love, by the extension of inborn spirituality into various experience and by the spontaneous play of an intuitive knowledge. Such an example cannot be generalised. Its object also was special and temporal, to exemplify in the great and decisive experience of a master-soul the truth, now most necessary to humanity, towards which

The fifth chapter of the Introduction to *The Synthesis of Yoga*, published in the *Arya* in 1914.

a world long divided into jarring sects and schools is with difficulty labouring, that all sects are forms and fragments of a single integral truth and all disciplines labour in their different ways towards one supreme experience. To know, be and possess the Divine is the one thing needful and it includes or leads up to all the rest; towards this sole good we have to drive and this attained, all the rest that the divine Will chooses for us, all necessary form and manifestation, will be added.

The synthesis we propose cannot, then, be arrived at either by combination in mass or by successive practice. It must therefore be effected by neglecting the forms and outsides of the Yogic disciplines and seizing rather on some central principle common to all which will include and utilise in the right place and proportion their particular principles, and on some central dynamic force which is the common secret of their divergent methods and capable therefore of organising a natural selection and combination of their varied energies and different utilities. This was the aim which we set before ourselves at first when we entered upon our comparative examination of the methods of Nature and the methods of Yoga and we now return to it with the possibility of hazarding some definite solution.

We observe, first, that there still exists in India a remarkable Yogic system which is in its nature synthetical and starts from a great central principle of Nature, a great dynamic force of Nature; but it is a Yoga apart, not a synthesis of other schools. This system is the way of the Tantra. Owing to certain of its developments Tantra has fallen into discredit with those who are not Tantrics; and especially owing to the developments of its left-hand path, the Vamamarga, which not content with exceeding the duality of virtue and sin and instead of replacing them by spontaneous rightness of action seemed sometimes to make a method of self-indulgence, a method of unrestrained social immorality. Nevertheless, in its origin, Tantra was a great and puissant system founded upon ideas which were at least partially true. Even its twofold division into the right-hand and left-hand paths, Dakshina Marga and Vama Marga, started from a certain profound perception. In the ancient symbolic sense of the words Dakshina and Vama, it was the distinction between the way of Knowledge and the way of Ananda, — Nature in man liberating itself by right discrimination in power and practice of its own energies, elements and potentialities and Nature in man liberating itself by joyous acceptance in power and practice of its own energies, elements and potentialities. But in both paths there was in the end an obscuration of principles, a deformation of symbols and a fall.

If, however, we leave aside, here also, the actual methods and practices and seek for the central principle, we find, first, that Tantra expressly differentiates itself from the Vedic methods of Yoga. In a sense, all the schools we have hitherto examined are Vedantic in their principle; their force is in knowledge, their method is knowledge, though it is not always discernment by the intellect, but may be, instead, the knowledge of the heart expressed in love and faith or a knowledge in the will working out through action. In all of them the lord of the Yoga is the Purusha, the Conscious Soul that knows, observes, attracts, governs. But in Tantra it is rather Prakriti, the Nature-Soul, the Energy, the Will-in-Power executive in the universe. It was by learning and applying the intimate secrets of this Will-in-Power, its method, its Tantra, that the Tantric Yogin pursued the aims of his discipline, — mastery, perfection, liberation, beatitude. Instead of drawing back from manifested Nature and its difficulties, he confronted them, seized and conquered. But in the end, as is the general tendency of Prakriti, Tantric Yoga largely lost its principle in its machinery and became a thing of formulae and occult mechanism still powerful when rightly used but fallen from the clarity of their original intention.

We have in this central Tantric conception one side of the truth, the worship of the Energy, the Shakti, as the sole effective force for all attainment. We get the other extreme in the Vedantic conception of the Shakti as a power of Illusion and in the search after the silent inactive Purusha as the means of liberation from the deceptions created by the active Energy. But in the integral conception the Conscious Soul is the Lord, the Nature-Soul is his executive Energy. Purusha is of the nature of Sat, the being of conscious self-existence pure and infinite; Shakti or Prakriti is of the nature of Chit, — it is power of the Purusha's self-conscious existence, pure and infinite. The relation of the two exists between the poles of rest and action. When the Energy is absorbed in the bliss of conscious self-existence, there is rest; when the Purusha pours itself out in the action of its Energy, there is action, creation and the enjoyment or Ananda of becoming. But if Ananda is the creator and begetter of all becoming, its method is Tapas or force of the Purusha's consciousness dwelling upon its own infinite potentiality in existence and producing from it truths of conception or real Ideas, *vijñāna*, which, proceeding from an omniscient and omnipotent Self-existence, have the surety of their own fulfilment and contain in themselves the nature and law of their own becoming in the terms of mind, life and matter. The eventual omnipotence of Tapas and the infallible fulfilment of the Idea are the very foundation of all Yoga. In man we render these terms by Will and Faith, — a will that is eventually self-effective because it is of the substance of Knowledge and a faith that is the reflex in the lower consciousness of a Truth or real Idea yet unrealised in the manifestation. It is this self-certainty of the Idea which is meant by the Gita when it says, *yo yac-chraddhaḥ sa eva saḥ*, 'whatever is a man's faith or the sure Idea in him, that he becomes.'

We see, then, what from the psychological point of view — and Yoga is nothing but practical psychology, — is the conception of Nature from which we have to start. It is the self-fulfilment of the Purusha through his Energy. But the movement of Nature is twofold, higher and lower, or, as we may choose to term it, divine and undivine. The distinction exists indeed for practical purposes only; for there is nothing that is not divine, and in a larger view it is as meaningless, verbally, as the distinction between natural and supernatural, for all things that are are natural. All things are in Nature and all things are in God. But, for practical purposes, there is a real distinction. The lower Nature, that which we know and are and must remain so long as the faith in us is not changed, acts through limitation and division, is of the nature of Ignorance and culminates in the life of the ego; but the higher Nature, that to which we aspire, acts by unification and transcendence of limitation, is of the nature of Knowledge and culminates in the life divine. The passage from the lower to the higher is the aim of Yoga; and this passage may effect itself by the rejection of the lower and escape into the higher, — the ordinary viewpoint, — or by the transformation of the lower and its elevation to the higher Nature. It is this, rather, that must be the aim of an integral Yoga.

But in either case it is always through something in the lower that we must rise into the higher existence, and the schools of Yoga each select their own point of departure or their own gate of escape. They specialise certain activities of the lower Prakriti and turn them towards the Divine. But the normal action of Nature in us is an integral movement in which the full complexity of all our elements is affected by and affects all our environments. The whole of life is the Yoga of Nature. The Yoga that we seek must also be an integral action of Nature, and the whole difference between the Yogin and the natural man will be this, that the Yogin seeks to substitute in himself for the integral action of the lower Nature working in and by ego and division the integral action of the higher Nature working in and by God and unity. If indeed our aim be only an escape from the world to God, synthesis is unnecessary and a waste of time; for then our sole practical aim must be to find out one path out of the thousand that lead to God, one shortest possible of short cuts, and not to linger exploring different paths that end in the same goal. But if our aim be a transformation of our integral being into the terms of God-existence, it is then that a synthesis becomes necessary.

The method we have to pursue, then, is to put our whole conscious being into relation and contact with the Divine and to call Him in to transform our entire being into His. Thus in a sense God Himself, the real Person in us, becomes the sadhaka of the sadhana[1] as well as the Master of the Yoga by whom the lower personality is used as the centre of a divine transfiguration and the instrument of its own perfection. In effect, the pressure of the Tapas, the force of consciousness in us dwelling in the Idea of the divine Nature upon that which we are in our entirety, produces its own realisation. The divine and all-knowing and all-effecting descends upon the limited and obscure, progressively illumines and energises the whole lower nature and substitutes its own action for all the terms of the inferior human light and mortal activity.

In psychological fact this method translates itself into the progressive surrender of the ego with its whole field and all its apparatus to the Beyond-ego with its vast and incalculable but always inevitable workings. Certainly, this is no short cut or easy

[1] *Sādhanā*, the practice by which perfection, *siddhi*, is attained; *sādhaka*, the Yogin who seeks by that practice the *siddhi*. [Sri Aurobindo's note]

sadhana. It requires a colossal faith, an absolute courage and above all an unflinching patience. For it implies three stages of which only the last can be wholly blissful or rapid, — the attempt of the ego to enter into contact with the Divine, the wide, full and therefore laborious preparation of the whole lower Nature by the divine working to receive and become the higher Nature, and the eventual transformation. In fact, however, the divine Strength, often unobserved and behind the veil, substitutes itself for our weakness and supports us through all our failings of faith, courage and patience. It 'makes the blind to see and the lame to stride over the hills.' The intellect becomes aware of a Law that beneficently insists and a succour that upholds; the heart speaks of a Master of all things and Friend of man or a universal Mother who upholds through all stumblings. Therefore this path is at once the most difficult imaginable and yet in comparison with the magnitude of its effort and object, the most easy and sure of all.

There are three outstanding features of this action of the higher when it works integrally on the lower nature. In the first place it does not act according to a fixed system and succession as in the specialised methods of Yoga, but with a sort of free, scattered and yet gradually intensive and purposeful working determined by the temperament of the individual in whom it operates, the helpful materials which his nature offers and the obstacles which it presents to purification and perfection. In a sense, therefore, each man in this path has his own method of Yoga. Yet are there certain broad lines of working common to all which enable us to construct not indeed a routine system, but yet some kind of Shastra or scientific method of the synthetic Yoga.

Secondly, the process, being integral, accepts our nature such as it stands organised by our past evolution and without rejecting anything essential compels all to undergo a divine change. Everything in us is seized by the hands of a mighty Artificer and transformed into a clear image of that which it now seeks confusedly to present. In that ever-progressive experience we begin to perceive how this lower manifestation is constituted and that everything in it, however seemingly deformed or petty or vile, is the more or less distorted or imperfect figure of some element or action in the harmony of the divine Nature. We begin to understand what the Vedic Rishis meant when they spoke of the human forefathers fashioning the gods as a smith forges the crude material in his smithy.

Thirdly, the divine Power in us uses all life as the means of this integral Yoga. Every experience and outer contact with our world-environment, however trifling or however disastrous, is used for the work, and every inner experience, even to the most repellent suffering or the most humiliating fall, becomes a step on the path to perfection. And we recognise in ourselves with opened eyes the method of God in the world, His purpose of light in the obscure, of might in the weak and fallen, of delight in what is grievous and miserable. We see the divine method to be the same in the lower and in the higher working; only in the one it is pursued tardily and obscurely through the subconscious in Nature in the other it becomes swift and self-conscious and the instrument confesses the hand of the Master. All life is a Yoga of Nature seeking to manifest God within itself. Yoga marks the stage at which this effort becomes capable of self-awareness and therefore of right completion in the individual. It is a gathering up and concentration of the movements dispersed and loosely combined in the lower evolution.

An integral method and an integral result. First, an integral realisation of Divine Being; not only a realisation of the One in its indistinguishable unity, but also in its multitude of aspects which are also necessary to the complete knowledge of it by the relative consciousness; not only realisation of unity in the Self, but of unity in the infinite diversity of activities, worlds and creatures.

Therefore, also, an integral liberation. Not only the freedom born of unbroken contact and identification of the individual being in all its parts with the Divine, *sāyujya mukti*, by which it can become free[2] even in its separation, even in the duality; not only the *sālokya mukti* by which the whole conscious existence dwells in the same status of being as the Divine, in the state of Sachchidananda; but also the acquisition of the divine nature by the transformation of this lower being into the human image of the divine, *sādharmya mukti*, and the complete and final release of all, the liberation of the consciousness from the transitory

2 As the Jivanmukta, who is entirely free even without dissolution of the bodily life in a final Samadhi. [Sri Aurobindo's note]

mould of the ego and its unification with the One Being, universal both in the world and the individual and transcendentally one both in the world and beyond all universe.

By this integral realisation and liberation, the perfect harmony of the results of Knowledge, Love and Works. For there is attained the complete release from ego and identification in being with the One in all and beyond all. But since the attaining consciousness is not limited by its attainment, we win also the unity in Beatitude and the harmonised diversity in Love, so that all relations of the play remain possible to us even while we retain on the heights of our being the eternal oneness with the Beloved. And by a similar wideness, being capable of a freedom in spirit that embraces life and does not depend upon withdrawal from life, we are able to become without egoism, bondage or reaction the channel in our mind and body for a divine action poured out freely upon the world.

The divine existence is of the nature not only of freedom, but of purity, beatitude and perfection. An integral purity which shall enable on the one hand the perfect reflection of the divine Being in ourselves and on the other the perfect outpouring of its Truth and Law in us in the terms of life and through the right functioning of the complex instrument we are in our outer parts, is the condition of an integral liberty. Its result is an integral beatitude, in which there becomes possible at once the Ananda of all that is in the world seen as symbols of the Divine and the Ananda of that which is not-world. And it prepares the integral perfection of our humanity as a type of the Divine in the conditions of the human manifestation, a perfection founded on a certain free universality of being, of love and joy, of play of knowledge and of play of will in power and will in unegoistic action. This integrality also can be attained by the integral Yoga.

Perfection includes perfection of mind and body, so that the highest results of Raja Yoga and Hatha Yoga should be contained in the widest formula of the synthesis finally to be effected by mankind. At any rate a full development of the general mental and physical faculties and experiences attainable by humanity through Yoga must be included in the scope of the integral method. Nor would these have any *raison d'être* unless employed for an integral mental and physical life. Such a mental and physical life would be in its nature a translation of the spiritual existence into its right mental and physical values. Thus we would arrive at a synthesis of the three degrees of Nature and of the three modes of human existence which she has evolved or is evolving. We would include in the scope of our liberated being and perfected modes of activity the material life, our base, and the mental life, our intermediate instrument.

Nor would the integrality to which we aspire be real or even possible, if it were confined to the individual. Since our divine perfection embraces the realisation of ourselves in being, in life and in love through others as well as through ourselves, the extension of our liberty and of its results in others would be the inevitable outcome as well as the broadest utility of our liberation and perfection. And the constant and inherent attempt of such an extension would be towards its increasing and ultimately complete generalisation in mankind.

The divinising of the normal material life of man and of his great secular attempt of mental and moral self-culture in the individual and the race by this integralisation of a widely perfect spiritual existence would thus be the crown alike of our individual and of our common effort. Such a consummation being no other than the kingdom of heaven within reproduced in the kingdom of heaven without, would be also the true fulfilment of the great dream cherished in different terms by the world's religions.

The widest synthesis of perfection possible to thought is the sole effort entirely worthy of those whose dedicated vision perceives that God dwells concealed in humanity.

Standards of Conduct and Spiritual Freedom

THE KNOWLEDGE on which the doer of works in Yoga has to found all his action and development has for the keystone of its structure a more and more concrete perception of unity, the living sense of an all-pervading oneness; he moves in the increasing consciousness of all existence as an indivisible whole: all work too is part of this divine indivisible whole. His personal action and its results can no longer be or seem a separate movement mainly or entirely determined by the egoistic 'free' will of an individual, himself separate in the mass. Our works are part of an indivisible cosmic action; they are put or, more accurately, put themselves into their place in the whole out of which they arise and their outcome is determined by forces that overpass us. That world action in its vast totality and in every petty detail is the indivisible movement of the One who manifests himself progressively in the cosmos..Man too becomes progressively conscious of the truth of himself and the truth of things in proportion as he awakens to this One within him and outside him and to the occult, miraculous and significant process of its forces in the motion of Nature. This action, this movement, is not confined even in ourselves and those around us to the little fragmentary portion of the cosmic activities of which we in our superficial consciousness are aware; it is supported by an immense underlying environing existence subliminal to our minds or subconscious, and it is attracted by an immense transcending existence which is superconscious to our nature. Our action arises, as we ourselves have emerged, out of a universality of which we are not aware; we give it a shape by our personal temperament, personal mind and will of thought or

Chapter 7 of the first part of *The Synthesis of Yoga*, published in the *Arya* in 1915. A revised version of the first part of the *Synthesis* was published in 1948.

force of impulse or desire; but the true truth of things, the true law of action exceeds these personal and human formations. Every standpoint, every man-made rule of action which ignores the indivisible totality of the cosmic movement, whatever its utility in external practice, is to the eye of spiritual Truth an imperfect view and a law of the Ignorance.

Even when we have arrived at some glimpse of this idea or succeeded in fixing it in our consciousness as a knowledge of the mind and a consequent attitude of the soul, it is difficult for us in our outward parts and active nature to square accounts between this universal standpoint and the claims of our personal opinion, our personal will, our personal emotion and desire. We are forced still to go on dealing with this indivisible movement as if it were a mass of impersonal material out of which we, the ego, the person, have to carve something according to our own will and mental fantasy by a personal struggle and effort. This is man's normal attitude towards his environment, actually false because our ego and its will are creations and puppets of the cosmic forces and it is only when we withdraw from ego into the consciousness of the divine Knowledge-Will of the Eternal who acts in them that we can be by a sort of deputation from above their master. And yet is this personal position the right attitude for man so long as he cherishes his individuality and has not yet fully developed it; for without this viewpoint and motive-force he cannot grow in his ego, cannot sufficiently develop and differentiate himself out of the subconscious or half-conscious universal mass-existence.

But the hold of this ego-consciousness upon our whole habit of existence is difficult to shake off when we have no longer need of the separative, the individualistic and aggressive stage of development, when we would proceed forward from this necessity of littleness in the child-soul to unity and universality, to the cosmic consciousness and beyond, to our transcendent spirit-stature. It is indispensable to recognise clearly, not only in our mode of thought but in our way of feeling, sensing, doing, that this movement, this universal action is not a helpless impersonal wave of being which lends itself to the will of any ego according to that ego's strength and insistence. It is the movement of a cosmic Being who is the Knower of his field, the steps of a Divinity who is the Master of his own progressive force of action. As the movement is one and indivisible, so he who is present in the movement is one, sole and indivisible. Not only all result is determined by him, but all initiation, action and process are dependent on the motion of his cosmic force and only belong secondarily and in their form to the creature.

But what then must be the spiritual position of the personal worker? What is his true relation in dynamic Nature to this one cosmic Being and this one total movement? He is a centre only — a centre of differentiation of the one personal consciousness, a centre of determination of the one total movement; his personality reflects in a wave of persistent individuality the one universal Person, the Transcendent, the Eternal. In the Ignorance it is always a broken and distorted reflection because the crest of the wave which is our conscious waking self throws back only an imperfect and falsified similitude of the divine Spirit. All our opinions, standards, formations, principles are only attempts to represent in this broken, reflecting and distorting mirror something of the universal and progressive total action and its many-sided movement towards some ultimate self-revelation of the Divine. Our mind represents it as best it can with a narrow approximation that becomes less and less inadequate in proportion as its thought grows in wideness and light and power; but it is always an approximation and not even a true partial figure. The Divine Will acts through the aeons to reveal progressively not only in the unity of the cosmos, not only in the collectivity of living and thinking creatures, but in the soul of each individual something of its divine Mystery and the hidden truth of the Infinite. Therefore there is in the cosmos, in the collectivity, in the individual, a rooted instinct or belief in its own perfectibility, a constant drive towards an ever increasing and more adequate and more harmonious self-development nearer to the secret truth of things. This effort is represented to the constructing mind of man by standards of knowledge, feeling, character, aesthesis and action, — rules, ideals, norms and laws that he essays to turn into universal dharmas.

*

* *

If we are to be free in the spirit, if we are to be subject only to the supreme Truth, we must discard the idea that our mental or moral laws are binding on the Infinite or that there can be anything sacrosanct, absolute or eternal even in the highest of our existing standards of conduct. To form higher and higher temporary standards as long as they are needed is to serve the Divine in his world march; to erect rigidly an absolute standard is to attempt the erection of a barrier against the eternal waters in their outflow. Once the nature-bound soul realises this truth, it is delivered from the duality of good and evil. For good is all that helps the individual and the world towards their divine fullness, and evil is all that retards or breaks up that increasing perfection. But since the perfection is progressive, evolutive in Time, good and evil are also shifting quantities and change from time to time their meaning and value. This thing which is evil now and in its present shape must be abandoned was once helpful and necessary to the general and individual progress. That other thing which we now regard as evil may well become in another form and arrangement an element in some future perfection. And on the spiritual level we transcend even this distinction, for we discover the purpose and divine utility of all these things that we call good and evil. Then have we to reject the falsehood in them and all that is distorted, ignorant and obscure in that which is called good no less than in that which is called evil. For we have then to accept only the true and the divine, but to make no other distinction in the eternal processes.

To those who can act only on a rigid standard, to those who can feel only the human and not the divine values, this truth may seem to be a dangerous concession which is likely to destroy the very foundation of morality, confuse all conduct and establish only chaos. Certainly, if the choice must be between an eternal and unchanging ethics and no ethics at all, it would have that result for man in his ignorance. But even on the human level, if we have light enough and flexibility enough to recognise that a standard of conduct may be temporary and yet necessary for its time and to observe it faithfully until it can be replaced by a better, then we suffer no such loss, but lose only the fanaticism of an imperfect and intolerant virtue. In its place we gain openness and a power of continual moral progression, charity, the capacity to enter into an understanding sympathy with all this world of struggling and stumbling creatures and by that charity a better right and a greater strength to help it upon its way. In the end where the human closes and the divine commences, where the mental disappears into the supramental consciousness and the finite precipitates itself into the infinite, all evil disappears into a transcendent divine Good which becomes universal on every plane of consciousness that it touches.

This, then, stands fixed for us that all standards by which we may seek to govern our conduct are only our temporary, imperfect and evolutive attempts to represent to ourselves our stumbling mental progress in the universal self-realisation towards which Nature moves. But the divine manifestation cannot be bound by our little rules and fragile sanctities; for the consciousness behind it is too vast for these things. Once we have grasped this fact, disconcerting enough to the absolutism of our reason, we shall better be able to put in their right place in regard to each other the successive standards that govern the different stages in the growth of the individual and the collective march of mankind. At the most general of them we may cast a passing glance. For we have to see how they stand in relation to that other standardless, spiritual and supramental mode of working for which Yoga seeks and to which it moves by the surrender of the individual to the divine Will and, more effectively, through his ascent by this surrender to the greater consciousness in which a certain identity with the dynamic Eternal becomes possible.

*
* *

There are four main standards of human conduct that make an ascending scale. The first is personal need, preference and desire; the second is the law and good of the collectivity; the third is an ideal ethic; the last is the highest divine law of the nature.

Man starts on the long career of his evolution with only the first two of these four to enlighten and lead him; for they constitute the law of his animal and vital existence and it is as the vital and physical animal man that he begins his progress. The true business of man upon earth is to express in the type of humanity a growing image of the Divine; whether knowingly or unknowingly, it is to this end that Nature is working in him under the thick veil of her inner and outer processes. But the material or animal man is ignorant of the inner aim of life; he knows only its needs and its desires and he has necessarily no other guide to what is required of him than his own perception of need and his own stirrings and pointings of desire. To satisfy his physical and vital demands and necessities before all things else and, in the next rank, whatever emotional or mental cravings or imaginations or dynamic notions rise in him must be the first natural rule of his conduct. The sole balancing or overpowering law that can modify or contradict this pressing natural claim is the demand put on him by the ideas, needs and desires of his family, community or tribe, the herd, the pack of which he is a member.

If man could live to himself, — and this he could only do if the development of the individual were the sole object of the Divine in the world, — this second law would not at all need to come into operation. But all existence proceeds by the mutual action and reaction of the whole and the parts, the need for each other of the constituents and the thing constituted, the interdependence of the group and the individuals of the group. In the language of Indian philosophy the Divine manifests himself always in the double form of the separative and the collective being, *vyaṣṭi, samaṣṭi*. Man, pressing after the growth of his separate individuality and its fullness and freedom, is unable to satisfy even his own personal needs and desires except in conjunction with other men; he is a whole in himself and yet incomplete without others. This obligation englobes his personal law of conduct in a group-law which arises from the formation of a lasting group-entity with a collective mind and life of its own to which his own embodied mind and life are subordinated as a transitory unit. And yet is there something in him immortal and free, not bound to this group-body which outlasts his own embodied existence but cannot outlast or claim to chain by its law his eternal spirit.

In itself this seemingly larger and overriding law is no more than an extension of the vital and animal principle that governs the individual elementary man; it is the law of the pack or herd. The individual identifies partially his life with the life of a certain number of other individuals with whom he is associated by birth, choice or circumstance. And since the existence of the group is necessary for his own existence and satisfaction, in time, if not from the first, its perservation, the fulfilment of its needs and the satisfaction of its collective notions, desires, habits of living, without which it would not hold together, must come to take a primary place. The satisfaction of personal idea and feeling, need and desire, propensity and habit has to be constantly subordinated, by the necessity of the situation and not from any moral or altruistic motive, to the satisfaction of the ideas and feelings, needs and desires, propensities and habits, not of this or that other individual or number of individuals, but of the society as a whole. This social need is the obscure matrix of morality and of man's ethical impulse.

It is not actually known that in any primitive times man lived to himself or with only his mate as do some of the animals. All record of him shows him to us as a social animal, not an isolated body and spirit. The law of the pack has always overriden his individual law of self-development; he seems always to have been born, to have lived, to have been formed as a unit in a mass. But logically and naturally from the psychological viewpoint the law of personal need and desire is primary, the social law comes in as a secondary and usurping power. Man has in him two distinct master impulses, the individualistic and the communal, a personal life and a social life, a personal motive of conduct and a social motive of conduct. The possibility of their opposition and the attempt to find their equation lie at the very roots of human civilisation and persist in other figures when he has passed beyond the vital animal into a highly individualised mental and spiritual progress.

The existence of a social law external to the individual is at different times a considerable advantage and a heavy disadvantage to the development of the divine in man. It is an advantage at first when man is crude and incapable of self-control and self-finding, because it erects a power other than that of his personal egoism through which that egoism may be induced or compelled to moderate its savage demands, to discipline its irrational and often violent movements and even to lose itself sometimes in a larger and less personal egoism. It is a disadvantage to the adult spirit ready to transcend the human formula because it is an external standard which seeks to impose itself on him from outside, and the condition of his perfection is that he shall grow from within and in an increasing freedom, not by the suppression but by the transcendence of his perfected individuality, not any longer by a law imposed on him that trains and disciplines his members but by the soul from within breaking through all previous forms to possess with its light and transmute his members.

*
* *

In the conflict of the claims of society with the claims of the individual two ideal and absolute solutions confront one another. There is the demand of the group that the individual should subordinate himself more or less completely or even lose his independent existence in the community, — the smaller must be immolated or self-offered to the larger unit. He must accept the need of the society as his own need, the desire of the society as his own desire; he must live not for himself but for the tribe, clan, commune or nation of which he is a member. The ideal and absolute solution from the individual's standpoint would be a society that existed not for itself, for its all-overriding collective purpose, but for the good of the individual and his fulfilment, for the greater and more perfect life of all its members. Representing as far as possible his best self and helping him to realise it, it would respect the freedom of each of its members and maintain itself not by law and force but by the free and spontaneous consent of its constituent persons. An ideal society of either kind does not exist anywhere and would be most difficult to create, more difficult still to keep in precarious existence so long as individual man clings to his egoism as the primary motive of existence. A general but not complete domination of the society over the individual is the easier way and it is the system that Nature from the first instinctively adopts and keeps in equilibrium by rigorous law, compelling custom and a careful indoctrination of the still subservient and ill-developed intelligence of the human creature.

In primitive societies the individual life is submitted to rigid and immobile communal custom and rule; this is the ancient and would-be eternal law of the human pack that tries always to masquerade as the everlasting decree of the Imperishable, *eṣa dharmaḥ sanātanaḥ*. And the ideal is not dead in the human mind; the most recent trend of human progress is to establish an enlarged and sumptuous edition of this ancient turn of collective living towards the enslavement of the human spirit. There is here a serious danger to the integral development of a greater truth upon earth and a greater life. For the desires and free seekings of the individual, however egoistic, however false or perverted they may be in their immediate form, contain in their obscure shell the seed of a development necessary to the whole; his searchings and stumblings have behind them a force that has to be kept and transmuted into the image of the divine ideal. That force needs to be enlightened and trained but must not be suppressed or harnessed exclusively to society's heavy cart-wheels. Individualism is as necessary to the final perfection as the power behind the group-spirit; the stifling of the individual may well be the stifling of the god in man. And in the present balance of humanity there is seldom any real danger of exaggerated individualism breaking up the social integer. There is continually a danger that the exaggerated pressure of the social mass by its heavy unenlightened mechanical weight may suppress or unduly discourage the free development of the individual spirit. For man in the individual can be more easily enlightened, conscious, open to clear influences; man the mass is still obscure, half-conscious, ruled by universal forces that escape its mastery and its knowledge.

Against this danger of suppression and immobilisation Nature in the individual reacts. It may react by an isolated resistance ranging from the instinctive and brutal revolt of the criminal to the complete negation of the solitary and ascetic. It may react by the assertion of an individualistic trend in the social idea, may impose it on the mass consciousness and establish a compromise between the individual and the social demand. But a compromise is not a solution; it only salves over the difficulty and in the end increases the complexity of the problem and multiplies its issues. A new principle has to be called in other and higher than the two conflicting instincts and powerful at once to override and to reconcile them. Above the natural individual law which sets up as our one standard of conduct the satisfaction of our individual needs, preferences and desires and the natural communal law which sets up as a superior standard the satisfaction of the needs, preferences and desires of the community as a whole, there had to arise the notion of an ideal moral law which is not the satisfaction of need and desire, but controls and even coerces or annuls them in the interests of an ideal order that is not animal, not vital and physical, but mental, a creation of the mind's seeking for light and knowledge and right rule and right movement and true order. The moment this notion becomes powerful in man, he begins to escape from the engrossing vital and material into the mental life; he climbs from the first to the second degree of the threefold ascent of Nature. His needs and desires themselves are touched with a more elevated light of purpose and the mental need, the aesthetic, intellectual and emotional desire begin to predominate over the demand of the physical and vital nature.

* * *

The natural law of conduct proceeds from a conflict to an equilibrium of forces, impulsions and desires; the higher ethical law proceeds by the development of the mental and moral nature towards a fixed internal standard or else a self-formed ideal of absolute qualities, — justice, righteousness, love, right reason, right power, beauty, light. It is therefore essentially an individual standard; it is not a creation of the mass mind. The thinker is the individual; it is he who calls out and throws into forms that which would otherwise remain subconscious in the amorphous human whole. The moral striver is also the individual; self-discipline, not under the yoke of an outer law, but in obedience to an internal light, is essentially an individual effort. But by positing his personal standard as the translation of an absolute moral ideal the thinker imposes it, not on himself alone, but on all the individuals whom his thought can reach and penetrate. And as the mass of individuals come more and more to accept it in idea if only in an imperfect practice or no practice, society also is compelled to obey the new orientation. It absorbs the ideative influence and tries, not with any striking success, to mould its institutions into new forms touched by these higher ideals. But always its instinct is to translate them into binding law, into pattern forms, into mechanic custom, into an external social compulsion upon its living units.

For, long after the individual has become partially free, a moral organism capable of conscious growth, aware of an inward life, eager for spiritual progress, society continues to be external in its methods, a material and economic organism, mechanical, more intent upon status and self-preservation than on growth and self-perfection. The greatest present triumph of the thinking and progressive individual over the instinctive and static society has been the power he has acquired by his thought-will to compel it to think also, to open itself to the idea of social justice and righteousness, communal sympathy and mutual compassion, to feel after the rule of reason rather than blind custom as the test of its institutions and to look on the mental and moral assent of its individuals as at least one essential element in the validity of its laws. Ideally at least, to consider light rather than force as its sanction, moral development and not vengeance or restraint as the object even of its penal action, is becoming just possible to the communal mind. The greatest future triumph of the thinker will come when he can persuade the individual integer and the collective whole to rest their life-relation and its union and stability upon a free and harmonious consent and self-adaptation, and shape and govern the external by the internal truth rather than to constrain the inner spirit by the tyranny of the external form and structure.

But even this success that he has gained is rather a thing in potentiality than in actual accomplishment. There is always a disharmony and a discord between the moral law in the individual and the law of his needs and desires, between the moral law proposed to society and the physical and vital needs, desires, customs, prejudices, interests and passions of the caste, the clan, the religious community, the society, the nation. The moralist erects in vain his absolute ethical standard and calls upon all to be faithful to it without regard to consequences. To him the needs and desires of the individual are invalid if they are in conflict with the moral law, and the social law has no claims upon him if it is opposed to his sense of right and denied by his conscience. This is his absolute solution for the individual that he shall cherish no desires and claims that are not consistent with love, truth and justice. He demands from the community or nation that it shall hold all things cheap, even its safety and its most pressing interests, in comparison with truth, justice, humanity and the highest good of the peoples.

No individual rises to these heights except in intense moments, no society yet created satisfies this ideal. And in the present state of morality and of human development none perhaps can or ought to satisfy it. Nature will not allow it, Nature knows that it should not be. The first reason is that our moral ideals are themselves for the most part ill-evolved, ignorant and arbitrary, mental constructions rather than transcriptions of the eternal truths of the spirit. Authoritative and dogmatic, they assert certain absolute standards in theory, but in practice every existing system of ethics proves either in application unworkable or is in fact a constant coming short of the absolute standard to which the ideal pretends. If our ethical system is a compromise or a makeshift, it gives at once a principle of justification to the further sterilising compromises which society and the individual hasten to make with it. And if it insists on absolute love, justice, right with an uncompromising insistence, it soars above the head of human possibility and is professed with lip homage but ignored in practice. Even it is found that it ignores other elements in humanity which equally insist on survival but refuse to come within the moral formula. For just as the individual law of desire contains within it invaluable elements of the infinite whole which have to be protected against the tyranny of the absorbing social idea, the innate impulses too both of individual and of collective man contain in them invaluable elements which escape the limits of any ethical formula yet discovered and are yet necessary to the fullness and harmony of an eventual divine perfection.

Moreover, absolute love, absolute justice, absolute right reason in their present application by a bewildered and imperfect humanity come easily to be conflicting principles. Justice often demands what love abhors. Right reason dispassionately considering the facts of nature and human relations in search of a satisfying norm or rule is unable to admit without modification either any reign of absolute justice or any reign of absolute love. And in fact man's absolute justice easily turns out to be in practice a sovereign injustice; for his mind, one-sided and rigid in its constructions, puts forward a one-sided partial and rigorous scheme or figure and claims for it totality and absoluteness and an application that ignores the subtler truth of things and the plasticity of life. All our standards turned into action either waver on a flux of compromises or err by this partiality and unelastic structure. Humanity sways from one orientation to another; the race moves upon a zigzag path led by conflicting claims and, on the whole, works out instinctively what Nature intends, but with much waste and suffering, rather than either what it desires or what it holds to be right or what the highest light from above demands from the embodied spirit.

*

* *

The fact is that when we have reached the cult of absolute ethical qualities and erected the categorical imperative of an ideal law, we have not come to the end of our search or touched the truth that delivers. There is, no doubt, something here that helps us to rise beyond limitation by the physical and vital man in us, an insistence that overpasses the individual and collective needs and desires of a humanity still bound to the living mud of Matter in which it took its roots, an aspiration that helps to develop the mental and moral being in us: this new sublimating element has been therefore an acquisition of great importance; its workings have marked a considerable step forward in the difficult evolution of terrestrial Nature. And behind the inadequacy of these ethical conceptions something too is concealed that does attach to a supreme Truth; there is here the glimmer of a light and power that are part of a yet unreached divine Nature. But the mental idea of these things is not that light and the moral formulation of them is not that power. These are only representative constructions of the mind that cannot embody the divine spirit which they vainly endeavour to imprison in their categorical formulas. Beyond the mental and moral being in us is a greater divine being that is spiritual and supramental; for it is only through a large spiritual plane where the mind's formulas dissolve in a white flame of direct inner experience that we can reach beyond mind and pass from its constructions to the vastness and freedom of the supramental realities. There alone can we touch the harmony of the divine powers that are poorly mispresented to our mind or framed into a false figure by the conflicting or wavering elements of the moral law. There alone the unification of the transformed vital and physical and the illumined mental man becomes possible in that supramental spirit which is at once the secret source and goal of our mind and life and body. There alone is there any possibility of an absolute justice, love and right — far other than that which we imagine — at one with each other in the light of a supreme divine knowledge. There alone can there be a reconciliation of the conflict between our members.

In other words there is, above society's external law and man's moral law and beyond them, though feebly and ignorantly aimed at by something within them, a larger truth of a vast unbound consciousness, a law divine towards which both these blind and gross formulations are progressive faltering steps that try to escape from the natural law of the animal to a more exalted light or universal rule. That divine standard, since the godhead in us is our spirit moving towards its own concealed perfection, must be a supreme spiritual law and truth of our nature. Again, as we are embodied beings in the world with a common existence and nature and yet individual souls capable of direct touch with the Transcendent, this supreme truth of ourselves must have a double character. It must be a law and truth that discovers the perfect movement, harmony, rhythm of a great spiritualised collective life and determines perfectly our relations with each being and all beings in Nature's varied oneness. It must be at the same time a law and truth that discovers to us at each moment the rhythm and exact steps of the direct expression of the Divine in the soul, mind, life, body of the individual creature.[1] And we find in experience that this supreme light and force of action in its highest expression is at once an imperative law and an absolute freedom. It is an imperative law because it governs by immutable Truth our every inner and outer movement. And yet at each moment and in each movement the absolute freedom of the Supreme handles the perfect plasticity of our conscious and liberated nature.

The ethical idealist tries to discover this supreme law in his own moral data, in the inferior powers and factors that belong to the mental and ethical formula. And to sustain and organise

[1] Therefore the Gita defines 'dharma', an expression which means more than either religion or morality, as action controlled by our essential manner of self-being. [Sri Aurobindo's note]

them he selects a fundamental principle of conduct essentially unsound and constructed by the intellect — utility, hedonism, reason, intuitive conscience or any other generalised standard. All such efforts are foredoomed to failure. Our inner nature is the progressive expression of the eternal Spirit and too complex a power to be tied down by a single dominant mental or moral principle. Only the supramental consciousness can reveal to its differing and conflicting forces their spiritual truth and harmonise their divergences.

The later religions endeavour to fix the type of a supreme truth of conduct, erect a system and declare God's law through the mouth of Avatar or prophet. These systems, more powerful and dynamic than the dry ethical idea, are yet for the most part no more than idealistic glorifications of the moral principle sanctified by religious emotion and the label of a superhuman origin. Some, like the extreme Christian ethic, are rejected by Nature because they insist unworkably on an impracticable absolute rule. Others prove in the end to be evolutionary compromises and become obsolete in the march of Time. The true divine law, unlike these mental counterfeits, cannot be a system of rigid ethical determinations that press into their cast-iron moulds all our life-movements. The law divine is truth of life and truth of the spirit and must take up with a free living plasticity and inspire with the direct touch of its eternal light each step of our action and all the complexity of our life-issues. It must act not as a rule and formula but as an enveloping and penetrating conscious presence that determines all our thoughts, activities, feelings, impulsions of will by its infallible power and knowledge.

The older religions erected their rule of the wise, their dicta of Manu or Confucius, a complex Shastra in which they attempted to combine the social rule and moral law with the declaration of certain eternal principles of our highest nature in some kind of uniting amalgam. All three were treated on the same ground as equally the expression of everlasting verities, *sanātana dharma*. But two of these elements are evolutionary and valid for a time, mental constructions, human readings of the will of the Eternal; the third, attached and subdued to certain social and moral formulas, had to share the fortunes of its forms. Either the Shastra grows obsolete and has to be progressively changed or finally cast away or else it stands as a rigid barrier to the self-development of the individual and the race. The Shastra erects a collective and external standard; it ignores the inner nature of the individual, the indeterminable elements of a secret spiritual force within him. But the nature of the individual will not be ignored; its demand is inexorable. The unrestrained indulgence of his outer impulses leads to anarchy and dissolution, but the suppression and coercion of his soul's freedom by a fixed and mechanical rule spells stagnation or an inner death. Not this coercion or determination from outside, but the free discovery of his highest spirit and the truth of an eternal movement is the supreme thing that he has to discover.

The higher ethical law is discovered by the individual in his mind and will and psychic sense and then extended to the race. The supreme law also must be discovered by the individual in his spirit. Then only, through a spiritual influence and not by the mental idea, can it be extended to others. A moral law can be imposed as a rule or an ideal on numbers of men who have not attained that level of consciousness or that fineness of mind and will and psychic sense in which it can become a reality to them and a living force. As an ideal it can be revered without any need of practice. As a rule it can be observed in its outsides even if the inner sense is missed altogether. The supramental and spiritual life cannot be mechanised in this way, it cannot be turned into a mental ideal or an external rule. It has its own great lines, but these must be made real, must be the workings of an active Power felt in the individual's consciousness and the transcriptions of an eternal Truth powerful to transform mind, life and body. And because it is thus real, effective, imperative, the generalisation of the supramental consciousness and the spiritual life is the sole force that can lead to individual and collective perfection in earth's highest creatures. Only by our coming into constant touch with the divine Consciousness and its absolute Truth can some form of the conscious Divine, the dynamic Absolute, take up our earth-existence and transform its strife, stumbling, sufferings and falsities into an image of the supreme Light, Power and Ananda.

The culmination of the soul's constant touch with the Supreme is that self-giving which we call surrender to the divine Will and immergence of the separated ego in the One who is all. A vast universality of soul and an intense unity with all is the base and fixed condition of the supramental consciousness and spiritual life. In that universality and unity alone can we find the supreme law of the divine manifestation in the life of the embodied spirit; in that alone can we discover the supreme motion and right play of our individual nature. In that alone can all these lower discords resolve themselves into a victorious harmony of the true relations between manifested beings who are portions of the one Godhead and children of one universal Mother.

*

* *

All conduct and action are part of the movement of a Power, a Force infinite and divine in its origin and secret sense and will even though the forms of it we see seem inconscient or ignorant, material, vital, mental, finite, which is working to bring out progressively something of the Divine and Infinite in the obscurity of the individual and collective nature. This power is leading towards the Light, but still through the Ignorance. It leads man first through his needs and desires; it guides him next through enlarged needs and desires modified and enlightened by a mental and moral ideal. It is preparing to lead him to a spiritual realisation that overrides these things and yet fulfils and reconciles them in all that is divinely true in their spirit and purpose. It transforms the needs and desires into a divine Will and Ananda. It transforms the mental and moral aspiration into the powers of Truth and Perfection that are beyond them. It substitutes for the divided straining of the individual nature, for the passion and strife of the separate ego, the calm, profound, harmonious and happy law of the universalised person within us, the central being, the spirit that is a portion of the supreme Spirit. This true Person in us, because it is universal, does not seek its separate gratification but only asks in its outward expression in Nature its growth to its real stature, the expression of its inner divine self, that transcendent spiritual power and presence within it which is one with all and in sympathy with each thing and creature and with all the collective personalities and powers of the divine existence, and yet it transcends them and is not bound by the egoism of any creature or collectivity or limited by the ignorant controls of their lower nature. This is the high realisation in front of all our seeking and striving, and it gives the sure promise of a perfect reconciliation and transmutation of all the elements of our nature. A pure, total and flawless action is possible only when that is effected and we have reached the height of this secret Godhead within us.

The perfect supramental action will not follow any single principle or limited rule. It is not likely to satisfy the standard either of the individual egoist or of any organised group-mind. It will conform to the demand neither of the positive practical man of the world nor of the formal moralist nor of the patriot nor of the sentimental philanthropist nor of the idealising philosopher. It will proceed by a spontaneous outflowing from the summits in the totality of an illumined and uplifted being, will and knowledge and not by the selected, calculated and standardised action which is all that the intellectual reason or ethical will can achieve. Its sole aim will be the expression of the divine in us and the keeping together of the world and its progress towards the Manifestation that is to be. This even will not be so much an aim and purpose as a spontaneous law of the being and an intuitive determination of the action by the Light of the divine Truth and its automatic influence. It will proceed like the action of Nature from a total will and knowledge behind her, but a will and knowledge enlightened in a conscious supreme Nature and no longer obscure in this ignorant Prakriti. It will be an action not bound by the dualities but full and large in the spirit's impartial joy of existence. The happy and inspired movement of a divine Power and Wisdom guiding and impelling us will replace the perplexities and stumblings of the suffering and ignorant ego.

If by some miracle of divine intervention all mankind at once could be raised to this level, we should have something on earth like the Golden Age of the traditions, Satya Yuga, the Age of Truth or true existence. For the sign of the Satya Yuga is that the Law is spontaneous and conscious in each creature and does its own works in a perfect harmony and freedom. Unity and universality, not separative division, would be the foundation of the consciousness of the race; love would be absolute; equality would be consistent with hierarchy and perfect in difference; absolute justice would be secured by the spontaneous action of the being in harmony with the truth of things and the truth of himself and others and therefore sure of true and right result; right reason, no longer mental but supramental, would be satisfied not by the observation of artificial standards but by the free automatic perception of right relations and their inevitable execution in the act. The quarrel between the individual and society or disastrous struggle between one community and another could not exist: the cosmic consciousness imbedded in embodied beings would assure a harmonious diversity in oneness.

In the actual state of humanity, it is the individual who must climb to this height as a pioneer and precursor. His isolation will necessarily give a determination and a form to his outward activities that must be quite other than those of a consciously divine collective action. The inner state, the root of his acts, will be the same; but the acts themselves may well be very different from what they would be on an earth liberated from ignorance. Nevertheless his consciousness and the divine mechanism of his conduct, if such a word can be used of so free a thing, would be such as has been described, free from that subjection to vital impurity and desire and wrong impulse which we call sin, unbound by that rule of prescribed moral formulas which we call virtue, spontaneously sure and pure and perfect in a greater consciousness than the mind's, governed in all its steps by the light and truth of the Spirit. But if a collectivity or group could be formed of those who had reached the supramental perfection, there indeed some divine creation could take shape; a new earth could descend that would be a new heaven, a world of supramental light could be created here amidst the receding darkness of this terrestrial ignorance.

The Cosmic Consciousness

To REALISE and unite oneself with the active Brahman is to exchange, perfectly or imperfectly according as the union is partial or complete, the individual for the cosmic consciousness. The ordinary existence of man is not only an individual but an egoistic consciousness; it is, that is to say, the individual soul or Jivatman identifying himself with the nodus of his mental, vital, physical experiences in the movement of universal Nature, that is to say, with his mind-created ego, and, less intimately, with the mind, life, body which receive the experiences. Less intimately, because of these he can say 'my mind, life, body,' he can regard them as himself, yet partly as not himself and something rather which he possesses and uses, but of the ego he says, It is I. By detaching himself from all identification with mind, life and body, he can get back from his ego to the consciousness of the true Individual, the Jivatman, who is the real possessor of mind, life and body.[1] Looking back from this Individual to that of which it is the representative and conscious figure, he can get back to the transcendent consciousness of pure Self, absolute

Chapter 15 of Part Two of *The Synthesis of Yoga*, published in the *Arya* in 1917 and revised shortly thereafter. The revised version, which will form part of the edition published in The Complete Works of Sri Aurobindo, is appearing here for the first time in print.

[1] There are various ways of detaching oneself from egoism by knowledge. The materialist way would be to see that mind, life, body are all or rather body manifesting phenomena of life and mind and the ego a mental fiction, and body again is merely a phenomenon of Nature, the universal Force. A kind of materialist Yoga is possible by which one could get rid of attachment to ego, mind, life, body and subordinate everything to the knowledge of Nature, the worship of Nature, the obedience to Nature. The Atheist has his religion, his jnana, bhakti, karmayoga. The Buddhist similarly denies the ego and sees life, mind, body as mere combinations and sanskaras; by detachment from these one arrives at Nirvana, annihilation in the Permanent. [Sri Aurobindo's note]

Existence or absolute Non-being, three poises of the same eternal Reality. But between the movement of universal Nature and this transcendent Existence, possessor of the one and cosmic self of the other, is the cosmic consciousness, the universal Purusha of whom all Nature is the Prakriti or active conscious Force. We can arrive at that, become that whether by breaking the walls of the ego laterally, as it were, and identifying oneself with all existences in the One, or else from above by realising the pure Self or absolute Existence in its outgoing, immanent, all-embracing, all-constituting self-knowledge and self-creative power.

The immanent, silent Self in all is the foundation of this cosmic consciousness for the experience of the mental being. It is the Witness pure and omnipresent who as the silent Conscious Soul of the cosmos regards all the activity of the universe; it is Sachchidananda for whose delight universal Nature displays the eternal procession of her works. We are aware of an unwounded Delight, a pure and perfect Presence, an infinite and self-contained Power present in ourselves and all things, not divided by their divisions, not affected by the stress and struggle of the cosmic manifestation; it is within it all, but it is superior to it all. Because of that all this exists, but that does not exist because of all this; it is too great to be limited by the movement in Time and Space which it inhabits and supports. This foundation enables us to possess in the security of the divine existence the whole universe within our own being. We are no longer limited and shut in by what we inhabit, but like the Divine contain in ourselves all that for the purpose of the movement of Nature we consent to inhabit. We are not mind or life or body, but the informing and sustaining Soul, silent, peaceful, eternal, which possesses them; and since we find this Soul everywhere sustaining and informing and possessing all lives and minds and bodies, we cease to regard it as a separate and individual being in our own. In it all this moves and acts; within all this it is stable and immutable. Having this, we possess our eternal self-existence at rest in its eternal consciousness and bliss.

Next we have to realise this silent Self as the Lord of all the action of universal Nature; we have to see that it is this same Self-existent who is displayed in the creative force of His eternal consciousness. All this action is only His power and knowledge and self-delight going abroad in His infinite being to do the works of His eternal wisdom and will. We shall realise the Divine, the eternal Self of all, first, as the source of all action and inaction, of all knowledge and ignorance, of all delight and suffering, of all good and evil, perfection and imperfection, of all force and form, of all the outgoing of Nature from the eternal divine Principle and of all the return of Nature towards the Divine. We shall realise it next as itself going abroad in its Power and Knowledge, — for the Power and Knowledge are itself, — not only the source of their works, but the creator and doer of their works, one in all existences; for the many souls of the universal manifestation are only faces of the one Divine, the many minds, lives, bodies are only His masks and disguises. We perceive each being to be the universal Narayana presenting to us many faces; we lose ourselves in that universality and perceive our own mind, life and body as only one presentation of the Self, while all whom we formerly conceived of as others, are now to our consciousness our self in other minds, lives and bodies. All force and idea and event and figure of things in the universe are only manifest degrees of this Self, values of the Divine in His eternal self-figuration. Thus viewing things and beings we may see them first as if they were parts and parcels of His divided being;[2] but the realisation and the knowledge are not complete unless we go beyond this idea of quality and space and division by which there comes the experience of less and more, large and small, part and whole, and see the whole Infinite everywhere; we must see the universe and each thing in the universe as in its existence and secret consciousness and power and delight the indivisible Divine in its entirety, however much the figure it makes to our minds may appear only as a partial manifestation. When we possess thus the Divine as at once the silent and surpassing Witness and the active Lord and all-constituting Being without making any division between these aspects, we possess the whole cosmic Divine, embrace all of the universal Self and Reality, are awake to the cosmic consciousness.

What will be the relation of our individual existence to this cosmic consciousness to which we have attained? For since we have still a mind and body and human life, our individual existence persists even though our separate individual consciousness

[2] The Gita speaks of the Jiva as a portion of the Lord. [Sri Aurobindo's note]

has been transcended. It is quite possible to realise the cosmic consciousness without becoming that; we can see it, that is to say, with the soul, feel it and dwell in it; we can even be united with it without becoming wholly one with it; in a word, we may preserve the individual consciousness of the Jivatman within the cosmic consciousness of the universal Self. We may preserve a yet greater distinctness between the two and enjoy the relations between them; we may remain, in a way, entirely the individual self while participating in the bliss and infinity of the universal Self. Or we may possess them both as a greater and lesser self, one we feel pouring itself out in the universal play of the divine consciousness and force, the other in the action of the same universal Being through our individual soul-centre or soul-form for the purposes of an individual play of mind, life and body. But the summit of this cosmic realisation by knowledge is always the power to dissolve the personality in universal being, to merge the individual in the cosmic consciousness, to liberate even the soul-form into the unity and universality of the Spirit. This is the *laya*, dissolution, or *mokṣa*, liberation, at which the Yoga of Knowledge aims. This may extend itself, as in the traditional Yoga, to the dissolution of mind, life and body itself into the silent Self or absolute Existence; but the essence of the liberation is the merging of the individual in the Infinite. When the Yogin no longer feels himself to be a consciousness situated in the body or limited by the mind, but has lost the sense of division in the boundlessness of an infinite consciousness, that which he set out to do is accomplished. Afterwards the retaining or non-retaining of the human life is a circumstance of no essential importance, for it is always the formless One who acts through its many forms of the mind and life and body and each soul is only one of the stations from which it chooses to watch and receive and actuate its own play.

That into which we merge ourselves in the cosmic consciousness is Sachchidananda. It is one eternal existence that we then are, one eternal Consciousness which sees its own works in us and others, one eternal Will or Force of that Consciousness which displays itself in infinite workings, one eternal Delight which has the joy of itself and all its workings. It is itself stable, immutable, timeless, spaceless, supreme and it is still itself in the infinity of its workings, not changed by their variations, not broken up by their multiplicity, not increased or diminished by their ebbings and flowings in the seas of Time and Space, not confused by their apparent contrarieties or limited by their divinely-willed limitations. Sachchidananda is the unity of the many-sidedness of manifested things, Sachchidananda is the eternal harmony of all their variations and oppositions, Sachchidananda is the infinite perfection which justifies their limitations and is the goal of their imperfections. So much for the essential relation; but we have to see also the practical results of this internal transformation.

It is evident that by dwelling in this cosmic consciousness our whole experience and valuation of everything in the universe will be radically changed. As individual egos we dwell in the Ignorance and judge everything by a broken, partial and personal standard of knowledge; we experience everything according to the capacity of a limited consciousness and force and are therefore unable to give a divine response or set the true value upon any part of cosmic experience. We experience limitation, weakness, incapacity, grief, pain, struggle and its contradictory emotions and we accept these things and their opposites as opposites in an eternal duality and cannot reconcile them in the eternity of an absolute good and happiness. We live by fragments of experience and judge by our fragmentary values each thing and the whole. When we try to arrive at absolute values we only promote some partial view of things to do duty for a totality in the divine workings; we then make believe that our fractions are integers and try to thrust our one-sided view-points into the catholicity of the all-vision of the Divine.

But by entering into the cosmic consciousness we begin to participate in that all-vision and see everything in the values of the Infinite and the One. Limitation itself, ignorance itself change their meaning for us. Ignorance changes into a particularising action of divine knowledge; strength and weakness and incapacity change into a free putting forth and holding back various measures of divine Force; joy and grief, pleasure and pain change into a mastering and a suffering of divine delight; struggle, losing its discords, becomes a balancing of forces and values in the divine harmony. We do not then suffer by the limitations of our mind, life and body; for we no longer live in these, even when we record and accept them, but in the infinity of the Spirit, and these we view in their right value and place and purpose in the manifestation, as degrees of the supreme being, conscious-force and delight of Sachchidananda veiling and manifesting Himself in the cosmos. We cease also to judge other men and things by their outward appearances and are delivered from hostile and contradictory ideas and emotions; for it is the soul that we see, the Divine that we seek and find in every thing and creature, and the rest has only a secondary value to us in a scheme of relations which exist now for us only as self-expressions of the Divine and not as having any absolute value in themselves. So too no event can disturb us, since the distinction of happy and unhappy, beneficent and maleficent happenings loses its force, and all is seen in its divine value and its divine purpose. Thus we arrive at a perfect liberation and an infinite equality. It is this consummation of which the Upanishad speaks when it says 'He in whom the self has become all existences, how shall he have delusion, whence shall he have grief who knows entirely[3] and sees in all things oneness.'

But this can be only when there is perfection in the cosmic consciousness, and that is difficult for the mental being. The mentality when it arrives at the idea or the realisation of the Spirit, the Divine, tends to break existence into two opposite halves, the lower and the higher existence. It sees on one side the Infinite, the Formless, the One, the Peace and Bliss, the Calm and Silence, the Absolute, the Vast and Pure; on the other it sees the finite, the world of forms, the jarring multiplicity, the strife and suffering and imperfect, unreal good, the tormented activity and futile success, the relative, the limited and vain and vile. To those who make this division and this opposition, complete liberation is only attainable in the peace of the One, in the featurelessness of the Infinite, in the non-becoming of the Absolute which is to them the only real being; to be free all values must be destroyed, all limitations not only transcended but abolished. They have the liberation of the divine rest, but not the liberty of the divine action; they enjoy the peace of the Transcendent, but not the cosmic bliss of the Transcendent. Their liberty depends upon abstention from the cosmic movement, it cannot dominate

[3] *vijānataḥ*. Vijnana is the knowledge of the One and the Many, by which the Many are seen in the terms of the One, in the infinite unifying Truth, Right, Vast of the divine existence. [Sri Aurobindo's note]

and possess cosmic existence itself. But it is also possible for them to realise and participate in the immanent as well as the transcendent peace. Still the division is not cured. The liberty they enjoy is that of the silent unacting Witness, not the liberty of the divine Master-consciousness which possesses all things, delights in all, casts itself into all forms of existence without fear of fall or loss or bondage or stain. All the rights of the Spirit are not yet possessed; there is still a denial, a limitation, a holding back from the entire oneness of all existence. The workings of Mind, Life, Body are viewed from the calm and peace of the spiritual planes of the mental being and are filled with that calm and peace; they are not possessed by and subjected to the law of the all-mastering Spirit.

All this is when the mental being takes its station in its own spiritual planes, in the mental planes of Sat, Chit, Ananda, and casts down their light and delight upon the lower existence. But there is possible the attempt at a kind of cosmic consciousness by dwelling on the lower planes themselves after breaking their limitations laterally, as we have said, and then calling down into them the light and largeness of the higher existence. Not only Spirit is one, but Mind, Life, Matter are one. There is one cosmic Mind, one cosmic Life, one cosmic Body. All the attempt of man to arrive at universal sympathy, universal love and the understanding and knowledge of the inner soul of other existences is an attempt to beat thin, breach and eventually break down by the power of the enlarging mind and heart the walls of the ego and arrive nearer to a cosmic oneness. And if we can by the mind and heart get at the touch of the Spirit, receive the powerful inrush of the Divine into this lower humanity and change our nature into a reflection of the divine nature by love, by universal joy, by oneness of mind with all Nature and all beings, we can break down the walls. Even our bodies are not really separate entities and therefore our very physical consciousness is capable of oneness with the physical consciousness of others and of the cosmos. The Yogin is able to feel his body one with all bodies, to be aware of and even to participate in their affections; he can feel constantly the unity of all Matter and be aware of his physical being as only a movement in its movement.[4] Still more

4 *jagatyām jagat*. Isha Upanishad. [Sri Aurobindo's note]

is it possible for him to feel constantly and normally the whole sea of the infinite life as his true vital existence and his own life as only a wave of that boundless surge. And more easily yet is it possible for him to unite himself in mind and heart with all existences, be aware of their desires, struggles, joys, sorrows, thoughts, impulses, in a sense as if they were his own, at least as occurring in his larger self hardly less intimately or quite as intimately as the movements of his own heart and mind. This too is a realisation of cosmic consciousness.

It may even seem as if it were the greatest oneness, since it accepts all that we can be sensible of in the mind-created world as our own. Sometimes one sees it spoken of as the highest achievement. Certainly, it is a great realisation and the path to a greater. It is that which the Gita speaks of as the accepting of all existences as if oneself whether in grief or in joy; it is the way of sympathetic oneness and infinite compassion which helps the Buddhist to arrive at his Nirvana. Still there are gradations and degrees. In the first stage the soul is still subject to the reactions of the duality, still subject therefore to the lower Prakriti; it is depressed or hurt by the cosmic suffering, elated by the cosmic joy. We suffer the joys of others, suffer their griefs; and this oneness can be carried even into the body, as in the story of the Indian saint who, seeing a bullock tortured in the field by its cruel owner, cried out with the creature's pain and the weal of the lash was found reproduced on his own flesh. But there must be a oneness with Sachchidananda in his freedom as well as with the subjection of the lower being to the reactions of Prakriti. This is achieved when the soul is free and superior to the cosmic reactions which are then felt only in the life, mind and body and as an inferior movement; the soul understands, accepts the experience, sympathises, but is not overpowered or affected, so that at last even the mind and body learn also to accept without being overpowered or even affected except on their surface. And the consummation of this movement is when the two spheres of existence are no longer divided and the mind, life and body obeying utterly the higher law grow into the spirit's freedom; free from the lower or ignorant response to the cosmic touches, their struggle and their subjection to the duality ceases. This does not mean insensibility to the subjection and struggles and sufferings of others, but it does mean a spiritual supremacy and freedom which enables one to understand perfectly, put the right values on things and heal from above instead of struggling from below. It does not inhibit the divine compassion and helpfulness, but it does inhibit the human and animal sorrow and suffering.

The link between the spiritual and the lower planes of the being is that which is called in the old Vedantic phraseology the *vijñāna* and which we may describe in our modern turn of language as the Truth-plane or the ideal mind or supermind. There the One and the Many meet and our being is freely open to the revealing light of the divine Truth and the inspiration of the divine Will and Knowledge. If we can break down the veil of the intellectual, emotional, sensational mind which our ordinary existence has built between us and the Divine, we can then take up through the Truth-mind all our mental, vital and physical experience and offer it up to the spiritual — this was the secret or mystic sense of the old Vedic 'sacrifice' — to be converted into the terms of the infinite truth of Sachchidananda, and we can receive the powers and illuminations of the infinite Existence in forms of a divine knowledge, will and delight to be imposed on our mentality, vitality, physical existence till the lower members are transformed into the perfect vessel of the higher nature. This was the double Vedic movement of the descent and birth of the gods in the human creature and the ascent of the human powers that struggle towards the divine knowledge, power and delight and climb into the godheads, the result of which was the possession of the One, the infinite, the beatific existence, the union with God, the Immortality. By possession of this ideal plane we break down entirely the opposition of the lower and the higher existence, the false gulf created by the Ignorance between the finite and the Infinite, God and Nature, the One and the Many, open the gates of the Divine, fulfil the individual in the complete harmony of the cosmic consciousness and realise in the cosmic being the epiphany of the transcendent Sachchidananda. And these results, which obtained on the supramental plane itself or beyond, would be the highest perfection of the human being, we can attain to partially, in a very modified way, in a sort of mental figure by awakening into activity on the corresponding plane of the mental nature. We can get a luminous shadow of that perfect harmony and light. But this belongs to another part of our subject; it is the Knowledge on which we must found our Yoga of self-perfection.

The Ananda Brahman

THE WAY of devotion in the integral synthetic Yoga will take the form of a seeking after the Divine through love and delight and a seizing with joy on all the ways of his being. It will find its acme in a perfect union of love and a perfect enjoyment of all the ways of the soul's intimacy with God. It may start from knowledge or it may start from works, but it will then turn knowledge into a joy of luminous union with the being of the Beloved and turn works into a joy of the active union of our being with the will and the power of being of the Beloved. Or it may start directly from love and delight; it will then take both these other things into itself and will develop them as part of the complete joy of oneness.

The beginning of the heart's attraction to the Divine may be impersonal, the touch of an impersonal joy in something universal or transcendent that has revealed itself directly or indirectly to our emotional or our aesthetic being or to our capacity of spiritual felicity. That which we thus grow aware of is the Ananda Brahman, the bliss existence. There is an adoration of an impersonal Delight and Beauty, of a pure and an infinite perfection to which we can give no name or form, a moved attraction of the soul to some ideal and infinite Presence, Power, existence in the world or beyond it, which in some way becomes psychologically or spiritually sensible to us and then more and more intimate and real. That is the call, the touch of the bliss existence upon us. Then to have always the joy and nearness of its presence, to know what it is, so as to satisfy the intellect and the intuitional mind of its constant reality, to put our passive and, so far as we can manage it, our active, our inner immortal and even our outer mortal being into perfect harmony with it,

Chapter 7 of the third part of the *Synthesis of Yoga*, published in the *Arya* in 1918.

grow into a necessity of our living. And to open ourselves to it is what we feel to be the one true happiness, to live into it the sole real perfection.

A transcendent Bliss, unimaginable and inexpressible by the mind and speech, is the nature of the Ineffable. That broods immanent and secret in the whole universe and in everything in the universe. Its presence is described as a secret ether of the bliss of being, of which the Scripture says that, if this were not, none could for a moment breathe or live. And this spiritual bliss is here also in our hearts. It is hidden in from the toil of the surface mind which catches only at weak and flawed translations of it into various mental, vital and physical forms of the joy of existence. But if the mind has once grown sufficiently subtle and pure in its receptions and not limited by the grosser nature of our outward responses to existence, we can take a reflection of it which will wear perhaps wholly or predominantly the hue of whatever is strongest in our nature. It may present itself first as a yearning for some universal Beauty which we feel in Nature and man and in all that is around us; or we may have the intuition of some transcendent Beauty of which all apparent beauty here is only a symbol. That is how it may come to those in whom the aesthetic being is developed and insistent and the instincts which, when they find form of expression, make the poet and artist, are predominant. Or it may be the sense of a divine spirit of love or else a helpful and compassionate infinite Presence in the universe or behind or beyond it which responds to us when we turn the need of our spirit towards it. So it may first show itself when the emotional being is intensely developed. It may come near to us in other ways, but always as a Power or Presence of delight, beauty, love or peace which touches the mind, but is beyond the forms these things take ordinarily in the mind.

For all joy, beauty, love, peace, delight are outflowings from the Ananda Brahman,—all delight of the spirit, the intellect, the imagination, aesthetic sense, ethical aspiration and satisfaction, action, life, the body. And through all ways of our being the Divine can touch us and make use of them to awaken and liberate the spirit. But to reach the Ananda Brahman in itself the mental reception of it must be subtilised, spiritualised, universalised, discharged of everything that is turbid and limiting. For when we draw quite near or enter into it, it is by an awakened spiritual sense of a transcendent and a universal Delight which exists within and yet behind and beyond the contradictions of the world and to which we can unite ourselves through a growing universal and spiritual or a transcendental ecstasy.

Ordinarily, the mind is satisfied with reflecting this Infinity we perceive or with feeling the sense of it within and without us, as an experience which, however frequent, yet remains exceptional. It seems in itself so satisfying and wonderful when it comes and our ordinary mind and the active life which we have to lead may seem to us so incompatible with it, that we may think it excessive to expect anything more. But the very spirit of Yoga is this, to make the exceptional normal, and to turn that which is above us and greater than our normal selves into our own constant consciousness. Therefore we should not hesitate to open ourselves more steadily to whatever experience of the Infinite we have, to purify and intensify it, to make it our object of constant thought and contemplation, till it becomes the originating power that acts in us, the Godhead we adore and embrace, our whole being is put into tune with it and it is made the very self of our being.

Our expeience of it has to be purified of any mental alloy in it, otherwise it departs, we cannot hold it. And part of this purification is that it shall cease to be dependent on any cause or exciting condition of mind; it must become its own cause and self-existent, source of all other delight, which will exist only by it, and not attached to any cosmic or other image or symbol through which we first came into contact with it. Our experience of it has to be constantly intensified and made more concentrated; otherwise we shall only reflect it in the mirror of the imperfect mind and not reach that point of uplifting and transfiguration by which we are carried beyond the mind into the ineffable bliss. Object of our constant thought and contemplation, it will turn all that is into itself, reveal itself as the universal Ananda Brahman and make all existence its outpouring. If we wait upon it for the inspiration of all our inner and our outer acts, it will become the joy of the Divine pouring itself through us in light and love and power on life and all that lives. Sought by the adoration and love of the soul, it reveals itself as the Godhead, we see in it the face of God and know the bliss of our Lover. Tuning our whole being to it, we grow into a happy perfection of likeness to it, a human rendering of the divine nature. And when it becomes in every way the self of our self, we are fulfilled in being and we bear the plenitude.

Brahman always reveals himself to us in three ways, within ourselves, above our plane, around us in the universe. Within us, there are two centres of the Purusha, the inner Soul through which he touches us to our awakening; there is the Purusha in the lotus of the heart which opens upward all our powers and the Purusha in the thousand-petalled lotus whence descend through the thought and will, opening the third eye in us, the lightnings of vision and the fire of the divine energy.[1] The bliss existence may come to us through either one of these centres. When the lotus of the heart breaks open, we feel a divine joy, love and peace expanding in us like a flower of light which irradiates the whole being. They can then unite themselves with their secret source, the Divine in our hearts, and adore him as in a temple; they can flow upwards to take possession of the thought and the will and break out upward towards the Transcendent; they stream out in thought and feeling and act towards all that is around us. But so long as our normal being offers any obstacle or is not wholly moulded into a response to this divine influence or an instrument of this divine possession, the experience will be intermittent and we may fall back constantly into our old mortal heart; but by repetition, *abhyāsa*, or by the force of our desire and adoration of the Divine, it will be progressively remoulded until this abnormal experience becomes our natural consciousness.

When the other upper lotus opens, the whole mind becomes full of a divine light, joy and power, behind which is the Divine, the Lord of our being on his throne with our soul beside him or drawn inward into his rays; all the thought and will become then a luminosity, power and ecstasy; in communication with the Transcendent, this can pour down towards our mortal members and flow by them outwards on the world. In this dawn too there are, as the Vedic mystics knew, our alternations of its day and night, our exiles from the light; but as we grow in the power

[1] The reference here is to the *cakras* or centres of tantric yoga, located in the subtle body. The highest *cakra*, the thousand-petalled lotus (*sahasradala padma*) opens upward from the top of the head. The 'third eye' or *ājñā cakra* lies between the two physical eyes. The lotus of the heart, *hṛt padma* or *anāhata cakra*, is in the centre of the chest.

to hold this new existence, we become able to look long on the sun from which this irradiation proceeds and in our inner being we can grow one body with it. Sometimes the rapidity of this change depends on the strength of our longing for the Divine thus revealed, and on the intensity of our force of seeking; but at others it proceeds rather by a passive surrender to the rhythms of his all-wise working which acts always by its own at first inscrutable method. But the latter becomes the foundation when our love and trust are complete and our whole being lies in the clasp of a Power that is perfect love and wisdom.

The Divine reveals himself in the world around us when we look upon that with a spiritual desire of delight that seeks him in all things. There is often a sudden opening by which the veil of forms is itself turned into a revelation. A universal spiritual Presence, a universal peace, a universal infinite Delight has manifested, immanent, embracing, all-penetrating. This presence by our love of it, our delight in it, our constant thought of it returns and grows upon us; it becomes the thing that we see and all else is only its habitation, form and symbol. Even all that is most outward, the body, the form, the sound, whatever our senses seize, are seen as this Presence; they cease to be physical and are changed into a substance of spirit. This transformation means a transformation of our own inner consciousness; we are taken by the surrounding Presence into itself and we become part of it. Our own mind, life, body become to us only its habitation and temple, a form of its working and an instrument of its self-expression. All is only soul and body of this delight.

This is the Divine seen around us and on our own physical plane. But he may reveal himself above. We see or feel him as a high-uplifted Presence, a great infinite of Ananda above us, — or in it, our Father in heaven, — and do not feel or see him in ourselves or around us. So long as we keep this vision, the mortality in us is quelled by that Immortality; it feels the light, power and joy and responds to it according to its capacity; or it feels the descent of the spirit and it is then for a time transformed or else uplifted into some lustre of reflection of the light and power; it becomes a vessel of the Ananda. But at other times it lapses into the old mortality and exists or works dully or pettily in the ruck of its earthly habits. The complete redemption comes by the descent of the divine Power into the human mind and body and the remoulding of their inner life into the divine image, — what the Vedic seers called the birth of the Son by the sacrifice. It is in fact by a continual sacrifice or offering, a sacrifice of adoration and aspiration, of works, of thought and knowledge, of the mounting flame of the Godward will that we build ourselves into the being of this Infinite.

When we possess firmly this consciousness of the Ananda Brahman in all of these three manifestations, above, within, around, we have the full oneness of it and embrace all existences in its delight, peace, joy and love; then all the worlds become the body of this self. But we have not the richest knowledge of this Ananda if it is only an impersonal presence, largeness or immanence that we feel, if our adoration has not been intimate enough for this Being to reveal to us out of its wide-extended joy the face and body and make us feel the hands of the Friend and Lover. Its impersonality is the blissful greatness of the Brahman, but from that can look out upon us the sweetness and intimate control of the divine Personality. For Ananda is the presence of the Self and Master of our being and the stream of its outflowing can be the pure joy of his Lila.

The Integral Perfection

A DIVINE perfection of the human being is our aim. We must know then first what are the essential elements that constitute man's total perfection; secondly, what we mean by a divine as distinguished from a human perfection of our being. That man as a being is capable of self-development and of some approach at least to an ideal standard of perfection which his mind is able to conceive, fix before it and pursue, is common ground to all thinking humanity, though it may be only the minority who concern themselves with this possibility as providing the one most important aim of life. But by some the ideal is conceived as a mundane change, by others as a religious conversion.

The mundane perfection is sometimes conceived of as something outward, social, a thing of action, a more rational dealing with our fellow-men and our environment, a better and more efficient citizenship and discharge of duties, a better, richer, kindlier and happier way of living, with a more just and more harmonious associated enjoyment of the opportunities of existence. By others again a more inner and subjective ideal is cherished, a clarifying and raising of the intelligence, will and reason, a heightening and ordering of power and capacity in the nature, a nobler ethical, a richer aesthetic, a finer emotional, a much healthier and better-governed vital and physical being. Sometimes one element is stressed, almost to the exclusion of the rest; sometimes, in wider and more well-balanced minds, the whole harmony is envisaged as a total perfection. A change of education and social institutions is the outward means adopted or an inner self-training and development is preferred as the true instrumentation. Or the two

Chapter 2 of the fourth part of the *Synthesis of Yoga*, published in the *Arya* in 1919.

aims may be clearly united, the perfection of the inner individual, the perfection of the outer living.

But the mundane aim takes for its field the present life and its opportunities; the religious aim on the contrary fixes before it the self-preparation for another existence after death, its commonest ideal is some kind of pure sainthood, its means a conversion of the imperfect or sinful human being by divine grace or through obedience to a law laid down by a scripture or else given by a religious founder. The aim of religion may include a social change, but it is then a change brought about by the acceptance of a common religious ideal and way of consecrated living, a brotherhood of the saints, a theocracy or kingdom of God reflecting on earth the kingdom of heaven.

The object of our synthetic Yoga must, in this respect too as in its other parts, be more integral and comprehensive, embrace all these elements or these tendencies of a larger impulse of self-perfection and harmonise them or rather unify, and in order to do that successfully it must seize on a truth which is wider than the ordinary religious and higher than the mundane principle. All life is a secret Yoga, an obscure growth of Nature towards the discovery and fulfilment of the divine principle hidden in her which becomes progressively less obscure, more self-conscient and luminous, more self-possessed in the human being by the opening of all his instruments of knowledge, will, action, life to the Spirit within him and in the world. Mind, life, body, all the forms of our nature are the means of this growth, but they find their last perfection only by opening out to something beyond them, first, because they are not the whole of what man is, secondly, because that other something which he is, is the key of his completeness and brings a light which discovers to him the whole high and large reality of his being.

Mind is fulfilled by a greater knowledge of which it is only a half-light, life discovers its meaning in a greater power and will of which it is the outward and as yet obscure functioning, body finds its last use as an instrument of a power of being of which it is a physical support and material starting-point. They have all themselves first to be developed and find out their ordinary possibilities; all our normal life is a trying of these possibilities and an opportunity for this preparatory and tentative self-training. But life cannot find its perfect self-fulfilment till it opens to that greater reality of being of which by this development of a richer power and a more sensitive use and capacity it becomes a well-prepared field of working.

Intellectual, volitional, ethical, emotional, aesthetic and physical training and improvement are all so much to the good, but they are only in the end a constant movement in a circle without any last delivering and illumining aim, unless they arrive at a point when they can open themselves to the power and presence of the Spirit and admit its direct workings. This direct working effects a conversion of the whole being which is the indispensable condition of our real perfection. To grow into the truth and power of the Spirit and by the direct action of that power to be made a fit channel of its self-expression, — a living of man in the Divine and a divine living of the Spirit in humanity, — will therefore be the principle and the whole object of an integral Yoga of self-perfection.

In the process of this change there must be by the very necessity of the effort two stages of its working. First, there will be the personal endeavour of the human being, as soon as he becomes aware by his soul, mind, heart of this divine possibility and turns towards it as the true object of life, to prepare himself for it and to get rid of all in him that belongs to a lower working, of all that stands in the way of his opening to the spiritual truth and its power, so as to possess by this liberation his spiritual being and turn all his natural movements into free means of its self-expression. It is by this turn that the self-conscious Yoga aware of its aim begins: there is a new awakening and an upward change of the life motive. So long as there is only an intellectual, ethical and other self-training for the now normal purposes of life which does not travel beyond the ordinary circle of working of mind, life and body, we are still only in the obscure and yet unillumined preparatory Yoga of Nature; we are still in pursuit of only an ordinary human perfection. A spiritual desire of the Divine and of the divine perfection, of a unity with him in all our being and a spiritual perfection in all our nature, is the effective sign of this change, the precursory power of a great integral conversion of our being and living.

By personal effort a precursory change, a preliminary conversion can be effected; it amounts to a greater or less spiritualising of our mental motives, our character and temperament, and a mastery, stilling or changed action of the vital and physical life. This converted subjectivity can be made the base of some communion or unity of the soul in mind with the Divine and some partial reflection of the divine nature in the mentality of the human being. That is as far as man can go by his unaided or indirectly aided effort, because that is an effort of mind and mind cannot climb beyond itself permanently: at most it arises to a spiritualised and idealised mentality. If it shoots up beyond that border, it loses hold of itself, loses hold of life, and arrives either at a trance of absorption or a passivity. A greater perfection can only be arrived at by a higher power entering in and taking up the whole action of the being. The second stage of this Yoga will therefore be a persistent giving up of all the action of the nature into the hands of this greater Power, a substitution of its influence, possession and working for the personal effort, until the Divine to whom we aspire becomes the direct master of the Yoga and effects the entire spiritual and ideal conversion of the being.

This double character of our Yoga raises it beyond the mundane ideal of perfection, while at the same time it goes too beyond the loftier, intenser, but much narrower religious formula. The mundane ideal regards man always as a mental, vital and physical being and it aims at a human perfection well within these limits, a perfection of mind, life and body, an expansion and refinement of the intellect and knowledge, of the will and power, of ethical character, aim and conduct, of aesthetic sensibility and creativeness, of emotional balanced poise and enjoyment, of vital and physical soundness, regulated action and just efficiency. It is a wide and full aim, but yet not sufficiently full and wide, because it ignores that other greater element of our being which the mind vaguely conceives as the spiritual element and leaves it either undeveloped or insufficiently satisfied as merely some high occasional or added derivatory experience, the result of the action of mind in its exceptional aspects or dependent upon mind for its presence and persistence. It can become a high aim when it seeks to develop the loftier and the larger reaches of our mentality, but yet not sufficiently high, because it does not aspire beyond mind to that of which our purest reason, our brightest mental intuition, our deepest mental sense and feeling, strongest mental will and power or ideal aim and purpose are only pale radiations. Its aim besides is limited to a terrestrial perfection of the normal human life.

A Yoga of integral perfection regards man as a divine spiritual being involved in mind, life and body; it aims therefore at a liberation and a perfection of his divine nature. It seeks to make an inner living in the perfectly developed spiritual being his constant intrinsic living and the spiritualised action of mind, life and body only its outward human expression. In order that this spiritual being may not be something vague and indefinable or else but imperfectly realised and dependent on the mental support and the mental limitations, it seeks to go beyond mind to the supramental knowledge, will, sense, feeling, intuition, dynamic initiation of vital and physical action, all that makes the native working of the spiritual being. It accepts human life, but takes account of the large supraterrestrial action behind the earthly material living, and it joins itself to the divine Being from whom the supreme origination of all these partial and lower states proceeds so that the whole of life may become aware of its divine source and feel in each action of knowledge, of will, of feeling, sense and body the divine originating impulse. It rejects nothing that is essential in the mundane aim, but enlarges it, finds and lives in its greater and its truer meaning now hidden from it, transfigures it from a limited, earthly and mortal thing to a figure of infinite, divine and immortal values.

The integral Yoga meets the religious ideal at several points, but goes beyond it in the sense of a greater wideness. The religious ideal looks, not only beyond this earth, but away from it to a heaven or even beyond all heavens to some kind of Nirvana. Its ideal of perfection is limited to whatever kind of inner or outer mutation will eventually serve the turning away of the soul from the human life to the beyond. Its ordinary idea of perfection is a religio-ethical change, a drastic purification of the active and the emotional being, often with an ascetic abrogation and rejection of the vital impulses as its completest reaching of excellence, and in any case a supraterrestrial motive and reward or result of a life of piety and right conduct. In so far as it admits a change of knowledge, will, aesthesis, it is in the sense of the turning of them to another object than the aims of human life and eventually brings a rejection of all earthly objects of aesthesis, will and knowledge. The method, whether it lays stress on personal effort or upon divine influence, on works and knowledge or upon grace, is not like the mundane a development, but rather a conversion; but in the end the aim is not a conversion of our mental and physical nature, but the putting on of a pure spiritual nature and being, and since that is not possible here on earth, it looks for its consummation by a transference to another world or a shuffling off of all cosmic existence.

But the integral Yoga founds itself on a conception of the spiritual being as an omnipresent existence, the fullness of which comes not essentially by a transference to other worlds or a cosmic self-extinction, but by a growth out of what we now are phenomenally into the consciousness of the omnipresent reality which we always are in the essence of our being. It substitutes for the form of religious piety its completer spiritual seeking of a divine union. It proceeds by a personal effort to a conversion through a divine influence and possession; but this divine grace, if we may so call it, is not simply a mysterious flow or touch coming from above, but the all-pervading act of a divine presence which we come to know within as the power of the highest Self and Master of our being entering into the soul and so possessing it that we not only feel it close to us and pressing upon our mortal nature, but live in its law, know that law, possess it as the whole power of our spiritualised nature. The conversion its action will effect is an integral conversion of our ethical being into the Truth and right of the divine nature, of our intellectual into the illumination of divine knowledge, our emotional into the divine love and unity, our dynamic and volitional into a working of the divine power, our aesthetic into a plenary reception and a creative enjoyment of divine beauty, not excluding even in the end a divine conversion of the vital and physical being. It regards all the previous life as an involuntary and unconscious or half conscious preparatory growing towards this change and Yoga as the voluntary and conscious effort and realisation of the change, by which all the aim of human existence in all its parts is fulfilled, even while it is transfigured. Admitting the supracosmic truth and life in worlds beyond, it admits too the terrestrial as a continued term of the one existence and a change of individual and communal life on earth as a strain of its divine meaning.

To open oneself to the supracosmic Divine is an essential condition of this integral perfection; to unite oneself with the universal Divine is another essential condition. Here the Yoga of self-perfection coincides with the Yogas of knowledge, works and devotion; for it is impossible to change the human nature into the divine or to make it an instrument of the divine knowledge, will and joy of existence, unless there is a union with the supreme Being, Consciousness and Bliss and a unity with its universal Self in all things and beings. A wholly separative possession of the divine nature by the human individual, as distinct from a self-withdrawn absorption in it, is not possible. But this unity will not be an inmost spiritual oneness qualified, so long as the human life lasts, by a separative existence in mind, life and body; the full perfection is a possession, through this spiritual unity, of unity too with the universal Mind, the universal Life, the universal Form which are the other constant terms of cosmic being. Moreover, since human life is still accepted as a self-expression of the realised Divine in man, there must be an action of the entire divine nature in our life; and this brings in the need of the supramental conversion which substitutes the native action of spiritual being for the imperfect action of the superficial nature and spiritualises and transfigures its mental, vital and physical parts by the spiritual ideality. These three elements, a union with the supreme Divine, unity with the universal Self, and a supramental life action from this transcendent origin and through this universality, but still with the individual as the soul-channel and natural instrument, constitute the essence of the integral divine perfection of the human being.

Karmayoga

I DO not mean by work action done in the ego and the ignorance, for the satisfaction of the ego and in the drive of rajasic desire. There can be no Karmayoga without the will to get rid of ego, rajas and desire, which are the seals of ignorance.

I do not mean philanthropy or the service of humanity or all the rest of the things — moral or idealistic — which the mind of man substitutes for the deeper truth of works.

I mean by work action done for the Divine and more and more in union with the Divine — for the Divine alone and nothing else. Naturally that is not easy at the beginning, any more than deep meditation and luminous knowledge are easy or even true love and bhakti are easy. But like the others it has to be begun in the right spirit and attitude, with the right will in you, then all the rest will come.

Works done in this spirit are quite as effective as bhakti or contemplation. One gets by the rejection of desire, rajas and ego a quietude and purity into which the Peace ineffable can descend; one gets by the dedication of one's will to the Divine, by the merging of one's will in the Divine Will the death of ego and the enlarging into the cosmic consciousness or else the uplifting into what is above the cosmic; one experiences the separation of Purusha from Prakriti and is liberated from the shackles of the outer nature; one becomes aware of one's inner being and sees the outer as an instrument; one feels the universal Force doing one's works and the Self or Purusha watching or witness but free; one feels all one's works taken from one and done by the universal or supreme Mother or by the Divine Power controlling and acting from behind the heart. By constant referring of all one's will

A letter written to a disciple in 1934 and later published in *Lights on Yoga* (1935) and *Letters on Yoga* (1972). Editorial title.

and works to the Divine, love and adoration grow, the psychic being comes forward. By the reference to the Power above, we can come to feel it above and its descent and the opening to an increasing consciousness and knowledge. Finally, works, bhakti and knowledge go together and self-perfection becomes possible — what we call the transformation of the nature.

These results certainly do not come all at once; they come more or less slowly, more or less completely according to the condition and growth of the being. There is no royal road to the divine realisation.

This is the Karmayoga laid down in the Gita as I have developed it for the integral spiritual life. It is founded not on speculation and reasoning but on experience. It does not exclude meditation and certainly does not exclude bhakti, for the self-offering to the Divine, the consecration of all oneself to the Divine which is the essence of this Karmayoga are essentially a movement of bhakti. Only it does exclude a life-fleeing exclusive meditation or an emotional bhakti shut up in its own inner dream taken as the whole movement of the yoga. One may have hours of pure absorbed meditation or of the inner motionless adoration and ecstasy, but they are not the whole of the integral yoga.

Bhakti

YOUR WHOLE-HEARTED acceptance of the Vaishnava idea and Bhakti becomes rather bewildering when it is coupled with an insistence that love cannot be given to the Divine until one has experience of the Divine.[1] For what is more common in the Vaishnava attitude than the joy of Bhakti for its own sake? 'Give me Bhakti,' it cries, 'whatever else you may keep from me. Even if it is long before I can meet you, even if you delay to manifest yourself, let my Bhakti, my seeking for you, my cry, my love, my adoration be always there.' How constantly the Bhakta has sung, 'All my life I have been seeking you and still you are not there, but still I seek and cannot cease to seek and love and adore.' If it were really impossible to love God unless you first experience him, how could this be? In fact, your mind seems to be putting the cart before the horse. One seeks after God first with persistence or with passion, one finds him afterwards, some sooner than others, but most after a long seeking. One does not find him first, then seek after him. Even a glimpse often comes only after long or fervent seeking. One has the love of God or at any rate some heart's desire for him and afterwards one becomes aware of God's love, its reply to the heart's desire, its response of the supreme joy and Ananda. One does not say to God, 'Show your love from the first, shower on me the experience of yourself, satisfy my demand, then I will see whether I can love you so long as you deserve it.' It is surely the seeker who must seek and love first, follow the quest, become impassioned for the Sought — then only does the veil move aside

A letter written in 1936 and later included in *Letters on Yoga*. Editorial title.

[1] The recipient of this letter was a disciple of Sri Aurobindo's who was also a devotee of Krishna. The 'Vaishnava idea' consists of devotion to and worship of the god Vishnu, particularly in the form of his incarnations Krishna and Rama.

and the Light appear and the Face manifest that alone can satisfy the soul after its long sojourn in the desert.

Then again you may say, 'Yes, but whether I love or not, I want, I have always wanted and now I want more and more, but I get nothing.' Yes, but wanting is not all. As you now begin to see, there are conditions that have to be met — like the purification of the heart. Your thesis was, 'Once I want God, God must manifest to me, come to me, at least give glimpses of himself to me, the real, solid, concrete experience, not mere vague things which I can't understand or value. God's Grace must answer my call for it, whether I yet deserve it or not — or else there is no Grace.' God's Grace may indeed do that in certain cases, but where does the 'must' come in? If God must do it, it is no longer God's Grace, but God's duty or an obligation or a contract or a treaty. The Divine looks into the heart and removes the veil at the moment which he knows to be the right moment to do it. You have laid stress on the Bhakti theory that one has only to call his name and he must reply, he must at once be there. Perhaps, but for whom is this true? For a certain kind of Bhakta surely who feels the power of the Name, who has the passion of the Name and puts it into his cry. If one is like that, then there may be the immediate reply — if not, one has to become like that, then there will be the reply. But some go on using the Name for years, before there is an answer. Ramakrishna himself got it after a few months, but what months! and what a condition he had to pass through before he got it! Still he succeeded quickly because he had a pure heart already — and that divine passion in it.

It is not surely the Bhakta but the man of knowledge who demands experience first. He can say, 'How can I know without experience?' but he too goes on seeking like Tota Puri even though for thirty years, striving for the decisive realisation.[2] It is really the man of intellect, the rationalist who says, 'Let God, if he exists, prove himself to me first, then I will believe, then I will make some serious and prolonged effort to explore him and see what he is like.'

[2] Tota Puri was the name of the yogi who initiated Ramakrishna Paramhansa into *sannyāsa*. He is said to have become *jivanmukta* or liberated in life as the result of austere spiritual practices for over forty years.

All this does not mean that experience is irrelevant to sadhana — I certainly cannot have said such a stupid thing. What I have said is that the love and seeking of the Divine can be and ordinarily is there before the experience comes — it is an instinct, an inherent longing in the soul and it comes up as soon as certain coverings of the soul disappear or begin to disappear. The next thing I have said is that it is better to get the nature ready first (the purified heart and all that) before the 'experiences' begin rather than the other way round and I base that on the many cases there have been of the danger of experiences before the heart and vital are ready for the true experience. Of course, in many cases there is a true experience first, a touch of the Grace, but it is not something that lasts and is always there but rather something that touches and withdraws and waits for the nature to get ready. But this is not in every case, not even in the majority of cases, I believe. One has to begin with the soul's inherent longing, then the struggle with the nature to get the temple ready, then the unveiling of the Image, the permanent Presence in the sanctuary.

Meditation

YOUR QUESTIONS cover the whole of a very wide field. It is therefore necessary to reply to them with some brevity, touching only on some principal points.

1. *What meditation exactly means.*

There are two words used in English to express the Indian idea of *dhyāna*, 'meditation' and 'contemplation'. Meditation means properly the concentration of the mind on a single train of ideas which work out a single subject. Contemplation means regarding mentally a single object, image, idea so that the knowledge about the object, image or idea may arise naturally in the mind by force of the concentration. Both these things are forms of *dhyāna*, for the principle of *dhyāna* is mental concentration whether in thought, vision or knowledge.

There are other forms of *dhyāna*. There is a passage in which Vivekananda advises you to stand back from your thoughts, let them occur in your mind as they will and simply observe them and see what they are. This may be called concentration in self-observation.[1]

This form leads to another, the emptying of all thought out of the mind so as to leave it a sort of pure vigilant blank on which the divine knowledge may come and imprint itself, undisturbed by the inferior thoughts of the ordinary human mind and with the clearness of a writing in white chalk on a blackboard. You will find that the Gita speaks of this rejection of all mental thought as one of the methods of yoga and even the method it seems to prefer. This may be called the *dhyāna* of liberation, as it frees

A letter written in 1914 to a correspondent who had posed a series of questions on meditation and related matters. Later included in *Letters on Yoga*. Editorial title.

[1] Swami Vivekananda, *Raja-Yoga*, chapter 6, in *The Complete Works of Swami Vivekananda*, vol. 1 (Calcutta: Adwaita Ashrama, 1989), 174–5.

the mind from slavery to the mechanical process of thinking and allows it to think or not to think, as it pleases and when it pleases, or to choose its own thoughts or else to go beyond thought to the pure perception of Truth called in our philosophy *Vijñāna*.

Meditation is the easiest process for the human mind, but the narrowest in its results; contemplation more difficult, but greater; self-observation and liberation from the chains of Thought the most difficult of all, but the widest and greatest in its fruits. One can choose any of them according to one's bent and capacity. The perfect method is to use them all, each in its own place and for its own object; but this would need a fixed faith and firm patience and a great energy of Will in the self-application to the yoga.

2. *What should be the object or ideas for meditation?*

Whatever is most consonant with your nature and highest aspirations. But if you ask me for an absolute answer, then I must say that Brahman is always the best object for meditation or contemplation and the idea on which the mind should fix is that of God in all, all in God and all as God. It does not matter essentially whether it is the Impersonal or the Personal God, or subjectively, the One Self. But this is the idea I have found the best, because it is the highest and embraces all other truths, whether truths of this world or of the other worlds or beyond all phenomenal existence, — 'All this is the Brahman.'

In the third issue of *Arya*, at the end of the second instalment of the Analysis of the Isha Upanishad, you will find a description of this vision of the [Brāhman][2] which may be of help to you in understanding the idea.

3. *Conditions internal and external that are most essential for meditation.*

There are no *essential* external conditions, but solitude and seclusion at the time of meditation as well as stillness of the body are helpful, sometimes almost necessary to the beginner. But one should not be bound by external conditions. Once the habit of meditation is formed, it should be made possible to do it in all circumstances, lying, sitting, walking, alone, in company, in silence or in the midst of noise etc.

[2] See Appendix next page. The passage, later published in the book *Isha Upanishad* (1920), appeared in the isssue of *Arya* that was being printed when this letter was written.

The first internal condition necessary is concentration of the will against the obstacles to meditation, i.e. wandering of the mind, forgetfulness, sleep, physical and nervous impatience and restlessness etc.

The second is an increasing purity and calm of the inner consciousness citta out of which thought and emotion arise, i.e. a freedom from all disturbing reactions, such as anger, grief, depression, anxiety about worldly happenings etc. Mental perfection and moral are always closely allied to each other.

APPENDIX

THE VISION OF THE BRAHMAN

The Upanishad teaches us how to perceive Brahman in the universe and in our self-existence.

We have to perceive Brahman comprehensively as both the Stable and the Moving. We must see It in eternal and immutable Spirit and in all the changing manifestations of universe and relativity.

We have to perceive all things in Space and Time, the far and the near, the immemorial Past, the immediate Present, the infinite Future with all their contents and happenings as the One Brahman.

We have to perceive Brahman as that which exceeds, contains and supports all individual things as well as all universe, transcendentally of Time and Space and Causality. We have to perceive It also as that which lives in and possesses the universe and all it contains.

This is the transcendental, universal and individual Brahman, Lord, Continent and Indwelling Spirit, which is the object of all Knowledge. Its realisation is the condition of perfection and the way of Immortality.

The Central Process of the Yoga

I HAVE said that the most decisive way for the Peace or the Silence to come is by a descent from above. In fact, in reality though not always in appearance, that is how they always come; — not in appearance always, because the sadhak is not always conscious of the process; he feels the peace settling in him or at least manifesting, but he has not been conscious how and whence it came. Yet it is the truth that all that belongs to the higher consciousness comes from above, not only the spiritual peace and silence, but the Light, the Power, the Knowledge, the higher seeing and thought, the Ananda come from above. It is also possible that up to a certain point they may come from within, but this is because the psychic being is open to them directly and they come first there and then reveal themselves in the rest of the being from the psychic or by its coming into the front. A disclosure from within or a descent from above, these are the two sovereign ways of the Yoga-siddhi. An effort of the external surface mind or emotions, a Tapasya of some kind may seem to build up some of these things, but the results are usually uncertain and fragmentary, compared to the result of the two radical ways. That is why in this yoga we insist always on an 'opening' — an opening inwards of the inner mind, vital, physical to the inmost part of us, the psychic, and an opening upwards to what is above the mind — as indispensable for the fruits of the sadhana.

The underlying reason for this is that this little mind, vital and body which we call ourselves is only a surface movement and not our 'self' at all. It is an external bit of personality put forward for one brief life, for the play of the Ignorance. It is

A letter written to a disciple in 1934 and later published in *Lights on Yoga* and *Letters on Yoga*. Editorial title.

equipped with an ignorant mind stumbling about in search of fragments of truth, an ignorant vital rushing about in search of fragments of pleasure, an obscure and mostly subconscious physical receiving the impacts of things and suffering rather than possessing a resultant pain or pleasure. All that is accepted until the mind gets disgusted and starts looking about for the real Truth of itself and things, the vital gets disgusted and begins wondering whether there is not such a thing as real bliss and the physical gets tired and wants liberation from itself and its pains and pleasures. Then it is possible for the little ignorant bit of personality to get back to its real Self and with it to these greater things — or else to extinction of itself, Nirvana.

The real Self is not anywhere on the surface but deep within and above. Within is the soul supporting an inner mind, inner vital, inner physical in which there is a capacity for universal wideness and with it for the things now asked for — direct contact with the truth of self and things, taste of a universal bliss, liberation from the imprisoned smallness and sufferings of the gross physical body. Even in Europe the existence of something behind the surface is now very frequently admitted, but its nature is mistaken and it is called subconscient or subliminal, while really it is very conscious in its own way and not subliminal but only behind the veil. It is, according to our psychology, connected with the small outer personality by certain centres of consciousness of which we become aware by yoga. Only a little of the inner being escapes through these centres into the outer life, but that little is the best part of ourselves and responsible for our art, poetry, philosophy, ideals, religious aspirations, efforts at knowledge and perfection. But the inner centres are for the most part closed or asleep — to open them and make them awake and active is one aim of yoga. As they open, the powers and possibilities of the inner being also are aroused in us; we awake first to a larger consciousness and then to a cosmic consciousness; we are no longer little separate personalities with limited lives but centres of a universal action and in direct contact with cosmic forces. Moreover, instead of being unwillingly playthings of the latter, as is the surface person, we can become to a certain extent conscious and masters of the play of nature — how far this goes depending on the development of the inner being and its opening upward to the higher spiritual levels. At the same time the opening of the heart centre releases the psychic being which proceeds to make us aware of the Divine within us and of the higher Truth above us.

For the highest spiritual Self is not even behind our personality and bodily existence but is above it and altogether exceeds it. The highest of the inner centres is in the head, just as the deepest is the heart; but the centre which opens directly to the Self is above the head, altogether outside the physical body, in what is called the subtle body, *sūkṣma śarīra*. This Self has two aspects and the results of realising it correspond to these two aspects. One is static, a condition of wide peace, freedom, silence: the silent Self is unaffected by any action or experience; it impartially supports them but does not seem to originate them at all, rather to stand back detached or unconcerned, *udāsīna*. The other aspect is dynamic and that is experienced as a cosmic Self or Spirit which not only supports but originates and contains the whole cosmic action—not only that part of it which concerns our physical selves but also all that is beyond it—this world and all other worlds, the supraphysical as well as the physical ranges of the universe. Moreover, we feel the Self as one in all; but also we feel it as above all, transcendent, surpassing all individual birth or cosmic existence. To get into the universal Self—one in all—is to be liberated from ego; ego either becomes a small instrumental circumstance in the consciousness or even disappears from our consciousness altogether. That is the extinction or Nirvana of the ego. To get into the transcendent self above all makes us capable of transcending altogether even cosmic consciousness and action—it can be the way to that complete liberation from the world-existence which is called also extinction, *laya, mokṣa, nirvāṇa*.

It must be noted however that the opening upward does not necessarily lead to peace, silence and Nirvana only. The sadhak becomes aware not only of a great, eventually an infinite peace, silence, wideness above us, above the head as it were and extending into all physical and supraphysical space, but also he can become aware of other things—a vast Force in which is all power, a vast Light in which is all knowledge, a vast Ananda in which is all bliss and rapture. At first they appear as something essential, indeterminate, absolute, simple, *kevala*: a Nirvana into any of these things seems possible. But we can come to see too that this Force contains all forces, this Light all lights, this Ananda all joy and bliss possible. And all this can descend into us. Any of them and all of them can come down, not peace alone; only the safest is to bring down first an absolute calm and peace, for that makes the descent of the rest more secure; otherwise it may be difficult for the external nature to contain or bear so much Force, Light, Knowledge or Ananda. All these things together make what we call the higher spiritual or Divine Consciousness. The psychic opening through the heart puts us primarily into connection with the individual Divine, the Divine in his inner relation with us; it is especially the source of love and bhakti. This upward opening puts us into direct relation with the whole Divine and can create in us the divine consciousness and a new birth or births of the spirit.

When the Peace is established, this higher or Divine Force from above can descend and work in us. It descends usually first into the head and liberates the inner mind centres, then into the heart centre and liberates fully the psychic and emotional being, then into the navel and other vital centres and liberates the inner vital, then into the Muladhara and below and liberates the inner physical being. It works at the same time for perfection as well as liberation; it takes up the whole nature part by part and deals with it, rejecting what has to be rejected, sublimating what has to be sublimated, creating what has to be created. It integrates, harmonises, establishes a new rhythm in the nature. It can bring down too a higher and yet higher force and range of the higher nature until, if that be the aim of the sadhana, it becomes possible to bring down the supramental force and existence. All this is prepared, assisted, farthered by the work of the psychic being in the heart centre; the more it is open, in front, active, the quicker, safer, easier the working of the Force can be. The more love and bhakti and surrender grow in the heart, the more rapid and perfect becomes the evolution of the sadhana. For the descent and transformation imply at the same time an increasing contact and union with the Divine.

That is the fundamental rationale of the sadhana. It will be evident that the two most important things here are the opening of the heart centre and the opening of the mind centres to all that is behind and above them. For the heart opens to the psychic being and the mind centres open to the higher consciousness and the nexus between the psychic being and the higher consciousness is the principal means of the siddhi. The first opening is effected by a concentration in the heart, a call to the Divine to manifest within us and through the psychic to take up and lead the whole nature. Aspiration, prayer, bhakti, love, surrender are the main supports of this part of the sadhana — accompanied by a rejection of all that stands in the way of what we aspire for. The second opening is effected by a concentration of the consciousness in the head (afterwards, above it) and an aspiration and call and a sustained will for the descent of the divine Peace, Power, Light, Knowledge, Ananda into the being — the Peace first or the Peace and Force together. Some indeed receive Light first or Ananda first or some sudden pouring down of knowledge. With some there is first an opening which reveals to them a vast infinite Silence, Force, Light or Bliss above them and afterwards either they ascend to that or these things begin to descend into the lower nature. With others there is either the descent, first into the head, then down to the heart level, then to the navel and below and through the whole body, or else an inexplicable opening — without any sense of descent — of peace, light, wideness or power, or else a horizontal opening into the cosmic consciousness or in a suddenly widened mind an outburst of knowledge. Whatever comes has to be welcomed — for there is no absolute rule for all — but if the peace has not come first, care must be taken not to swell oneself in exultation or lose the balance. The capital movement however is when the Divine Force or Shakti, the power of the Mother comes down and takes hold, for then the organization of the consciousness begins and the larger foundation of the yoga.

The result of the concentration is not usually immediate — though to some there comes a swift and sudden outflowering; but with most there is a time longer or shorter of adaptation or preparation, especially if the nature has not been prepared already to some extent by aspiration and Tapasya. The coming of the result can sometimes be aided by associating with the concentration one of the processes of the old yoga. There is the Adwaita process of the way of knowledge — one rejects from oneself the identification with the mind, vital, body, saying continually 'I am not the mind', 'I am not the vital', 'I am not the body', seeing these things as separate from one's real self — and after a time one feels all the mental, vital, physical processes and the very sense of mind, vital, body becoming externalised, an outer action, while within and detached from them there grows the sense of a separate self-existent being which opens into the realisation of the cosmic and transcendent spirit. There is also the method — a very powerful method — of the Sankhyas, the separation of the Purusha and the Prakriti. One enforces on the mind the position of the Witness — all action of mind, vital, physical becomes an outer play which is not myself or mine, but belongs to Nature and has been enforced on an outer me. I am the witness Purusha; I am silent, detached, not bound by any of these things. There grows up in consequence a division in the being; the sadhak feels within him the growth of a calm silent separate consciousness which feels itself quite apart from the surface play of the mind and the vital and physical Nature. Usually when this takes place, it is possible very rapidly to bring down the peace of the higher consciousness and the action of the higher Force and the full march of the yoga. But often the Force itself comes down first in response to the concentration and call and then, if these things are necessary, it does them and uses any other means or process that is helpful or indispensable.

One thing more. In this process of the descent from above and the working it is most important not to rely entirely on oneself, but to rely on the guidance of the Guru and to refer all that happens to his judgment and arbitration and decision. For it often happens that the forces of the lower nature are stimulated and excited by the descent and want to mix with it and turn it to their profit. It often happens too that some Power or Powers undivine in their nature present themselves as the Supreme Lord or as the Divine Mother and claim the being's service and surrender. If these things are accepted, there will be an extremely disastrous consequence. If indeed there is the assent of the sadhak to the Divine working alone and the submission or surrender to that guidance, then all can go smoothly. This assent and a rejection of all egoistic forces or forces that appeal to the ego are the safeguard throughout the sadhana. But the ways of nature are full of snares, the disguises of the ego are innumerable, the illusions of the Powers of Darkness, Rakshasi Maya, are extraordinarily skilful; the reason is an insufficient guide and often turns traitor; vital desire is always with us tempting to follow any alluring call.

This is the reason why in this yoga we insist so much on what we call Samarpana — rather inadequately rendered by the English word surrender. If the heart centre is fully opened and the psychic is always in control, then there is no question; all is safe. But the psychic can at any moment be veiled by a lower upsurge. It is only a few who are exempt from these dangers and it is precisely those to whom surrender is easily possible. The guidance of one who himself is by identity or represents the Divine is in this difficult endeavour imperative and indispensable.

What I have written may help you to get some clear idea of what I mean by the central process of the yoga. I have written at some length but, naturally, could cover only the fundamental things. Whatever belongs to circumstance and detail must arise as one works out the method, or rather as it works itself out — for the last is what usually happens when there is an effective beginning of the action of the sadhana.

The Novelty of the Integral Yoga

BY TRANSFORMATION I do not mean some change of the nature — I do not mean, for instance, sainthood or ethical perfection or yogic siddhis (like the Tantrik's) or a transcendental *(cinmaya)* body. I use transformation in a special sense, a change of consciousness radical and complete and of a certain specific kind which is so conceived as to bring about a strong and assured step forward in the spiritual evolution of the being of a greater and higher kind and of a larger sweep and completeness than what took place when a mentalised being first appeared in a vital and material animal world. If anything short of that takes place or at least if a real beginning is not made on that basis, a fundamental progress towards this fulfilment, then my object is not accomplished. A partial realisation, something mixed and inconclusive, does not meet the demand I make on life and yoga.

Light of realisation is not the same thing as Descent. Realisation by itself does not necessarily transform the being as a whole; it may bring only an opening or heightening or widening of the consciousness at the top so as to realise something in the Purusha part without any radical change in the parts of Prakriti. One may have some light of realisation at the spiritual summit of the consciousness but the parts below remain what they were. I have seen any number of instances of that. There must be a descent of the light not merely into the mind or part of it but into all the being down to the physical and below before a real transformation can take place. A light in the mind may spiritualise or otherwise change the mind or part of it in one way or another, but it need not change the vital nature; a light in the vital may purify and enlarge the vital movements or else silence and

A letter written to a disciple in 1935 and later published in *Letters on Yoga*.

immobilise the vital being, but leave the body and the physical consciousness as it was, or even leave it inert or shake its balance. And the descent of Light is not enough, it must be the descent of the whole higher consciousness, its Peace, Power, Knowledge, Love, Ananda. Moreover, the descent may be enough to liberate, but not to perfect, or it may be enough to make a great change in the inner being, while the outer remains an imperfect instrument, clumsy, sick or unexpressive. Finally, transformation effected by the sadhana cannot be complete unless it is a supramentalisation of the being. Psychicisation is not enough, it is only a beginning; spiritualisation and the descent of the higher consciousness is not enough, it is only a middle term; the ultimate achievement needs the action of the supramental Consciousness and Force. Something less than that may very well be considered enough by the individual, but it is not enough for the earth-consciousness to take the definitive stride forward it must take at one time or another.

I have never said that my yoga was something brand new in all its elements. I have called it the integral yoga and that means that it takes up the essence and many processes of the old yogas — its newness is in its aim, standpoint and the totality of its method. In the earlier stages which is all I deal with in books like the 'Riddle' or the 'Lights' or in the new book to be published[1] there is nothing in it that distinguishes it from the old yogas except the aim underlying its comprehensiveness, the spirit in its movements and the ultimate significance it keeps before it — also the scheme of its psychology and its workings: but as that was not and could not be developed systematically or schematically in these letters, it has not been grasped by those who are not already acquainted with it by mental familiarity or some amount of practice. The detail or method of the later stages of the yoga which go into little known or untrodden regions, I have not made public and I do not at present intend to do so.

I know very well also that there have been seemingly allied ideals and anticipations — the perfectibility of the race, certain Tantric sadhanas, the effort after a complete physical siddhi by

[1] *The Riddle of This World* (1933), *Lights on Yoga* (1935), and *Bases of Yoga* (1936): three collections of letters dealing with the foundations of Sri Aurobindo's yoga.

certain schools of yoga, etc., etc. I have alluded to these things myself and have put forth the view that the spiritual past of the race has been a preparation of Nature not merely for attaining the Divine beyond the world, but also for this very step forward which the evolution of the earth-consciousness has still to make. I do not therefore care in the least — even though these ideals were, up to some extent parallel, yet not identical with mine — whether this yoga and its aim and method are accepted as new or not; that is in itself a trifling matter. That it should be recognised as true in itself by those who can accept or practise it and should make itself true by achievement is the one thing important; it does not matter if it is called new or a repetition or revival of the old which was forgotten. I laid emphasis on it as new in a letter to certain sadhaks so as to explain to them that a repetition of the aim and idea of the old yogas was not enough in my eyes, that I was putting forward a thing to be achieved that has not yet been achieved, not yet clearly visualised, even though it is the natural but still secret outcome of all the past spiritual endeavour.

It is new as compared with the old yogas:

1. Because it aims not at a departure out of world and life into Heaven or Nirvana, but at a change of life and existence, not as something subordinate or incidental, but as a distinct and central object. If there is a descent in other yogas, yet it is only an incident on the way or resulting from the ascent — the ascent is the real thing. Here the ascent is the first step, but it is a means for the descent. It is the descent of the new consciousness attained by the ascent that is the stamp and seal of the sadhana. Even the Tantra and Vaishnavism end in the release from life; here the object is the divine fulfilment of life.

2. Because the object sought after is not an individual achievement of divine realisation for the sake of the individual, but something to be gained for the earth-consciousness here, a cosmic, not solely a supra-cosmic achievement. The thing to be gained also is the bringing in of a Power of Consciousness (the supramental) not yet organised or active directly in earth-nature, even in the spiritual life, but yet to be organised and made directly active.

3. Because a method has been preconized for achieving this purpose which is as total and integral as the aim set before it, viz.,

the total and integral change of the consciousness and nature, taking up old methods but only as a part action and present aid to others that are distinctive. I have not found this method (as a whole) or anything like it professed or realised in the old yogas. If I had, I should not have wasted my time in hewing out a road and in thirty years of search and inner creation when I could have hastened home safely to my goal in an easy canter over paths already blazed out, laid down, perfectly mapped, macadamised, made secure and public. Our yoga is not a retreading of old walks, but a spiritual adventure.

Part Six
Poetry of the Spirit

The *mantra* as I have tried to describe it in *The Future Poetry* is a word of power and light that comes from the Overmind inspiration or from some very high plane of Intuition. Its characteristics are a language that conveys infinitely more than the mere surface sense of the words seems to indicate, a rhythm that means even more than the language and is born out of the infinite and disappears into it, and the power to convey not merely the mental, vital or physical contents or indications or values of the thing uttered, but its significance and figure in some fundamental and original consciousness which is behind all these and greater.

Extract from a letter

PART SIX consists of an essay in which Sri Aurobindo sets forth his idea of the nature of poetry, a selection of short poems and a canto from the epic *Savitri*.

- In *The Essence of Poetry*, a chapter from *The Future Poetry*, Sri Aurobindo explains his idea that the greatest poetry, whatever its theme, approaches the power of the *mantra* or word that reveals the veiled Reality.
- *Selected Short Poems*. 'Invitation' was written by Sri Aurobindo in Alipore Jail (1908–9) and published after his release. The next four poems, although written as 'metrical experiments', are among his most beautiful and significant poetic achievements. 'Trance', written in 1933, was published the next year with a note explaining that metrically it was 'an experiment in the use of quantitative foot measures'. 'Ocean Oneness' and 'Descent' (1942) are written in quantitative metres on the Greek model, alcaics and sapphics respectively. The metre of 'Thought the Paraclete' (written 1934) has similarities to the Latin hendecasyllable. The Greek word 'paraclete', meaning 'one called to help', 'intercessor', is borrowed from Christian theology, where it is applied to the Holy Spirit. 'Transformation' and 'Nirvana' appeared in 1934; the other six sonnets, written in 1938 and 1939, were first published posthumously. All eight are first-person accounts of experiences of the mystic path.
- *Savitri: A Legend and a Symbol*, an epic poem of almost 24,000 lines, was written by Sri Aurobindo over a period of 35 years. In a letter of 1936 he said that he used it 'as a means of ascension. I began with it on a certain mental level, each time I could reach a higher level I rewrote from that level'. *Savitri* is based on the story of Savitri and Satyavan as told in the Mahabharata. In Sri Aurobindo's recounting, Savitri is an incarnation of the Divine Mother brought down to earth by the aspiration of the sage Aswapati. Savitri marries Satyavan, who after a year of bliss is taken away by the Lord of Death. In 'The Book of Yoga', from which this selection is taken, Savitri, having foreknowledge of the coming tragedy, seeks for and discovers her soul, with whose help she will face and overcome Death.
- Appendix: *The Fifteenth of August 1947*. A message broadcast by All India Radio, Tiruchchirappalli, on 14 August 1947, the day before India became independent. See the general introduction.

The Essence of Poetry

WHAT THEN is the nature of poetry, its essential law? what is the highest power we can demand from it, what the supreme music that the human mind, reaching up and in and out to its own widest breadths, deepest depths and topmost summits, can extract from this self-expressive instrument? and how out of that does there arise the possibility of its use as the *mantra* of the Real? Not that we need spend any energy in a vain effort to define anything so profound, elusive and indefinable as the breath of poetic creation; to take the myriad-stringed harp of Saraswati to pieces for the purpose of scientific analysis is a narrow and barren amusement. But we stand in need of some guiding intuitions, some helpful descriptions which will serve to enlighten our search; to fix in that way, not by definition, but by description, the essential things in poetry is neither an impossible, nor an unprofitable endeavour.

We meet here two common enough errors, to one of which the ordinary uninstructed mind is most liable, to the other the too instructed critic or the too intellectually conscientious artist or craftsman. To the ordinary mind, judging poetry without really entering into it, it looks as if it were nothing more than an aesthetic pleasure of the imagination, the intellect and the ear, a sort of elevated pastime. If that were all, we need not have wasted time in seeking for its spirit, its inner aim, its deeper law. Anything pretty, pleasant and melodious with a beautiful idea in it would serve our turn; a song of Anacreon or a plaint of Mimnermus would be as satisfying to the poetic sense as the Oedipus, Agamemnon or Odyssey, for from this point of view

Chapter 2 of *The Future Poetry*, published in the *Arya* in 1918. *The Future Poetry* was subsequently revised and published posthumously in 1953.

they might well strike us as equally and even, one might contend, more perfect in their light but exquisite unity and brevity.[1] Pleasure, certainly, we expect from poetry as from all art; but the external sensible and even the inner imaginative pleasure are only first elements. For these must not only be refined in order to meet the highest requirements of the intelligence, the imagination and the ear; but afterwards they have to be still farther heightened and in their nature raised beyond even their own noblest levels, so that they may become the support for something greater beyond them; otherwise they cannot lead to the height on which lives the Mantra.

For neither the intelligence, the imagination nor the ear are the true or at least the deepest or highest recipients of the poetic delight, even as they are not its true or highest creators; they are only its channels and instruments: the true creator, the true hearer is the soul. The more rapidly and transparently the rest do their work of transmission, the less they make of their separate claim to satisfaction, the more directly the word reaches and sinks deep into the soul, the greater the poetry. Therefore poetry has not really done its work, at least its highest work, until it has raised the pleasure of the instrument and transmuted it into the deeper delight of the soul. A divine Ananda,[2] a delight interpretative, creative, revealing, formative, — one might almost say, an inverse reflection of the joy which the universal Soul felt in its great release of energy when it rang out into the rhythmic forms of the universe the spiritual truth, the large interpretative idea, the life, the power, the emotion of things packed into an original creative vision, — such spiritual joy is that which the soul of the poet feels and which, when he can conquer the human difficulties of his task, he succeeds in pouring also into all those who are prepared to receive it. This delight is not merely a godlike pastime; it is a great formative and illuminative power.

1 Mimnermus (fl. 630 BCE) and Anacreon (563–478 BCE) were Greek poets who treated love and similar themes in lyric and elegiac metres. The *Oedipus Rex* and *Agamemnon* are major tragedies by Sophocles (496–406 BCE) and Aeschylus (525–456 BCE) respectively, the *Odyssey* one of the two epics attributed to Homer.

2 Ananda, in the language of Indian spiritual experience, is the essential delight which the Infinite feels in itself and in its creation. By the infinite Self's Ananda all exists, for the Self's Ananda all was made. [Sri Aurobindo's note]

The critic — of a certain type — or the intellectually conscientious artist will, on the other hand, often talk as if poetry were mainly a matter of a faultlessly correct or at most an exquisite technique. Certainly, in all art good technique is the first step towards perfection; but there are so many other steps, there is a whole world beyond before you can get near to what you seek; so much so that even a deficient correctness of execution will not prevent an intense and gifted soul from creating great poetry which keeps its hold on the centuries. Moreover, technique, however indispensable, occupies a smaller field perhaps in poetry than in any other art, — first, because its instrument, the rhythmic word, is fuller of subtle and immaterial elements; then because, the most complex, flexible, variously suggestive of all the instruments of the artistic creator, it has more — almost infinite — possibilities in many directions than any other. The rhythmic word has a subtly sensible element, its sound value, a quite immaterial element, its significance or thought value, and both of these again, its sound and its sense, have separately and together a soul value, a direct spiritual power, which is infinitely the most important thing about them. And though this comes to birth with a small element subject to the laws of technique, yet almost immediately, almost at the beginning of its flight, its power soars up beyond the province of any laws of mechanical construction: and this form of speech carries in it on its summits an element which draws close to the empire of the ineffable.

Poetry rather determines its own form; the form is not imposed on it by any law mechanical or external to it. The poet least of all artists needs to create with his eye fixed anxiously on the technique of his art. He has to possess it, no doubt; but in the heat of creation the intellectual sense of it becomes a subordinate action or even a mere undertone in his mind, and in his best moments he is permitted, in a way, to forget it altogether. For then the perfection of his sound-movement and style come entirely as the spontaneous form of his soul: that utters itself in an inspired rhythm and an innate, a revealed word, even as the universal Soul created the harmonies of the universe out of the power of the word secret and eternal within him, leaving the mechanical work to be done in a surge of hidden spiritual excitement by the subconscient part of his Nature. It is this highest speech which is the supreme poetic utterance, the immortal element in his poetry, and a little of it is enough to save the rest of his work from oblivion. *Svalpam apyasya dharmasya!*

This power makes the rhythmic word of the poet the highest form of speech available to man for the expression whether of his self-vision or of his world-vision. It is noticeable that even the deepest experience, the pure spiritual which enters into things that can never be wholly expressed, still, when it does try to express them and not merely to explain them intellectually, tends instinctively to use, often the rhythmic forms, almost always the manner of speech characteristic of poetry. But poetry attempts to extend this manner of vision and utterance to all experience, even the most objective, and therefore it has a natural urge towards the expression of something in the object beyond its mere appearances, even when these seem outwardly to be all that it is enjoying.

We may usefully cast a glance, not at the last inexpressible secret, but at the first elements of this heightening and intensity peculiar to poetic utterance. Ordinary speech uses language mostly for a limited practical utility of communication; it uses it for life and for the expression of ideas and feelings necessary or useful to life. In doing so, we treat words as conventional signs for ideas with nothing but a perfunctory attention to their natural force, much as we use any kind of common machine or simple implement; we treat them as if, though useful for life, they were themselves without life. When we wish to put a more vital power into them, we have to lend it to them out of ourselves, by marked intonations of the voice, by the emotional force or vital energy we throw into the sound so as to infuse into the conventional word-sign something which is not inherent in itself. But if we go back earlier in the history of language and still more if we look into its origins, we shall, I think, find that it was not always so with human speech. Words had not only a real and vivid life of their own, but the speaker was more conscious of it than we can possibly be with our mechanised and sophisticated intellects. This arose from the primitive nature of language which, probably, in its first movement was not intended, — or shall we say, did not intend, — so much to stand for distinct ideas of the intelligence as for feelings, sensations, broad indefinite mental impressions with minute shades of quality in them which we do not now care to pursue. The intellectual sense in its precision must have been a secondary element which grew more dominant as language evolved along with the evolving intelligence.

For the reason why sound came to express fixed ideas, lies not in any natural and inherent equivalence between the sound and its intellectual sense, for there is none, — intellectually any sound might express any sense, if men were agreed on a conventional equivalence between them; it started from an indefinable quality or property in the sound to raise certain vibrations in the life-soul of the human creature, in his sensational, his emotional, his crude mental being. An example may indicate more clearly what I mean. The word wolf, the origin of which is no longer present to our minds, denotes to our intelligence a certain living object and that is all, the rest we have to do for ourselves: the Sanskrit word *vṛka*, 'tearer', came in the end to do the same thing, but originally it expressed the sensational relation between the wolf and man which most affected the man's life, and it did so by a certain quality in the sound which readily associated it with the sensation of tearing. This must have given early language a powerful life, a concrete vigour, in one direction a natural poetic force which it has lost, however greatly it has gained in precision, clarity, utility.

Now, poetry goes back in a way and recovers, though in another fashion, as much as it can of this original element. It does this partly by a stress on the image replacing the old sensational concreteness, partly by a greater attention to the suggestive force of the sound, its life, its power, the mental impression it carries. It associates this with the definitive thought value contributed by the intelligence and increases both by each other. In that way it succeeds at the same time in carrying up the power of speech to the direct expression of a higher reach of experience than the intellectual or vital. For it brings out not only the definitive intellectual value of the word, not only its power of emotion and sensation, its vital suggestion, but through and beyond these aids its soul-suggestion, its spirit. So poetry arrives at the indication of infinite meanings beyond the finite intellectual meaning the word carries. It expresses not only the life-soul of man as did the primitive word, not only the ideas of his intelligence for which speech now usually serves, but the experience, the vision, the ideas, as we may say, of the higher and wider soul in him. Making them real to our life-soul as well as present to our intellect, it opens to us by the word the doors of the Spirit.

Prose style carries speech to a much higher power than its ordinary use, but it differs from poetry in not making this yet greater attempt. For it takes its stand firmly on the intellectual value of the word. It uses rhythms which ordinary speech neglects, and aims at a general fluid harmony of movement. It seeks to associate words agreeably and luminously so as at once to please and to clarify the intelligence. It strives after a more accurate, subtle, flexible and satisfying expression than the rough methods of ordinary speech care to compass. A higher adequacy of speech is its first object. Beyond this adequacy it may aim at a greater forcefulness and effectiveness by various devices of speech, by many rhetorical means for heightening the stress of its intellectual appeal. Passing beyond this first limit, this just or strong, but always restrained measure, it may admit a more emphatic rhythm, more directly and powerfully stimulate the emotion, appeal to a more vivid aesthetic sense. It may even make such a free or rich use of images as to suggest an outward approximation to the manner of poetry; but it employs them decoratively, as ornaments, *alaṅkāra*, or for their effective value in giving a stronger intellectual vision of the thing or the thought it describes or defines; it does not use the image for that profounder and more living vision for which the poet is always seeking. And always it has its eye on its chief hearer and judge, the intelligence, and calls in other powers only as important aids to capture his suffrage. Reason and taste, two powers of the intelligence, are rightly the supreme gods of the prose stylist, while to the poet they are only minor deities.

If it goes beyond these limits, approaches in its measures a more striking rhythmic balance, uses images for sheer vision, opens itself to a mightier breath of speech, prose style passes beyond its normal province and approaches or even enters the confines of poetry. It becomes poetical prose or even poetry itself using the apparent forms of prose as a disguise or a loose apparel. A high or a fine adequacy, effectivity, intellectual illuminativeness and a carefully tempered aesthetic satisfaction are the natural and proper powers of its speech. But the privilege of the poet is to go beyond and discover that more intense illumination of speech, that inspired word and supreme inevitable utterance, in which there meets the unity of a divine rhythmic movement with a depth of sense and a power of infinite suggestion welling up directly from the fountain-heads of the spirit within us. He may not always or often find it, but to seek for it is the law or at least the highest trend of his utterance, and when he can not only find it, but cast into it some deeply revealed truth of the spirit itself, he utters the *mantra*.

But always, whether in the search or the finding, the whole style and rhythm of poetry are the expression and movement which come from us out of a certain spiritual excitement caused by a vision in the soul of which it is eager to deliver itself. The vision may be of anything in Nature or God or man or the life of creatures or the life of things; it may be a vision of force and action, or of sensible beauty, or of truth of thought, or of emotion and pleasure and pain, of this life or the life beyond. It is sufficient that it is the soul which sees and the eye, sense, heart and thought-mind become the passive instruments of the soul. Then we get the real, the high poetry. But if what acts is too much an excitement of the intellect, the imagination, the emotions, the vital activities seeking rhythmical and forceful expression, without that greater spiritual excitement embracing them, or if all these are not sufficiently sunk into the soul, steeped in it, fused in it, and the expression does not come out purified and uplifted by a sort of spiritual transmutation, then we fall to lower levels of poetry and get work of a much more doubtful immortality. And when the appeal is altogether to the lower things in us, to the mere mind, we arrive outside the true domain of poetry; we approach the confines of prose or get prose itself masking in the apparent forms of poetry, and the work is distinguished from prose style only or mainly by its mechanical elements, a good verse form and perhaps a more compact, catching or energetic expression than the prose writer will ordinarily permit to the easier and looser balance of his speech. It will not have at all or not sufficiently the true essence of poetry.

For in all things that speech can express there are two elements, the outward or instrumental and the real or spiritual. In thought, for instance, there is the intellectual idea, that which the intelligence makes precise and definite to us, and the soul-idea, that which exceeds the intellectual and brings us into nearness or identity with the whole reality of the thing expressed. Equally in emotion, it is not the mere emotion itself the poet seeks, but the soul of emotion, that in it for the delight of which the soul in us and the world desires or accepts emotional experience. So too with the poetical sense of objects, the poet's attempt to embody in his speech truth of life or truth of Nature. It is this greater truth and its delight and beauty for which he is seeking, beauty which is truth and truth beauty and therefore a joy for ever, because it brings us the delight of the soul in the discovery of its own deeper realities. This greater element the more timid and temperate speech of prose can sometimes shadow out to us, but the heightened and fearless style of poetry makes it close and living and the higher cadences of poetry carry in on their wings what the style by itself could not bring. This is the source of that intensity which is the stamp of poetical speech and of the poetical movement. It comes from the stress of the soul-vision behind the word; it is the spiritual excitement of a rhythmic voyage of self-discovery among the magic islands of form and name in these inner and outer worlds.

Selected Short Poems

Invitation

With wind and the weather beating round me
Up to the hill and the moorland I go.
Who will come with me? Who will climb with me?
Wade through the brook and tramp through the snow?

Not in the petty circle of cities
Cramped by your doors and your walls I dwell;
Over me God is blue in the welkin,
Against me the wind and the storm rebel.

I sport with solitude here in my regions,
Of misadventure have made me a friend.
Who would live largely? Who would live freely?
Here to the wind-swept uplands ascend.

I am the lord of tempest and mountain,
I am the Spirit of freedom and pride.
Stark must he be and a kinsman to danger
Who shares my kingdom and walks at my side.

Trance

A naked and silver-pointed star
    Floating near the halo of the moon;
A storm-rack, the pale sky's fringe and bar,
    Over waters stilling into swoon.

My mind is awake in stirless trance,
    Hushed my heart, a burden of delight;
Dispelled is the senses' flicker-dance,
    Mute the body aureate with light.

O star of creation pure and free,
    Halo-moon of ecstasy unknown,
Storm-breath of the soul-change yet to be,
    Ocean-self enraptured and alone!

Ocean Oneness

Silence is round me, wideness ineffable;
White birds on the ocean diving and wandering;
    A soundless sea on a voiceless heaven,
        Azure on azure, is mutely gazing.

Identified with silence and boundlessness
My spirit widens clasping the universe
    Till all that seemed becomes the Real,
        One in a mighty and single vastness.

Someone broods there nameless and bodiless,
Conscious and lonely, deathless and infinite,
    And, sole in a still eternal rapture,
        Gathers all things to his heart for ever.

Descent

All my cells thrill swept by a surge of splendour,
Soul and body stir with a mighty rapture,
Light and still more light like an ocean billows
Over me, round me.

Rigid, stonelike, fixed like a hill or statue,
Vast my body feels and upbears the world's weight;
Dire the large descent of the Godhead enters
Limbs that are mortal.

Voiceless, thronged, Infinity crowds upon me;
Presses down a glory of power eternal;
Mind and heart grow one with the cosmic wideness;
Stilled are earth's murmurs.

Swiftly, swiftly crossing the golden spaces
Knowledge leaps, a torrent of rapid lightnings;
Thoughts that left the Ineffable's flaming mansions,
Blaze in my spirit.

Slow the heart-beats' rhythm like a giant hammer's;
Missioned voices drive to me from God's doorway
Words that live not save upon Nature's summits,
Ecstasy's chariots.

All the world is changed to a single oneness;
Souls undying, infinite forces, meeting,
Join in God-dance weaving a seamless Nature,
Rhythm of the Deathless.

Mind and heart and body, one harp of being,
Cry that anthem, finding the notes eternal, —
Light and might and bliss and immortal wisdom
Clasping for ever.

Thought the Paraclete

As some bright archangel in vision flies
Plunged in dream-caught spirit immensities,
Past the long green crests of the seas of life,
Past the orange skies of the mystic mind
Flew my thought self-lost in the vasts of God.
Sleepless wide great glimmering wings of wind
Bore the gold-red seeking of feet that trod
Space and Time's mute vanishing ends. The face
Lustred, pale-blue-lined of the hippogriff,
Eremite, sole, daring the bourneless ways,
Over world-bare summits of timeless being
Gleamed; the deep twilights of the world-abyss
Failed below. Sun-realms of supernal seeing,
Crimson-white mooned oceans of pauseless bliss
Drew its vague heart-yearning with voices sweet.
Hungering, large-souled to surprise the unconned
Secrets white-fire-veiled of the last Beyond,
Crossing power-swept silences rapture-stunned,
Climbing high far ethers eternal-sunned,
Thought the great-winged wanderer paraclete
Disappeared slow-singing a flame-word rune.
Self was left, lone, limitless, nude, immune.

Transformation

My breath runs in a subtle rhythmic stream;
It fills my members with a might divine:
I have drunk the Infinite like a giant's wine.
Time is my drama or my pageant dream.
Now are my illumined cells joy's flaming scheme
And changed my thrilled and branching nerves to fine
Channels of rapture opal and hyaline
For the influx of the Unknown and the Supreme.

I am no more a vassal of the flesh,
A slave to Nature and her leaden rule;
I am caught no more in the senses' narrow mesh.
My soul unhorizoned widens to measureless sight,
My body is God's happy living tool,
My spirit a vast sun of deathless light.

Nirvana

All is abolished but the mute Alone.
The mind from thought released, the heart from grief
Grow inexistent now beyond belief;
There is no I, no Nature, known-unknown.
The city, a shadow picture without tone,
Floats, quivers unreal; forms without relief
Flow, a cinema's vacant shapes; like a reef
Foundering in shoreless gulfs the world is done.

Only the illimitable Permanent
Is here. A Peace stupendous, featureless, still,
Replaces all, — what once was I, in It
A silent unnamed emptiness content
Either to fade in the Unknowable
Or thrill with the luminous seas of the Infinite.

The Indwelling Universal

I contain the wide world in my soul's embrace:
In me Arcturus and Belphegor burn.
To whatsoever living form I turn
I see my own body with another face.

All eyes that look on me are my sole eyes;
The one heart that beats within all breasts is mine.
The world's happiness flows through me like wine,
Its million sorrows are my agonies.

Yet all its acts are only waves that pass
Upon my surface; inly for ever still,
Unborn I sit, timeless, intangible;
All things are shadows in my tranquil glass.

My vast transcendence holds the cosmic whirl;
I am hid in it as in the sea a pearl.

Bliss of Identity

All Nature is taught in radiant ways to move,
All beings are in myself embraced.
O fiery boundless Heart of joy and love,
How art thou beating in a mortal's breast!

It is Thy rapture flaming through my nerves
And all my cells and atoms thrill with Thee;
My body Thy vessel is and only serves
As a living wine-cup of Thy ecstasy.

I am a centre of Thy golden light
And I its vast and vague circumference;
Thou art my soul great, luminous and white
And Thine my mind and will and glowing sense.

Thy spirit's infinite b[illegible] I feel in me;
My life is a throb of Thy eternity.

The Pilgrim of the Night

I made an assignation with the Night;
In the abyss was fixed our rendezvous:
In my breast carrying God's deathless light
I came her dark and dangerous heart to woo.

I left the glory of the illumined Mind
And the calm rapture of the divinised soul
And travelled through a vastness dim and blind
To the grey shore where her ignorant waters roll.

I walk by the chill wave through the dull slime
And still that weary journeying knows no end;
Lost is the lustrous godhead beyond Time,
There comes no voice of the celestial Friend,

And yet I know my footprints' track shall be
A pathway towards Immortality.

Liberation

I have thrown from me the whirling dance of mind
And stand now in the spirit's silence free;
Timeless and deathless beyond creature-kind,
The centre of my own eternity.

I have escaped and the small self is dead;
I am immortal, alone, ineffable;
I have gone out from the universe I made,
And have grown nameless and immeasurable.

My mind is hushed in a wide and endless light,
My heart a solitude of delight and peace,
My sense unsnared by touch and sound and sight,
My body a point in white infinities.

I am the one Being's sole immobile Bliss:
No one I am, I who am all that is.

Krishna

At last I find a meaning of soul's birth
  Into this universe terrible and sweet,
I who have felt the hungry heart of earth
  Aspiring beyond heaven to Krishna's feet.

I have seen the beauty of immortal eyes,
  And heard the passion of the Lover's flute,
And known a deathless ecstasy's surprise
  And sorrow in my heart for ever mute.

Nearer and nearer now the music draws,
  Life shudders with a strange felicity;
All Nature is a wide enamoured pause
  Hoping her lord to touch, to clasp, to be.

For this one moment lived the ages past;
The world now throbs fulfilled in me at last.

The Word of the Silence

A bare impersonal hush is now my mind,
  A world of sight clear and inimitable,
A volume of silence by a Godhead signed,
  A greatness pure of thought, virgin of will.

Once on its pages Ignorance could write
  In a scribble of intellect the blind guess of Time
And cast gleam-messages of ephemeral light,
  A food for souls that wander on Nature's rim.

But now I listen to a greater Word
  Born from the mute unseen omniscient Ray:
The Voice that only Silence' ear has heard
  Leaps missioned from an eternal glory of Day.

All turns from a wideness and unbroken peace
To a tumult of joy in a sea of wide release.

Savitri

The Finding of the Soul

Onward she passed seeking the soul's mystic cave.
At first she stepped into a night of God.
The light was quenched that helps the labouring world,
The power that struggles and stumbles in our life;
This inefficient mind gave up its thoughts,
The striving heart its unavailing hopes.
All knowledge failed and the Idea's forms
And Wisdom screened in awe her lowly head
Feeling a Truth too great for thought or speech,
Formless, ineffable, for ever the same.
An innocent and holy Ignorance
Adored like one who worships formless God
The unseen Light she could not claim nor own.
In a simple purity of emptiness
Her mind knelt down before the unknowable.
All was abolished save her naked self
And the prostrate yearning of her surrendered heart:
There was no strength in her, no pride of force;
The lofty burning of desire had sunk
Ashamed, a vanity of separate self,
The hope of spiritual greatness fled,
Salvation she asked not nor a heavenly crown:
Humility seemed now too proud a state.
Her self was nothing, God alone was all,
Yet God she knew not but only knew he was.
A sacred darkness brooded now within,
The world was a deep darkness great and nude.
This void held more than all the teeming worlds,
This blank felt more than all that Time has borne,
This dark knew dumbly, immensely the Unknown.

But all was formless, voiceless, infinite.
As might a shadow walk in a shadowy scene,
A small nought passing through a mightier Nought,
A night of person in a bare outline
Crossing a fathomless impersonal Night,
Silent she moved, empty and absolute.
In endless Time her soul reached a wide end,
The spaceless Vast became her spirit's place.
At last a change approached, the emptiness broke;
A wave rippled within, the world had stirred;
Once more her inner self became her space.
There was felt a blissful nearness to the goal;
Heaven leaned low to kiss the sacred hill,
The air trembled with passion and delight.
A rose of splendour on a tree of dreams,
The face of Dawn out of mooned twilight grew.
Day came, priest of a sacrifice of joy
Into the worshipping silence of her world;
He carried immortal lustre as his robe,
Trailed heaven like a purple scarf and wore
As his vermilion caste-mark a red sun.
As if an old remembered dream come true,
She recognised in her prophetic mind
The imperishable lustre of that sky,
The tremulous sweetness of that happy air
And, covered from mind's view and life's approach,
The mystic cavern in the sacred hill
And knew the dwelling of her secret soul.
As if in some Elysian occult depth,
Truth's last retreat from thought's profaning touch,
As if in a rock-temple's solitude hid,
God's refuge from an ignorant worshipping world,
It lay withdrawn even from life's inner sense,
Receding from the entangled heart's desire.
A marvellous brooding twilight met the eyes
And a holy stillness held that voiceless space.
An awful dimness wrapped the great rock-doors
Carved in the massive stone of Matter's trance.
Two golden serpents round the lintel curled,
Enveloping it with their pure and dreadful strength,

Looked out with wisdom's deep and luminous eyes.
An eagle covered it with wide conquering wings:
Flames of self-lost immobile reverie,
Doves crowded the grey musing cornices
Like sculptured postures of white-bosomed peace.
Across the threshold's sleep she entered in
And found herself amid great figures of gods
Conscious in stone and living without breath,
Watching with fixed regard the soul of man,
Executive figures of the cosmic self,
World-symbols of immutable potency.
On the walls covered with significant shapes
Looked at her the life-scene of man and beast
And the high meaning of the life of gods,
The power and necessity of these numberless worlds,
And faces of beings and stretches of world-space
Spoke the succinct and inexhaustible
Hieratic message of the climbing planes.
In their immensitude signing infinity
They were the extension of the self of God
And housed, impassively receiving all,
His figures and his small and mighty acts
And his passion and his birth and life and death
And his return to immortality.
To the abiding and eternal is their climb,
To the pure existence everywhere the same,
To the sheer consciousness and the absolute force
And the unimaginable and formless bliss,
To the mirth in Time and the timeless mystery
Of the triune being who is all and one
And yet is no one but himself apart.
There was no step of breathing men, no sound,
Only the living nearness of the soul.
Yet all the worlds and God himself were there,
For every symbol was a reality
And brought the presence which had given it life.
All this she saw and inly felt and knew
Not by some thought of mind but by the self.
A light not born of sun or moon or fire,
A light that dwelt within and saw within

Shedding an intimate visibility
Made secrecy more revealing than the word:
Our sight and sense are a fallible gaze and touch
And only the spirit's vision is wholly true.
As thus she passed in that mysterious place
Through room and room, through door and rock-hewn door,
She felt herself made one with all she saw.
A sealed identity within her woke;
She knew herself the Beloved of the Supreme:
These Gods and Goddesses were he and she:
The Mother was she of Beauty and Delight,
The Word in Brahma's vast creating clasp,
The World-Puissance on almighty Shiva's lap,—
The Master and the Mother of all lives
Watching the worlds their twin regard had made,
And Krishna and Radha for ever entwined in bliss,
The Adorer and Adored self-lost and one.
In the last chamber on a golden seat
One sat whose shape no vision could define;
Only one felt the world's unattainable fount,
A Power of which she was a straying Force,
An invisible Beauty, goal of the world's desire,
A Sun of which all knowledge is a beam,
A Greatness without whom no life could be.
Thence all departed into silent self,
And all became formless and pure and bare.
Then through a tunnel dug in the last rock
She came out where there shone a deathless sun.
A house was there all made of flame and light
And crossing a wall of doorless living fire
There suddenly she met her secret soul.

A being stood immortal in transience,
Deathless dallying with momentary things,
In whose wide eyes of tranquil happiness
Which pity and sorrow could not abrogate
Infinity turned its gaze on finite shapes:
Observer of the silent steps of the hours,
Eternity upheld the minute's acts
And the passing scenes of the Everlasting's play.

In the mystery of its selecting will,
In the Divine Comedy a participant,
The Spirit's conscious representative,
God's delegate in our humanity,
Comrade of the universe, the Transcendent's ray,
She had come into the mortal body's room
To play at ball with Time and Circumstance.
A joy in the world her master movement here,
The passion of the game lighted her eyes:
A smile on her lips welcomed earth's bliss and grief,
A laugh was her return to pleasure and pain.
All things she saw as a masquerade of Truth
Disguised in the costumes of Ignorance,
Crossing the years to immortality;
All she could front with the strong spirit's peace.
But since she knows the toil of mind and life
As a mother feels and shares her children's lives,
She puts forth a small portion of herself,
A being no bigger than the thumb of man
Into a hidden region of the heart
To face the pang and to forget the bliss,
To share the suffering and endure earth's wounds
And labour mid the labour of the stars.
This in us laughs and weeps, suffers the stroke,
Exults in victory, struggles for the crown;
Identified with the mind and body and life,
It takes on itself their anguish and defeat,
Bleeds with Fate's whips and hangs upon the cross,
Yet is the unwounded and immortal self
Supporting the actor in the human scene.
Through this she sends us her glory and her powers,
Pushes to wisdom's heights, through misery's gulfs;
She gives us strength to do our daily task
And sympathy that partakes of others' grief
And the little strength we have to help our race,
We who must fill the role of the universe
Acting itself out in a slight human shape
And on our shoulders carry the struggling world.
This is in us the godhead small and marred;
In this human portion of divinity

She seats the greatness of the Soul in Time
To uplift from light to light, from power to power,
Till on a heavenly peak it stands, a king.
In body weak, in its heart an invincible might,
It climbs stumbling, held up by an unseen hand,
A toiling spirit in a mortal shape.
Here in this chamber of flame and light they met;
They looked upon each other, knew themselves,
The secret deity and its human part,
The calm immortal and the struggling soul.
Then with a magic transformation's speed
They rushed into each other and grew one.

Once more she was human upon earthly soil
In the muttering night amid the rain-swept woods
And the rude cottage where she sat in trance:
That subtle world withdrew deeply within
Behind the sun-veil of the inner sight.
But now the half-opened lotus bud of her heart
Had bloomed and stood disclosed to the earthly ray;
In an image shone revealed her secret soul.
There was no wall severing the soul and mind,
No mystic fence guarding from the claims of life.
In its deep lotus home her being sat
As if on concentration's marble seat,
Calling the mighty Mother of the worlds
To make this earthly tenement her house.
As in a flash from a supernal light,
A living image of the original Power,
A face, a form came down into her heart
And made of it its temple and pure abode.
But when its feet had touched the quivering bloom,
A mighty movement rocked the inner space
As if a world were shaken and found its soul:
Out of the Inconscient's soulless mindless night
A flaming Serpent rose released from sleep.
It rose billowing its coils and stood erect
And climbing mightily, stormily on its way
It touched her centres with its flaming mouth;
As if a fiery kiss had broken their sleep,

They bloomed and laughed surcharged with light and bliss.
Then at the crown it joined the Eternal's space.
In the flower of the head, in the flower of Matter's base,
In each divine stronghold and Nature-knot
It held together the mystic stream which joins
The viewless summits with the unseen depths,
The string of forts that make the frail defence
Safeguarding us against the enormous world,
Our lines of self-expression in its Vast.
An image sat of the original Power
Wearing the mighty Mother's form and face.
Armed, bearer of the weapon and the sign
Whose occult might no magic can imitate,
Manifold yet one she sat, a guardian force:
A saviour gesture stretched her lifted arm,
And symbol of some native cosmic strength,
A sacred beast lay prone below her feet,
A silent flame-eyed mass of living force.
All underwent a high celestial change:
Breaking the black Inconscient's blind mute wall,
Effacing the circles of the Ignorance,
Powers and divinities burst flaming forth;
Each part of the being trembling with delight
Lay overwhelmed with tides of happiness
And saw her hand in every circumstance
And felt her touch in every limb and cell.
In the country of the lotus of the head
Which thinking mind has made its busy space,
In the castle of the lotus twixt the brows
Whence it shoots the arrows of its sight and will,
In the passage of the lotus of the throat
Where speech must rise and the expressing mind
And the heart's impulse run towards word and act,
A glad uplift and a new working came.
The immortal's thoughts displaced our bounded view,
The immortal's thoughts earth's drab idea and sense;
All things now bore a deeper heavenlier sense.
A glad clear harmony marked their truth's outline,
Reset the balance and measures of the world.
Each shape showed its occult design, unveiled

God's meaning in it for which it was made
And the vivid splendour of his artist thought.
A channel of the mighty Mother's choice,
The immortal's will took into its calm control
Our blind or erring government of life;
A loose republic once of wants and needs,
Then bowed to the uncertain sovereign mind,
Life now obeyed to a diviner rule
And every act became an act of God.
In the kingdom of the lotus of the heart
Love chanting its pure hymeneal hymn
Made life and body mirrors of sacred joy
And all the emotions gave themselves to God.
In the navel lotus' broad imperial range
Its proud ambitions and its master lusts
Were tamed into instruments of a great calm sway
To do a work of God on earthly soil.
In the narrow nether centre's petty parts
Its childish game of daily dwarf desires
Was changed into a sweet and boisterous play,
A romp of little gods with life in Time.
In the deep place where once the Serpent slept,
There came a grip on Matter's giant powers
For large utilities in life's little space;
A firm ground was made for Heaven's descending might.
Behind all reigned her sovereign deathless soul:
Casting aside its veil of Ignorance,
Allied to gods and cosmic beings and powers
It built the harmony of its human state;
Surrendered into the great World-Mother's hands
Only she obeyed her sole supreme behest
In the enigma of the Inconscient's world.
A secret soul behind supporting all
Is master and witness of our ignorant life,
Admits the Person's look and Nature's role.
But once the hidden doors are flung apart
Then the veiled king steps out in Nature's front;
A Light comes down into the Ignorance,
Its heavy painful knot loosens its grasp:
The mind becomes a mastered instrument

And life a hue and figure of the soul.
All happily grows towards knowledge and towards bliss.
A divine Puissance then takes Nature's place
And pushes the movements of our body and mind;
Possessor of our passionate hopes and dreams,
The beloved despot of our thoughts and acts,
She streams into us with her unbound force,
Into mortal limbs the Immortal's rapture and power.
An inner law of beauty shapes our lives;
Our words become the natural speech of Truth,
Each thought is a ripple on a sea of Light.
Then sin and virtue leave the cosmic lists;
They struggle no more in our delivered hearts:
Our acts chime with God's simple natural good
Or serve the rule of a supernal Right.
All moods unlovely, evil and untrue
Forsake their stations in fierce disarray
And hide their shame in the subconscient's dusk.
Then lifts the mind a cry of victory:
'O soul, my soul, we have created Heaven,
Within we have found the kingdom here of God,
His fortress built in a loud ignorant world.
Our life is entrenched between two rivers of Light,
We have turned space into a gulf of peace
And made the body a Capitol of bliss.
What more, what more, if more must still be done?'
In the slow process of the evolving spirit,
In the brief stade between a death and birth
A first perfection's stage is reached at last;
Out of the wood and stone of our nature's stuff
A temple is shaped where the high gods could live.
Even if the struggling world is left outside
One man's perfection still can save the world.
There is won a new proximity to the skies,
A first betrothal of the Earth to Heaven,
A deep concordat between Truth and Life:
A camp of God is pitched in human time.

APPENDIX

The Fifteenth of August 1947

August 15th, 1947 is the birthday of free India. It marks for her the end of an old era, the beginning of a new age. But we can also make it by our life and acts as a free nation an important date in a new age opening for the whole world, for the political, social, cultural and spiritual future of humanity.

August 15th is my own birthday and it is naturally gratifying to me that it should have assumed this vast significance. I take this coincidence, not as a fortuitous accident, but as the sanction and seal of the Divine Force that guides my steps on the work with which I began life, the beginning of its full fruition. Indeed, on this day I can watch almost all the world-movements which I hoped to see fulfilled in my lifetime, though then they looked like impracticable dreams, arriving at fruition or on their way to achievement. In all these movements free India may well play a large part and take a leading position.

The first of these dreams was a revolutionary movement which would create a free and united India. India today is free but she has not achieved unity. At one moment it almost seemed as if in the very act of liberation she would fall back into the chaos of separate States which preceded the British conquest. But fortunately it now seems probable that this danger will be averted and a large and powerful, though not yet a complete union will be established. Also, the wisely drastic policy of the Constituent Assembly has made it probable that the problem of the depressed classes will be solved without schism or fissure. But the old communal division into Hindus and Muslims seems now to have hardened into a permanent political division of

A message broadcast by All India Radio, Tiruchchirappalli, on 14 August 1947. See the General Introduction.

the country. It is to be hoped that this settled fact will not be accepted as settled for ever or as anything more than a temporary expedient. For if it lasts, India may be seriously weakened, even crippled: civil strife may remain always possible, possible even a new invasion and foreign conquest. India's internal development and prosperity may be impeded, her position among the nations weakened, her destiny impaired or even frustrated. This must not be; the partition must go. Let us hope that that may come about naturally, by an increasing recognition of the necessity not only of peace and concord but of common action, by the practice of common action and the creation of means for that purpose. In this way unity may finally come about under whatever form — the exact form may have a pragmatic but not a fundamental importance. But by whatever means, in whatever way, the division must go; unity must and will be achieved, for it is necessary for the greatness of India's future.

Another dream was for the resurgence and liberation of the peoples of Asia and her return to her great role in the progress of human civilisation. Asia has arisen; large parts are now quite free or are at this moment being liberated: its other still subject or partly subject parts are moving through whatever struggles towards freedom. Only a little has to be done and that will be done today or tomorrow. There India has her part to play and has begun to play it with an energy and ability which already indicate the measure of her possibilities and the place she can take in the council of the nations.

The third dream was a world-union forming the outer basis of a fairer, brighter and nobler life for all mankind. That unification of the human world is under way; there is an imperfect initiation organised but struggling against tremendous difficulties. But the momentum is there and it must inevitably increase and conquer. Here too India has begun to play a prominent part and, if she can develop that larger statesmanship which is not limited by the present facts and immediate possibilities but looks into the future and brings it nearer, her presence may make all the difference between a slow and timid and a bold and swift development. A catastrophe may intervene and interrupt or destroy what is being done, but even then the final result is sure. For unification is a necessity of Nature, an inevitable movement. Its necessity for the nations is also clear, for without it the freedom of the small nations may be at any moment in peril and the life even of the large and powerful nations insecure. The unification is therefore to the interests of all, and only human imbecility and stupid selfishness can prevent it; but these cannot stand for ever against the necessity of Nature and the Divine Will. But an outward basis is not enough; there must grow up an international spirit and outlook, international forms and institutions must appear, perhaps such developments as dual or multilateral citizenship, willed interchange or voluntary fusion of cultures. Nationalism will have fulfilled itself and lost its militancy and would no longer find these things incompatible with self-preservation and the integrality of its outlook. A new spirit of oneness will take hold of the human race.

Another dream, the spiritual gift of India to the world has already begun. India's spirituality is entering Europe and America in an ever increasing measure. That movement will grow; amid the disasters of the time more and more eyes are turning towards her with hope and there is even an increasing resort not only to her teachings, but to her psychic and spiritual practice.

The final dream was a step in evolution which would raise man to a higher and larger consciousness and begin the solution of the problems which have perplexed and vexed him since he first began to think and to dream of individual perfection and a perfect society. This is still a personal hope and an idea, an ideal which has begun to take hold both in India and in the West on forward-looking minds. The difficulties in the way are more formidable than in any other field of endeavour, but difficulties were made to be overcome and if the Supreme Will is there, they will be overcome. Here too, if this evolution is to take place, since it must proceed through a growth of the spirit and the inner consciousness, the initiative can come from India and, although the scope must be universal, the central movement may be hers.

Such is the content which I put into this date of India's liberation; whether or how far this hope will be justified depends upon the new and free India.

Further Reading

Most of Sri Aurobindo's prose works first appeared in instalments in the journals *Karmayogin* (1909–10) and *Arya* (1914–21). Between 1918 and 1950 revised editions of five of the major works and many shorter works were published as books. During the 1930s some short collections of letters were published. A fairly complete edition of letters in four volumes was issued between 1947 and 1951. Three collections of poetry and two translations from the Sanskrit appeared between 1898 and 1924; two more volumes of poetry came out in 1936 and 1946. In 1950–1 the epic *Savitri* appeared in two volumes. A number of different works were issued posthumously between 1951 and 1994. By this time the number of separate titles exceeded one hundred.

Between 1953 and 1962 an attempt was made to publish Sri Aurobindo's major works in a uniform edition. Eight titles were issued at that time. In 1972, on the occasion of Sri Aurobindo's centenary, all works then available were published in twenty-nine volumes (with an additional reference volume) under the name Sri Aurobindo Birth Centenary Library (SABCL). This remains the most complete and authoritative edition of Sri Aurobindo's works. Most of the SABCL volumes have been reprinted in smaller format. In 1995 the Sri Aurobindo Ashram announced plans to bring out The Complete Works of Sri Aurobindo (CWSA) in thirty-four volumes with an additional reference volume. When completed around the turn of the century, this will become the standard edition. In what follows I will refer to the SABCL edition except where it does not contain an adequate text of the writing concerned, or when the CWSA edition is or will soon be available. Unless otherwise noted the publisher is Sri Aurobindo Ashram, Pondicherry.

A Brief Guide to Sri Aurobindo's Works

Political Writings. Sri Aurobindo's political writings and speeches from the 1906–8 period and before are reproduced in SABCL volume 1, *Bande Mataram: Early Political Writings—1*. Political writings and speeches from 1909–10 are reproduced in SABCL volume 2, *Karmayogin: Early Political Writings—2*. *Bande Mataram* is available as a separate book.

The best introduction to this material is *On Nationalism* (1996), a compilation of writings and speeches from both periods.

Writings in Bengali. Sri Aurobindo's original writings in Bengali on political and other subjects, first collected in SABCL volume 4, now appear in *Bangla Rachana*.

Poetry and Literature. Virtually all of Sri Aurobindo's poetry excluding *Savitri* is reproduced in *Collected Poems*, SABCL volume 5 (available as a separate book). The epic *Savitri*, volumes 28 and 29 of SABCL, was issued in a new edition in 1993. *Collected Plays and Short Stories* occupies SABCL volumes 6 and 7 (available as separate books). Sri Aurobindo's translations from Sanskrit, Bengali and other languages appear in *Translations*, SABCL volume 8. Most of his early literary prose is collected in *The Harmony of Virtue and Other Writings*, SABCL volume 3. *On the Mahabharata* (1991, reprinted 1996) is a collection of his writings on and translations from Vyasa's epic. *The Future Poetry*, SABCL volume 9, was issued in a new corrected edition containing the author's revisions in 1985 (reprinted 1994). The author's *Letters on Poetry, Literature and Art*, published in SABCL along with *The Future Poetry*, is now available as a separate book.

Sri Aurobindo's sonnets provide a good introduction to the poetry. A complete edition, published under the title *Sonnets* in 1980, is available in a new impression. The new edition of *Savitri* is essential reading for all serious students of Sri Aurobindo's works.

Writings on the Indian Tradition. Sri Aurobindo's principal writings on Indian culture are *The Renaissance in India* (available as a separate booklet) and *A Defence of Indian Culture*. Between 1972 and 1996 these two works and some other essays appeared under the editorial title *The Foundations of Indian Culture*, SABCL volume 14. In CWSA the same writings will appear under the original titles. Sri Aurobindo's writings on the principal texts of the Indian spiritual tradition are contained in four volumes: writings on and translations from the Rig-veda in *The Secret of the Veda* (SABCL volume 10, available as a separate book), translations of hymns to Agni from the Rig-veda in *Hymns to the Mystic Fire* (SABCL volume 11, available as a separate book), translations of and commentaries on the Upanishads in *The Upanishads* (SABCL volume 12, available in a new edition (1981, reprinted 1994)), and *Essays on the Gita* (SABCL volume 13, now available in a new edition reproducing the CWSA text).

The most accessible of these books is *Essays on the Gita*, always the most popular of Sri Aurobindo's major works. Equally interesting to the student of Indian religion, philosophy or yoga are his commentaries on the Isha Upanishad and Kena Upanishad, which are available as separate booklets.

Political and Social Theory. Sri Aurobindo's three major works on political science and sociology, *The Ideal of Human Unity*, *The Human Cycle*, and *War and Self-Determination*, were published together as volume 15 of SABCL. They are available in this form as a separate book.

The Human Cycle is the most important of these works for the general reader.

Philosophy. Sri Aurobindo's main philosophical work is *The Life Divine*, volumes 18 and 19 of SABCL (available as a separate book). Philosophical essays published during his lifetime, including *The Problem of Rebirth* and *The Supramental Manifestation Upon Earth*, were published in SABCL volume 16, *The Supramental Manifestation and Other Writings*, which is available as a separate book in a new edition. In CWSA the same material will be published as *Essays in Philosophy and Yoga*. Most philosophical essays not published during Sri Aurobindo's lifetime appeared in SABCL volume 17, *The Hour of God and Other Writings*. In 1994 a new edition of this material, reedited and enlarged, was published as *Essays Divine and Human*. This arrangement and title will be retained in CWSA.

Some of the essays in *The Supramental Manifestation/Essays in Philosophy and Yoga* provide a more accessible introduction to aspects of Sri Aurobindo's philosophy than *The Life Divine*. Several of these essays appear also in short booklets like *Evolution* and *The Superman*. Some of the longer pieces in *Essays Divine and Human* are of great interest.

Yoga. *The Synthesis of Yoga*, volumes 20 and 21 of SABCL, is Sri Aurobindo's principal work on yoga. The three volumes of *Letters on Yoga* are more detailed and more accessible. The short book *The Mother* is a powerful series of meditations on the *yoga-shakti*. In SABCL volume 25 this was published together with Sri Aurobindo's *Letters on the Mother* (available as a separate book). *On Himself* (SABCL volume 26, available separately) contains Sri Aurobindo's autobiographical letters and notes, and is of considerable interest both to students of Indian history and to those interested in Sri Aurobindo's yoga.

A good introduction to Sri Aurobindo's yoga is *The Integral Yoga* (1993), a selection of letters.

Reference Works

The reference volume of SABCL (volume 30) contains a fairly complete index, a glossary of Sanskrit and other Indian terms, and some useful lists and tables.

Glossary of Terms in Sri Aurobindo's Writings (second impression, 1994) contains a reprint of the glossary in the SABCL reference volume, as well as a selection of passages in which Sri Aurobindo explains the principal terms of his philosophy and yoga.

Glossary and Index of Proper Names in Sri Aurobindo's Works (1989) contains information on over 5000 proper names referred to by Sri Aurobindo.

Biographies

A. B. Purani, *The Life of Sri Aurobindo*. Fourth edition (Pondicherry: Sri Aurobindo Ashram, 1978). Written by a direct disciple, this work gives the basic biographical information, and contains some documentary appendixes.

K.R. Srinivasa Iyengar, *Sri Aurobindo: A Biography and a History.* Fourth edition (Pondicherry: Sri Aurobindo Ashram, 1985). The author, a noted literary critic, provides a detailed biographical narrative and expositions of Sri Aurobindo's major works.
Peter Heehs, *Sri Aurobindo: A Brief Biography* (Delhi: Oxford University Press, 1989). A relatively short work based on primary documents.

STUDIES

A large number of articles and books about Sri Aurobindo and his writings have been published. Many of them may prove to be ephemeral. The list that follows is very selective. Preference has been given to books that maintain a high level of scholarship.

General. Robert A. McDermott, ed., *Six Pillars: Introductions to the Major Works of Sri Aurobindo* (Chambersburg, PA: Wilson Books, 1974). Contains excellent essays on six of Sri Aurobindo's major works.
Haridas Chaudhuri and Frederic Spiegelberg, eds., *The Integral Philosophy of Sri Aurobindo* (London: George Allen and Unwin, 1960). An earlier collection of essays; contributors include Pitirim Sorokin and J. N. Mohanty.
Satprem, *Sri Aurobindo or the Adventure of Consciousness*, translated from the French by Luc Venet (New York: Institute for Evolutionary Research, 1984). A popular study weaving together biographical and expository material, with many well-chosen quotations.
The Mother, *On Thoughts and Aphorisms*, translated from the French (Pondicherry: Sri Aurobindo Ashram, 1977). Commentaries on a brief but important work of Sri Aurobindo's by his collaborator. Many of the Mother's other works, for example *Conversations* (Pondicherry: Sri Aurobindo Ashram, 1982), provide clear and accessible accounts of the integral yoga.

Philosophy. Stephen H. Phillips, *Aurobindo's Philosophy of Brahman* (Leiden: E. J. Brill, 1986). A critical yet sympathetic study of Sri Aurobindo's metaphysics by an American philosopher and Sanskritist.
J.N. Mohanty, *Essays on Indian Philosophy Traditional and Modern* (Delhi: Oxford University Press, 1993). Contains three

essays on Sri Aurobindo by a philosopher with an international reputation.

Satya Prakash Singh, *Sri Aurobindo and Whitehead on the Nature of God* (Aligarh: Vigyan Prakashan, 1972). One of the most interesting of the many comparative studies that have been published.

S.K. Maiṭra, *An Introduction to the Philosophy of Sri Aurobindo* (Calcutta: The Culture Publishers, 1941). A brief study of *The Life Divine.*

Political and Social Thought. V. P. Varma, *The Political Philosophy of Sri Aurobindo*. Second edition (Delhi: Motilal Banarsidass, 1976). Still the best introduction to the subject.

D.P. Chattopadhyaya, *History, Society and Polity: Integral Sociology of Sri Aurobindo* (New Delhi: Macmillan, 1976). By an academic who was a cabinet minister.

Poetry. K.D. Sethna, *The Poetic Genius of Sri Aurobindo*. Second edition (Pondicherry: Sri Aurobindo Ashram, 1974). Essays by a poet and critic who was a close disciple of Sri Aurobindo's.

Sources of Selections

Unless otherwise specified, references are to volumes and pages of the Sri Aurobindo Birth Centenary Library (SABCL) edition. Whenever possible texts have been made to accord with the new Collected Works of Sri Aurobindo (CWSA) edition. See Further Reading for details.

The Spiritual Revolution, 16: 393–4.

1. NATIONALISM AND BEYOND
Epigraph, 2: 126-7; New Lamps for Old, 1: 15–19; The Doctrine of Passive Resistance, 1: 85–9; The Present Situation, 1: 652–65; Uttarpara Speech, CWSA 8: 3–12; The Ideal of the Karmayogin, CWSA 8: 23–28; Letter to Joseph Baptista, 26: 429–31; Letter to Balakrishna Shivaram Munje, 26: 432–4.

2. THE INDIAN TRADITION AND THE FUTURE
Epigraph, 22:88; 'Is India Civilised?', CWSA 20: 55–66; The Evolution of Indian Spirituality, CWSA 20: 196–213; The Secret of the Veda: The Problem and its Solution, 10: 1–7; Readings in the Taittiriya Upanishad, 12: 347–51; Kena Upanishad: A Last Word, 12: 1–7; The Core of the Gita's Meaning, CWSA 19: 562–7; The Renaissance in India, CWSA 20: 3–16; Indian Civilisation and the Evolutionary Future, CWSA 20: 79–93.

3. THE INDIVIDUAL, SOCIETY AND HUMANITY
Epigraph, 20: 187; The Turn towards Unity: Its Necessity and Dangers, 15: 263–6; The Ideal of Human Unity: Summary and Conclusion, 15: 548–55; A Note, *Bulletin of the SAICE* 28, 2 (April 1976): 82–4; The Cycle of Society, 15: 3–10; The Advent and Progress of the Spiritual Age, 15: 246-54.

4. THE EVOLUTION OF CONSCIOUSNESS
Epigraph, 19: 1070; The Teaching of Sri Aurobindo, 26: 95-7; The Human Aspiration, 18: 1–4; The Two Negations: The Materialist Denial, 18: 6–16; The Two Negations: The Refusal of the Ascetic, 18: 17–24; Man and the Evolution, 19: 824–47; Man and the Supermind, *Essays Divine and Human* (*EDH*): 163–4; The Involved and Evolving Godhead, *EDH*: 169–72; The Evolution of Consciousness, *EDH*: 173–7; Rebirth, 16: 79–88; Rebirth and Karma, 16: 153–61; Rebirth and Personality, 22: 451–2; Metaphysical Thought and the Supreme Truth 22: 157– 61.

5. YOGA AND LIFE
Epigraph, 14: 404; Life and Yoga, 20: 1–4; The Synthesis of the Systems, 20: 36–44; Standards of Conduct and Spiritual Freedom, 20: 177–96; The Cosmic Consciousness, 20: 392–400; The Ananda Brahman, 21: 567–72; The Integral Perfection, 21: 590–6; Karmayoga, 23: 528–9; Bhakti, 23: 787–8; Meditation, 23: 721-3; The Central Process of the Yoga, 24: 1163–70; The Novelty of the Integral Yoga, 22: 99–101.

6. POETRY
Epigraph, 9: 369–70; The Essence of Poetry, CWSA 26: 11–18; Invitation, 5: 39; Trance, 5: 572; Ocean Oneness, 5: 557; Descent, 5: 563; Thought the Paraclete, 5: 582; Transformation, 5: 161; Nirvana, 5: 161; The Indwelling Universal, 5: 131; Bliss of Identity, 5: 135; The Pilgrim of the Night, 5: 132; Liberation, 5: 133; Krishna, 5: 139; The Word of the Silence, 5: 141; Savitri: The Finding of the Soul, CWSA 34: 522–31.

Appendix: The Fifteenth of August 1947, 26: 404–6.

Chronology

1872 August 15	Birth in Calcutta. Third son of Kristo Dhone Ghose, a physician in government service, and Swarnalotta Ghose, eldest daughter of Rajnarain Bose, the head of the Adi Brahmo Samaj.
1872–7	In Rangpur, eastern Bengal (now Bangladesh).
1877–9	At Loreto Convent School, Darjeeling.
1879	Taken to England. He and his brothers placed in the charge of the Rev. William Drewett, a Congregational clergyman of Manchester.
1879–84	In Manchester. The two older boys attend Manchester Grammar School; Aurobindo is tutored at home by Mr and Mrs Drewett.
1884–9	In London. Scholarship student at St Paul's School.
1890 July	Admitted as a probationer to the Indian Civil Service.
1890–2	Scholarship student at King's College, Cambridge. Studies simultaneously the civil service and classical curricula.
1892 May	Passes the first part of the classical tripos (honours degree examination) in the first class.
August	Passes the Indian Civil Service final examination.
November	Rejected from the civil service owing to his inability to pass the riding examination.

December	Obtains employment in the service of the Maharaja of Baroda.
1893 February	Returns to India.
1893–1906	In the Baroda State service, at first in various administrative departments, then professor of French and English in the Baroda College, then private secretary or *huzur kamdar* of the Maharaja, finally vice-principal of the college.
1893–4	*New Lamps for Old*, a series of articles on the Indian National Congress, published in Bombay.
1898	*Songs to Myrtilla*, a collection of poems, privately printed.
1901 April	Marriage to Mrinalini Bose in Calcutta.
1902–3	Begins to organize a revolutionary group in Bengal and to contact advanced nationalist politicians in western India.
1902 July	'The Age of Kalidasa', an article, published in the *Indian Review* (Madras).
1905	Begins the practice of *yoga*.
1905 October	Partition of Bengal goes into effect.
1906 February	Goes to Bengal, begins to participate in the anti-Partition movement.
August	Becomes principal of the newly founded Bengal National College. Begins to write for the nationalist journal *Bande Mataram*.
December	Active at the Calcutta session of the Indian National Congress.
1907 April	Publishes *The Doctrine of Passive Resistance* in *Bande Mataram*.
August	Arrested on the charge of sedition for articles printed in *Bande Mataram*; released on bail.
September	Acquitted. From this point comes forward as the leader of the Nationalist or Extremist Party in Bengal.

	December	A leader of the Extremists at the Surat session of the Indian Nationalist Congress. Conflict between Extremists and Moderates ends in a violent clash.
1908	January	Meets with V.B. Lele, a Maharashtrian yogi. Has his first decisive spiritual realization.
	Jan. – April	Delivers many speeches.
	May	Arrested as implicated in the terrorist activities of a group led by his brother Barindrakumar; charged with conspiracy to wage war against the king. Until May 1909 an undertrial prisoner in Alipore Jail, near Calcutta; spends most of his time in meditation, has many spiritual experiences.
1909	May 6	Acquitted. His brother condemned to the gallows, later transported to the Andamans.
	May 30	Speech at Uttarpara, Bengal. Many other speeches delivered before November.
	June 19	Starts *Karmayogin*, a weekly political and cultural journal in English. Writes most of its articles.
	August 23	Starts *Dharma*, a weekly political and cultural journal in Bengali. Writes many of its articles.
1910	February	Goes secretly to Chandernagore, a French enclave north of Calcutta.
	April 4	Arrives by ship in Pondicherry, the capital of French India. The same day a warrant issued in Calcutta charging him with sedition for an article published in *Karmayogin*.
	November	Article found not seditious. Announces his presence in Pondicherry and his retirement from active politics.
1914	August 15	First issue of *Arya*, a 'review of pure philosophy'. Most of his major works brought out in monthly instalments in this journal before it ceases publication in January 1921.

1920	August	Offered the presidentship of the Indian National Congress; declines.
1926	November	After a decisive spiritual realization withdraws from direct contact with most others. The community of seekers (*ashram*) that had grown up around him put in the hands of the Mother (Mirra Alfassa).
1930–8		Extensive correspondence with members of the ashram and some outsiders.
1938	November	Fractures his thigh. Limited contact with a few disciples begins; two of them record and later publish his talks.
1939–40		Revision and book publication of *The Life Divine*.
1940		Supports Allies during World War II. In 1942 recommends the acceptance of the Cripps Proposal offering India self-government after the war.
1947	August 15	Liberation of India. His message broadcast by All India Radio.
1948		Publication of revised version of *The Synthesis of Yoga*, Part I.
1949		Publication of revised version of *The Human Cycle*.
1950		Publication of revised version of *The Ideal of Human Unity*.
	December 5	Death after a brief illness.

Glossary

Words are Sanskrit unless otherwise indicated. Words and phrases defined by Sri Aurobindo where they occur have been omitted.

ādeś, adesh, (inner) command.
ānanda, delight of existence.
aṇur hyeṣa dharmaḥ, for subtle is the law of it.
āścaryam, mystery.
asura, titan, hostile being.
avatāra, incarnation of God.
Babu, old term for a Hindu, especially a Bengali, gentleman.
Bande Mataram, Bengali pronunciation of *vande mātaram*, 'Salutation to the Mother', the first words of a song by the novelist Bankim Chandra Chatterjee (1838–94); the phrase was taken up by Bengali nationalists as a sort of war-cry; Bipin Chandra Pal used it as the name of the English-language daily newspaper he founded in 1906.
bhakta, a lover and devotee of the Divine.
bhakti, love for the Divine, devotion to the Divine.
brahman, the Reality, the Eternal, the Infinite; the One besides whom there is nothing else existent.
brāhmaṇas, a portion of the Vedas containing rules for the right performance of rituals, etc.
brahmavidya, the knowledge of brahman.
Brahmin, properly *brāhmaṇa*, a member of the highest of the four orders (see *caturvarṇa*), the man of learning and thought and knowledge.
Brindavan, the place where the young Sri Krishna danced with the *gopis* or cow-herdesses.
caturvarṇa (Chaturvarna), the fourfold order of ancient Indian society: *brāhmaṇas, ksatriyas, vaiśyas, śūdras*. See *The Cycle of Society* for a discussion by Sri Aurobindo.

chhotalok (Bengali), 'little people', a disparaging term for the lower classes.

cit (Chit), consciousness.

cinmaya, composed of consciousness, transcendental.

daitya, demon.

dakṣiṇamārga, the right-hand (*dakṣiṇa*) path of Tantra, the way of knowledge.

darśana (Darshana), philosophy.

dharma, law of being; sometimes used as an equivalent of the English term 'religion'.

eppur si muove (Italian), 'and yet it moves'.

eṣa dharmaḥ sanātanaḥ, this is the eternal law.

Gokul, the village where Krishna was brought up.

guru, spiritual teacher.

hājat (Hindustani), lockup in a police station.

haṭhayoga, a system of yoga that uses the body and vital functionings as its instruments.

hṛdaye guhāyām, in the secret heart cave (a Vedic allusion).

jeu d'esprit (French), a humorous literary trifle.

jīvātman, the self in the living being; individual self.

karma, action, especially action determining the nature and eventuality of the soul's repeated existences.

kevala, absolute, simple.

Kṛṣṇa (Krishna), a god, regarded as an incarnation of Vishnu; in the Bhagavad Gita he is the charioteer and guide of the hero Arjuna.

kṣatriya, a member of the second of the four orders (see *caturvarṇa*), the man of power and action.

Kurukshetra, the field where the great battle of the Mahabharata was fought.

laya, dissolution of the individual soul in the infinite.

līlā, play; the creation seen as the play of the divine.

mantra, sacred verbal formula.

Manu, the Thinker; the traditional author of a famous Hindu lawbook.

māyā, the power of self-illusion in *brahman*.

mokṣa, liberation.

mūlādhāra, root-vessel, the lowest of the subtle centres or *cakras*.

Nārāyaṇa, a name of Vishnu or Krishna, who, as the God in

man, lives constantly associated in a dual unity with Nara, the human being.

nāsti anto vistarasya me, there is no end to My self-extension (spoken by Krishna in the Bhagavad Gita).

nirvāṇa, extinction, not necessarily of all being, but of being as we know it.

prakṛti (Prakriti), nature, executive or working force.

Puranic, having to do with the Puranas, legendary stories of the Hindus.

puruṣa (Purusha), person, conscious being; essential being supporting the play of Prakriti.

rāja-śakti, political power.

rājayoga, a system of yoga that makes use of mental askesis to open up the divine life on all its planes.

rākṣasī māyā, illusion of the powers of darkness.

ṛtasya panthāḥ, the path of the Truth (a Vedic allusion).

ryot (Hindustani), cultivator, peasant.

sabhā, society, association.

saccidānanda (Sachchidananda), existence-consciousness-bliss.

sādhaka, one who practices a *sādhana*.

sādhana, the practice of yoga; any system of yogic practice.

śakti (Shakti), energy, power; the divine in Her form of power; any female consort of a male deity.

samarpaṇa, complete self-offering, surrender.

samaṣṭi, the collectivity.

sanātana dharma, the eternal law; the eternal religion; used, especially since the mid-nineteenth century, as a Sanskrit equivalent of the English term 'Hinduism'.

sandhi, joint.

Sāṅkhyas, those who profess the analytical philosophy known as Sankhya or 'enumeration'.

sannyāsin, an ascetic.

Saraswati, the Muse and goddess of wisdom, learning and the arts and crafts.

śāstra (Shastra), scripture.

sat, being, existence.

Satya Yuga, the Age of Truth, the Golden Age.

Shakti, see *śakti*.

Shastra, see *śāstra*.

śūdra (Shudra), a member of the lowest of the four orders (see

caturvarṇa), the man fit only for unskilled labour and service.
Sūrya, the Sun-god.
svabhāva (swabhava), own-nature, essential nature of being of each becoming.
svadharma, own law of being.
svalpam apyasya dharmasya, only a little of this *dharma*. . . (an allusion to a phrase in the Bhagavad Gita).
svarāj (Swaraj) self-government; during the freedom movement the term was used by some Extremist politicians as the equivalent of political independence, but by the Moderates to refer at most to self-government within the British Empire.
swabhava, swadharma, see ***svabhāva, svadharma***.
Tantra, the yogic system based on the *tantras*.
tantras, a class of Sanskrit texts, many of which deal with the Divine as Shakti or Power.
tapasyā, concentration of the will and energy to control and change mind, life and body.
tato na vicikitsate, debates not thereafter.
theos ouk estin alla gignetai (Greek), God is not being but becoming.
udāsīna, seated above and indifferent.
Vaishnavism, the devotional system that regards Vishnu, especially in His incarnations Krishna or Rama, as the Supreme.
vaiśya, a member of the third of the four orders (see ***caturvarṇa***), the economic man, producer and wealth-getter.
vāmamārga, the left-hand (*vāma*) path of the Tantra, the way of *ānanda*; it includes certain practices that have 'fallen into discredit with those who are not Tantrics'.
Vāsudeva, a name of Krishna.
Vedānta, a system of philosophy based on the Upanishads.
vijñāna, real Idea, divine mind, supermind.
vyaṣṭi, the individual.
yoga, union with the divine; a method for attaining such union.
yoga-siddhi, perfection in yoga.
yuga, an age.
yugadharma, the best ideal (*dharma*) of the age.